Nationality and Citizenship
in Revolutionary France

Nationality and Citizenship in Revolutionary France

The Treatment of Foreigners 1789–1799

MICHAEL RAPPORT

CLARENDON PRESS · OXFORD

OXFORD

UNIVERSITY PRESS

Great Clarendon Street, Oxford OX2 6DP

Oxford University Press is a department of the University of Oxford.
It furthers the University's objective of excellence in research, scholarship,
and education by publishing worldwide in

Oxford New York

Athens Auckland Bangkok Bogotá Buenos Aires Calcutta
Cape Town Chennai Dar es Salaam Delhi Florence Hong Kong Istanbul
Karachi Kuala Lumpur Madrid Melbourne Mexico City Mumbai
Nairobi Paris São Paulo Singapore Taipei Tokyo Toronto Warsaw
and associated companies in Berlin Ibadan

Oxford is a registered trade mark of Oxford University Press
in the UK and certain other countries

Published in the United States
by Oxford University Press Inc., New York

© Mike Rapport 2000

The moral rights of the author have been asserted
Database right Oxford University Press (maker)

First published 2000

British Library Cataloguing in Publication Data

Data available

Library of Congress Cataloging in Publication Data

Data available

ISBN 0-19-820845-6

1 3 5 7 9 10 8 6 4 2

Typeset by Joshua Associates Ltd., Oxford
Printed in Great Britain
on acid-free paper by
Biddles Ltd.,
Guildford and King's Lynn

For HELEN

Preface

Alexis de Tocqueville wrote:

The French Revolution aspired to be world-wide and its effect was to erase all the old national frontiers from the map. We find it uniting and dividing men throughout the world, without regard to national traditions, temperaments, laws, and mother tongues, sometimes leading them to regard compatriots as foes and foreigners as their kinsmen. Or, perhaps, it would be truer to say that it created a common intellectual fatherland whose citizenship was open to men of every nationality and in which racial distinctions were obliterated.

No one reading these words at the beginning of the twenty-first century need be reminded of the tensions which exist, in so many ways, between globalization, notions of universal human rights, ethnic and religious identities, citizenship and nationhood. This book was written in the 1990s, when old identities and notions of nationality and citizenship have been challenged by such developments as the end of the cold war, European integration, and the break up of both Yugoslavia and the Soviet Union. Much of the research for this book was carried out in France in 1991–3, a period marked by the referendum on the Maastricht treaty and by often fiery debates on immigration and naturalization. Two hundred years after the event, some of the central issues posed by the French Revolution are still relevant today: how to define the nation and its membership; the rights of citizenship and its limits; the balance between universal rights on the one hand and national and cultural traditions on the other. A study of foreigners in France during the Revolution might help to explain how, at one of the fountainheads of these questions, people tried to find answers.

This book originated as a thesis and has undergone many mutations. I have therefore accumulated intellectual and personal debts which I can barely service, let alone repay. The first is to William Doyle, who was my supervisor at the University of Bristol. His broad knowledge of both French and European history was brought to bear in his highly constructive comments.

He was patient with both my sprawling draft chapters and the somewhat erratic pace by which the thesis was completed. The brainstorming sessions which we had were extremely enjoyable—as was the hospitality which he and Christine extended in the nerve-wracking days around my viva. It was an honour and a pleasure to work under his alert eye.

Since 1994, I have been fortunate to have taught in two institutions which have lively groups of historians. I have found friends and colleagues whose company I enjoy and who have, in many different ways, contributed to this work. Friends in both the History section at the University of Sunderland and the History Department at the University of Stirling have helped hone my ideas. They are simply too many to be listed, but I should mention those who read parts of this book and made helpful remarks, namely Emma Macleod, George Peden, and David Bebbington. Teaching has helped me keep one eye on the broader issues and the context into which my work on foreigners should be placed. I am therefore grateful to my students, particularly those in my final year classes on revolutionary Europe, who strengthened my belief that teaching and research should feed each other in a symbiotic relationship.

I have also received much help from beyond the breathtaking haven for students, tutors, rabbits, and ducks which is the University of Stirling's campus. Norman Hampson has been very generous in his advice and encouragement. He allowed me to roam freely across academic pastures where his expertise is widely respected and generously shared his ideas and knowledge. I have also benefited from the leads and often thrusting questions put to me by Timothy Blanning and John Whittam at my viva. The annual conference of the Society for the Study of French History has proved to be a sociable and fertile ground for friendly advice and ideas. Edna Lemay allowed me to attend her seminar at the École des Hautes Études en Sciences Sociales in Paris and, in my first ever paper, to test my earliest thoughts on this subject. Comments and questions which followed papers given at the Institute of Historical Research in London, at the Enlightenment Seminar organized by the Voltaire Foundation and the Faculty of Modern History at Oxford University, and at my alma mater, the University of Edinburgh, have also contributed heavily to this work.

I am particularly grateful to staff at the Archives Nationales, the Ministère des Affaires Étrangères, the Service Historique de l'Armée de Terre, the Bibliothèque Nationale, and the Bibliothèque Historique de la Ville de Paris. In Britain, I should thank staff at the libraries of the Universities of Stirling, Bristol, Sunderland, Glasgow, and Edinburgh; at the British Library and Institute of Historical Research in London; and at the National Library of Scotland and Christine Johnson at the Scottish Catholic Archives in Edinburgh.

Until taking up my first post at Sunderland, this research was funded by a Major State Studentship from the British Academy, for which I am extremely grateful. The peripatetic nature of my career has meant that I abused the hospitality of many people, including Ian Wei and my cousins, the McLarens, in Bristol, and, until we found a home in Scotland, my mother-in-law, Elizabeth Comerford. Research trips to London have been made especially pleasurable by the friendship and hospitality of Ross and Nina Bryson. My parents on both sides of the Atlantic, George, my father, and Jane Rapport and Anita, my mother, and Mike Radford, have provided help of all kinds. My father is not an academic, but he has kept me on my toes with his broad knowledge of history. Late-night conversations with my mother and Mike have kept me up to speed on the view from France. The support of all four over the past few years has been immeasurable.

Finally, the one person who has lived and breathed this book from start to finish is my wife, Helen. We were together in Paris as I did my research, which made it one of the most memorable times of my life. Helen has her own passionate views on nationality and nationalism and, as we never agree on anything, has been a lively foil for my arguments. Her own historical knowledge, especially of Scotland, has, at many points, lent its perspective to this book. She has put up with my obsession with the French Revolution more than I deserve. Her friendship, companionship, love, understanding, and intellect make this her work as much as it is mine.

M.G.R.

Stirling
August 1999

Contents

Abbreviations

ADP	Affaires Diverses Politiques (within Ministère des Affaires Étrangères, Paris)
AhRf	*Annales historiques de la Révolution française*
AN	Archives Nationales, Paris
AP	*Archives parlementaires de 1787 à 1860. Recueil complet des débats législatifs et politiques des chambres françaises*, 1ère sér., 96 vols. (Paris, 1877–1990)
AP/2	*Archives Parlementaires. Recueil complet des débats législatifs et politiques des chambres françaises de 1800 à 1860*, 2ème sér., 127 vols. (Paris, 1862–1913)
CP	Correspondance Politique (within Ministère des Affaires Étrangères, Paris)
Isambert	Isambert, Jourdan, and Decrusy, *Recueil général des anciennes lois françaises depuis l'an 420 jusqu'à la Révolution de 1789*, 31 vols. (Paris, 1822–33)
MAE	Ministère des Affaires Étrangères, Paris
MD	Mémoires et Documents
Moniteur	*Gazette Nationale, ou le Moniteur Universel*
SCA	Scottish Catholic Archives, Edinburgh
SHAT	Service Historique de l'Armée de Terre, Vincennes

Introduction

At 4 o'clock in the afternoon on 4 Germinal in the Year II of the Republic (24 March 1794), eighteen prisoners passed through an unassuming grille which led from the Conciergerie prison into the courtyard of the Palais de Justice, in the heart of Paris. Their hands were bound behind with cord, the collars of their shirts torn off, and their hair cut short in order to expose the neck. A vast, murmuring crowd, fenced out by the tall, iron gates which separated the courtyard from the street beyond, let out a roar as the captives emerged. The prisoners filed towards four open carts which awaited them, arguing bitterly amongst themselves. One, named Jacques-René Hébert, could barely walk: his elegant clothes dishevelled, his face livid with terror, he was supported by two gaolers. This pitiful sight was a stark contrast to the Hébert who had written fierce polemics demanding the shedding of more blood, more than the current Terror was already spilling. A couple of the prisoners, however, remained calm, courageously holding their fear in check. One of these was a German named Anacharsis Cloots, a onetime baron who even now preached his doctrine of a universal, world republic. Although a Prussian subject by origin, he had been elected a member of the French National Convention, the legislature of the first French Republic, in September 1792. Yet he associated far too closely to the extreme left-wing opposition to the government, grouped around Hébert. Consequently, Cloots was expelled from the Convention on 25 December 1793, along with another famous foreign deputy, Thomas Paine, who had been involved with the moderates, the outlawed Girondins. The official reason for their expulsion from the legislature was that they were foreigners and so were not fit to represent the French people. Both men, having lost their parliamentary immunity, were arrested within days. If Paine languished in prison until after the Terror, he was the lucky one. Cloots now stood convicted, along with the seventeen others, of treason. He was the second prisoner to climb into

the carts and, when his associates had all mounted, the vehicles
rumbled through the courtyard gates. As the convoy emerged,
people surged forward to catch a glimpse of the people who, they
had been told, were counter-revolutionaries. Cloots never lost
his composure as the carts made their agonizingly ponderous
journey, through the press of the crowd, towards the place de la
Révolution and the guillotine. When his turn came, he stepped
up onto the scaffold, crying out 'Hurrah for the fraternity of
nations! Long live the Republic of the world!'

The revolutionary government thus killed off the motley
group of extremists who are known as the Hébertists. Besides
Cloots, there were two other foreigners among them, a Belgian
financier called Pierre Proli and a Dutch banker named Joannes
de Kock. Six days later, the government turned to destroy its
critics on the right, the Dantonists or Indulgents who, in contrast
to Hébert, sought to end the Terror. Four foreigners also died
with this group: the Frey brothers from Moravia, their Danish
associate, and a Spanish adventurer named Guzman. With the
most vocal opposition destroyed, the government, embodied in
the Committee of Public Safety and the Committee of General
Security, sought to consolidate its hold on the Republic by
persuading the Convention to vote through a package of policing
measures, on 15 and 16 April, the law of 26–7 Germinal. The
government's spokesman, the young, pale, and immaculately
dressed Louis Antoine Saint-Just, urged the legislators to purge
Paris, seaports, and frontier towns of aristocrats—and foreigners. Not content with the earlier act denying foreigners the right
to sit as deputies in the Convention, the government also
demanded that foreigners be barred from political clubs, from
local revolutionary committees, and from the elected local
assemblies of the rural communes and the urban sections.[1]
Foreigners, therefore, were to be excluded both from key centres
of French social and economic life and, above all, from involvement in every level of French politics. 'You must build a city,'
declared Saint-Just, 'of citizens who will be friends, who will be
hospitable and brothers.'[2] It seemed very clear that this city was
to be an exclusively French community. Some foreigners paid

---

[1] *Archives parlementaires de 1787 à 1860: Recueil complet des débats législatifs et
politiques des chambres françaises*, 1ère sér., 96 vols. (Paris, 1877–1990), lxxxviii. 613–
22, 647–50.   [2] Ibid. lxxxviii. 615.

the ultimate price for trying to meddle with the creation of this new order.

Yet this was the same Revolution which, scarcely four years previously, had opened with such liberating promise—and not just for France. It seemed to many enthusiastic observers and participants, including Cloots, that in founding a new order on the basis of natural rights, the French Revolution was sending a message to all humankind. People everywhere were being called upon to recognize that every person, by the simple virtue of being born human, shared in the same essential rights, such as liberty, property, and resistance to oppression. The revolutionaries used the term 'cosmopolitanism' when applying these ideals to foreigners. The roots of cosmopolitanism were diverse, including religious ideas which stressed mankind's common humanity, economic thinking which emphasized the universal moral and material benefits of commerce, and theories of natural rights. In the eighteenth century, these influences produced a number of works, such as those of the abbé de Saint-Pierre, who proposed a plan for universal and perpetual peace, and of Voltaire, who denounced the excesses of war and religious persecution. The influence of Rousseau led some revolutionaries to pursue notions of 'natural rights' to their logical conclusion, claiming that, as they pertained to the very nature of man, so they were universal.

For a brief period after 1789, cosmopolitanism's apparent antithesis, 'patriotism', actually overlapped with it. The meaning of patriotism was traditionally bound to aristocratic notions of honour, service to the king, and provincial loyalties. In the political clashes of the later eighteenth century, and particularly after the Maupeou crisis of 1771, a more radical sense of patriotism arose. Patriots were those who claimed to put the interests of the country as a whole before the partisan wishes of the allegedly despotic government. By 1789, this patriotism entailed an assault on privilege, because it raised barriers between the different sections of society. The *patrie* was not just one's native land, but a place where the new, egalitarian order would flourish, where the people enjoyed civil equality and liberty, which meant freedom from arbitrary government and the exercise of political rights. Patriotism was therefore a political virtue which focused on the domestic affairs of the state and did not necessarily imply the expansion or elevation of France at the expense of other peoples. Indeed, favourable images of 'free' countries such as Britain and, above all, the nascent United States, could be used by French patriots as a means of comparison to highlight the shortcomings of the Ancien Régime in France. For this reason, there was nothing contradictory about being a *cosmopolite* and a *patriote*. Nor was a 'foreign patriot' an oxymoron during the French Revolution: they were foreigners who sought to do good for their own countries, while drawing inspiration from the ideals being proclaimed in France.

The people, whose interests patriots sought to promote, were referred to as the 'nation'. In 1789, the old ties of loyalty to king and province crumbled and, in their place, the revolutionaries expected the people to find their identity, their rights, and obligations through membership of the nation, the community of equal citizens. It was the nation, through its representatives, which was to decide the form and structure of the state. This elevation of the nation as the source of sovereignty did not, initially, entail aggression against foreigners. In the early years of the Revolution, a desire to nourish and enrich the nation combined with cosmopolitan idealism to lead the National Assembly to pass decrees encouraging the participation and assimilation of foreigners in French society. On 6 August 1790, Bertrand Barère, who was later to be one of Saint-Just's colleagues on the Committee of Public Safety, enjoined the National Assembly:

So let foreigners come to find in France a homeland; let them live here, let them enjoy liberty while they are alive, and their children their benevolence after their death. . . . The sale of national property will bring wealthy purchasers and new proprietors to France, who, in paying our taxes, will increase the mass of public riches, will augment our industry, animate our agriculture and commerce and finish by adopting free France *as their patrie*.[3]

In the space of a few years, the French Revolution seemed to have passed from this inclusive view of the new order to the one envisaged by Saint-Just, which excluded along lines of nationality.[4]

---

[3] *AP* xvii. 629.

[4] For a fuller discussion of patriotism and cosmopolitanism, see N. Hampson, 'The idea of the Nation in Revolutionary France', in A. Forrest and P. Jones (eds.),

I. THE HISTORICAL PROBLEM: UNIVERSAL RIGHTS AGAINST THE NATION-STATE

At the end of the First World War, Albert Mathiez focused on this passage of the Revolution from its early, cosmopolitan flourish to an exclusive nationalism. He published a book whose arguments and tone were heavily influenced both by the horrific conflict which had maimed Europe and by the Bolshevik Revolution. *La Révolution et les étrangers: Cosmopolitisme et défense nationale* was the first study dedicated entirely to the experience of foreigners in revolutionary France. Mathiez drew comparisons between the Europe of 1789 and of 1914. He claimed that in both years the French people saw themselves as 'citizens of the human race'. Mathiez saw similarities between the socialist internationalism of the early twentieth century and the cosmopolitanism of the eighteenth.[5] The First World War and the Russian Revolution led Mathiez to discuss the tension between cosmopolitanism and patriotism and the emergence of nationalism.

He argues that, in the early years of the Revolution, French patriots 'took their role seriously as the instructors of nations, as the protectors of the oppressed. . . . In every foreigner, they saw a brother, a slightly inferior brother to whom they would be the charitable and generous tutors.' Yet, with the political crisis of the summer of 1791, provoked by Louis XVI's unsuccessful dash for the border, this pacific cosmopolitanism gave way to a more militant kind. Foreign patriots, backed by the Girondins, were encouraged to distribute propaganda among their country-men, while their Girondin friends campaigned for a war to liberate Europe. Mathiez can scarcely conceal his dislike for this development: 'foreigners were never more pampered, more exalted than . . . when we were engaged in a fight to the death against their countries of origin'. For the first year of the war, no

Reshaping France: Town, Country and Region during the French Revolution (Manchester, 1991); Hampson, 'La Patrie', in C. Lucas (ed.), *The French Revolution and the Creation of Modern Political Culture*, ii. *The Political Culture of the French Revolution* (Oxford, 1988); M. Rapport, 'The Treatment of Foreigners in Revolutionary France, 1789–1797', Ph.D. thesis (Bristol, 1997), 76–134.

[5] A. Mathiez, *La Révolution et les étrangers: Cosmopolitisme et défense nationale* (Paris, 1918), 1–3.

security measures were taken against foreigners. These same people were therefore allowed to have undue influence in revolutionary politics and 'this abnormal situation could not continue without serious disadvantages'. Even when the revolutionaries understood this, they tried to reconcile their cosmopolitan ideology with the demands of national security, refusing to take reprisals against enemy subjects when their governments mistreated French citizens. Eventually, circumstances discredited cosmopolitanism and forced the revolutionaries to act against foreigners.[6] In his study of the popular movement, Albert Soboul follows this interpretation, arguing that 'the foreign war and the intensification of the fight rapidly gave popular attitudes a nationalist and xenophobic character, which became marked from the late summer of 1793 . . . the *sans-culottes* classed foreigners as suspects and treated them as such'.[7]

In 1793, the rejection of the Revolution by peoples 'liberated' by the French, renewed defeats at the hands of the coalition and internal troubles led the revolutionaries to take the first general measures against foreigners. These circumstances ensured that, for Mathiez, 'distrust of foreigners was the order of the day' and that 'cosmopolitanism retreated daily'. The overthrow of the Girondins in June naturally made matters worse. The problems faced by the Revolution deepened over the summer and nationalism stirred. The ultimate expression of this development was the Terror, which for Mathiez was nothing other than a 'state of siege', entailing the suspension of civil liberties and, above all, the arrest of enemy subjects and the seizure of their property. He suggests that, as revolutionary ideology lost its cosmopolitanism and focused on the defence of the nation itself ('republican defence and national defence . . . merged'), so an exclusive, chauvinistic form of nationalism was born. This development occurred because foreigners' involvement in revolutionary politics tended be with the opposition to the revolutionary government, namely the Hébertists and the Dantonists. It was this fratricidal conflict which put unwelcome foreigners at the heart of politics, both in reality and in the revolutionary imagination.

---

[6] Mathiez, *La Révolution et les étrangers*, 29, 60–1, 72, 81, 91.

[7] *Les Sans-Culottes parisiens en l'An II: Histoire politique et sociale des sections de Paris, 2 juin 1793–9 thermidor an II* (La Roche-sur-Yon, 1958), 208.

This development caused the government to complete its repressive legislation against foreigners. Mathiez does not, however, claim that this was anything more than 'the *awakening* of nationalism'. He recognizes that the whole panoply of revolutionary laws against foreigners did not amount to the same severity exercised against all enemy aliens by the belligerent powers in 1914. 'By that,' he concludes elegiacally, 'one can measure how far civilization has marched a century later.'[8]

In contrast to Mathiez, who explained the demise of cosmopolitanism largely through force of circumstances, Hannah Arendt identified the main problem within revolutionary ideology itself. Writing in 1949, she argued that the tension between the Revolution's promise of universal rights and the more exclusive idea of the nation was present from the very beginning:

The French Revolution combined the declaration of the Rights of Man with the demand for national sovereignty. The same essential rights which were at once claimed as the inalienable heritage of all human beings *and* as the specific heritage of specific nations, the same nation was at once declared to be subject to laws, which supposedly would flow from the Rights of Man, *and* sovereign, that is, bound by no universal law and acknowledging nothing superior to itself. The practical outcome of this contradiction was that from then on human rights were protected and enforced only as national rights.[9]

This contradiction certainly existed within French revolutionary ideology. The revolutionaries claimed that all people shared natural rights, which were the same anywhere in the world. Yet to make such universal claims implied that national boundaries—and nationality itself—were superfluous. The revolutionaries, however, usually gained legitimacy for their acts not by appealing to all humanity, but to the nation which would have certain territorial boundaries. Geographical limits to the French nation implied some exclusion. People born outside France had other loyalties and obligations, so only French people could enjoy full rights in France. Thus French citizens were differentiated from foreigners. The latter were still considered to have natural rights, but they could only be realized as the political

---

[8] Mathiez, *La Révolution et les étrangers*, 123–6, 132–3, 137, 147, 162–3, 171–2, 177, 181.
[9] H. Arendt, *The Origins of Totalitarianism*, 3rd edn. (London, 1967), 230.

rights of citizenship in their own countries. Jean-Jacques Rousseau, advising the Poles on their new constitution in 1772,
expressed this in the extremest of terms. He wrote that love of
the particular laws and freedom offered by the *patrie* is the mark
of a true republican: 'once he is alone, he is nothing; once he no
longer has a *patrie*, he no longer exists and he is better off
dead'.[10]

Human beings, in other words, only enjoy their full rights
when they are citizens in a particular country. Citizenship is the
legal membership of a state. A state is comprised of the political
and administrative structures which protect the entitlement of its
citizens to certain social and political rights, as well as enforcing
their duties. When they stray beyond the geographical limits of
their state's authority (in other words, when they leave their own
country) people carry their original citizenship with them and,
when abroad, do not share the same political or even social rights
as their hosts. Citizenship has both legal and geographical
boundaries and those frontiers usually define the limits of the
nation.[11] For Arendt, writing shortly after the Holocaust, this
implied that 'the world found nothing sacred in the abstract
nakedness of being human'.[12]

Almost fifty years after Arendt was writing, and seventy years
on from Mathiez, Europe has faced new problems which make
relevant once more the tension between the Revolution's universalist claims and the limits set by citizenship within the
nation-state. In response to the social and political issues raised
by mass immigration, the upsurge of nationalism in Europe,
often in its ugliest and most brutal form, and the challenges
posed to identities and citizenship by European integration,
sociologists, political scientists, and philosophers are debating
the issues of national identity, access to citizenship, and the
integration of foreigners.[13] In France, historians of the French

---

[10] J.-J. Rousseau, 'Considérations sur le gouvernement de Pologne et sur sa
réformation projettée', in *Œuvres Complètes* (Paris, 1964), iii. 966.
[11] R. Brubaker, *Citizenship and Nationhood in France and Germany* (Cambridge,
Mass., 1992), p. x. [12] Arendt, *Origins of Totalitarianism*, 299.
[13] C. Mouffe (ed.), *Dimensions of Radical Democracy: Pluralism, Citizenship,
Community* (London, 1992); O. Le Cour Grandmaison and C. Withol de
Wenden, *Les Étrangers dans la cité: Expériences européennes* (Paris, 1993); J. Kristeva,
Strangers to Ourselves, tr. L. S. Roudiez (New York, 1991); J. Kristeva, *Nations
without Nationalism*, tr. L. S. Roudiez (New York, 1993).

Revolution, such as Florence Gauthier and Sophie Wahnich, have made their contributions. Gauthier has investigated the question raised by Hannah Arendt in 1949: how did the revolutionaries reconcile their claims to universal human rights with their insistence on the nation as the source of sovereignty? She argues that, by 1795, references to universal, natural rights disappeared from revolutionary ideology, to be replaced by the notion of the rights of man in society.[14] This implied that the notion of the unity of mankind, bound together by the sharing of the same fundamental rights, was superseded by the importance of being a citizen in a particular nation. Men could only enjoy their full rights in the society of which they were members. Beyond their own nation, they were merely human, devoid of political rights and protected only by the varying degrees of civil law, the tolerance of their hosts, and the practices of inter-national law. This intellectual development in revolutionary France marked a substantial retreat from cosmopolitanism towards nationalism.

Sophie Wahnich, in a book entitled *L'Impossible Citoyen*, has sought to look at revolutionary discourse (or the ideology, language, and the values conveyed by that rhetoric) regarding foreigners. In a sophisticated analysis of the speeches, petitions, and addresses of revolutionaries, she seeks to illuminate the modern-day questions posed by immigrants in France. By investigating 'that side of the past which might be reassuring' she hopes to find 'the bases upon which foreigners can be welcomed'. Far from being reassuring, however, Wahnich finds that the universalism of the rights of man could not easily be reconciled with the national limits of citizenship.[15]

In fact, during the Terror (Wahnich's primary, but not exclusive, focus), the revolutionaries actually explained the exclusion of foreigners with reference to the universality of their principles. By August 1793, when the Republic was struggling for its very survival against the coalition and its domestic enemies, 'it was no longer a matter of liberating peoples, but of defending the only nation which incarnated the

---

[14] F. Gauthier, *Triomphe et mort du droit naturel en Révolution 1789–1795–1802* (Paris, 1992), 9.
[15] S. Wahnich, *L'Impossible Citoyen: L'Étranger dans le discours de la Révolution française* (Paris, 1997), 9.

principles of liberty against a conspiracy which incarnated the principles of despotism'. If this meant that the interests of humanity were bound up with those of France, then there were two implications: either all foreigners, by the simple fact of not being French, were enemies, or those foreigners who supported France were friends to humanity and, therefore, to the nation. If one chose to believe the latter, then, given the fact that there were also French people who opposed the Revolution, the battlelines of friend and foe cut across nationality. Foreigners, therefore, were not simply those from countries outside France. French people opposed to the Revolution were also referred to as 'foreigners': quite literally, by their very opposition, they had stepped outside the regenerated community of citizens. Louis XVI, the nobility, the rebels of the Vendée, and then republican opponents of the revolutionary government were therefore liable to be destroyed as foreign enemies. The problem, however, was that it was not always certain who were friends and who were foes. It was, above all, this need to classify foreigners and French people alike as suspects or not which led to foreigners being targeted by laws which sought to control their movements and make them more visible to public scrutiny. If all those opposed to the Revolution were regarded as foreigners, then it was easy to suppose that all foreigners were enemies. For Wahnich, they were 'the first great guilty ones'. In this atmosphere, even foreigners who were recognized as friends could be stigmatized as traitors. With their surveillance and policing measures against foreigners, the revolutionaries institutionalized suspicion and xenophobia.[16]

These developments closed off participation in revolutionary politics to foreigners. There was no place for such outsiders in the political life of the *patrie*. It was this closure which led to the expulsion of Thomas Paine and Cloots from the Convention on 25 December 1793 and, ultimately, to the ban on foreigners from participating in political clubs and local committees by the law of 26–7 Germinal. In this way, the revolutionaries succeeded in purging the embarrassing reminders of their earlier, universal pretensions. For a foreigner, it was no longer good enough to adhere to the political orthodoxy of the Revolution to share in

---

[16] Wahnich, *L'Impossible Citoyen*, 28–33, 122, 151.

the rights of citizenship, one had to be part of the sovereign French people as well. The limits of citizenship, Wahnich suggests, at last coincided with the frontier of nationality.[17]

Wahnich concludes from her analysis of revolutionary language that the exclusion of foreigners cannot be explained merely by reference to the circumstances of the war, as Mathiez does.[18] Rather, the implications were always present in revolutionary ideology. The war, Wahnich admits, certainly led the revolutionaries to reconsider their behaviour towards foreigners, but it was not the war which formulated the language and concepts which dictated how they would respond to the crisis. Those rhetorical and ideological devices were already present. It was not the war which led to the exclusion of foreigners from the Convention and from popular societies; nor was it because the term 'foreigner' was being applied to all enemies of the Revolution. It was because the revolutionaries were seeking to define the limits of citizenship—and in doing so, decided to restrict sovereignty to those who were clearly French. Ultimately, the idea of natural rights went underground: what remained of the universalist dream was simply used to justify France's own interests and, above all, her European hegemony.[19]

This necessarily brief overview of Wahnich's arguments can do little justice to their nuances and sophistication. Her work owes much to recent developments in the historiography of the French Revolution. Since the 'Revisionist' assault on interpretations which, in varying degrees, rested on economic and social determinism, politics, and culture have become the focus of the work of historians. In turn, this development has spawned various interpretations, as historians seek to explain the origins, course, and effects of the Revolution in terms of politics, culture, and their social context.[20]

Among the most important of these developments are interpretations which place ideology and rhetoric at the heart of the Revolution. Wahnich's book is undoubtedly of this ilk, which can be traced to François Furet's *Interpreting the French Revolution.*

---

[17] Ibid. 160–1, 200, 231–2, 352.
[18] Mathiez, *La Révolution et les étrangers*, 81, 121–2, 172.
[19] Wahnich, *L'Impossible Citoyen*, 351–2, 361.
[20] P. Jones (ed.), *The French Revolution in Social and Political Perspective* (London, 1996), 1–10.

Furet argues that the Revolution substituted the absolutism of the monarchy with the absolutism of popular sovereignty. This process led revolutionary politicians, soaked in Rousseauist political thought, to try to mirror what they claimed to be the will of the people. The 'general will' could not be divided. Any attempt to represent sectional or personal interests was not only pernicious, but counter-revolutionary. The claims of the Revolution for the absolute power of the people denied the possibility of pluralist politics. In this 'new democratic conviction that the general, or national, will could not be publicly opposed by special interests',[21] opposition was regarded as selfish, sinister, and conspiratorial, the nemesis of the supposed transparency of the popular will. The logical products of this denial of political pluralism were a punitive mentality, the justification of violence, and the Terror. Such atrocities, Furet argues, were the product of revolutionary ideology rather than a simple reaction to circumstances. They were inherent in the Revolution from the moment the sovereignty of the nation was accepted as its guiding principle.[22]

Other historians, such as Lynn Hunt in her *Politics, Culture, and Class in the French Revolution,* have expanded on Furet's work by looking at the various expressions of revolutionary ideology in rhetoric, symbolism, and ritual and at the people who practised politics. In placing political ideology in a broader social and cultural context, Hunt supports many of Furet's suggestions. She accepts the potency of revolutionary ideology as the dynamic which drove the Revolution along its path to Terror. Yet Hunt also argues that 'although the Terror followed logically from the principles enunciated in revolutionary rhetoric, it was not the only possible deduction from those principles'. She shares, however, Furet's generally pessimistic prognosis of the course of the Revolution.[23]

In her examination of revolutionary discourse on foreigners, Wahnich's interpretation tends to lend weight to the analyses of Furet and Hunt. The surveillance, arrest, and expulsion of

---

[21] F. Furet, *Interpreting the French Revolution,* tr. E. Forster (Cambridge, 1981), 53.

[22] Ibid. 25, 39, 46–56.

[23] L. Hunt, *Politics, Culture, and Class in the French Revolution* (London, 1986), 19–51.

foreigners in the Terror occurred as the logical outcome of revolutionary ideology and language. In the case of foreigners, it was the product of the irreconcilable tension between universalism and the idea of the nation. The exclusion of foreigners was, above all, the result of nationality becoming the essential criterion for citizenship.

There is, however, still room for a study of foreigners in revolutionary France, for three reasons. First, the radical interpretations proposed by Furet and Hunt, emphasizing ideology and culture, have led some historians to identify 'the creation of modern political culture' as the main achievement of the Revolution. Among the most important frames of reference in the new politics were the citizen and the nation. Such terms, however, had to be defined: who was to be included, and who excluded? Research on this issue has taken different forms, including discussions of citizenship, popular sovereignty, patriotism, and elections. Historians working in these areas have naturally been drawn to study the limits of revolutionary citizenship and the ways in which excluded groups challenged these boundaries. The political and social rights of women, Jews, blacks, the poor, and the aristocracy were all subjects of debate and action among the revolutionaries as they defined the extent of citizenship.

The study of women in the French Revolution has offered potent examples of how the revolutionaries restricted access to political rights and how, in response, some of those excluded challenged those limits. Joan Landes's work in this area offers a potential parallel to the revolutionary experience of foreigners. Explicitly adopting Jürgen Habermas's concept of the 'bourgeois public sphere', she argues that, in the Revolution, the absolute monarchy gave way to 'a more pervasive gendering of the public sphere'. Despite the patriarchal character of the Ancien Régime, women influenced and participated in politics, in their roles at court, in literary salons, in the traditions of popular protest, and even in formal political activities such as the elections to the Estates-General. Such exclusion from the public sphere which women experienced did not seem exceptional because few men or women enjoyed political rights anyway. Although the breakdown of authority in 1789 and the crisis of 1793 opened the public sphere to all forms of political expression, in which women played a prominent role, ultimately they were deliberately and explicitly excluded by the revolutionaries. This exclusion from the political life of the new order was 'central to its incarnation . . . the bourgeois public sphere is essentially, not just contingently, masculinist. . . . The Republic was constructed against women, not just without them.' In the bourgeois view of universal natural rights, men were seen as political creatures, while women were regarded as naturally domestic. Yet the idea that rights were universal allowed feminists to expose the discrepancies between principle and practice: republican ideology had a capacity 'to encompass both feminist and antifeminist alternatives'.[24]

Landes's work raises the question as to how far the revolutionaries deliberately sought to define the nation not only without certain groups, but also in opposition to them. Darline Gay Levy offers another possible approach. For her, 'the meanings assigned to citizenship by participants in this political drama were staggeringly diverse, often competing and conflicting . . . all meanings of French revolutionary citizenship . . . were plural and unstable, marked by complex internal tensions and fissures'.[25] This raises another tempting perspective on exclusion: that, for much of the French Revolution, ideas of citizenship were in flux and were being constantly challenged. If the limits which defined the new order were fluctuating, then perhaps foreigners, like French women, found ways to test these boundaries.

The ideas mooted by Landes and Levy raise important questions about the denial of rights to groups on the limits of the body politic. Was the new order deliberately defined so as to exclude foreigners, to become Saint-Just's republican 'city' of brothers? Or were notions of citizenship and even of nationality still oscillating and open to challenge by those on its fringes? A consideration as to how foreigners actually fared, as opposed to their treatment in revolutionary rhetoric, might reveal another dimension to the revolutionary experience of defining citizenship and nationality. How foreigners were treated in practice might indicate how far the revolutionaries succeeded in aligning

[24] J. Landes, *Women and the Public Sphere in the Age of the French Revolution* (Ithaca, NY, 1988), 2, 4–7, 12–13, 20–1, 105–7.

[25] D. G. Levy, 'Women's Revolutionary Citizenship in Action, 1791: Setting the Boundaries', in R. Waldinger, P. Dawson, and I. Woloch (eds.), *The French Revolution and the Meaning of Citizenship* (Westport, Conn., 1993), 169, 182.

citizenship with nationality. This current work aims to show that there were not only contradictions within revolutionary ideology, as identified by Arendt, Gauthier, and Wahnich, but there was also a gap between what the revolutionaries said and what they actually did.

Secondly, discussions on the creation of modern political culture have led to debate over just how novel the political structures and practices of the Revolution actually were. If much of François Furet's work owes an explicit debt to the Tocquevillian approach which stresses continuities, he claims that in ideological terms the Revolution represented a complete break with the past: the old France was a kingdom of subjects whose place was determined by privilege, while the new France was a nation of equal citizens. Furet subsequently argued that this break with the past led the revolutionaries to innovate and so 1789 was the 'birth of political modernity'.[26] For some historians, this modernity is an ongoing process, whereby the Revolution has provided subsequent generations with 'master narratives' upon which current political and social action can draw for experience and example. Others have found the modernity of the Revolution in the creation of a political framework in which, above all, social and economic questions are debated and where the tension lies between an urge for social justice and demands for political freedom.[27] Sophie Wahnich has significantly identified the Revolution's modernity in its exposure of the contradictions between the universal and the local, between being human and being a citizen.[28] The modernity thesis has not been accepted by all historians. In recent works, both Peter Jones and Malcolm Crook argue for the persistence of older forms and customs within French revolutionary politics.[29] Albert Mathiez, while seeing in the Terrorist measures against foreigners the birth of nationalism, suggests that the acts themselves were a far cry from behaviour of governments towards enemy aliens in the total wars of the

[26] P. M. Jones, *Reform and Revolution in France: The Politics of Transition, 1774– 1791* (Cambridge, 1995), 2.

[27] F. Fehér, 'Introduction', *The French Revolution and the Birth of Modernity* (Berkeley, Calif., 1990), 3–10.

[28] Wahnich, *L'Impossible Citoyen*, 352.

[29] Jones, *Reform and Revolution in France*; M. Crook, *Elections in the French Revolution: An Apprenticeship in Democracy, 1789–1799* (Cambridge, 1996).

twentieth century. An examination of the treatment of foreigners might, therefore, also contribute to the question of rupture or continuity in the revolutionary creation of modern political practice.

Finally, historiographical developments outside the field of the French Revolution have produced stimulating work on identity of various kinds.[30] Different attitudes towards foreigners are ways of emphasizing the separateness, or even uniqueness, of one's homeland. The study of the identity of any people is consequently incomplete without some consideration for the way in which it regards its neighbours and treats foreigners among it. Theodore Zeldin has written that 'France was defined as a nation not only by the policies of its rulers—or, alternatively, by the peculiarities of the provinces from which it was formed—but also by the way it distinguished itself from the nations that surround it. To understand France, one must appreciate the complexity of its attitudes towards foreigners.'[31] Any study of identity, because of the very nature of its slow evolution, must take a long-term perspective. It is hoped, however, that in taking a snapshot of a ten-year period in which the French treatment of foreigners underwent many mutations, some tentative remarks might be offered on the Revolution's impact on French identity. Before the examination of foreigners begins, it is necessary to describe what nationality and citizenship meant in eighteenth-century France.

2. THE FRENCH IDEA OF THE NATION IN THE EIGHTEENTH CENTURY

A modern state usually gives the rights of citizenship to those people who are recognized as members of the nation—or nations, as in the case of the United Kingdom and the former USSR—which fall under its authority. A nation is a people which identifies itself as a distinct political or ethnic community, which often claims control over its own domestic and external

---

[30] E. Weber, *Peasants into Frenchmen: The Modernization of Rural France, 1870–1914* (Stanford, Calif., 1976); L. Colley, *Britons: Forging the Nation 1707–1837* (London, 1994).

[31] *France 1848–1945: Intellect and Pride* (Oxford, 1980), 86.

affairs. Consequently, how each state defines who are members of the nation and who are not carries great weight. The French approach, often described as 'assimilationist', is rooted in the historical development of the French state.

In 1694, the *Dictionnaire de l'Académie* defined the nation as 'all the inhabitants of the same state, of the same country who live under the same laws and use the same language'.[32] If the monarchy had insisted on this last point, then the people over whom it claimed sovereignty would never have constituted a nation. Linguistically, religiously, and culturally, the subjects of the French king were a diverse group of people. Language and custom, above all, could not be a determinant of Frenchness. The inhabitants of Alsace, for example, were very different from others in the French kingdom. In July 1789, Arthur Young remarked on how striking it was 'to cross a great range of mountains; to enter a level plain, inhabited by a people totally distinct and different from France, with manners, language, ideas, prejudices, and habits all different'. He commented that 'I found myself to all appearance veritably in Germany . . . here not one person in a hundred has a word of French.'[33] Earlier in his circuitous travels, he observed that the inhabitants of Roussillon in the south 'are Spaniards in language and in customs, but they are under a French government'.[34] Furthermore, Basque was spoken along the western Pyrenees and Breton in Lower Brittany. Conversely, French was spoken in Brabant, under Austrian sovereignty. French language and the culture stemming from it could not, therefore, be one of the prime legal criteria for French nationality.

Similarly, religion was not a factor, despite the theoretical commitment of the French monarchy to extirpate heresy. It is true that, to be naturalized, a foreigner had in theory to convert to Catholicism, but this practice became rarer over the course of the eighteenth century. The king tolerated Jews and Protestants among his subjects, even if they were 'second class' behind Catholics. Ethnicity and race excluded Jews and blacks from the full privileges and protection of the law under the Ancien

[32] Brubaker, *Citizenship and Nationhood*, 192 n.
[33] A. Young, *Travels in France during the Years 1787, 1788 and 1789*, ed. C. Maxwell (Cambridge, 1929), 180.
[34] Ibid. 38.

Régime, but French contemporaries still saw them as subjects of the king of France, if only, for one, as a religious and racial minority to be grudgingly tolerated and, for the other, as a racial group to be subjected to segregation, enslavement, and brutal exploitation. The Ashkenazim Jews in Alsace and Lorraine spoke Yiddish between themselves, as well as the French or German dialects of their immediate locality. There was also a population of these Jews in Paris. Those of the south, in Avignon, the Comtat-Venaissin, Bordeaux, and Bayonne, were Sephardim and were more assimilated. The Jews of Bordeaux and Saint-Esprit, a suburb of Bayonne, had arrived from Portugal in the sixteenth century (and were therefore sometimes referred to as 'Portuguese Jews'). They often presented themselves as Catholics, while privately observing their original religious faith. The 20,000 Ashkenazim Jews in Alsace, however, were forced to live in separate ghettos in small villages, mainly in the north. These people were forbidden to live in the larger towns, so that there were only four Jewish families in Strasbourg in 1789. The edict of 1784 gave them the right to live in 182 small towns and villages in Alsace, but, as they were not allowed to employ Christians, they had to work the land themselves. The Jews also suffered from a deep-rooted anti-Semitism which erupted during the peasant uprisings in the summer of 1789.[35] With their segregation, their limited choice of residence, and the denial of other social rights, the Jews were among the least privileged subjects in metropolitan France. Their legal situation, however, was better than the conditions suffered by the slaves in France's overseas colonies.

Blacks were enslaved there because of their race, although they were still considered subjects of the king of France. This is not to say that both creole and African slaves accepted this and believed that they were French. The varieties of *gens de couleur* and black slaves in the French colonies presented a mosaic of African, creole, and French culture, which eventually developed, at least in Haiti, into a separate political identity. Yet, before the Revolution, whites in the colonies determined an individual's place in the social hierarchy by assessing the different mixtures of race which he or she carried: black, white, indigenous indian.

---

[35] E. Hartmann, *La Révolution française en Alsace et en Lorraine* (Paris, 1990), 27–9.

The various proportions of 'blood' were described with bizarre precision in an outlandish terminology.[36] Meanwhile, the authorities in metropolitan France regarded all inhabitants of the colonies, slave, free black, and white, as subjects of the king, albeit indirectly, through the brutal medium of the plantation owners. The monarchy was, in theory, the supreme recourse of justice for slaves. Louis XIV's *Code Noir* allowed slaves to complain about their treatment to the royal *procureur-général*, while subjecting them to absolute obedience to their owners. In practice, the code did not reflect the realities of plantation life.[37]

Yet the idea that all inhabitants of the French empire were the king's subjects was reinforced by the fact that freed blacks automatically assumed the *qualité de français*, without needing letters of naturalization. The 'freedom principle', first declared by the *parlement* of Paris in 1571, that 'there are no slaves in France' meant that those brought into the kingdom by their owners were to be freed automatically and allowed to live like other subjects. When, in 1738, a slave from Saint-Domingue named Jean Boucaux won his freedom before the Admiralty Court, his lawyer never mentioned his race, but argued that he was French 'because he was born the subject of our monarch; equal, as much by humanity as by the religion which he professes; and citizen because he lives with us and among us'. Likewise, in 1762, the *procureur du roi* upheld the 'freedom principle' of French soil on the grounds that 'every slave on entering France is free like all other subjects of the king'. This is not to say that racial anxieties were absent. Louis XVI was worried even by the small numbers of blacks who arrived in the kingdom, so the government issued the *Déclaration pour la police des Noirs* in 1777, prohibiting the entry of all blacks and *gens de couleur*. Those brought to France by their owners were to stay in depots in their port of arrival. This edict used explicitly racial categories rather than the term 'slaves' because, as the naval minister, Sartine, explained, the *parlement* of Paris could not refuse to register the order on the grounds of the 'freedom

---

[36] A. Césaire, *Toussaint Louverture: La Révolution française et le problème colonial* (Paris, 1961), 31.

[37] H. M. Beckles, 'Social and Political Control in the Slave Society', in F. W. Knight (ed.), *General History of the Caribbean*, iii. *The Slave Societies of the Caribbean* (Basingstoke, 1997), 200–1.

principle'. The following year saw a ban on interracial marriage.[38]

Such sinister attempts at stemming the trickle of non-whites into France were accompanied by anxieties about the 'corruption' of French blood. These measures suggest that, if the absolute monarchy was willing to count blacks and people of mixed race among its subjects, it would much rather have kept them in its distant colonies. Whether or not the laws were applied with any vigour (and the evidence suggests that they were not[39]), it does appear that, legally, the monarchy was coming close to defining metropolitan France as a racially closed community of subjects. In fact, it never went that far. The black population which existed in Paris, small as it was, appeared to be well-integrated into French society. Most often, blacks were free, working as domestics, masons, carpenters, upholsterers, labourers, shopkeepers and enjoyed the same level of literacy as their white counterparts in the same occupations.[40] At the very best, while they undoubtedly suffered from racial abuse, free blacks in France were treated and fared legally like other subjects of the king. At the worst, blacks were enslaved in the colonies, forced to submit to the *Code Noir*, barred entry into metropolitan France, and compelled to absolute obedience to their immediate owners. Social status and corporate identity were defined in Ancien Régime by privilege, or absence of it. In this social arrangement, enslaved blacks were the most underprivileged of all the king's subjects.

The unequal distribution of privilege could accommodate a wide variety of linguistic, ethnic, and religious groups. The facts of race and religious observance did not determine French nationality, but they did dictate the degree of privilege and civil freedom one enjoyed. What bound together the French kingdom and empire was the monarchy itself, or rather the assumption that ultimately all those born on the domains of the French king were subject to his laws, and received his protection in return for their obedience. Legal, linguistic, reli-

[38] S. Peabody, *'There are no Slaves in France': The Political Culture of Race and Slavery in the Ancien Régime* (New York, 1996), 3–8, 36, 91, 128–9.

[39] P. H. Boulle, 'Les Gens de couleur à Paris à la veille de la Révolution', in M. Vovelle (ed.), *L'Image de la Révolution française: Congrès Mondial pour le Bicentenaire de la Révolution, Sorbonne, Paris 6–12 juillet 1989*, 4 vols. (Paris, 1990), i. 159–60.   [40] Ibid. 162–3.

gious, cultural, and ethnic differences between subjects were not anomalous to eighteenth-century jurists, because they were related to the very nature of Ancien Régime society. Privilege, or absence of it, distinguished the various individuals, guilds, corporations, towns, and provinces from each other. In this corporate society, what tied them all together was obedience to the same king. Their Frenchness was defined by the vertical ties of ultimate loyalty to the monarchy, while they remained separate and distinct from each other because of differences in privilege.[41] During the elections to the Estates-General in 1789, some provinces even resisted the idea that they formed part of the kingdom of France, invoking a purely dynastic link to the French crown. The Estates of Navarre, for example, were scandalized at being treated as anything other than a separate kingdom.[42]

None the less, Navarre was still subject to royal authority. To have been born under that authority was to be a *régnicole*, a natural subject of the king. It was assumed that one tacitly accepted the king's protection and offered obedience to his laws in return. French nationality, therefore, was determined by one's birth on the dominions of the French crown, while a foreigner was defined baldly as 'he who is born outside the Kingdom'.[43] Even this simple formula immediately posed problems, because no one knew precisely where the frontiers of the French kingdom lay. Anne-Robert de Turgot, as controller-general of finances from 1774 to 1776, set up a Topographical Bureau which would mark out the limits of French territory. The task was not a simple one. In Lorraine, for example, it was not clear where the possessions of the king of France ended and those of the elector of Trier began.[44] Border arrangements were still being discussed with princes of the Holy Roman Empire in the mid-1780s.[45]

[41] M. P. Fitzsimmons, 'The National Assembly and the Invention of Citizenship', in R. Waldinger, P. Dawson, and I. Woloch, *The French Revolution and the Meaning of Citizenship* (Westport, Conn., 1993), 29.

[42] Jones, *Reform and Revolution*, 13–14.

[43] C.-J. de Ferrière, *Dictionnaire de droit pratique contenant l'explication des termes de droit, d'ordonnances, de coutumes et de pratique: Avec les jurisdictions de France*, 2 vols. (Toulouse, 1779), i. 658.

[44] Jones, *Reform and Revolution*, 13.

[45] Archives Nationales, K//2033; F/7/4399; P. Sahlins, 'Natural Frontiers Revisited: France's Boundaries since the Seventeenth Century', *American Historical Review*, 95 (1990), 1440–1.

To complicate matters further, the French monarchy periodi-
cally laid claim to territory beyond its existing frontiers, and
could treat those who were technically living under the sovereignty of another prince as its own subjects. The Comtat-
Venaissin and Avignon were papal territories enclaved in the
south of France. Both areas were ceded to the pope, the Comtat
in 1275 and Avignon in 1348. In 1789, as the British traveller
Dr Edward Rigby discovered, Avignon 'still belongs to the Pope
. . . we were therefore required to take a passport on leaving it'.[46]
Yet the border was far from insurmountable for the papal
subjects: in 1348, Philip VI declared the Avignonnais and the
Venaissins to be French and this was confirmed in 1540. By
these edicts, inhabitants of the enclaves could even hold ecclesiastical benefices in France, a privilege otherwise denied to all
but *régnicoles* by the Blois ordinance of 1579.[47] Culturally and
linguistically, too, the inhabitants had much in common with the
people who lived in the kingdom of France itself. In all aspects of
French life, therefore, Avignonnais and Venaissins were in
practical terms completely indistinct from *régnicoles*: quite
simply, they were not treated as foreigners. In a similar fashion,
from 1702 the inhabitants of Savoy were treated as *régnicoles*,
although they were subjects of the king of Sardinia.[48] Such
rulings were dictated by the monarchy's desire to justify and
reinforce older claims on the territory concerned.

There were also regions within France over which the king laid
claim to sovereignty, but in which he recognized certain legal
jurisdictions of foreign princes, as in the enclaves of Alsace.
France won possession of the province with the treaty of
Westphalia in 1648, but accepted some of the legal and fiscal
rights of the princes of the Holy Roman Empire, who owned
estates and fiefdoms there. Such privileges varied from one lord
to another, but they included the appointment of judges and
clergy, the imposition of taxes, and the levying of dues.[49] The

---

[46] E. Rigby, *Dr. Rigby's Letters from France, etc., in 1789* (London, 1880), 126.

[47] R. Villers, 'La Condition des étrangers en France dans les trois derniers siècles
de la monarchie', *Recueils de la Société Jean Bodin*, x. *L'Étranger* (Brussels, 1958), 144,
148; Isambert, Jourdan, and Decrusy, *Recueil général des Anciennes lois françaises
depuis l'an 420 jusqu'à la Révolution de 1789*, 31 vols. (Paris, 1822–33), xii. 743.

[48] J. Boizet, 'Les Lettres de naturalité sous l'Ancien régime', Thèse de droit (Paris,
1943), 51.

[49] AN, F/7/4399.

population of these enclaves therefore owed obedience not only to the king of France, but also to their German lord.

For the Ancien Régime in Europe, such overlaps of authority were not unusual. Some European sovereigns did seek to wrap their dynastic lands into continuous territorial parcels, but the weight of tradition, prescription, and international treaties—the *droit public* of Europe—led most people to accept such apparent anomalies as existed in Avignon, the Comtat, Savoy, and Alsace. The question as to what constituted French nationality boiled down to whom one owed ultimate allegiance. Jews, although weighed down by heavy-handed regulations which prevented them from assimilating, were under the final protection and command of the king of France. Black slaves in the colonies, mainly African in culture and subject to the immediate, hard and inflexible will of the planters, were also forced to submit theoretically to the distant French crown. In cases such as Alsace, the papal enclaves, and Savoy, the *droit public* of Europe determined the principle, if not the practice, of nationality. If the people of Alsace owed their first obedience to their immediate masters in the Holy Roman Empire, at another level they were considered French rather than German because their ultimate overlord was the king of France. This arrangement did not, however, preclude disputes over the precise extent of French sovereignty in Alsace.[50] Meanwhile, and despite their naturalization by the French monarchy, inhabitants of the papal enclaves and of Savoy were legally foreigners. In practice, of course, the subjects in question may have felt differently and behaved accordingly: an Avignonnais, technically a foreigner, had more in common with a French-speaking subject of Louis XVI than did a German-speaking Alsatian. Yet people born in France were assumed to have made the commitment of loyalty to the king. This territorial basis of nationality was referred to as the *droit de sol*, and included those born in France of foreign parents, and children born abroad of French parents, provided that they returned to live permanently in the kingdom.

The revolutionaries aimed to create a new civic order based on the abolition of distinctions of birth and privilege among all

---

[50] P. Muret, 'L'Affaire des princes possessionnés d'Alsace et les origines du conflit entre la Révolution et l'Empire', *Revue d'histoire moderne et contemporaine*, 1 (1899–1900), 434–9.

citizens. At the same time, they made the nation, rather than the king, the source of political legitimacy. Both developments redefined the relationship of the citizen to the state. The abolition of privilege on 4 August 1789, the administrative division of the kingdom into departments, the emancipation of Protestants, Jews, and, eventually, blacks theoretically erased the old legal sources of social differentiation. People's loyalty and identity were now expected to focus on the entire French people, rather than one's corporation, guild, town, province, religious, linguistic, or ethnic group. What defined French nationality was no longer loyalty to a monarch, but rather to the nation, the community of citizens who shared the same rights within the same territorial limits.

In this respect, the Revolution inherited from the Ancien Régime the tendency to define French nationality only in political terms. Emmanuel Sieyès described the nation in 1789 simply as 'a body of associates living under a common law and represented by the same *legislature*'.[51] On the one hand, this confirmed the assimilationist tendency in the definition of French nationality, which could encompass anyone who sought to participate and contribute to the life of the nation. On the other hand, this idea was not only dictated by principles. To insist on language, ethnicity, or religion as a basis for nationality would have made France as it was in 1789 merely a state rather than a nation, and a state constructed from a variety of 'nations' or peoples who might demand, on the basis of the Revolution's own ideology, their own rights to self-determination. In any case, the one short-lived attempt to impose linguistic conformity on all French citizens, by the law of 20 July 1794, floundered because it was unworkable.[52] Defining the nation as a cultural entity was impossible in practice. If the Revolution represented a break with the past in terms of the transfer of sovereignty from king to nation, there was continuity in the definition of membership of the nation, and in the motivation for it.

The Revolution also inherited the same problems of drawing a

---

[51] E. Sieyès, *Qu'est-ce que le tiers état?*, ed. J.-D. Bredin (Paris, 1988), 40.

[52] *AP*, xciii. 367–8; M. Lyons, 'Regionalism and Linguistic Conformity in the French Revolution', in A. Forrest and P. Jones, *Reshaping France* (Manchester, 1991), 185, 188.

geographical line of demarcation between French and foreigners. Unlike the Ancien Régime, the absolute pretensions of the principle of national sovereignty could not accommodate such overlaps of jurisdiction as existed in Alsace. Nor could it resist for long the demands of Avignon and the Comtat-Venaissin for 'reunion' with France, as they were apparently the expressed will of the people of those enclaves. In these cases, the Revolution sharpened the focus in the definition of French nationality by denying the legitimacy of the apparent anomalies tolerated by the old European *droit public*. More problematic was the fact that the political boundaries of the French nation were in flux for most of the revolutionary period, because of the war. This meant that the limits of French nationality still remained unclear. When revolutionary armies surged into Belgium and the Rhineland, first at the end of 1792 and again in the summer of 1794, the revolutionaries laid claim to both areas, which naturally included Flemish and German speakers. Early in 1793, the Convention accepted the mainly extorted 'plebiscites' from Belgian and Liégeois communes for 'reunion' with France. Henceforth, the Belgians and the Liégeois might have expected to be considered French citizens. Yet when the Austrians reconquered their territory, the revolutionary authorities treated Belgians and Liégeois in France ambiguously. Sometimes they were deemed French citizens, but on other occasions they were treated as foreigners. They were exempt from the confiscation of foreigners' property, decreed on 7 September 1793, on the grounds that they were French. On 25 December, however, Maximilien Robespierre had them excepted from the law expelling foreigners from elected office, not because they were considered French citizens, but because they fulfilled their functions honourably.[53]

The nationality of Belgians and Liégeois was decided only when their countries were formally annexed by France on 1 October 1795. This annexation and the forced cession by the Empire of the left bank of the Rhine in December 1798 represented victories for the proponents of France's 'natural frontiers' or *grandes limites*. They also made, in theory at least, French citizens out of people who spoke Flemish and German. Appeals to nature justified these expanded limits of the Republic and,

[53] *AP*, lxxiii. 504; lxxxii. 304.

tellingly, if the Rhine was France's 'natural' frontier, nature herself had not preordained nations to speak the same language. As the revolutionaries created a new state and a new political culture, therefore, the very people whom they sought to regenerate by these changes remained fluid both in definition and in fact. This definition of the nation, however, was crucial for determining who should have the rights of citizenship. For the revolutionaries, citizenship depended first of all on nationality. In every constitution of the 1790s, a precondition for the exercise of the rights of citizenship was either birth on French soil, or, for foreigners, a period of residence followed by naturalization. One had to be defined as French before one could claim political rights. In fact, while they used the terms *nation* and *national* lavishly, the revolutionaries rarely, if ever, spoke of *nationalité*,[54] because the term was almost redundant. To be French was simply to have claims to the rights and duties of citizenship within French territory.

The condition of membership of the contractual community was that one either sacrificed or made secondary all other sources of collective identity. Any legal identity which drew immutable distinctions between citizens and which therefore divided the sovereign nation were to be levelled. Allegiance to another sovereign was to be renounced; membership of hereditary orders was to be relinquished; insistence on a separate corporate identity within the nation, whether religious, linguistic, or ethnic, was to be abandoned. Nothing was to obstruct the relationship of the individual with the nation, an idea which was famously expressed by the deputy to the Constituent Assembly, Clermont-Tonnerre, on 26 August 1789, speaking in favour of emancipating the Jews: 'We must refuse everything to the Jews as a *Nation*, and grant them everything as *individuals*, they must be neither a political body, nor an order, within the State, they must be individual citizens.'[55] Within the revolutionary nation, each citizen had the same worth and dignity as the other and each was equally liable

[54] J. Godechot, 'The New Concept of the Nation and its Diffusion in Europe', in O. Dann and J. Dinwiddy (eds.), *Nationalism in the Age of the French Revolution* (London, 1988), 13–14.
[55] J. Godechot, 'La Révolution française et les juifs', *Annales historiques de la Révolution française*, 48 (1976), 56.

to the same laws. When citizens formed themselves into exclusive associations which stressed characteristics common only to each group, the sovereign nation was divided and became, like the Ancien Régime, a mere collection of corporations, each with their own special privileges before the law. The tacit contract, of emancipation in return for assimilation, left little room for any public identity other than that of being a citizen. Religious, ethnic, and cultural identities were to be relegated to private life.

It was this principle which enabled some Jewish leaders to argue that they were not foreigners, but French citizens who, as individuals, merely had a different faith. Zalkind Hourwitz, a Jew of Polish origin, anticipated Clermont-Tonnerre's statement by suggesting that the cultural characteristics which differentiated Jews from other French subjects arose precisely because of the laws which restricted their behaviour and prevented them from realizing their full potential as citizens. Suppress those laws, his argument ran, and Jews would assimilate with the French people.[56] The revolutionaries accepted this and, when Jews were accorded full civil and political rights on 27 September 1791, the National Assembly implicitly rejected the view of the conservative cleric Maury, that 'calling Jews citizens would be like saying that without letters of naturalization and without ceasing to be English and Danish, the English and Danish could become French'.[57] The emancipation decreed by the Constituent Assembly did not, of course, destroy long-held anti-Semitism. It did, however, stress that, at a legal level, nationality was not to be defined ethnically or linguistically and emphasized the secularism of the new state. Yet, as many Ashkenazim Jews did not easily assimilate, it left them exposed to persecution, during local manifestations of the anti-religious movement in 1793, as a separate, religious group reluctant to embrace the national community.[58] The apparent reluctance to embrace cultural pluralism, implicit in the assimilationist ideal,

[56] L. Hunt, *The French Revolution and Human Rights: A Brief Documentary History* (New York, 1996), 48–50.

[57] Ibid. 89.

[58] G. Kates, 'Jews into Frenchmen: Nationality and Representation in Revolutionary France', in Fehér, *The French Revolution and the Birth of Modernity* (Berkeley, Calif., 1990), 103–15; Godechot, 'La Révolution française et les juifs', 60–70; R. Necheles, 'L'Emancipation des juifs 1787–1795', *AhRf* 48 (1976), 79–80.

has brought the revolutionary concept of the nation under attack in modern French politics.[59]

Perhaps the greatest failure of the practical application of the assimilationist ideal, however, came over the problem of race and slavery in the colonies. The issue was forced by the slave insurrection in Saint-Domingue which began in August 1791. It culminated in a full-scale revolution which led to the establishment of the independent Haitian republic in 1804. One of the responses of the French Revolution was to abolish slavery on 4 February 1794, proclaiming that all men in the empire 'without distinction of colour' were to be considered French citizens, enjoying all the rights assured by the constitution.[60] Blacks did not need to be naturalized to assume such political rights, because, as inhabitants of the French empire, they were automatically French. Yet most of the slaves in the Antilles had been born in Africa and so were culturally and linguistically African, mixed perhaps with some creole influences. By giving them French citizenship, even if it had not considered or planned it that way, the Convention was defining French nationality in a way which could accommodate all manner of races. The revolutionaries were not naturalizing blacks, but merely recognizing that, as inhabitants of French territory, they were citizens equal to whites. For all the expediency behind the decree, it ensured that French citizenship would not be limited on the basis of race.

It is doubtful, however, that most of the insurgents regarded themselves as French. Their culture was predominantly African. They naturally proclaimed their loyalty to those powers which seemed to offer the best promise of freedom. So, while retaining their own identities, the Haitian revolutionaries went over to the French only when they abolished slavery.[61] Conversely, when Napoleon Bonaparte tried to reintroduce slavery in 1802, the Haitians rebelled once more and won their independence. In trying to enslave the very people whom the Convention had once

[59] J. F. Hollifield, 'Immigration and Modernization', in J. F. Hollifield and G. Ross (eds.), *Searching for the New France* (London, 1991), 113–50.

[60] Hunt, *The French Revolution and Human Rights*, 116.

[61] M. Craton, 'Forms of Resistance to Slavery', in Knight, *General History of the Caribbean*, iii. 244–8; J. K. Thornton, '"I am the Subject of the King of Congo": African Political Ideology and the Haitian Revolution', *Journal of World History*, 4 (1993), 181–214. I am grateful to Robin Law for this last reference.

claimed as French citizens, Bonaparte forced the people of Haiti to become, quite literally, foreigners: members of an independent state seeking to assert their own 'Afro-Antillean' identity.[62]

Blacks, women, Jews, and other excluded groups all challenged the limits of citizenship in the revolutionary decade, with varying degrees of success and with different results. These people, or at least their leaders and their supporters, could argue for greater rights of participation in politics and in society both by claiming membership of the broad, French nation and by reminding legislators of their universal, natural rights. Foreigners could base their claims on the latter, but not on the former. Yet, while most foreigners accepted the need for naturalization before they assumed the rights of citizenship, a small number either held public office or found ways of participating in revolutionary politics without becoming French citizens. For most foreigners in 1789, however, the aim was not to obtain further access to politics and the state, but to preserve what positions they already had in those structures. For the problem which foreigners posed to the revolutionary idea of the nation was that they served the French monarchy in the army, in administration, in finance, and in the church in capacities which appeared to contradict the idea that only citizens should enjoy such rights and bear such duties. While the privileged, corporate structure of Ancien Régime society allowed foreigners to serve the king in the French state without any apparent anomaly, the revolutionary notion of the sovereignty of the nation implied that they be excluded from such roles.

These 'nationalizing' tendencies in revolutionary ideology were frequently expressed in the 1790s, but they were never fully applied because the revolutionaries were realistic enough to understand the practical problems which they faced. Financial, economic, diplomatic, and military crises led the revolutionaries to retain the skills, money, and manpower offered by foreigners. While their decisions may have been explained or justified with reference to revolutionary principles, they were not necessarily driven by those ideas. Consequently, as this study aims to show, the revolutionaries fell short of excluding all foreigners from

---

[62] F. W. Knight, *The Caribbean: The Genesis of a Fragmented Nationalism* (New York, 1978), 158.

participation in revolutionary politics and from the structures of the state. Nor did they, in practice, shut foreigners out from the broader social and economic life in France, even in the dark, xenophobic days of the Terror. In short, they never built the exclusively French 'city' envisaged by Saint-Just.

To Live Free, to Die a Slave:
Foreigners in Ancien Régime France

On a December morning in 1750, a funeral procession left the white-towered Renaissance château of Chambord. A carriage, draped in black and built specially for the occasion, was drawn by six cloaked horses. The coffin was attended by equerries, pages, valets, lackeys, and guards. This cortège was escorted by one hundred horsemen, bristling with sabres, carbines, lances, and brightly dressed as dragoons, uhlans, and Tartars—a reflection of their diverse and exotic origins, from Africa to eastern Europe. The procession was made rarer by its destination, the Lutheran chapel of Saint-Thomas in Strasbourg.

The man honoured in this way was Maurice de Saxe, marshal of France, duke of Courland and son of the elector of Saxony, Frederick-Augustus, later Augustus II of Poland. The cavalrymen escorting the coffin were once his own, part of his thousand-strong regiment of horse, the Saxe-Volontaire. Maurice's final journey would take two months. On its way through the garrison towns of north-eastern France, church bells tolled solemnly and guards of honour presented arms. In the countryside, small clusters of curious peasants followed in respectful silence. When the convoy finally reached Strasbourg on 8 February, it was greeted with twelve cannon shots and attended by notables of Alsace, non-commissioned officers of the Saxe-Volontaire, four lieutenant-generals, and no less than forty-three Protestant pastors. The entire garrison of the city lined the route from the Porte de France to the chapel. Banners were lowered as the carriage rumbled by and drums, covered with black crêpe, quietly rolled. After the funeral service, the crowds which had massed in the street were allowed to file past the tomb, either to pay homage to the marshal or to satisfy their curiosity.

The bill for this deference to a Protestant foreigner, as

Maurice de Saxe was never naturalized despite thirty years' service to the French crown, was footed by the royal treasury.[1] This favour bestowed by Louis XV was only the last of many. Besides his rank of *maréchal de France*, de Saxe had also been granted a pension, Chambord, the governorship of Alsace, the right to enter the Louvre in a horsedrawn coach, and, significantly in a court still meticulously governed by etiquette, the right to sit when in audience with the king.[2] He had been granted permission, unlike many other foreigners, to dispose of his property to whomsoever he pleased.[3] With such favours, it might have been that Maurice de Saxe never felt the need to be naturalized. The absence of naturalization also allowed Maurice to remain a Protestant, even while occupying some of the highest military and administrative positions in the Catholic kingdom. De Saxe, however, had no need to convert to Catholicism, let alone be naturalized, to prove his loyalty to the French crown. He had won the trust of Louis XV and immense popularity amongst the people at large, thanks mainly to his victory at Fontenoy in 1745. Equally important for the king, however, was his fidelity. Maurice had refused the tempting offer from his half-brother, Augustus III of Poland, to assume command of his army in the War of Polish Succession (1733–5). The Saxon Protestant replied that he had served the king of France for thirteen years and would not now abandon him. As French policy dictated support for Augustus's rival, Stanisław Leszczyński, Maurice found himself duty-bound to fight against his blood-relative, with whom he was not reconciled until 1736. It was such loyalty, as well as his success on the battlefield, that made de Saxe's status as a foreigner a minor consideration.

There were others like him in eighteenth-century France. As a Protestant, the Genevan banker Jacques Necker was denied entry into the royal council and excluded from the post of *contrôleur-général* of finances, but he still took charge of them with a different title, as *directeur-général*, from 1776 to 1781 and again from 1788 to 1790. He never converted to Catholicism and he was never naturalized, unlike one of his predecessors, the

---

[1] F. Hulot, *Le Maréchal de Saxe* (Paris, 1989), 266–8; E. Fieffé, *Histoire des troupes étrangères au service de France*, 2 vols. (Paris, 1854), i. 280–2.

[2] Hulot, *Saxe*, 176.

[3] Isambert, xxii. 185.

Scottish Protestant John Law.[4] Both Necker and de Saxe remained Protestants and foreigners, but they reached the pinnacles of the French state. What mattered was not their nationality, but rather the personal ties of service and loyalty between monarch and servant. Their respect for these bonds, and the recognition of their value to the state, gave de Saxe and Necker the credentials required for the highest positions in the kingdom without having to undergo a religious conversion or naturalization. Necker and de Saxe were, however, remarkable exceptions. The privileges which de Saxe and Necker enjoyed underscored the disadvantages which humbler foreigners usually faced in France.

While there were rules and obstacles which theoretically applied to all foreigners, the main legal divide was not one of nationality. What mattered to a foreigner, as much as the fact of not being French, was the function which he or she performed in French society, and the privileges and obstacles which that function presented to them. Privilege defined relationships between the component parts of Ancien Régime society, and different foreigners enjoyed different benefits and confronted a variety of difficulties, depending upon their occupation. Naturalization, inheritance laws, religious and legal obstacles affected all foreigners, but not equally from one to the next. Foreign soldiers, clergymen, artists, intellectuals, political exiles, merchants, manufacturers, bankers, and poverty-stricken migrants all enjoyed or suffered differing degrees of privilege and disabilities depending on a variety of factors. Among those factors was their country of origin, religious affiliation, and, crucially, occupation.

I

The most important of these practices was the *droit d'aubaine*, by which the property of dead foreigners reverted to the king, unless they left heirs born in France.[5] Even naturalized foreigners were

[4] R. D. Harris, *Necker: Reform Statesman of the Ancien Régime* (Berkeley, Calif., 1979), 1–2.

[5] For a fuller discussion, see J.-F. Dubost and P. Sahlins, *Et si on faisait payer les*

subject to the *aubaine* if they had no *régnicole* inheritors, or if they had failed to write a will. The assumption behind this 'tyranny', growled a fuming Tobias Smollett in 1763, was that as foreigners had acquired their property in France, 'it would be unjust to convey it to another country'. French jurists cited this reason, but added that a distinction existed between the *droit des gens*, laws which applied to all people and all nations everywhere, and the *droit civil*, which applied only to the citizens of a specific country. Under the former, foreigners were able to do everything necessary to live and work, because these were natural to all human beings. All legal acts relating to death, however, such as wills and testaments, fell into the realm of the *droit civil* and were applicable only to French subjects.[6]

Why foreigners could provide for their families while alive, but not at death, was explained with reference to Roman law, whereby foreigners 'live free, but die as slaves'.[7] In Rome, freemen had the right to trade, while slaves did not. The application of this principle in eighteenth-century France meant that living foreigners could enter contracts and exchange wealth, but in death they were unable to dispose freely of their estate because they fell to the lowly status of slaves. Despite this appeal to Roman law, the actual origins of the *droit d'aubaine* are obscure. In the eighteenth century, *aubain* was a legal term to describe a foreigner and a government memorandum of 1785 traced the word back to the Carolingian age. It was explained that the term described any outsider who had settled on a lord's domain and who was liable to *mainmorte*.[8] Over the centuries, *mainmorte* took a variety of forms, one of which was the right of the *seigneur* to seize the property of a deceased vassal whose children were no longer resident on his domain. The fact that *mainmorte* was practised in many parts of western Europe might explain why the *droit d'aubaine*, if it was linked to *mainmorte*, existed not only in France, but in Germany and elsewhere.

Etrangers? Louis XIV, les immigrés et quelques autres (Paris, 1999), 64–96; M. Rapport, '"A Languishing Branch of the Old Tree of Feudalism": The Death, Resurrection and Final Burial of the *Droit d'Aubaine* in France', *French History*, 14/1 (2000), 13–40.

[6] T. Smollett, *Travels through France and Italy* (London, 1907), 9; Ferrière, *Dictionnaire*, i. 142, 585–6.

[7] Ferrière, *Dictionnaire*, i. 141–2.

[8] Archives de la Ministère des Affaires Étrangères (MAE), Affaires Diverses Politiques (ADP), France, 1.

Right up to its abolition in 1790, the *droit d'aubaine* was not applied uniformly from province to province, or even from town to town. Exemptions and different rules limited its impact across the kingdom, particularly in regions only recently absorbed by the French crown. The bishoprics of Metz, Toul, and Verdun claimed that the *aubaine* did not apply to them, while the ports of Marseille and Dunkirk had privileges which exempted their foreigners from this *droit*.[9] In response to a questionnaire on legal practices circulated by chancellor d'Aguesseau in August 1738, the *parlements* of Toulouse and Besançon claimed the inapplicability of the *droit d'aubaine* for, respectively, Languedoc and the Franche-Comté. Other *parlements* placed limitations on the extent to which the *droit d'aubaine* applied. These same jurisdictions used their freedom from the *aubaine* to claim exemptions from a special tax imposed by a money-starved Louis XIV on foreigners in 1697. In the process, the *droit d'aubaine* became an issue in the struggle between the centralizing tendencies of the monarchy and provincial institutions seeking to uphold local privileges.[10]

The monarchy itself granted exemptions from the *aubaine* to encourage the assimilation of desirable foreigners. Merchants in Bordeaux and at the fairs of the Champagne and Lyon benefited from such privileges, although they applied only to their merchandise. Artisans and manufacturers, such as those in the Gobelins and Beauvais tapestry works, were freed from the *aubaine*, as were foreign mercenaries, such as Swiss troops and the *Garde écossaise*.[11] To avoid any embarrassing incidents, foreign ambassadors were exempt, although this dispensation applied only to their movable wealth. For equally diplomatic reasons, the *droit* was never levied on other sovereigns.[12]

Despite its limits in practice, the *aubaine*'s links to 'feudalism' made it a sitting target for enlightened opinion. Montesquieu and the *Encyclopédie* were sharply critical for both humanitarian

---

[9] Ibid.; C. Danjou, *La Condition civile de l'étranger dans les trois derniers siècles de la monarchie* (Paris, 1939), 109–11.

[10] M. Folain-Le Bras, 'Un projet d'ordonnance du chancelier Daguesseau: Étude de quelques incapacités de donner et de recevoir sous l'Ancien Régime', Thèse pour le doctorat (Paris, 1941), 68–84; Dubost and Sahlins, *Et si on faisait payer les étrangers?*, 83.

[11] MAE, ADP, France, 1.

[12] Ferrière, *Dictionnaire*, i. 592–3; Danjou, *Condition civile*, 100–2.

and economic reasons,[13] while the Physiocrats Letrône, Turgot, and Dupont de Nemours regarded the *aubaine* as an obstacle to the free disposal of wealth and to the naturalization of foreign skills in the kingdom. By the end of the Ancien Régime, it was not only Physiocrats who agreed that the *aubaine* was counter-productive, bringing very little to the royal coffers while discouraging economic development. Necker and his rival Calonne both proposed its abolition in the 1780s. Yet if, in the last two decades of the absolute monarchy, the *droit d'aubaine* was regarded with hostility within government circles, it was not abolished outright. Instead, there was a flurry of treaties with individual sovereigns for its reciprocal abolition, beginning in the mid-1770s. These treaties were not the first diplomatic initiatives to mitigate the effects of the *aubaine* for specific nationalities, but the entry of Turgot into the government in 1774 marked the beginning of a flood of negotiations and edicts which dramatically reduced the scope of the *droit*. Of the seventy-nine Ancien Régime treaties and edicts modifying or abolishing the *droit d'aubaine* for various nationalities, mainly subjects of German princes, thirty-four were signed between Turgot's rise to power and the Revolution.[14]

Before Turgot, the abolition of the *aubaine* for certain nationalities was seen primarily in political terms, as a means of showing favour to the subjects of a particular monarch. Abolition for Spanish subjects in 1760 came when the *pacte de famille* between the two Bourbon houses was about to be renewed. The agreement between Louis XV and Maria-Theresa to free their respective subjects from the *aubaine* in 1766 was explicitly intended to cement the unpopular Franco-Austrian alliance of ten years previously.[15] Such diplomatic motives never entirely disappeared, but Turgot and then Necker, while not sharing the same economic thinking, both regarded the *aubaine* mainly in economic terms, as an obstruction to trade and industrial advancement. Calonne, the last Ancien Régime minister to try

---

[13] C.-L. de S. Montesquieu, *De l'esprit des loix* (Amsterdam and Leipzig, 1758), book xxi, ch. 17; D. Diderot and J. d'Alembert, *Encyclopédie, ou dictionnaire raisonné des sciences, des arts et des métiers, par une société des gens de lettres*, 23 vols. and 4 suppls. (Neuchâtel, 1751–77), i. 863; vi. 71.

[14] MAE, ADP, France, 1.

[15] AN, K//2033; MAE, ADP, France, 1.

to tackle the issue, believed that abolition would help to create the conditions for long-term growth in the French economy. The hectic activity after 1774 was therefore due, initially, to the Physiocratic ideas injected into the French government by Turgot during his brief tenure of power, which lasted until 1776. It was continued as his successors, although they did not share his economic philosophy, sought to stimulate the French economy in order to steer the monarchy through its grave financial difficulties.

Yet when both Necker in 1780 and Calonne in 1786 proposed outright and unilateral abolition, these schemes were buried.[16] These failures suggest that the monarchy was unwilling to lose the *droit d'aubaine* as the diplomatic bargaining chip which it had played for decades. Moreover, the principle of reciprocity, which pervaded every treaty made with foreign sovereigns on the *aubaine*, was deeply entrenched in broader Ancien Régime concepts of international law. The *droit des gens* demanded the mutual execution of treaties by the parties concerned. It also allowed governments to treat foreigners in the same way as their own subjects were treated abroad. By emphasizing reciprocity on the *aubaine*, the French government always retained the possibility of reimposing it on the subjects of princes who failed to honour their obligations. This embedded principle may explain why few in the French government were ever willing to countenance unilateral abolition of the *droit d'aubaine*.

The emphasis on reciprocity belies the claim that by the Revolution the *droit d'aubaine* had all but disappeared in France.[17] Furthermore, many treaties did not abolish all restrictions on foreigners' inheritances. Many German princes in particular retained the *Abzug* or *Abschoß*, which usually amounted to 10 per cent of the value of inheritances exported from their lands. Under the conditions of reciprocity, therefore, the king of France could also exercise this right, called in French the *droit de détraction*, on subjects from thirty different German states, as well as Austria, Portugal, Britain, and Poland. Other modifications, such as those in favour of the British in 1739 and Swedes in

---

[16] MAE, ADP, France, 1.

[17] Villers, 'Condition des étrangers', 150; J. Mathorez, *Les Étrangers en France sous l'Ancien Régime: Histoire de la formation de la population française*, 2 vols. (Paris, 1919–21), i. 139.

1784, abolished the *aubaine* only for movable goods, while others only allowed foreigners to *inherit* estates by testament, not bequeath them. The range of treaties was so diverse that when the Restoration monarchy reviewed the *droit* in 1818, the foreign ministry categorized no less than ten different classes of agreement between France and other sovereigns up to 1789.[18] If the *aubaine* was dying out by 1789, it was doing so in a very irregular way and the monarchy showed that it had no intention of abolishing it completely. That gesture was left to the revolutionaries.

Another restriction on the lives of foreigners in France was more successfully overcome by government initiative. Many foreigners came from countries where the established religion was not Catholicism, but Protestantism and, in rarer cases, Judaism, Orthodox Christianity, or Islam. Since the revocation of the Edict of Nantes in 1685, the government had sought to maintain religious orthodoxy, while enticing often heretical foreigners who offered their expertise and wealth. As early as 1686, Louis XIV was passing edicts in an attempt to encourage foreign Protestants to remain or move to France.[19] Religious toleration was offered, but precautions were taken to ensure that French subjects were not exposed to the 'errors' of other faiths.

Thanks to the concessions won between 1715 and 1729 by their ambassador Hop, Dutch Protestants in Paris were assured decent burial and freedom of worship, but only in the embassy chapel. Royal soldiers were posted outside, with orders to arrest those French subjects who were too keen to satisfy their curiosity about 'the errors of Calvinism *chez le sieur Hop*'.[20] Foreign Protestants of all nationalities were guaranteed a Christian burial when Louis XIV gave them permission to bury their dead in France and declared that a site would be designated in Paris for this purpose. Yet it took a persistent petitioning campaign by Protestant foreigners in Paris, who had been reduced to holding funerals in private gardens or in the semi-rural area behind the Invalides, to persuade the Regency to provide a burial ground in 1720. The edict was hedged in by precautions which would ensure that no French subjects would be encouraged to dissent from Catholicism: the *arrêt* stressed

---

[18] MAE, ADP, France, 1.   [19] Ibid. 7.   [20] Mathorez, *Étrangers*, ii. 325–6.

that Protestant burials could not serve as a pretext for foreigners to practise their faith publicly. To ensure that none of the Protestant contagion spilt over onto the streets of Paris and infected the king's subjects, funerals were to be performed without ceremony and within the hours designated by the *lieutenant-général de police*. No French subjects were allowed to attend. Furthermore, the edict insisted that the cemetery be enclosed behind a high wall and guarded by a *concierge*. This last condition was originally intended as a prophylactic to shield French people from Protestantism, but it also served to protect the cemetery from desecration by irate Catholics. When the site was first opened near the Porte Saint-Martin, it was not enclosed and the first corpse to be buried, that of the Saxon plenipotentiary minister, was exhumed at night by a mob and horribly mutilated. The government was finally spurred into building the wall and posting the guard.[21]

The practice of burying foreign Protestants in separate burial sites persisted into the 1780s. Edward Rigby, visiting Vienne on 27 July 1789, described 'a singular place, something like an apartment in a rock', where he saw a monument to a young Englishman who had died about a year earlier and been 'buried in unholy and ignoble ground', so 'leave had been obtained to appropriate this place to the interment of strangers, and of those who had professed a foreign religion'.[22] Otherwise, the alternative was to transport the body out of the kingdom and to do so required the special permission of the king, particularly if the relatives of the deceased were to avoid insult piled onto grief by having to pay customs, excise, or other *droits* in the process.[23]

Besides restrictions on worship and burial, non-Catholic foreigners also faced other civil disabilities, which sometimes threatened career progress. A colleague of the German engraver Johann Georg Wille, named Schmidt, could not be accepted into the Académie royale de peinture because of his Protestantism, until Louis XV gave him special dispensation in 1742. The Swedish portrait painter, Alexander Roslin, received a similar favour.[24] Their experience is revealing. The monarchy, for all its

---

[21] MAE, ADP, France, 7. [22] Rigby, *Letters*, 121–2.
[23] MAE, ADP, France, 7.
[24] J.-G. Wille, *Mémoires et journal de Jean-Georges Wille, graveur du roi*, 3 vols. (Paris, 1857), i. 82; Mathorez, *Étrangers*, ii. 372.

apparent Catholic orthodoxy, was willing to waive religious conditions imposed on foreigners if it thought their potential was worth such a concession. Furthermore, the crown was not entirely dogmatic in its Catholicism when it came to converts from Geneva. The king had an agreement with this city-state for the repatriation of children who slipped across the frontier in order to change faith. If the Genevan parents appealed to the French government, their Calvinist children, if under the age of 17 and seeking conversion to Catholicism, could be carted back to face their wrath. Young French Catholics who committed the offence in the opposite direction were equally liable to be hauled back to their families.[25]

By the 1780s, growing religious tolerance in the French government loosened some of the restrictions on foreigners' worship. At first, treaties with specific countries permitted some of them to practise their faith freely, as in the commercial treaty with Britain in 1786 and the treaty of navigation and commerce with Russia in 1787.[26] This freedom to worship was however restricted to private observance, a condition probably dictated as much by a concern for public order as by a desire to preserve Catholic orthodoxy. In November 1787, civil rights were granted to all Protestants in the kingdom, so by 1789 the question of religious tolerance was no longer an issue for most non-Catholic foreigners in France. The minority of foreign Jews, Muslims, and Orthodox Christians had to wait until the Revolution for their full emancipation.

If advances had been made in the conditions of foreigners as regards their inheritance rights and religious toleration, other restrictions remained firmly in place. The *cautio judicatum solvi*, for example, was a deposit which a foreign plaintiff had to pay when taking court action against a French defendant. This deposit was to ensure that the foreigner could pay the legal costs and penalties should his case fail. French jurists claimed that, without it, foreigners might be able to sue whomever they pleased with impunity, as they could easily run away home if the case turned against them. The *cautio judicatum solvi*, payable in both the first instance and on appeal, did not apply either to

---

[25] MAE, ADP, France, 14.   [26] Isambert, xxviii. 291–2, 317.

foreigners who had sufficient real estate in France, or to commercial disputes. The plaintiff could alternatively present a third party willing to pay any expenses and fines. The deposit was not demanded of foreign defendants, on the grounds that self-defence was natural to all human beings.[27]

More onerous was the *contrainte par corps* for civil (as opposed to commercial) debts. Imprisonment for debt was abolished for French subjects by the ordinance of 1667, but was retained for foreigners to prevent them from fleeing the kingdom in order to avoid honouring their payments. Foreign debtors were in fact caught in a legal pincer, as they were also denied the right to obtain from the chancellery the *lettres de répi* (from the word *répit*, respite). These granted French debtors, who had suffered considerable losses, a delay in which to raise sufficient funds to pay off their creditors, before any legal action could be taken. Foreigners were also denied what was known as 'le refuge des misérables', the *cession de biens*, whereby a debtor unable to make financial payments could hand over his property as payment in kind.[28] Foreign debtors therefore went to prison until they came up with the necessary funds to placate their creditors. On 13 July 1789, Rigby witnessed the release from La Force of an unfortunate Irish nobleman, Lord Massareene, who was said to have been held in prison for twenty-three years for debts of between 15,000 and 20,000 *livres*. It does seem that, if Massareene's time in prison was exaggerated by rumour, it was not by much.[29] Occasionally the crown could grant letters of safe-conduct, which allowed foreign debtors to collect their property and sort out their affairs without being arrested.[30]

Beyond the financial and legal disabilities, foreigners were, in theory, also denied any important role in government, church, and judiciary. It was considered dangerous (and contrary to the *droit civil*) to give foreigners any authority which they could use against the interests of the kingdom. Ordinances dating to the sixteenth century barred foreigners from holding ecclesiastical positions,[31] but by the eighteenth century these laws were being

[27] Danjou, *Condition civile*, 34.   [28] Ferrière, *Dictionnaire*, i. 142, 272.
[29] Rigby, *Letters*, 52; J. G. Alger, *Englishmen in the French Revolution* (London, 1889), 3–8.
[30] MAE, Correspondance Politique (CP), Allemagne, 659; MAE, ADP, France, 14.
[31] Villers, 'Condition des étrangers', 144; Danjou, *Condition civile*, 51–2.

ignored or circumvented. In the machinery of state, foreigners were not allowed to become tax farmers. A declaration of 1651 by the *parlement* of Paris banned all foreigners 'even naturalized' from the *conseil du roi*. While this measure was aimed at Cardinal Mazarin, Necker fell foul of it, resigning in 1781 ostensibly because he was refused a place in the *conseil d'état*. None the less, both he and John Law still played leading roles in the administration of the royal finances.[32] Foreigners were barred from the judiciary and were not allowed to become barristers. In certain commercial spheres, too, the role of foreigners was hedged in by extra regulations. A foreigner could not, for example, run a banking business in France without paying a deposit of 150,000 *livres* every five years.[33]

On top of these legal restrictions, foreigners were also subject to police surveillance, especially in Paris and fortress towns, even if it was discreet and haphazardly executed. On entering Paris by postal carriage, foreigners had their names recorded by the *maîtres des portes* and the owners of *hôtels* and *chambres garnis* were required to keep a register of their guests for scrutiny by the police, who would send a report every three days to the ministry of foreign affairs. There, officials would compare the registers of the *maîtres des portes* with those of the hoteliers to get an idea as to the number and types of foreigners in the city. In Paris, however, these procedures were not adhered to strictly. A memorandum in the foreign ministry complained in August 1782 that the records kept by hoteliers 'are incomplete, incorrect and almost indecipherable'. As not all foreigners entered the city by the postal carriages, not all arrivals were easily verified by the authorities. Furthermore, there was no means by which the police or the government could know of foreigners who were staying in the homes of friends or associates.[34] It was quite possible for determined foreigners to disappear from the sight of the police.

For this reason, it was suggested that foreign visitors in Paris be subjected to the same system as existed in fortress towns. There, at every gate, there were *consignes* where the names of every foreigner arriving by whatever mode of transport were

---

[32] Danjou, *Condition civile*, 49; Isambert, xvii. 243; W. Doyle, *Origins of the French Revolution* (Oxford, 1980), 58.
[33] Danjou, *Condition civile*, 51–2.   [34] MAE, ADP, France, 14.

recorded, as well as the address at which they planned to stay. These registers were forwarded to the military commandant and the magistrates. Meanwhile, all inhabitants were obliged to give written details of the foreigners who were staying with them within twenty-four hours, or be liable to a fine. These details were deposited in a locked box at the *hôtel de ville* and were then compared with the registers submitted by the *consignes*. The foreign ministry suggested that, while the immensity of the city of Paris made the establishment of *consignes* at every entrance impractical, a box similar to those in fortress towns could be placed in every *quartier*. Every person, without exception, should be obliged to supply details of foreign guests, for the perusal of the *lieutenant-général de police*.[35] Nothing seems to have come of this proposal, but the fact that it was made suggests that certain sections of the government were concerned with keeping a watchful eye over foreigners in the kingdom's largest city. Up to the Revolution, daily reports arrived at the ministry of foreign affairs giving the names, nationality, and lodgings of certain foreigners who had arrived in Paris and details of their intentions and travel plans.[36] If the Revolution later established an extensive surveillance system, some of the methods can be traced to the Ancien Régime.

Yet the intensity of this watchfulness should not be overstated. Passports existed, but were not the documents recognizable today. They were either issued by the government to foreigners as a way of obtaining passage out of the country without harassment, or were a means by which a foreign ambassador accredited a fellow subject with his protection. In his entire period of service as American minister to France, from 1785 to 1789, Thomas Jefferson issued only 132 passports and, as many were only valid for a matter of weeks or months, many of them were renewals.[37] In contrast, such was the fear and suspicion stirred by the migrant poor, whether French or foreign, that they were subject to more controls than wealthier travellers. If they were to avoid trouble from the authorities, they were to carry 'passports', issued in their village of origin stating their purpose and their destination, or an *aveu* which was a statement of good

---

[35] Ibid.
[36] Ibid. 8.
[37] T. Jefferson, *The Papers of Thomas Jefferson*, ed. J. P. Boyd and W. H. Gaines, 21 vols. (Princeton, 1950–83), xv. 483–7.

character written by their priest or a local official. The well-organized Savoyards were among those who would be expected to bear such documents.[38]

Yet in wartime the information gathered about wealthier foreigners could be used by the government to great effect. In theory, enemy subjects could be expelled, arrested as hostages, or have their wealth seized. In practice, the measures taken varied from conflict to conflict and between the nationalities involved. While the French government recognized that there were limits placed by the *droit des gens* on what actions could be taken against enemy subjects, these limits were never defined with any precision. In 1733, a foreign ministry memorandum advised the government that 'there are no certain rules which define precisely all that is permitted or not permitted in wartime'. The *droit des gens* allowed sovereigns to do everything they could to prevent the enemy from waging war, but their measures should not be motivated 'by a pure spirit of vengeance'. Such behaviour would not bring peace any closer and would encourage the opposition to exert its *droit de représailles*. This last right was generally believed to belong to any sovereign who could respond in kind to the unfair treatment of his subjects in a foreign country. The memorandum concluded that the government could seize all merchandise and vessels which could be used against the French in wartime. The authorities could also intern all enemy naval and army officers 'as a form of precaution, by virtue of the *droit des gens*'. Merchants and everyday goods were protected to a greater extent, because they worked for 'the common advantage of all nations'. The government could only take measures which prevented enemy agents and spies from using commerce as a cover for their machinations. As a precaution, therefore, merchants should be given between three to nine months to leave the country, but their non-military goods could not be confiscated because they might be trading on behalf of neutral or friendly nations. All these precautions were subject to the principle of reciprocity. The French could go further in their measures only in reprisal for any harsher treatment of French subjects abroad.[39]

[38] O. Hufton, *The Poor of Eighteenth-Century France 1750–1789* (Oxford, 1974), 98, 228–9.

[39] MAE, *Mémoires et documents*, Allemagne, 94.

The restraints put on government action against enemy subjects looked good on paper, but the problem in practice was defining precisely the terms. Almost any form of merchandise or any vessel could be deemed to be useful to the enemy's war effort. Consequently, in the reign of Louis XIV the Dutch, except for those in Bordeaux, found themselves expelled in 1672, while in 1688 all their ships and property were confiscated along with those of Spanish subjects. Meanwhile, Austrian notables in Paris were seized as hostages or expelled from the kingdom.[40] In the eighteenth century, despite the number of wars the age witnessed, such 'precautions' taken as a general measure were rare, possibly because they were considered counter-productive in that they disrupted commerce. British subjects were expelled at the outbreak of the Seven Years War, but at the same time all foreigners, including the British, were offered an absolute guarantee that their state *rentes* would not be touched, a concession dictated by financial considerations. At France's intervention in the American War of Independence, the government stressed its right to exact reprisals on British subjects, but not to take any pre-emptive measures.[41] In practice, however, the French did seize British shipping as a precaution. Such seizures could include the hapless passengers and crew, as the Dutch merchants Paul van de Serre and Girard Meyners found to their outrage in 1779. Their British-built ship, owned in partnership with the British captain, was seized in the Mediterranean by a French frigate, although it was flagged as a Dutch vessel.[42]

This spiky issue of maritime prizes was the same for both the Ancien Régime and the Revolution. French regulations for the seizure of enemy shipping were laid down in 1695 and 1778 and they were adopted, with only small changes, by the Republic. The state awarded to individual shipowners *lettres de marque*, which either gave them permission to arm their ships for war, or to act as corsairs. In the latter case, captains were allowed to wage *guerre de course*, or warfare on enemy maritime traffic, and to capture merchantmen and enemy cargoes, including those

---

[40] Isambert, xix. 12; xx. 66, 70, 76–7; Mathorez, *Étrangers*, i. 137.
[41] Isambert, xxv. 331, 353; Mathorez, *Étrangers*, i. 137; M. Marion, *Dictionnaire des Institutions de la France aux XVIIe et XVIIIe siècles* (Paris, 1984), 225.
[42] AN, T//507–8.

being carried on neutral vessels. A special agreement between France and Britain protected fishing boats from these predators. Otherwise, corsairs had to follow precise procedures in the chase, seizure, and homeward carriage of their booty. The prize had to be recognized as legal by the port authorities (or, during the Revolution, the *juge de paix*). Neutrals caught carrying enemy goods could appeal, but while waiting for the final decision the authorities held onto the vessel and its load. If the goods were perishable, they could be sold off.[43] In the heat of the chase and capture, the regulations could easily be ignored, which is why there were so many disputes both before and after 1789. Foreigners did have some protection in the form of consuls. These foreign officials were sometimes chosen by their government from among merchants or landowners already in France, or they were diplomats appointed to act specifically in a consular role. They were expected to look after the interests of their countrymen, particularly in commerce, but also to provide assistance when they were legally challenged in civil and criminal cases.[44] The eighteenth century saw a growth of consulates in France, both in number and in the importance assigned to their role. In 1716, there was no list of consuls in the *Almanach Royal*. In 1774, fourteen different countries were listed as having between them sixty-two consuls and vice-consuls scattered around the different French cities and ports, some of them very small. By 1789, the list had expanded to include twenty-two countries, with no less than 219 consuls and vice-consuls across the kingdom.[45]

Unless he was Maurice de Saxe or Jacques Necker, the only sure way for a foreigner to escape all the legal and civil disabilities was to become a French subject by applying for *lettres de naturalité*. In the hands of the crown, naturalization could be used as an instrument with which to attract foreigners to France. The king granted *lettres de naturalité générales* to specific types of foreign artisans in certain manufactures or projects, or to soldiers who fulfilled certain conditions. The assumption was that these foreigners were of enough utility to

[43] U. Bonnel, *La France et les États-Unis et la guerre de course (1797–1815)* (Paris, 1961), 44–7.
[44] Danjou, *Condition civile*, 87–8.
[45] *Almanach Royal* (1716); (1774), 438–41; (1789), 182–90.

the king for the usual procedures for individual naturalization to be waived. The ultimate aim of these general letters, of course, was to enhance French wealth and power.[46]

The key to individual *lettres de naturalité*—and thereby to French nationality—was an expression of loyalty by a foreigner to his or her new sovereign. Such loyalty was usually, but not always, demonstrated in two ways: by conversion to Catholicism and by permanent residence in France. The king of France swore at his coronation to stamp out heresy and so in theory he could not accept among his subjects people of any religion except Catholicism. Lefèvre de la Planche wrote that 'everyone in France is presumed Catholic',[47] but in practice being French did not necessarily entail such orthodoxy, as the existence of Jewish and Protestant subjects testifies. Perhaps in recognition of the near impossibility of imposing orthodoxy, both Louis XV and Louis XVI tended to waive the demands for conversion, by according a *dispense de catholicité*. The crown, however, was not indifferent to religion as a basis of nationality. *Dispenses de catholicité* tended to be granted only to other Christians. In those rare cases where foreign Jews and Muslims applied for *lettres de naturalité*, they declared their conversion to the Catholic faith. Furthermore, if some Protestants escaped the need to convert, others did not.[48] The engraver Johann Georg Wille, a Protestant born in Königsberg, became Catholic before his naturalization in 1758.[49] An enthusiastic Jean Lampe of Danzig prostrated himself on his naturalization in 1779, rejecting 'the errors of Calvinism, which he had the misfortune to suck in with his mother's milk'.[50] The second proof of loyalty, residence in France, was not a condition prior to naturalization, but a foreigner, once naturalized, was legally bound to stay in the kingdom for the rest of his life. Although a voyage abroad 'with the intention to return' did not endanger his naturalization, a prolonged absence did. The king could waive the condition of residence, however, by granting a *dispense d'incolat*. Those who received this privilege were usually those who had shown enough loyalty to the king, by sacrifice or service, that they had no need

---

[46] Folain-Le Bras, 'Un projet d'ordonnance', 51; Mathorez, *Étrangers*, i. 99; Danjou, *Condition civile*, 88, 90, 96.

[47] Boizet, 'Lettres de naturalité', 78.

[48] Ibid. 80–2.   [49] Wille, *Mémoires*, i. 163, 175; Mathorez, *Étrangers*, ii. 132.

[50] Boizet, 'Lettres de naturalité', 81.

to live in France. Other dispensations were granted to magnates, probably in recognition of their duties in their country of origin.[51]

The importance of *lettres de naturalité* was that they symbolized the adoption by the king of his new subject. They were a sign of the personal ties of loyalty which bound the subject to the monarch. For a foreigner, the registration of the *lettres de naturalité* confirmed both 'the abdication of his old country' and 'the true acceptance and fulfilment of the King's grace'.[52] Naturalization was therefore symbolic of the two-way process of loyalty and obedience offered by the subject and of protection provided by the king. It was the acceptance of these mutual obligations which determined the new nationality of a foreigner. For people born as French subjects, it was assumed that these obligations were implicit. These personal ties between ruler and subject defined nationality.

The general treatment of foreigners in France varied according to their specific nationality, their religion, and specific exceptions granted by the monarchy. Under the Ancien Régime, however, where social status was determined largely by privilege, the main determinant of the conditions in which foreigners lived was their occupation. Foreigners participated in almost every major aspect of French society, including the army, the clergy, intellectual and artistic life, and the economy. There were also political refugees and those who were considered less desirable, the migrant poor.

II

'Keep the foreign regiments, those which I have here are . . . strong and complete; they deny troops to the enemy; spare our own subjects and [so] one man has the same use as three of the kingdom's subjects.'[53] It might not be surprising that the person who wrote this favourable opinion of foreign soldiers at the end of the War of Austrian Succession was Maurice de Saxe, but he

---

[51] Boizet, 'Lettres de naturalité', 72–7.
[52] Ibid. 19.
[53] R. Haas, *Un régiment suisse au service de France: Bettens 1672–1792* (Pont l'Abbé, 1967), 33.

was merely citing what was conventional wisdom for most governments in early modern Europe.[54] In time of war, one of the quickest and easiest ways of expanding the armed forces was to raise mercenaries who were already trained and experienced and who were loyal so long as they were paid. Some foreigners in French service, such as the Irish regiments, were not mercenaries. The regiments in the Irish Brigade had served France since the Williamite war, which finished with the evacuation of 20,000 Irish troops by Louis XIV in 1691.[55] The Swiss had a long tradition in the French army, dating back to the treaty of Perpetual Peace between the French monarchy and the Swiss Confederation in 1516.

By 1789, there were thirty-two foreign regiments in the French army, out of a total of 172, twenty-four of which were infantry (twelve Swiss, eight German, three Irish, and one Liégeois) and eight of which were cavalry (one German, one Irish, and six Hussar, which were theoretically Hungarian). In addition, a seventh of the troops in the twelve light infantry battalions in the French army were foreigners, mostly from the Italian states and concentrated in the battalions of the Chasseurs Royaux-Corses and the Chasseurs Corses.[56] Many of these regiments were founded generations before the Revolution, but as their members became increasingly assimilated into French society, the genuinely foreign element in them dwindled. Of all such units in France, the Swiss remained the most exclusively foreign, but even they were only three-quarters Swiss: the rest were men of other nationalities and 200–300 were French.[57] The varied composition of foreign regiments makes a figure for the total number of foreign troops in 1789 hard to calculate. Moreover, a third of all foreigners in the infantry were scattered among regular French units. One estimate places the figure at less than 8 per cent of all the French infantry outside the Swiss

---

[54] M. S. Anderson, *War and Society in Europe of the Old Regime, 1618–1789* (London, 1988), 51.

[55] MAE, ADP, France, 10; J. G. Simms, 'The Irish on the Continent, 1691–1800', in T. W. Moody and W. E. Vaughan (eds.), *A New History of Ireland*, iv. *Eighteenth-Century Ireland 1691–1800* (Oxford, 1986), 633.

[56] S. F. Scott, *The Response of the Royal Army to the French Revolution: The Role and Development of the Line Army, 1787–93* (Oxford, 1978), 5–6, 12–13, 115–16, 217–24; Fieffé, *Histoire des troupes étrangères*, i. 393–420.

[57] Scott, *Response of the Royal Army*, 13.

regiments, one-seventh in the light infantry, and 6 per cent in the cavalry.[58] If this figure were to be accepted, then taking the total number of troops in the Royal Army as 156,000 in 1789, of which approximately 13,770 were Swiss,[59] a reasonable estimate of the number or foreign troops in the Royal Army might be around 24,000, or just over 15 per cent of the army, a figure which confirms the more conservative contemporary estimates.[60]

The value which the French monarchy placed on these foreign troops is reflected in the high rates of pay, the fostering of an *esprit de corps* and the privileges granted to certain foreign units. Foreign troops were paid more than their French counterparts,[61] both because of the desire to attract quality foreign troops into the royal army and because to reduce this pay would lead to an exodus of disgruntled soldiers, which actually happened in the Irish regiments in 1697. An *esprit de corps* was encouraged by the retention of the 'national' character of each foreign regiment. Each had its own distinctive uniforms and carried special emblems on parade and in battle. The Swiss units wore red coats, as distinct from the Bourbon white, while the banners of the Irish regiments bore the harp. It is said that in 1789, when as little as 10 per cent of the Irish Brigade were actually from the British Isles, the officers still gave orders in Gaelic. In the Hussars, where only 6 per cent of the soldiers were actually foreign in 1789, French recruits were still taught to curse in Hungarian.[62]

The privileges granted foreign troops by the monarchy gave them a status superior to that normally attained by soldiers and none were more privileged than the Swiss. The *capitulations* negotiated between the French king and the Swiss cantons laid out the terms and conditions of service and they guaranteed a wide range of special rights for Swiss troops. They were granted fiscal immunities which included an exemption from the *droit*

---

[58] Scott, *Response of the Royal Army*, 12–13.

[59] Ibid. 5–6; E. Maradan, 'L'Échec de la propagande du club helvetique auprès du Régiment des Gardes 1789–1791', in M. Vovelle (ed.), *Paris et la Révolution* (Paris, 1989), 254.   [60] *AP* x. 519.

[61] J.-P. Poussou, 'Un monde plein', in Y. Lequin (ed.), *Histoire des étrangers et de l'immigration en France* (Paris, 1992), 202; *AP* ix. 261–2.

[62] Fieffé, *Histoire des troupes étrangères*, i. 279; Scott, *Response of the Royal Army*, 13.

d'aubaine and taxes such as the *taille*. When they owned land, they paid the same taxation as the French nobility.[63] The Swiss also had judicial privileges: when sued by French subjects, Swiss soldiers could have the case heard by a court consisting entirely of their own officers, as their legal jurisdiction was considered to be their regiment.[64] There was some dispute as to whether or not this privilege included criminal cases, but soldiers of the élite company of the *Cent-Suisses*, the king's personal bodyguard, were tried before their own officers for crimes against French civilians, including murder.[65]

The Swiss were granted religious toleration, a crucial point if the French wished to recruit from the Protestant cantons. In practice, Protestants in the Swiss regiments found that to obtain further favours, such as admission to the Invalides on their retirement, a timely conversion to Catholicism was practical if not compulsory. This was particularly true in the earlier part of the eighteenth century: in the 1720s, Swiss Protestants in the Invalides were told that they could enter and remain only if they converted.[66] In 1760, however, the duc de Choiseul, minister of foreign affairs, proposed to establish separate companies of Protestant pensioners in the Invalides, probably to conform more closely to the *capitulations*.

If the government was willing to pay the price of maintaining foreign regiments in the French army, the population at large was less so. The privileged position of the foreign regiments, while justifiable in the eyes of the state, was a source of grievance for French people, as a clutch of *cahiers de doléances* of 1789 revealed. Particularly galling was the knowledge that foreign troops were paid more than their compatriots for the same service to the king. Another complaint was that the use of foreigners in the army denied employment to French subjects. Others grumbled that the foreigners' conditions of service prevented their deployment overseas, so that, despite their higher cost, they were of limited use.[67] This claim, while not true for the Irish regiments, which served in the American War

---

[63] Haas, *Régiment suisse*, 4.

[64] J. Chagniot, *Paris et l'armée au XVIIIe siècle: Étude politique et sociale* (Paris, 1985), 366.

[65] AN, Z/1R/7.   [66] Chagniot, *Paris*, 367.

[67] *AP* iii. 735; iv. 766; v. 790; vi. 43.

of Independence, was certainly correct for the Swiss, whose *capitulations* stipulated that they should not be shipped overseas.

There is plenty of evidence that foreign troops assimilated into French society to a great extent, or at least fraternized with locals. Foreign soldiers often found temporary work and many of the *soldats-cultivateurs* who worked plots of land around Paris were Swiss. Others toiled as sharecroppers, as field-hands, or patrolled as guards of granaries. Retirement from foreign regiments often led to assimilation into French civilian society, although former soldiers traditionally took up certain types of jobs. Grizzled Swiss veterans were known for establishing cabarets, for working as *suisses de porte*, or gatekeepers in the *hôtels* of the wealthy, and as church guards.[68] In their leisure hours, foreign soldiers frequented bars and cabarets, sometimes in defiance of restrictions placed on them by barracking.[69] Marriages between foreign soldiers and French women were frequent—and married life could indeed be bliss as it could mean an escape from the confinements of military life. Such trysts did cause problems with jealous locals. The young men of Argenteuil and Saint-Denis, both towns in which Swiss Guards were quartered, once demanded that the troops be sent elsewhere, because they could not compete with their glamorous rivals for the attentions of local women.[70]

On the other hand, these points of contact with the French population became rarer in the last decades of the Ancien Régime, mainly as a result of the army reforms initiated by Choiseul between 1763 and 1765. As minister of war (merely one of his numerous portfolios), he stressed the humanity of the soldier who, in return, was expected to adopt a more professional attitude by applying himself exclusively to military tasks, which meant increasing segregation from civilians, more barracking, less billeting, and less work outside military duties.

While some of these developments reduced some sources of tension between soldiers and civilians, such as billeting, they also accentuated the isolation of foreign troops in France. Of course, all soldiers, whether French or foreign, enjoyed less contact with

---

[68] Chagniot, *Paris*, 367; J. Godechot, *La Grande Nation: L'Expansion révolutionnaire de la France dans le monde de 1789 à 1799*, 2nd edn. (Paris, 1983), 92.

[69] Chagniot, *Paris*, 420.

[70] Ibid. 420–1, 438; Haas, *Régiment suisse*, 5.

the local population than before. Furthermore, the rift between soldier and civilian could become a gaping chasm when the former was employed by the authorities against rioters and protesters in times of civil unrest. For the foreign soldier, however, the isolation from civilian life was even greater, owing sometimes to linguistic barriers and more often to the privileges extended to them. These conditions meant that, by the Revolution, there was a widespread belief that foreign troops were far more likely than their French comrades to be the unquestioning tools in the hands of the authorities. In 1789, twenty-nine general *cahiers de doléances* called for the 'nationalization' of the army, which meant the disbandment of the foreign regiments.[71] In July 1789, the suspicion that foreign troops were the passive instruments of the monarchy was confirmed.

III

Like foreign soldiers, the foreign Catholic clergy who practised in France were to become suspect during the Revolution. Their presence in France was largely a legacy of the persecution of Catholics in Protestant countries since the Reformation, particularly in Britain and Ireland. By 1789, there were no less than eighteen monasteries and convents for Irish or British inmates. Of those, ten were for English women (four Benedictine convents, four Poor Clares, one Augustinian, and one Immaculate Conception) and eight were men's monasteries (three English Benedictine, two Irish Franciscan, one English Franciscan, and two Irish Capuchin). There were also twelve educational institutions intended primarily as seminaries for those who aspired to the priesthood or to become missionaries to the British Isles. They included seven Irish, two Scots, and three English colleges. Most of these cloisters and seminaries had been founded between the later sixteenth and mid-seventeenth centuries. There were also foreigners who became secular clergymen, attending to the needs of laymen around France. In 1772, for

[71] B. F. Hyslop, *French Nationalism in 1789 According to the General Cahiers* (New York, 1968), appendix; *AP* iii. 569, 735; iv. 338, 666, 766; v. 541, 791; vi. 43, 294, 370.

example, there were fifteen Irishmen who were parish clergy in the diocese of Bordeaux and by 1789 there were about forty Irish priests living in the dioceses of Bordeaux and Bazas.[72] This number seems exceptional, but elsewhere in France a handful of foreign priests served as private confessors, as tutors, or as chaplains attached to the army. The Irish College in Paris boasted that its graduates often became 'chaplains and inter-preters to the French armies, as MM. d'Orléans, de Guichon, de la Motte-Picquet and Rochambeau can testify'.[73]

These clerics were refugees, driven from Britain and Ireland by the Reformation, the successive defeats of the Jacobites, and by penal laws against Catholics. In France, they sought to follow their vocation and to be trained as missionaries for the salvation of both Catholic souls and Protestant heretics in the British Isles. France, in particular, attracted them for a number of reasons, besides its Catholicism. First, the centre of the Jacobite cause was for a long time the palace at Saint-Germain-en-Laye. There, James II/VII's queen, Mary of Modena, made special efforts to persuade the Gallican clergy to help exiled ecclesiastics find positions and financial help. Saint-Germain therefore became a centre of patronage for Catholic clergy from the British Isles. In return, the ecclesiastical refugees offered both moral and prac-tical support to the Stuarts. More alumni of the Scots College in Paris fought for the Jacobites than were ordained priests.[74] Secondly, France was close to the British Isles and was linked to them by trade routes served by Irish and British merchants resident in the major French ports. This proximity had two advantages. On the one hand, it made travel cheaper for postulants, students, priests, and missionaries. On the other, it allowed the exiled clergy to keep abreast of developments in the British Isles.[75]

Many of these religious establishments acted as seminaries

---

[72] P. Loupès, 'Les Ecclésiastiques irlandais dans le Diocèse de Bordeaux sous l'Ancien Régime', in Fédération Historique du Sud-Ouest, *Bordeaux et les Îles britanniques du XIIIe au XXe siècle: Actes du Colloque, York, 1973* (Bordeaux, 1975), 88; Loupès, 'The Irish Clergy of the Diocese of Bordeaux during the Revolution', in D. Dickson and H. Gough (eds.), *Ireland and the French Revolution* (Dublin, 1990), 28.

[73] AN, D/XIX/30.

[74] B. M. Halloran, *The Scots College Paris 1603–1792* (Edinburgh, 1997), 80.

[75] AN, G/9/66 (1–3).

and ran courses to train priests and missionaries. The English Franciscan monastery at Douai, for example, offered classes in theology and philosophy.[76] One of the main subjects of study in the Scots College in Paris was 'the Scottish language, in order to exercise fruitfully the functions of missionaries in Scotland', although the College did not only train priests.[77] Crucially, none of the houses were meant to admit French people, because missionaries from the British Isles were 'the most capable of speaking the language, of knowing the morals, character and customs' of the countries concerned.[78] To be a teacher or student in the Scots College in Paris, one had to be born in Scotland and be a Catholic.[79] At Dieulouard, the English Benedictines drew all their recruits from England.[80] Such policies ensured that the foreign religious houses in France actually retained a genuinely foreign character.

If members of these establishments were in France because they were pushed there by persecution at home, the French authorities had their own reasons to welcome and perpetuate their presence. There may have been a political motive, at least until the mid-eighteenth century. Should the Jacobites have been successful in restoring the Stuarts, the Catholic clergy would have found themselves in some demand in the British Isles and might have played an important part in winning hearts and minds for the Stuarts and their French allies.

The English friar, Augustus Moore, naturally offered the government other good reasons for supporting the foreign clergy. In 1766, he defended the English Benedictine college and monastery at Douai before the Gallican church's Commission of Regulars, which had just begun its task of reviewing monasticism in France. He beamed, rather weakly, that the English order sought to 'make itself useful to the public by its wishes and by its most ardent prayers'.[81] Yet claims for the pastoral care offered by foreigners could be supported in the calculations made by the French clergy. In 1770, for example, the Commission accepted the argument of the English Carmelites, who were seeking to establish a seminary in Boulogne, that they would be able to fill the vacuum left by the closure of the Minimes' house in Boulogne. Both the

---

[76] Ibid. [77] AN, H/3/2561/A. [78] AN, G/9/66 (1–3).
[79] AN, H/3/2561/A. [80] AN, G/9/66 (1–3). [81] Ibid.

officials of the *sénéchaussée* and the bishop of Boulogne pointed out that the buildings were located in 'one of the most populated districts of that town, where there are only two other men's convents, both of which have precious few friars'.[82]

Moreover, in showing *largesse* to the stricken martyrs of persecution, the monarchy was reinforcing its prestige as an institution founded on the Catholic faith. The foreign clergy were to reciprocate any favours by perpetuating this image. Many of the *lettres patentes* which allowed foreign clerics to set up houses stress the part they were to play in supporting the Most Christian King.[83] The monarchy's Catholic image needed some polishing after the expulsion of the Jesuits in 1764 and because, between 1766 and 1784, the Commission of Regulars closed down hundreds of small, uneconomic religious houses. So when the English Carmelites applied to take over the buildings of the Minimes in Boulogne, the Commission saw a means of replying to 'the accusation of destroying everything'.[84]

The foreign clergy had been known, however, to participate in movements which threatened the orthodoxy of the Gallican church. As Prefect of Studies from 1718 to 1727, Thomas Innes modelled his teaching at the Scots College in Paris on the Jansenist practices of the Port-Royal and was promptly accused of heresy. The charges may have over-exaggerated the intensity of his commitment to Jansenism and his accusers were initially driven by murky, personal, and financial motives. On the other hand, at least eleven students opposed *Unigenitus*, the papal bull which condemned Jansenism in 1713, and Innes himself was a 'conscientious objector'[85] to the bull. The college itself was known to the police as a centre for the diffusion of the *Nouvelles ecclésiastiques*, the underground Jansenist newspaper.[86]

Fortunately, there were other reasons for the church and state to welcome the foreign clergy. Still speaking of the English establishment at Douai, Moore pointed to 'the thousands of *livres* which it has spent in that town, and the foreigners whom it attracts there'. This suggestion reflected the common assump-

---

[82] AN, G/9/66 (1–3).   [83] Ibid.   [84] Ibid.
[85] J. F. McMillan, 'Thomas Innes and the Bull "Unigenitus"', *Innes Review*, 33 (1982), 23.
[86] J. F. McMillan, 'Scottish Catholics and the Jansenist Controversy: The Case Reopened', *Innes Review*, 32 (1981), 30.

tion that foreigners spent money which benefited the French economy. The English Benedictines at Dieulouard claimed, gloriously if implausibly, to have introduced beer brewing to Lorraine.[87] The religious establishments certainly provided local tradesmen with business. By the spring of 1790, the twenty English nuns of the Immaculate Conception on the rue de Charenton in Paris owed 20,312 *livres*, mostly to various craftsmen and mainly for repairs to the convent buildings and the properties which they rented out.[88] In the summer of 1790, among the debts of the twenty-one not-so-abstemious English Augustinian nuns of the rue des Fossés-Saint-Victor, an impressive 1,539 *livres* for beer was owed to Santerre, the brewer and future commander of the Paris National Guard.[89]

With the apparent advantages to be drawn from foreign religious establishments, the monarchy and church alike were willing to grant certain concessions which made the foreign clergy a particularly privileged group among foreigners in France. Such privileges sometimes included special *lettres de naturalité* enabling foreign clergy to hold benefices. These letters had the specific purpose of allowing them to administer parishes as any French priest could. Sometimes, letters were granted to entire religious communities. Care was taken, however, to ensure that the Gallican church was not adulterated by too many foreigners. The letters usually stated that the beneficiary could not employ foreign curates, although this condition was not always obeyed in practice.[90]

Both the Gallican church and the secular authorities also granted the foreign clergy special financial privileges and exemptions. In 1700, Louis XIV exempted the English Benedictines of Dieulouard from the *salines*, the tax raised, like the *gabelle* elsewhere, on salt in the north-eastern provinces.[91] Four years after their establishment in 1603, the Irish seminarists in Bordeaux were allowed by their founder, Archbishop François de Sourdis, to carry the dead at funerals in order to earn their keep. By 1774, however, this 'privilege' was no longer regarded as such. The superior, Martin Glynn, travelled around the British Isles to raise enough money by 1780, not only to reconstruct a

---

[87] AN, G/9/66 (1–3).   [88] AN, S//4616.   [89] Ibid.
[90] AN, G/9/66 (1–3); Ferrière, *Dictionnaire*, ii. 152–3; Loupès, 'Ecclésiastiques irlandais', 91–2.   [91] AN, G/9/66 (1–3).

crumbling wing of their buildings, but also to free the Irish from what was now seen as the humiliation of having to work as pallbearers.[92] Those studying for the priesthood at the Irish College at Lille were allowed to take collections at church doors and, like their counterparts in Bordeaux, were permitted to carry the dead at funerals. In 1711, the municipality of Lille made the latter a right exclusive to the Irish seminarians.[93]

The French church and state also provided some financial support to the foreign establishments. Such funding was limited, not least because the government made it very clear that the foreigners should not become charges of the state. An analysis of the fixed annual revenue of eleven of the English establishments in France shows that the church provided on average only 7 per cent of their annual income, while the state accounted for 10 per cent. The Gallican church gave the foreign establishments financial support in three ways: it might provide them with lump sums of money for investment; it could make an engagement to pay an annual grant, in cash or kind, to individual establishments; and it could grant them property. Royal donations came in four different forms: the king could grant pensions to the establishments or to individual clerics; he also donated annual alms to various houses; he allowed foreign clergy to share in government handouts to the church; and, finally, he granted rebates on certain taxes and dues. The bulk of their revenue, however, came from their property (50 per cent) and their investments (33 per cent), usually *rentes*. The vast majority, if not all, of the original funds for this wealth came from English sources.[94] Likewise, in 1790, Alexander Gordon, principal of the Scots College, Paris, claimed that its revenue stemmed entirely from the donations and fees paid by Scots.[95]

For the bulk of foreign establishments, therefore, funding mainly came from such sources as the orders' movable wealth, spirited across the Channel during its flight from persecution, donations from wealthy Catholic benefactors, students' fees, the dowries of nuns, and the endowments or pensions brought by

[92] Loupès, 'Ecclésiastiques irlandais', 82.

[93] C. Giblin, 'The Irish Colleges on the Continent', in L. Swords (ed.), *The Irish-French Connection 1578–1978* (Paris, 1978), 19.

[94] AN, G/9/66 (1–3); D/XIX/30; S//4616; S//4619.

[95] J. Black, 'The Archives of the Scots College Paris on the Eve of their Destruction', *Innes Review*, 43 (1992), 56.

novices. This money was invested in property and bonds, but not always successfully. By 1766, a disastrous blend of disruption caused by the Seven Years War, ill-advised investments, the high price of staples in France, and the cost of repairs to its dilapidating buildings forced the English College at Douai to contract debts of 18,000 *livres*.[96] The Scots College in Paris hired out six houses which it owned in the city, but up to 40 per cent of the revenue was spent on maintaining the properties.[97]

Contact between foreign clergy and local people varied from one order to the next, depending upon their rules and function. The strict cloistering of the English Clarists would not have encouraged frequent interaction,[98] but most of the foreign religious orders claimed to be preachers, teachers, and dispensers of charity among local people. The English Franciscans of Douai claimed to fulfil a catalogue of duties, including 'visiting the sick, helping the dying, hearing confessions, both in the town and in the country'.[99] Some of the convents undertook to give French children a basic education not geared exclusively to religious life. The English Clarists at Gravelines declared in December 1789 that they received as pupils 'English and French *Demoiselles* without discrimination; they teach the latter English, which is presently part of the French curriculum'.[100]

Too many ties between the foreigners and locals could lead to a degree of assimilation which was regarded as unsuitable for people intended to return to the British Isles as missionaries. Those seminarians at the Irish College in Paris who arrived while still young forgot Gaelic, but became fluent in French. They were less inclined to leave France, so that between 1694 and 1734 only twenty-five missionaries left to serve in Ireland. To counteract such a possibility at the Scots College in Paris, students attending classes at the University were expected to go as a group, escorted by the beady-eyed Prefect of Studies, and were expected to return to the college immediately afterwards.[101] Contact with the outside world, with all its temptations and distractions, was to be minimized.

---

[96] AN, G/9/66 (1–3).
[97] Halloran, *Scots College*, 23–4.
[98] AN, G/9/66 (1–3).   [99] Ibid.
[100] D/XIX/30.
[101] Giblin, 'Irish Colleges', 15; Halloran, *Scots College*, 22.

Those of the foreign clergy who were cut off from French lay people, either through the language barrier or because of the rules of their order, do not seem to have been respected or resented any more than other ecclesiastics. Hostility between French laymen and foreign clerics did sometimes erupt, as in Bordeaux in 1759. There, a fight broke out between members of the Irish College and the local *confrèrie* of barrel-makers, when both organizations, with remarkably poor timing, tried to bury one of their dead at the same church at the same time.[102] It is not clear, however, that the *tonneliers* were motivated either by anticlericalism or by xenophobia.

It is certain that the presence of foreign clergy could provoke outbursts of xenophobia among local people, although such outbursts appear to have been rare. In July 1769 the petition of the English Carmelites to establish themselves in Boulogne was opposed by some of the municipal officers, who had convinced themselves that an English institution would act as a Trojan horse for sinister foreign interests. It was claimed that British merchants would use the friars as their agents in the port and they would be the eyes of the British cabinet. Such fantasies were brushed off by the Commission of Regulars, which argued that Catholic exiles were hardly likely to assist either Protestant merchants or the British government.[103] This response served to underline the commitment of the Ancien Régime to tolerating the existence of foreign Catholic clergy in France, provided, of course, that they did not become a charge on the state, or threaten the orthodoxy of the Gallican church.

IV

Catholic refugees were not the only foreign students and teachers in France. There were others in French institutions, from as far afield as Brazil, Russia, and even China. The Universities of Montpellier and Bordeaux accepted several Brazilian students, mostly from the rich province of Minas Geraïs, to study medicine. When José Joachim de Maïa, one of the future leaders of the 1789 uprising against Portuguese rule, graduated from

---

[102] Loupès, 'Ecclésiastiques Irlandais', 94.   [103] AN, G/9/66 (1–3).

Montpellier as a doctor of medicine in 1787, he took his degree with ten other foreigners who had origins as diverse as the United States, Smyrna in Turkey, and Lima in Peru.[104] The University of Angers boasted Polish and German scholars studying law and French, while in the nearby Académie d'équitation, of 334 *académiciens* taught between 1755 and 1792, no less than 201 whose nationalities are known were foreigners.[105] At the University of Strasbourg 'many Germans and Englishmen come to study'.[106] Between 1785 and 1787, of one hundred students of 'distinction' (unfortunately meaning of social standing rather than academic merit, although the two are not always mutually exclusive) at the school of medicine, forty-four were Russian. Goethe, himself studying law at Strasbourg, recognized the medical faculty there as the best of them all and he attended classes in chemistry, anatomy, and clinical medicine.[107] Between 1751 and 1766, two Chinese students, Ko and Yang, were sent by the Jesuit mission to Paris for their education, presumably for training as Christian missionaries in China.[108]

Foreign students received little or no financial aid from either the French state or the church, as bursaries were only offered to French students.[109] Foreigners could, of course, set up their own endowments, as happened with the Scots College which supported four students, but they usually studied in France at the expense of their parents, as was the case with the thirty boarders at the English College at Douai in 1766.[110] In 1761 Johann Georg Wille received as students two Russians (one a Cossack), who had been given bursaries by the tsarina to study art in Paris. Other Russian students lived, depending upon their means, in modest townhouses or with fruit-sellers, cobblers, or wig-makers.[111]

For those students and intellectuals who were not in France for religious reasons, the attractions of the kingdom, and Paris in particular, lay in its reputation as a European cultural hub. Many

---

[104] V. Chacon, 'Étudiants brésiliens à Montpellier et Révolution française', *AhRf* 62 (1990), 485–92; Mathorez, *Étrangers*, i. 104.

[105] Mathorez, *Étrangers*, i. 105.

[106] N. M. Karamzin, *Voyage en France 1789–1790*, tr. A. Legrelle (Paris, 1885), 8.

[107] W. Goethe, *The Autobiography of Goethe. Truth and Poetry: From my Life*, tr. P. Godwin, 2 vols. (London, 1847), i. 144, 156; ii. 2–3.

[108] Mathorez, *Étrangers*, i. 308, 381; ii. 34.

[109] Danjou, *Condition civile*, 51–2.

[110] AN, G/9/66 (1–3).

[111] Wille, *Mémoires*, i. 172; Mathorez, *Étrangers*, i. 309.

contemporaries regarded Enlightenment Europe as *l'Europe française*. This term was first coined in 1777 by the Marquis Carracioli, the Neapolitan ambassador to Versailles, as a means of describing the cultural prevalence of France at the time. This dominance was largely due to the use of French as the international language of diplomacy and cultural exchange, but it was not always accepted willingly and it certainly frustrated writers in other languages who sought to raise theirs to an equal status.[112] Moreover, the apparent importance of French language and culture among the European élites should not be allowed to detract from the important cultural and linguistic differences which separated the *philosophes* from the *Aufklärer* and the *illuminati*.[113] Still, the artistic and literary importance of French culture in Europe played an important part in attracting foreigners to Paris. The young Wille arrived in Strasbourg in 1736 on his way to Paris. When his companion decided that he would not continue the journey, Wille tried in vain to persuade his friend to reconsider, saying that 'a period in Paris would profit him and earn his reputation'.[114] Wille did not, however, continue on his own. He was accompanied by Schmidt, another artist, and by a Moravian cabinetmaker who quickly found work in the *faubourg* Saint-Antoine. Schmidt rapidly made his reputation and in 1742 was elected to the Académie royale de peinture on the strength of his engravings and then became, like Wille after him, a *graveur du Roi*. Others came to France to study under French masters: Jacques-Louis David counted at least twenty-seven foreign pupils, from North America to Russia. Between 1758 and 1789, thirty Russian students worked under the painters and sculptors of Paris. As Wille established his reputation as an engraver, he eventually became an integral part of the network of cultural exchange, friendship, and rivalries sometimes referred to at the time as the 'republic of letters'. His journal in the 1750s and 1760s drops famous names like confetti. He was forever being visited by artists and patrons from across Europe at his home on rue de la Harpe.[115]

---

[112] L. Réau, *L'Europe française au siècle des Lumières* (Paris, 1971), 9, 261–2.

[113] T. C. W. Blanning, *Reform and Revolution in Mainz, 1743–1803* (Cambridge, 1974), 1–3.   [114] Wille, *Mémoires*, i. 48.

[115] Ibid. i. 60–1, 82, 115; Réau, *L'Europe française*, 345–6; Mathorez, *Étrangers*, i. 309.

The 'republic of letters' naturally included writers and scientists as well as artists. Of the 120 *encyclopédistes* whose identity is known, at least fifteen were born abroad, although they did not all come to France.[116] Other foreign writers came to Paris, sometimes with a mission of their own in response to French cultural hegemony. Grimm, for example, arrived in Paris in 1748 with his pupil, the count von Schönberg, with a view to 'unite French charm and taste with German genius' and he stayed for over forty years. Paul-Jérémie Bitaubé, born in Königsberg in 1732, translated the *Iliad* into French and became a friend of d'Alembert, who urged him to come to Paris, where he was elected to the Académie des Inscriptions. In 1784, the Genevan Jacques Mallet du Pan arrived in Paris to be author–editor of the political section of Panckoucke's *Mercure de France*, which had the official privilege to print news. Neither he nor his publisher saw anything amiss about a foreigner assuming a role influential in the shaping of French public opinion. Certain *salons* became associated with foreigners: Madame de Geoffrin's was a rallying-point for those Poles who clustered around Count Stanisław Poniatowski before he became king of Poland in 1764. She also received Hume and Kaunitz. Her rival, Madame du Deffand, counted Horace Walpole and the Count Bernstorff of Denmark among her guests. Madame de Boufflers, who was a correspondent of Gustav III, became the favoured hostess for Swedes in Paris, while Madame d'Holbach assembled Galiani, Grimm, Beccaria, and Sterne.[117]

Science was also regarded in cosmopolitan terms. Among the seventy-six members of the Académie des sciences eight members could be foreign. As Nikolai Karamzin observed, 'foreigners consider it a great honour to be members of this Parisian Academy'.[118] Benjamin Franklin mixed with French scientists there during his stay in Paris between 1776 and 1785. He was appointed with Lavoisier to a committee to investigate Mesmerism and the climax was his embrace with Voltaire at the

[116] F. A. Kafker, 'Paris, centre principal de l'entreprise encyclopédique', in Vovelle, *Paris et la Révolution*, 203.

[117] J.-P. Poussou, 'Les Internationales de l'"honnête homme"', in Lequin, *Histoire des étrangers*, 282; F. Acomb, *Mallet du Pan (1749–1800): A Career in Political Journalism* (Durham, NC, 1973), 156, 158–9; Mathorez, *Étrangers*, i. 251–2; ii. 136, 379; Réau, *L'Europe française*, 267–70.

[118] Karamzin, *Voyage*, 171.

Academy in 1778.[119] Franklin, of course, had both scientific renown because of his lightning-rod and had broader popularity because of his plain, but carefully cultivated, manners and dress, which made him the quintessential 'American', straight from the Rousseauistic simplicity and honesty of the New World.[120] Of course, the extensive contacts made in the 'republic of letters' tended to be built up by the successful artists and intellectuals who had established a reputation. This form of cosmopolitanism was very much an élite phenomenon. Nor was it universally appreciated. A wealthy aristocrat from Cleves, Jean-Baptiste Cloots, was a francophile and disciple of Voltaire. He settled in Paris in 1775 and became embroiled in the religious debates with his defence of the *philosophes*. The police took notice of his rabid anticlericalism in 1785 and he was forced to flee. At his trial in 1794, he would describe himself proudly as 'burnable in Rome, hangable in London, and breakable on the wheel in Vienna'.[121] The authorities patronized and basked in the reflected glory of *l'Europe française* only for as long as its participants did not challenge too explicitly the existing political or moral order.

It was not only the police who did not always welcome the intrusion of foreigners into French cultural life. Many of these intellectuals viewed French society with an overly critical eye and injured French self-esteem. The usually 'cosmopolitan' Louis-Sébastien Mercier warned his fellow-countrymen to beware of those foreigners who were the self-appointed critics of French customs: 'do not doubt that they are amassing materials for little satires which they will write against the French'.[122] Mercier's warning reflects a concern for how foreigners perceived his countrymen. Such anxieties were, however, one of the prices to be paid for cultural vitality. If France was one of the epicentres of European civilization, it had to expect criticism as well as praise. Some towns suffered from this scrutiny: between 1763

[119] R. R. Palmer, *The Age of the Democratic Revolution: A Political History of Europe and America, 1760–1800*, 2 vols. (Princeton, 1959–64), i. 250.

[120] P. Higonnet, *Sister Republics: The Origins of French and American Republicanism* (Cambridge, Mass., 1988), 135, 178.

[121] G. P. Gooch, *Germany and the French Revolution* (London, 1920), 321–2; Mathiez, *La Révolution et les étrangers*, 48–50; M. Slavin, *The Hébertistes to the Guillotine: Anatomy of a 'Conspiracy' in Revolutionary France* (Baton Rouge, La., 1994), 190–1.

[122] L.-S. Mercier, *Le Tableau de Paris*, ed. J. Kaplow (Paris, 1989), 172.

and 1789, Montpellier lost pride of place to Nice as the resort of wealthy British tourists. Its fate had not been helped by the comments published by British travellers, most notably Smollett, who claimed to have been poisoned by garlic and (worse) being served tea without milk.[123]

With France, and Paris in particular, as a major cultural focus, its many notable foreign visitors would reinforce certain elements in French identity and politics. For one, the highly publicized visits of Franklin and other Americans to France helped to reinforce the impression, in 1789, that the French Revolution was directly related to its sister in America. For many of the revolutionaries who had worked as publicists, journalists, writers, and scientists, the international focus of Paris and the notion of a 'republic of letters' suggested that all men were brothers. Combined with the highly charged politics of the Revolution itself, the 'cosmopolitanism' of some of these intellectuals was to inspire the notion of a 'crusade for universal liberty' in 1792, which many of the original participants in the pacific exchange of ideas would reject in horror. An exception was Cloots, who in 1785 published a tract urging the French government to set its sights on 'the natural limit of the Gauls', the Rhine frontier.[124] For many of the artists and intellectuals, however, the improvement of humanity was to remain in the moral sphere of human endeavour and even to be restricted to the educated élites. It was not to be transformed into political action.

V

France did, however, attract individuals and groups who had failed in their political endeavours abroad. Over the course of the eighteenth century, they varied in their aims and ideology, from the absolutist and often Catholic Jacobites in the first half of the century to the radical Genevans and Dutch in the 1780s. The Jacobites had come from the British Isles since the Revolution of 1688–9. They included soldiers shipped from Ireland in 1691,

[123] M. Sacquin, 'Les Anglais à Montpellier et à Nice pendant la seconde moitié du siècle', *Dix-huitième siècle*, 13 (1981), 292.
[124] Mathiez, *La Révolution et les étrangers*, 50.

Catholic clergy who suddenly found themselves no longer tolerated after the respite under James II/VII, and the Jacobite court, which settled at Saint-Germain-en-Laye. The obvious attractions of France for Jacobites were its proximity to the British Isles, its Catholicism, and the support the government was likely to give to their cause. Between 1688 and 1760, the French occasionally gave assistance to the Jacobites, although the last real hope of the Stuarts perished at Culloden in 1746. Jacobites used France as a base for their activities against Britain: the Walsh family of Saint-Malo used their knowledge of British coastal waters in their privateering raids.[125]

After the failure of the uprising of 1745–6, many of those Jacobites who escaped limped to France and there received some help from the French government. D'Argenson, the foreign minister, issued private instructions regarding an ordinance of 15 February 1746, which had raised two Scots infantry regiments for service in Scotland. He now promised that those who had joined the units would be given posts in the French army. After the final defeat in April, a large number of Scottish officers did flee to France and received, not army commissions, but handouts from the government to support them in their exile.[126] There was good reason to pamper the Jacobites: in the increasingly unlikely event of a Stuart restoration, the few hundred thousand *livres* spent supporting them in France would reap dividends in terms of gratitude once the Jacobites were in power.

For all the apparent amity between the Jacobite court and the French government, the exiles were still watched carefully by agents reporting to the foreign ministry. One report by d'Eguilles, dated 30 July 1746, gives details about leading Scottish, Irish, and English Jacobites in Paris, of whom to be wary and, significantly, who still had influence with the prince and who was now entirely dependent upon him for their livelihood.[127] Charles Edward Stuart was eventually imprisoned at Vincennes in 1748 and then expelled from France as a condition of the peace of Aix-la-Chapelle. With the Jacobite exiles, as with other refugees, *raison d'état* took precedence over ideological affinity.

Rival groups of Polish exiles appeared in France, surrounding

---

[125] Simms, 'The Irish', 643.   [126] MAE, MD, Angleterre, 79.   [127] Ibid.

different candidates for the throne. In a foreshadowing of the more brutal factional struggles among radical exiles during the Revolution, the supporters of the ultimately successful Russian candidate, Stanisław Poniatowski, sparred with those who backed Xavier de Saxe, son of Augustus III. The focal points for these groups were, respectively, the *salon* of Madame de Geoffrin and Xavier de Saxe himself, who settled in Paris once his bid for election had failed. The Geoffrin set had somewhat more success than the Jacobite exiles in influencing French policy. Although in 1764 the government backed Xavier rather than Poniatowski, de Geoffrin used her influence at court to arrange a meeting between Prince Sulkowski and Sainte-Foy, the foreign minister. This contact led to official French acknowledgement of Stanisław as king of Poland in 1766.[128]

The crucial difference between the Jacobites and Poniatowski's supporters was, of course, that the latter were politically successful. This meant that diplomatic necessity made pawns of the powerless Jacobite exiles, while the Poniatowski entourage in Paris, who had Russian backing, were suddenly more substantial pieces in the international game. In another anticipation of revolutionary politics, the status and importance of political exiles was determined less by ideology than by the demands of international politics.

Given this pragmatic approach, the French government's toleration of the Genevan *Représentants* who fled to France after 1782 is surprising, the more so because the French had provided troops to oust them in the first place. Yet exiles such as Étienne Clavière, Étienne Dumont, and Jacques-Antoine Du Roveray enjoyed a remarkably high profile in France in the 1780s, despite the king's order given in June 1782 that 'no *Représentant* be allowed to cross the frontier'. In July, Vergennes accused the Genevan 'insurgents' of being British agents. Clavière, however, worked through his acquaintances Mirabeau and Brissot to further both his political and financial ambitions and thereby enjoyed much publicity in France. He engaged in pamphleteering battles involving, among other institutions, the *caisse d'escompte*, and the Paris *compagnie des eaux*. His campaign against the latter got him into trouble with the authorities, but he

---

[128] Mathorez, *Étrangers*, i. 245–59.

remained in France and enriched himself further through shrewd investments. In August 1788, he was made *administrateur-général* of the royal life assurance company. For an exile still apparently committed to the overthrow of a regime guaranteed by the French government, Clavière had assumed a very public role, sometimes aided and abetted by the French government itself. Perhaps the reason behind the authorities' tolerance was the occasional use to which his financial expertise could be put. For Calonne, Clavière had served a useful purpose in his campaigns against financial interests, such as the *caisse d'escompte*, and they had a mutual enemy in Necker. Clavière's closest Genevan associates, Dumont and Du Roveray, did not arrive in Paris until 1789, by which time the government was concerned with far more important matters than the presence of three Genevan dissidents on its territory.[129]

The Dutch 'Patriots' were more openly welcomed by the French government, despite their commitment to overthrow or at least limit the powers of the Stadholder. Having fled from the Prussian invasion of the United Provinces in September 1787, they were the largest single group of political exiles established in France before the Revolution. By the summer of 1789, there were about 5,000 Patriots clustering in Paris and northern towns such as Saint-Omer, Gravelines, Dunkirk, and Watten. Why they should be tolerated by the French monarchy in such large numbers can be put down to practical politics. The strategic and commercial importance of the Netherlands was obvious to France as well as to Britain. Like the Jacobite exiles, they were a ready-made corps of leadership who might be expected to impose francophile policies should their political fortunes change. For the Patriots' part, the French were still their best hope of support in Europe. In Brussels, they established a commission with the clear, if long-winded, objective to 'support and defend the interests of the Patriot nation at the court of the King of France and to press with especial vigour for armed assistance to help re-establish the downtrodden liberties of the nation'. Despite the ideological divide between the exiles and the monarchy, both sides could see mutual advantage in maintaining

---

[129] J. Bénétruy, *L'Atelier de Mirabeau: Quatre proscrits genevois dans la tourmente révolutionnaire* (Paris, 1962), 25, 31, 96, 104–15, 137; D. Jarrett, *The Begetters of Revolution: England's Involvement with France, 1759–1789* (London, 1973), 209–10.

relations with each other. The Patriots, however, had to tread a treacherous path between their 'democratic' language and the practical necessity of retaining French support: the one could not be entirely accommodated without some damage to the other.[130]

They seem to have avoided the pitfalls, for the Dutch exiles were soon receiving handouts of cash from the French government. In 1788, Johan Valckenaer, one of the Patriot leaders in France, had persuaded Lambert, the French minister responsible for the Dutch refugees, to provide subsidies towards the fugitives' keep. The usual allocation was 14 *livres* on arrival in France. Unfortunately for all concerned, management of the pensions was devolved onto Coert Lambertus van Beijma, Valckenaer's rival. Van Beijma's mismanagement of the French pensions, coupled with his refusal to allow the government to inspect the accounts, put those very funds in jeopardy. Lambert imposed a deadline at the end of 1788, after which no new arrivals in France would be eligible for money. Repeated demands for the opening of the registers for government inspection were not met until 1790.[131] The fracture among the Dutch Patriots in France would persist into the French Revolution, with bitter consequences.

The Ancien Régime approach to political refugees was based on political necessity. While ideological affinity may have hidden this fundamental motive in the case of the Jacobites, the use which the French crown had for Clavière and the Dutch Patriots made it more obvious. The policies of the French Revolution were to be similar, although the basic pressures of practical politics would be hidden by the ideological pretensions of both the exiles and the revolutionaries. Yet, under both the monarchy and the Republic, diplomatic tact and ideological conformity helped to make relations between refugees and government smoother and the latter more inclined to be generous. The peculiar circumstances of the Revolution, however, were to exaggerate the need for political orthodoxy to an unprecedented extreme. For all the apparent rupture with the past in 1789, the

---

[130] S. Schama, *Patriots and Liberators: Revolution in the Netherlands 1780–1813*, 2nd edn. (London, 1992), 106, 123–4, 144–6; T. C. W. Blanning, *The Origins of the French Revolutionary Wars* (London, 1986), 47–8; Godechot, *Grande Nation*, 93.

[131] Schama, *Patriots and Liberators*, 144–6, 669 n. 24; *AP* xvii. 377–8.

policies of the Revolution towards political exiles were dictated by the same concerns which confronted the ministers of the absolute monarchy. These considerations included the refugees' potential in furthering French interests abroad and some assurance that their presence posed no threat to French domestic and external security.

VI

Those foreigners who contributed to the economy were encouraged to settle in France, possibly more than any other type. The establishment of foreign manufacturers, merchants, and financiers was nothing new. In the previous century, the mercantilism of Louis XIV's minister, Colbert, and the Sun King's efforts to build up the French navy, had led the government to invite or attract foreigners with expertise in specific areas.[132] The eighteenth century witnessed a continuity in these policies, with new skills and technology being imported in various ways, both foul and fair, particularly from Britain from the 1720s, as the French government sought to make good the technological gap which was widening between the two countries.[133]

Among the fair means by which industrial techniques came to France was through the legitimate migration of foreign artisans and manufacturers, such as Christoff-Philipp Oberkampf or, in some cases, through the adoption of those who felt persecuted or restricted in their home country, like John Kay and John Holker. The fouler method was to lure (the wonderful French word was *débaucher*) skilled workers and entrepreneurs with promises of plump bounties and profits. Among those seduced were Michael Alcock, William Wilkinson, and John Badger.

Artisans who travelled to France with their skills could form a substantial proportion of the population in some neighbourhoods. By 1789, perhaps 4 per cent of the *faubourg* Saint-Antoine was foreign-born, half from Germany. The artisans of

---

[132] J.-P. Poussou, 'À l'école des autres', in Lequin, *Histoire des étrangers*, 235–6.

[133] J. R. Harris, *Industrial Espionage and Technology Transfer: Britain and France in the Eighteenth Century* (Aldershot, 1998), 7; P. Mathias, 'Skills and the Diffusion of Innovations from Britain in the Eighteenth Century', *Transactions of the Royal Historical Society*, 5th ser. 25 (1975), 93–113.

this nationality contributed greatly to the reputation of the quarter for cabinetmaking, while craftsmen from Brabant and Liège worked on other furniture and in metalwork and textiles. The small group of Italians, mainly from Tuscany, made figurines.[134] These craftsmen worked with traditional methods in an area renowned for its artisanal life. Others, however, brought new technology to France, or helped in new developments. Christoff-Philipp Oberkampf belonged to this last category.

Born in 1738 at Vaihingen-an-der-Enz, 17 miles north-west of Stuttgart, Oberkampf came to France after being brought to Basle by his father, a calico dyer, where he began his apprenticeship as an *indienneur*, a printer of the fine cotton cloths imported from Asia. In 1758, he deserted his father and in Mulhouse met an agent for the factory of Jacques-Daniel Cottin at the Arsenal in Paris. After a trial period, Oberkampf was signed on for three years as a colour-maker. This method of recruitment by French manufacturers, particularly from among foreigners, was not unusual when certain skills and knowledge were in short supply. Adept dyers and printers of fine cloths were scarce in France in the mid-eighteenth century, because the import of *indiennes* had been illegal since 1686 in order to protect the producers of *étoffes nationales*, such as Lyonnais silks and Norman woollens. These restrictions started to lift after 1750 and Cottin seized the opportunity, leasing buildings in the Arsenal from 1754 to dye cotton using indigo. Over half a century of restrictions meant that local talent for this promising industry was non-existent, so Cottin was forced to look to areas of Europe where the activity was well-developed, such as Switzerland and western Germany. Oberkampf had precisely the sort of skills which Cottin required.[135]

Unlike Oberkampf, John Holker from Lancashire had no choice but to come to France. A Catholic, he joined the Jacobite army in 1745 and after his capture was sentenced to death. With his dramatic escape to France in 1746, he brought his expertise

[134] R. Monnier, *Le Faubourg Saint-Antoine (1789–1815)* (Paris, 1981), 33–4, 71, 302.
[135] S. Chassagne, *Oberkampf: Un entrepreneur capitaliste au siècle des Lumières* (Paris, 1980), 21–30; S. D. Chapman and S. Chassagne, *European Textile Printers in the Eighteenth Century: A Study of Peel and Oberkampf* (London, 1981), 104–8, 113–15.

in textiles obtained during his partnership in a Manchester calendering firm. His knowledge of textiles impressed Marc Morel, an inspector of manufactures for the government's *bureau de commerce*, who introduced him to Daniel-Charles Trudaine of the bureau in 1751. That year, he was employed as an agent for the illicit recruitment of British expertise. Holker was also made a partner in two innovative Rouen firms, one for the manufacture of cotton velvet, the other for calendering and 'English' finishing of cloth. The intention was to integrate Holker into these firms, which would employ defecting British artisans, who in turn would train French workers in their methods. The imported artisans would also be circulated among several firms, to spread the new techniques and to avoid, as Trudaine hoped, the creation of monopolies. As with Oberkampf, Holker and the workers he lured over from Britain had skills which were lacking in France, but which were in great demand. In September 1754, the cloth-finishing business in which Holker was involved became a privileged *manufacture royale* and a centre for the diffusion of the new methods in France. It employed ninety-two workers, of whom twenty were British. In 1755, Holker's achievements were rewarded by his appointment as an inspector of foreign manufactures for the *bureau de commerce*. He used this position to entice more skilled artisans and manufacturers to France. Many such artisans were more easily assimilated into French society, as they were often recruited from among Holker's Jacobite—and therefore often Catholic—connections. Otherwise, the artisans had to be promised religious toleration.[136]

The transfer of technology was driven by the desire to keep apace of Britain's rapid economic development, but military considerations also entered the equation. The *bureau de commerce* was all too aware of advances made in the industrializing regions of France's great rival. The bureau's agents, such as Gabriel Jars and Marchant de la Houillère, gained access to British manu-

---

[136] J. R. Harris, 'John Holker: A Lancashire Jacobite in French Industry', *Newcomen Society Transactions*, 64 (1992–3), 132–5; Harris, *Industrial Espionage*, 43–78; A. P. Wadsworth and J. de L. Mann, *The Cotton Trade and Industrial Lancashire, 1600–1780* (Manchester, 1931), 196–7; W. O. Henderson, *Britain and Industrial Europe, 1750–1870: Studies in British Influence on the Industrial Revolution in Western Europe*, 3rd edn. (Leicester, 1972), 14–17; C. C. Gillispie, *Science and Polity in France at the End of the Old Régime* (Princeton, 1980), 420–4.

factures and returned with reports on new techniques.[137] While
these experts could not disguise their enthusiasm for the developments, their missions were often driven by alarm: de la
Houillère was sent to Staffordshire in 1775 to discover how the
British cast their cannon. He was struck by the advantages which
the British navy drew from the Wilkinson brothers' methods of
founding iron and boring the barrels for artillery pieces. He set
about luring William, the younger Wilkinson, to France.[138]

The traffic in artisans and technology was certainly a seller's
market, not only because the skills and methods were in great
demand, but also because workers and manufacturers who left
home were often running grave risks, owing to laws prohibiting
the export of machinery and the emigration of skilled workers. In
1756, Michael Alcock's wife was arrested in London with four
artisans on their way back to France from Birmingham. Nine
years later, another recruiter for the Alcock family, William
Hyde, was nearly killed with a worker when, in a shoot-out in
an inn on the road to London, a bullet passed through his night
cap.[139] In order to attract and then retain the defectors which
they so craved, the French authorities had to pay handsome
sums, grant concessions, and, in some cases, show inexhaustible
patience. The prickly John Kay, inventor of the flying shuttle,
had fled Britain in 1747, either to escape the mob violence
wherever he tried to introduce his creation, or because of his
unsuccessful defence of his patent rights. Until his death in 1779,
he spent fitful periods in France, where his quarrelsome tem-
perament and ambition made him a difficult man to deal with.
The French government had to be generous, however, because
'to leave him without recompense would be to disgust foreigners
from bringing their industry into the kingdom'.[140]

The government did achieve some success in enticing foreign
entrepreneurs. In 1753, John Badger was brought to Lyon by
Holker to produce watered silk. In return, he received one *louis* a
week for subsistence on route, the supply of all the necessary
machinery and tools, a guinea a week paid to his wife in London
during his absence, a promise to look after his widow and two

---

[137] Henderson, *Britain and Industrial Europe*, 5.
[138] AN, F/12/1300.
[139] AN, F/12/1315a.
[140] Wadsworth and Mann, *Cotton Trade*, 465.

children should he die before his enterprise was established, and either a pension or a fourteen-year monopoly once he had produced 'watered fabrics as beautiful as those of England'.[141] In Staffordshire, de la Houllière played on what he saw as the 'the spirit of gain, too common in that Nation' and won over William Wilkinson. He offered the ironmaster an advance of 50,000 *livres* towards a foundry in France, 200–300 guineas for his moving expenses and a further 50,000 *livres* on the production of the first twelve working cannon.[142] Wilkinson also received an annual pension of 12,000 *livres* on his arrival in France in 1777.[143]

Such enticements were not restricted to the manufacturers themselves, as artisans were also required to set up the establishments and then to train local people in the necessary skills and techniques. Michael Alcock, for example, had established a manufacture of hardware such as buttons, candlesticks, buckles, and locks at La Charité-sur-Loire in 1756. In order to draw the required workers from Birmingham, special concessions were offered to encourage them to make the hazardous journey. Workers at La Charité were exempt from the *droit d'aubaine*, all personal taxes, from service in the *milice*, and from billeting. Holker further suggested that 150 *livres* be awarded as a bounty to Alcock's son, Joseph, for every worker he brought over from Britain. The artisans themselves were offered 'gratifications' for their move to France. To ensure their own assimilation, Michael's sons converted to Catholicism.[144]

The manufacturers and the artisans did prosper, both in establishing successful factories and in spreading the skills and techniques in France. At the end of 1759, Oberkampf entered into a partnership with three entrepreneurs to set up a calico-printing plant at Jouy near Versailles. Despite some teething problems, by 1787 Oberkampf had become the sole owner at Jouy. Just over 9 per cent of his workers were drawn from abroad and his overseers were recruited either from among his own family or from Germany.[145]

---

[141] AN, F/12/1442.   [142] AN, F/12/1300.
[143] Henderson, *Britain and Industrial Europe*, 40.
[144] AN, F/12/1315a; Harris, *Industrial Espionage*, 185.
[145] AN, F/12/876; Chapman and Chassagne, *European Textile Printers*, 121, 127, 176–8.

Oberkampf, however, was not obliged to train French artisans to perform all the necessary tasks. His was a private enterprise, only getting the title of *manufacture royale* in 1784. Holker and the others, meanwhile, owed their businesses to the support of the *bureau de commerce* and were expected to teach the French new techniques. Success was chequered. John Kay's shuttle was tested in Normandy and was adopted in at least one of the *manufactures royales*, but progress in its adoption was slow and by 1790 its use had been dropped altogether.[146] Likewise John Badger's attempts to introduce new silk methods to Lyon were met with difficulties in finding the right parts for the machinery and raw materials, which left the enterprise dependent upon imports from Britain, defeating the whole object of the exercise. Holker still persuaded the government to provide Badger with a subsidy to train French workers in finishing heavy woollens.[147]

In contrast to these failures, Holker himself expanded from his *manufacture royale* at Saint-Sever, outside Rouen, to set up other plants at Vernon, Elbeuf, and Pont de l'Arche. Saint-Sever produced the tools and machinery which could be moved elsewhere and French artisans learnt to build the looms and jennies. He encouraged other British manufacturers to come to France with new designs. John Milne and his three sons answered the call and, with Calonne's encouragement, finally produced a water-frame at Passy in 1787.[148] The Alcocks, too, disseminated their skills, although not always in the way they anticipated. When, in 1760, one of their French associates, Frenais, broke away after an angry dispute, he set up his own manufacture of buttons in Paris, taking with him two trained-up French workers, who were offered 48 *livres* bounty. The Alcocks expanded their own enterprise by establishing a new manufacture at Roanne in 1765 and then Michael set up a steelworks at Villefray in 1767.[149] By 1788, William Wilkinson had a manufacture at Indret on the Loire near Nantes and at Le Creusot, where Arthur Young reported that he employed between 500 and 600 workers—all but two of them French.[150]

---

[146] Wadsworth and Mann, *Cotton Trade*, 460, 466.

[147] Harris, 'John Holker', 136; Henderson, *Britain and Industrial Europe*, 21.

[148] Gillispie, *Science and Polity*, 423–4; Henderson, *Britain and Industrial Europe*, 17, 22; Harris, *Industrial Espionage*, 377.

[149] AN, F/12/1315a.   [150] Young, *Travels in France*, 199.

As a further means of enriching the kingdom, colonies of foreign merchants in the great maritime towns of France were allowed to grow. In Bordeaux in 1777, there were no less than 111 foreign merchants and commercial agents, with Germans being the most important group at fifty-two, followed by the 'Jacobite' *anglo-irlandais*, the Dutch, Swedes, Danes, and Swiss. In Marseille ten years later, of 209 foreign Protestant *négociants*, 157 were Swiss.[151] These merchants were considered an integral part of the network of French commerce.

To encourage trade, therefore, the French government extended special privileges to the foreign mercantile colonies, such as exemptions from the *droit d'aubaine* and general decrees of naturalization. Despite such measures, which might have encouraged the assimilation of merchants into the broader French community, many persisted in doing business with their own countrymen. This might be explained by the merchants' habits of acting as agents or partners for their compatriots, which reinforced the foreign commercial networks into which the government wanted French merchants to break. Many foreign merchants who made enough money then sank it into landed property, and this is particularly true of the Jacobite exiles from the British Isles after mid-century.[152]

The government was also willing to develop some of France's primary industries, particularly in fishing. Nantucket whalers arrived in Dunkirk in May 1786, when three ships sailed in from across the Atlantic, the fruit of an agreement between a Quaker named William Roth and the French government. Roth had promised to bring ten to twelve whalers to Dunkirk, while the French naval minister, the *maréchal* de Castries, offered a bounty of 50 *livres* for every tonnage of ship brought and a guarantee of their freedom to worship. By 1788, there were three Nantucket shipowners in Dunkirk, managing eight whalers between them.[153] Meanwhile, Catalan fishermen had long used Marseille

---

[151] J.-P. Poussou, 'Mobilité et migrations', in J. Dupâquier, *Histoire de la population française*, 4 vols. (Paris, 1988), ii. 135.

[152] Simms, 'The Irish', 647; J.-P. Poussou, 'Recherches sur l'immigration anglo-irlandaise à Bordeaux au XVIIIe siècle', in *Bordeaux et les Îles britanniques*, 71–2; R. Hayes, 'Liens irlandais avec Bordeaux', in R. Hayes, C. Preston, and J. Weygand, *Les Irlandais en Aquitaine* (Bordeaux, 1971), 11–18.

[153] C. Pfister-Langanay, *Ports, navires et négociants à Dunkerque (1662–1792)* (Dunkirk, 1985), 270–2.

as a seasonal port for their fishing expeditions, with special privileges dating back to the reign of Louis XIV. The rights of Spanish fishermen in French waters were confirmed by the *pacte de famille* of 1761, but this ensured that, by the time of the Revolution, their relationship with French fishermen would be stormy.

The presence of such foreigners in France had clear advantages for the government. They brought with them skills and methods which the French would otherwise have lacked, thereby enriching the kingdom (and the tax base) and helping France in its commercial rivalry with Britain. The dividends which the government hoped to reap made it willing to spend a lot of time, money, and effort in attracting the right people to France and in keeping them there. Unlike foreign refugees and even clergy, the artisans, manufacturers, merchants, and fishermen tended to avoid politics and so, while some of them were difficult, they were never perceived as posing a threat to the established order. This pattern of behaviour was to be altered only slightly during the Revolution.

Banking and finance, however, were so tied up with the state that those foreigners who participated could not always avoid embroilment in the politics of the court. The involvement of foreign bankers in French administration could have its advantages, as they drew on wide sources of credit. The Genevan Necker, for example, was barely 24 when he and another Genevan, George-Tobied Thellusson, were given the management of the bank of Isaac Vernet in 1756. By 1770, when the two Genevans took over actual ownership, the bank *Thellusson, Necker & Compagnie* was one of the largest Protestant banks in Europe, with contacts among the vast European network of Huguenot, Genevan, Swiss, Dutch, and British bankers.[154] The vast majority of correspondents of Necker's banking rival and compatriot, Isaac Panchaud, were also abroad, especially in the Netherlands, while those in France were foreigners, mostly British and Swiss, including the Neuchâtelois, Jean-Frédéric Perregaux.[155]

The connections of Necker and Panchaud were useful to the

---

[154] H. Lüthy, *La Banque Protestante en France, de la révocation de l'Édit de Nantes à la Révolution*, 2 vols. (Paris, 1959–61), ii. 230–1, 315.

[155] Ibid. ii. 425–6

French government when it came to raising much-needed loans, or placating the monarchy's foreign creditors.[156] For the French monarchy to have such an asset explains why the government was willing to create the post of Director-General of Finance to allow Necker control of the royal purse-strings. When Necker was deposed after his first ministry in 1781, the monarchy was not short of similar contacts and it was Panchaud who took over, not as Director-General of Finance, but as financial adviser to Necker's replacement, Joly de Fleury. Panchaud, in turn, used his Amsterdam contacts to float loans for the monarchy.[157]

Furthermore, foreign bankers could bring expertise and ideas which encouraged the development of Paris as a financial centre. It was Panchaud who, in 1776, masterminded the creation of the *caisse d'escompte*, a banking institution which was to become of key importance in the last years of the Ancien Régime and a matter of bitter political feuding in the early Revolution. Its primary purpose was to enhance commerce by discounting letters of exchange, but it also acted as a bank dealing with the expenses and revenue of *notaires*, bankers, and merchants.[158]

Foreign involvement in French finance fed the paranoia of those who saw in the international Protestant banking network a threat to French (and Catholic) interests. There was plenty of evidence to suggest the interference of foreign bankers in French domestic affairs. Both Necker and Panchaud raised money for the French government by selling *rentes viagères*, bonds which paid interest until the holders died. As foreign financiers subscribed to these schemes, Necker's enemies could claim that he had sold France out to foreign capitalists.[159] Furthermore, perhaps owing to the nature of Panchaud's correspondents, all but two of the members of the *caisse d'escompte*'s first board were foreigners.[160] Suspicion of foreign bankers deepened when the threadbare state of the monarchy's finances came to light in the late 1780s. By then, the belief that foreign financiers were manipulating both the government and the destiny of France had wide appeal. With the continued involvement of foreign

[156] Jarrett, *Begetters of Revolution*, 159.
[157] Ibid. 173.
[158] Lüthy, *Banque Protestante*, ii. 433–5.
[159] Jarrett, *Begetters of Revolution*, 171–2.
[160] Lüthy, *Banque Protestante*, ii. 421, 437.

bankers, and the indebtedness of the French state to foreign creditors, it was perhaps inevitable that suspicion of these financiers should persist into the Revolution, sometimes fatally.

If foreign manufacturers, artisans, fishermen, merchants, and bankers helped to generate wealth in the French economy, there were others who contributed in smaller ways. Migrant labour was driven by the 'economy of makeshifts' which demanded that, in order to prevent their families from going hungry even in normal times, the poor needed an extra job, be it through seasonal migration, begging, or smuggling. Migration, pushed by high birth rates and limited agricultural resources, brought to the large cities labourers from all parts of France and Europe, but especially from Savoy.[161] In Paris, Savoyards emerged from their lodgings in the *quartiers* of the Ville Neuve near the Porte Saint-Denis, or in the *faubourgs* Saint-Jacques and Saint-Marcel to work the streets as lamplighters, messengers, chimney-sweeps, shoe-shiners, sawyers, or even as *décrotteurs*, people who earned their keep by scraping mud off people's boots. Savoyard women worked in Lyon as *tireuses de cordes* for the silk weavers.[162] They were stereotyped for their poverty: 'Savoyard' became a generic term for anyone who performed dirty and menial tasks in the streets.[163] Johann Georg Wille stumbled across a group of chimney-sweeps in their sordid lodgings and he concluded instantly that they were Savoyards:

I entered a house whose entrance, filled with refuse, already shocked me; but, out of pure curiosity, I went further, where I saw a large room, blackened with smoke and soiled on every side. These were the lodgings of a company of little chimney-sweeps from Savoy, each of whom had the pleasure of sleeping on a mean bed of chopped straw, for two *sols* rent a night, paid in advance. Oh! How quickly I fled from that miserable cavern![164]

The authorities twitched with suspicion towards the Savoyards, as they did towards the labouring poor in general. Savoyards were occasionally fingered for involvement in the

---

[161] Hufton, *Poor of Eighteenth-Century France*, 15, 71–3, 83.

[162] J. Kaplow, *The Names of Kings: The Parisian Laboring Poor in the Eighteenth Century* (New York, 1972), 33, 43, 52; Mercier, *Tableau de Paris*, 142, 144.

[163] J. Kaplow, 'Sur la population flottante de Paris à la fin de l'Ancien Régime', *AhRf* 39 (1967), 3.

[164] Wille, *Mémoires*, i. 89.

more boisterous political demonstrations. When the *parlement* of Paris was recalled in 1774, the celebrations went on into the early hours of the morning and the guard had to force the crowd from the courtyard of the Palais de Justice. It was reported by the officer in charge that Savoyards were among those ejected.[165] The Savoyards worked long hours, however, being among the first on the streets at 5 o'clock in the morning and staying out until late at night.[166] Mercier stressed that, poor as they were, they saved money 'to send some home to their poor relations each year' and he praised them as 'models of filial love'.[167] Mercier was not exaggerating: annually, towards the end of the eighteenth century, up to 40,000 people returned to Savoy with varying amounts of money saved up. Moreover, some were skilled artisans and *colporteurs* who had become small *commerçants* with their own shops.[168]

Savoyards, despite speaking French, retained a distinct identity. Mercier observed that 'they always distinguish themselves by their love for their country and for their relations', perhaps in common with expatriates everywhere. They were often organized in a self-regulating community which kept them out of trouble with the authorities: 'the oldest have the right to watch over the youngest . . . they have been seen to inflict justice on one of their number who had been thieving; they tried and hanged him'.[169] Never fully integrated, the Savoyards were none the less an important part of French urban life.

At the very bottom of the social pile, however, were those who provoked not just suspicion, but outright hostility: migrant beggars. Judging by arrests ordered by the commissioners of the Châtelet during the economic crisis of 1788, few foreign beggars appear to have made it to Paris,[170] but they certainly existed in greater numbers in the provinces. Beggars and migrant workers were sometimes one and the same as they made their way across the countryside in search of work. The same economic factors which drove the Savoyards to seek low-

---

[165] Kaplow, *Names of Kings*, 156.
[166] Karamzin, *Voyage*, 92; Mercier, *Tableau de Paris*, 142.
[167] Mercier, *Tableau de Paris*, 142.
[168] J. Nicolas, *La Savoie au 18ᵉ siècle: Noblesse et bourgeoisie*, 2 vols. (Paris, 1978), ii. 937.
[169] Mercier, *Tableau de Paris*, 142.
[170] Kaplow, 'Population flottante', 10–11.

paid labour in France forced others live by charity. Occasionally the problem provoked the authorities into action at the highest level. Between 1780 and 1783, twenty-one beggars, mostly from northern Italy, were arrested in France at places as diverse as Poitou, Angers, Rennes, Pau, Besançon, and Aix-en-Provence. What linked them together was that they all carried false letters from religious orders permitting them to beg for alms. They were forged by an enterprising schoolmaster in the Val de Styr in Switzerland. He had acquired copies of official monastic stamps and made wood-block imitations. On 17 April, the king gave orders for the expulsion of all foreign beggars in France, including even genuine foreign friars who sought alms. By 29 April, more than sixty friars were arrested and ordered to leave the country.[171] If real peripatetic brothers were expelled along with beggars, it reflects the authorities' determination to get rid of those who seemed to threaten public order.

VII

The contrasting treatment of different types of foreigners in France before 1789 shows that they were encouraged to settle in France where they were deemed of utility to the state. Such uses could be obvious: foreign troops defended the kingdom; political refugees could be played as pawns in the game of European diplomacy; manufacturers, artisans, and merchants enriched the country. Less obvious was the reinforcement of the prestige of the monarchy, either through enhancing its Catholic image by tolerating foreign clergy, or by seeking a reflection of its glory through patronizing foreigners in the arts and sciences.

Yet the state also had to balance its use of foreigners with other considerations, such as domestic stability and diplomacy. Open as the Ancien Régime was to the contributions of foreigners, it was also ready to dispense with them, or at least control their activities, when practical politics dictated. The state sought to prevent the foreign clergy from becoming financially dependent on the crown and, in order to preserve the essentially French fabric of the Gallican church, it tried to stop foreign priests from

---

[171] MAE, ADP, France, 12.

appointing foreign vicars. Despite its interest in a Stuart restoration in Britain, the French government discarded the Jacobites when broader diplomatic pressures so required. The absolute monarchy was pragmatic in its approach to foreigners, an expediency which helps to explain why the *droit d'aubaine* was not unilaterally and completely abolished in France before 1789. While it recognized the potential economic benefits of such a measure, the government was unwilling to ease restrictions on foreigners while French subjects abroad remained liable to similar impositions.

The treatment of foreigners under the Ancien Régime depended on their role in French society. The variations conformed to the entire social structure of the Ancien Régime, in which people were organized into corporate groups based on function, with varying degrees of privilege. In these circumstances, the nationality of foreigners mattered less than loyalty and obedience to the king and, above all, the part they performed in the kingdom.

The Revolution presented an ideological challenge to this corporate society, by abolishing the multitude of privileges which defined these groups. In making the nation the essential source of identity, the Revolution put into question the role of foreigners who had long enjoyed a privileged position in various branches of French state and society. Ideology, however, concealed the fact that the fundamental pressures which had faced the Ancien Régime remained the same. The revolutionaries were not doctrinaires who blindly applied their principles regardless of the consequences. Instead, when they dealt with the problems posed by foreigners, they were as sensitive to the financial, political, and diplomatic implications as the Ancien Régime had been. For this reason, the Revolution witnessed a good deal of continuity from the absolute monarchy in its ways of dealing with foreigners.

2

Foreigners under the
Constituent Assembly

A blustery, rainy day in Paris, 14 July 1790 was the first anniversary of the fall of the Bastille. It was celebrated across France with oaths of loyalty to the nation, the law, and the constitution. In the capital, units of National Guards from all over France were marshalled on the Champ de Mars. Beyond these phalanxes of citizen-soldiers were spectators assembled on rows of benches and archways rising above the field like a classical stadium. Probably 350,000 people gathered in this open-air ceremony. Among them was a young British woman named Helen Maria Williams, who had arrived in Paris the day before. She was not merely a curious tourist. In London, she was already on the way to establishing a literary reputation and she had close associations with radical Whigs and Unitarian dissenters. She was already predisposed to be deeply affected by what she was to see in France.[1] At the *Fête de la Fédération*, she was not disappointed:

You will not suspect that I was an indifferent witness of such a scene. Oh no! this was not a time in which the distinctions of country were remembered. It was the triumph of human kind; it was man asserting the noblest privileges of his nature; and it required but the common feelings of humanity to become in that moment a citizen of the world. . . . I too, though but a sojourner in their land, rejoiced in their happiness, joined the universal voice, and repeated with all my heart and soul, 'Vive la nation!'[2]

Williams expressed what many foreigners felt that summer. The Revolution in France had global significance because the French had not asserted historical, prescriptive claims, but their

---

[1] L. D. Woodward, *Une Anglaise amie de la Révolution française: Hélène Maria Williams et ses amis* (Paris, 1930), 27–33.

[2] H. M. Williams, *Letters Written in France in the Summer of 1790* (London, 1790), 13–14, 21.

rights purely and simply as human beings. When it came to the reality of foreigners in general, however, the revolutionaries were faced with a myriad of pressures which often exerted their force in different directions. The cosmopolitan implications of the rights of man were often restrained by the revolutionaries, aware as they were of France's own political and military limitations. When the Constituent Assembly embarked on its reform of France and was faced with the privileges of certain types of foreigners, it could not sweep them aside as easily as it did those belonging to French people, because often those privileges had been based on diplomatic considerations. Such concerns prevented the full application of the nationalizing tendencies and the egalitarian ideals of 1789 under the Constituent Assembly.

I

If Williams saw herself as a citizen of the world, the Constituent Assembly was faced with the reality of defining the limits of the French nation and how membership could be acquired. It inherited from the Ancien Régime a situation which was far from clear-cut. While one of the prerequisites for the exercise of political rights was French nationality, some foreigners acquired a voice in the elections to the Estates-General. The Genevan Étienne Dumont attended the elections in the *quartier* of Filles-Saint-Thomas.[3] In the assemblies of the nobility of Gex, Quesnoy, and Avesnes, foreign owners of fiefs claimed a right to representation. The keeper of the seals decided on each occasion that representation was the prerogative of property-owners, irrespective of nationality. On 14 July 1789, however, the National Assembly heard a report contesting the right of the bishops of Ypres and Tournay to sit as deputies and decided six days later that those bishops should not have been elected as they were foreigners.[4] The vast majority of foreigners in France remained without the suffrage and very few tried to vote or to represent their order in the Estates.

[3] E. Dumont, *Souvenirs sur Mirabeau et sur les deux premières assemblées législatives*, ed. J. Bénétruy (Paris, 1951), 45.
[4] Sieyès, *Qu'est-ce que le tiers état?*, 61–2; J. Portemer, 'L'Étranger dans le droit de la Révolution française', *Recueils de la Société Jean Bodin*, x. 536 n.

On 20 October, the Constituent Assembly stressed that, for a foreigner to acquire political rights, he would first have to assume French nationality. The first condition of an 'active' citizen was to have 'been born French or become French'. This raised the question as to how a foreigner could qualify: surely, asked the baron de Beaumetz, the Assembly had no intention of retaining the old system of *lettres de naturalité*, which implied bonds between king and subject, rather than between citizens? The Constituent did not rescind the Ancien Régime letters, but sought to snatch the initiative of naturalization away from the king and place it in the hands of the nation or its representatives. The lawyer Guy Target of the *comité de constitution* gave expression to this transfer of sovereignty when he suggested that the Assembly draw up fixed conditions for naturalization.[5]

The Constituent had emphasized that the exercise of citizenship was dependent, first of all, on nationality. Yet a few foreigners had voted in 1789 and there were more who had served in municipalities under the Ancien Régime. They were to lose their eligibility for communal and departmental administration, a disenfranchisement which sat uneasily with the universal implications of the rights of man. Target saluted their services on 30 April 1790: 'some have been officials in the old municipalities; others are officers in the National Guard: all have taken the civic oath'. The solution was to encourage such foreigners to become legally French, thus 'you will acquire yet more friends to a constitution which wants to make all men happy'.[6] The naturalization law voted that same day was, among others things, an attempt to assimilate more fully those foreigners already involved in the workings of the French state. As such, it worked: the Dutch Patriot Jan-Antonie Daverhoult and the Genevan exile Étienne Clavière were naturalized before standing for election to the Legislative Assembly in 1791, the former successfully, the latter not.[7]

The very conditions of naturalization were aimed at assuring the loyalty of such people: on assuming French nationality, they had to take the civic oath, which was a public display of adherence to the Revolution. The revolutionaries were aware

[5] *AP* ix. 469–70.
[6] *AP* xv. 245.
[7] Mathiez, *La Révolution et les étrangers*, 31.

that an oath on its own was no real guarantee of commitment to the new order. Consequently, foreigners were also required to have a material stake in the country. They had to have lived in France continuously for five years. They must have acquired property or established agricultural or commercial concerns. The targets of the decree were not the multitude of poor migrants who swept chimneys and chopped wood in French cities. The expected beneficiaries were those who could enrich France through commerce, industry, or agriculture and who would easily qualify for the political rights of 'active' citizenship. Indeed, the only way in which a propertyless foreigner could hope to become a French citizen was through marriage to a French woman, which assumed a commitment to staying in France. The social basis of the law was an effort to attract wealth and to avoid the assimilation of those who might either have lacked commitment or threatened social stability.[8]

Naturalization, however, became a legal right for all those who fulfilled the required conditions: it was no longer a royal prerogative. The new law represented the transfer of sovereignty from king to the nation. It also suggested that the nation was being defined as a community of citizens sharing the same civil rights—even if those citizens were classed either as 'active' or 'inactive'. Naturalization became the expression both of a desire by a foreigner to join the national community and of the nation's acceptance of the foreigner as a citizen. French nationality was therefore based on individuals recognizing each other as compatriots: it represented the abandonment of Ancien Régime corporate society, bound together by loyalty to a king. Article 4 enabled the legislature to naturalize any foreigner at its own discretion 'with no other condition than that of fixing their domicile in France and taking the civic oath'.[9] This reservation was an expression of the cosmopolitanism of the Constituent Assembly, but also stressed the absolute sovereignty of the nation, whose representatives were empowered to make exceptions to the rule.

The Constitution also determined how nationality could be transmitted from one generation to the next. In doing so, it retained an important tradition of the Ancien Régime, *ius soli*,

---

[8] *AP* xv. 245.   [9] *AP* xxxii. 527.

whereby nationality was determined by the territory upon which one was born. Those born in France of parents of any nationality were recognized as French citizens if they settled permanently there. Children born abroad of a French father were also considered French citizens, provided they returned to live in France and took the civic oath. While this suggested *ius sanguinis*, or the inheritance of nationality by 'blood', it was in fact another aspect of the old regime practice of *ius soli*, because the provision applied only to the first generation, who were then compelled to live on French soil.

Language was not a consideration. The law made no reference to a need to speak French, probably for the very practical reason that any linguistic condition would literally denationalize the peoples of whole French provinces such as Alsace, Brittany, and Gascony. The law on nationality was also devoid of any religious conditions. By the late eighteenth century, the absolute monarchy itself had rarely insisted on a religious conversion and all Protestants were given full civil rights on 19 November 1787. The cemetery for foreign Protestants in Paris was now redundant and was closed without a whimper in 1791.[10] Yet the lack of religious content in the new regulations was not devoid of meaning. Days after rejecting Dom Gerle's motion to declare Catholicism the national religion, the Constituent was consciously trying to shape a secular order which did not exclude anyone on the basis of faith. The final version of the decree which appeared in the Constitution of 1791 renounced the persecution of the Huguenots by offering reintegration into French society in the most generous of terms. Anyone who could prove that they had an ancestor, no matter how remote, who had been exiled for religious beliefs could become a French citizen on moving to France and taking the civic oath.[11]

The retention of *ius soli* and the rejection of language and religion as preconditions offered an inclusive definition of French nationality. A person did not need to have French parents or 'blood' in order to become a citizen. Membership of the nation was open to all regardless of ethnic background: all that was required was the fulfilment of certain legal prerequisites which assured their assimilation into the new civic order. This

---

[10] MAE, ADP, France, 7.   [11] *AP* xxxii. 527.

ideal of citizenship was not only based on universalist ideas. The haphazard, historical formation of the French state, with all its linguistic, religious, and cultural differences, made a broad definition of nationality not only desirable, but necessary. Moreover, the Constituent sought to exclude transients and poor foreign vagrants. The disinherited and the rootless were not considered worthy of French citizenship. They were, however, excluded precisely because they were poor, not because they were foreign, in the same way that the poorest French people were denied the political rights of 'active' citizenship.[12] For all its pragmatism, the law on naturalization still stands as a milestone in the civic definition of nationality: it was based not on ethnicity, religion, or language, but on a theoretical contract between citizens.

Not all foreigners could or would be naturalized, which raised the question of their legal treatment while in France. The Constitution of 1791 declared that foreigners 'are subject to the same criminal and policing laws as French citizens . . . their person, their property, their industry, their religion are similarly protected by the law'.[13] While the *droit des gens* still existed as the unwritten code determining relations between states and their conduct towards each others' citizens, the decision to give legal parity to foreigners within France eradicated, in theory at least, the traditional division between *droit des gens* and *droit civil*. The fate of the *droit d'aubaine* was called into question.

When Barère rose in the name of the *comité des domaines* on 6 August 1790 and demanded complete abolition, he met little opposition. His arguments were little different to those used by those Ancien Régime ministers who had requested a similar measure. He suggested that the *droits d'aubaine* and *de détraction* yielded a tiny amount of revenue, while abolition would encourage foreigners to invest in *biens nationaux*, commerce, industry, and agriculture. He stressed the economic and fiscal benefits the measure would bring at such a cheap price. Of course, Barère embellished his speech with plenty of references to the cosmopolitan implications of the rights of man. The *aubaine* was an insult 'to natural law and to the *droit des gens*'. He recoiled in horror at the old justification for the exclusion of

---

[12] Wahnich, *L'Impossible Citoyen*, 72.   [13] *AP* xxxii. 541.

foreigners from the full protection of civil law: '*He lives free, but dies a serf*: that is the atrocious maxim which the representatives of a free people must rush to erase from its laws.' He finished with a cosmopolitan flourish, 'Today, France must open herself to all peoples of the earth.'[14]

The abolition of the *droit d'aubaine* represented the admission of foreigners to the *droit civil*. The measure was dictated primarily by French economic and fiscal interests, the perceptions of which had not changed very much between the old and the new regimes. The difference, however, lay in the way in which those interests were expressed: wrapped in the language of cosmopolitanism, the abolition of the *droit d'aubaine* had instant appeal among the deputies. Only one sought to limit the decree, which in the end was voted unanimously with little discussion.[15] For the time being, the revolutionaries' cosmopolitan ideology and their view of what was right for the state coincided. From the point of view of foreigners, the significance of the abolition of 1790 was that it made no demands of reciprocity and that it abolished the *droit de détraction*. This was a path which the absolute monarchy had been unwilling to tread. The *aubaine* brought little revenue to the state's coffers, but its demise was symbolic of the new order's attitudes towards foreigners and their place in society.

Despite the claims of the Constitution to give foreigners legal treatment equal with French citizens, two Ancien Régime practices remained in force. The *cautio judicatum solvi* was not abolished and nor was the *contrainte par corps* for foreign debtors, until the Convention did so, between 9 and 12 March 1793, with Danton arguing that no one should be forced to give their own person as collateral.[16] In a sinister foretaste of what was to come, certain police measures singled out foreigners, or strangers, for special attention. In April 1790, the commune of Villeneuve-de-Berg in the Vivarais enacted emergency rules regarding all visitors to the town. Outsiders had to register with the municipality on arrival, 'under pain of being arrested and regarded as suspect persons'. National Guards and special citizens' patrols were to ensure that the rules were enforced. These measures

---

[14] *AP* xvii. 628–9.
[15] *AP* xvii. 629.
[16] *AP* lx. 13–14; Portemer, 'L'Étranger', 549.

were aimed at all strangers, whether French or foreign, but they hint at a reflex of suspicion and surveillance which emerged in times of crisis.[17] It was, however, a local response to fears of disturbance, arising from the insecurity felt by many interim municipal authorities. The elections of May and June put the new communal and departmental authorities in place and soothed these anxieties. The measures taken were not revolutionary either, in the sense that they were new or determined by revolutionary principles. In their reaction, it was natural for local officials to fall back on trusted eighteenth-century methods of surveillance, such as registers and patrols. In future times of anxiety, the revolutionaries would respond in the same way, reverting to old practices first, before feeling pressed to innovate.

On balance, when foreigners were not treated equally with French citizens before the law, it was usually in their favour. When an outburst of xenophobia provoked by the flight to Varennes led the National Assembly to close the frontiers on 21 June 1791, discretion ruled a week later. The Assembly decided that arrests of foreigners on the frontiers would be commercially and diplomatically counter-productive.[18] Unlike French citizens, foreigners were permitted to leave France on production of a valid passport issued by a French municipality or the foreign minister.[19] While passports were later an ominous way of controlling the movements of foreigners and citizens alike, for now they were a means of exempting foreigners from restrictions on cross-border movement.

The Constituent Assembly took a practical approach to the general conditions of foreigners in France. While they proclaimed high principles, in reality the revolutionaries were led not by ideology but by their view of national interest. In these early years of the Revolution, those perceptions led them to encourage the assimilation of foreigners. Political, economic, fiscal, and diplomatic considerations demanded flexibility in the application of revolutionary principles. This flexibility could work both in favour and against foreigners. While the Constituent abolished the *droit d'aubaine*, it retained the *contrainte par*

---

[17] Wahnich, *L'Impossible Citoyen*, 84–6.
[18] *AP* xxvii. 385–6.
[19] *AP* xxvii. 358–9, 563.

corps and the *cautio judicatum solvi*, presumably because of the same legal justifications presented under the Ancien Régime. The revolutionaries understood that the application of all the sweeping changes to foreigners would have diplomatic and economic consequences and so made the necessary exemptions in their favour. Foreign troops and foreign clergy best illustrate this point.

II

The behaviour of foreign troops during the collapse of the absolute monarchy left them under a heavy, rumbling cloud of suspicion. To both the authorities and the people alike, they seemed to be loyal to their aristocratic officers and to the old order. The high proportion of foreign troops in the military build-up around Paris and Versailles (5,800 out of 17,000 new arrivals) from 13 April 1789 encouraged wild speculation and rumour.[20] The day after the fall of the Bastille, Mirabeau rose in the National Assembly and denounced 'those foreign satellites' whose presence was 'the prelude to a Saint Bartholomew [massacre]'.[21]

The foreign troops, with their reputation for iron discipline and obedience, may have caused consternation among the French population, but in fact they seem to have been as affected by the political instability as French units.[22] There were important exceptions, such as the Royal-Allemand cavalry and the Hussars. For the former, the officers and men found solidarity in the face of popular enmity which followed the events of 12 July.[23] On that day, the horsemen rampaged through the Parisian crowds in the Tuileries gardens, sabres drawn. Families returning from their Sunday strolls in the Bois de Boulogne were caught up in the confusion. The involvement of foreign soldiers in such dramatic manifestations of loyalty to the old regime determined popular attitudes towards them, regardless of the realities of desertion and indiscipline in other foreign units. What

---

[20] Scott, *Response of the Royal Army*, 51–5.
[21] *Gazette Nationale, ou Le Moniteur Universel* (15–16 July 1789).
[22] Scott, *Response of the Royal Army*, 58, 61.
[23] Ibid. 61.

was remembered was the charge of the Royal-Allemand cavalry on 12 July, not the refusal of the Swiss Châteauvieux regiment to fight against the people. The baron de Besenval, the commander of the troops in and around Paris, later praised the restraint of the Germans up to the moment they galloped into the crowd,[24] but the civilian population had a more sinister idea of their intentions and they were encouraged in this by the press. 'Three German regiments with their cannon went to the *porte d'Enfer*', the *Moniteur* insisted, choosing an appropriately named scene for the appearance of the Germanic hordes.[25] People also remembered that Swiss troops (from the Salis-Samade regiment), in addition to French invalids, had fired from the ramparts of the Bastille into the crowd on 14 July.[26] If eventually de Launay had been willing to capitulate, the Swiss commander, Louis de Flue, was not.[27]

The plight of foreign troops in France during the Revolution was that, if they insisted on retaining their distinctiveness and continued in their loyalty to the crown, they would continue to incur the odium of the people and of the new authorities. If, however, they declared their loyalty to the nation and the new order, they were betraying their own conditions of service and even their own governments. Meanwhile, the dramatic experiences at the hands of foreign troops and popular hostility evident in the *cahiers de doléances* put pressure on the revolutionaries to consider very carefully their continued service in the French army.

In the Constituent Assembly, a number of deputies sought to forestall the counter-revolutionary potential of the army by speaking in favour of different forms of national service, which naturally excluded foreigners. On 18 September 1789, Louis de Noailles stressed that the army ought to be considered as part of the citizenry, all of whom should be prepared to serve in the military. The army was a guarantor of public order, but it should never act against the nation except in cases laid down by law.

---

[24] P.-V. Besenval, *Mémoires de M. le baron de Besenval*, 3 vols. (Paris, 1805), iii. 411.

[25] *Moniteur* (17–20 July 1789).

[26] J. Bodin, *Les Suisses au service de la France de Louis XI à la Légion étrangère* (Paris, 1988), 246.

[27] 'Relation de la Prise de la Bastille, le 14 juillet 1789, par un de ses défenseurs', *Revue Rétrospective*, ière sér. 4 (1834), 291.

Foreign regiments, however, knew only 'a blind obedience' and were therefore a threat to the new constitution.[28]

The egalitarian definition of citizenship allowed no special privileges for any section of society and it admitted no one except citizens to full participation in the state. These ideas were voiced less than three months later by Noailles's colleague on the Assembly's military committee, Dubois-Crancé. On 12 December, he seized on the phrase of the old regime military reformer, Guibert, and declared that 'every citizen must be a soldier, and every soldier a citizen', which left little room for foreigners.[29] Those who did not opt to join the national community neither shared the same political rights as citizens, nor the same duties.

Yet circumstances did not allow the revolutionaries to exercise their principles to their logical extent. If Dubois-Crancé's bill did not become law, this was not because the deputies (except for some on the right) objected to the principle of excluding foreigners from service, but because they preferred to continue to rely for the time being on the professional line army already in existence.[30] The revolutionaries recognized the need to maintain the forces against both internal disorder and, as France now posed a tempting, soft target, the possibility of foreign invasion.[31] With disintegrating discipline and alarming rates of desertion, the army appeared to be bleeding to death at a precarious moment. In such circumstances, most revolutionaries were reluctant to dismiss well-disciplined foreign regiments.

On 18 September 1789, the *comité militaire* therefore proposed that while no more foreign troops be recruited, those units already serving be kept under new titles. The Swiss, of course, presented a special case: unlike most other foreign regiments, they served the king of France by virtue of treaties and capitulations with their respective governments. It would have been diplomatically disruptive to have disbanded the Swiss regiments and so Noailles insisted that the treaties with the cantons be respected. Even Dubois-Crancé, for all his enthusiasm for 'a truly national conscription', conceded this point.[32] These arguments won over hostility towards foreign troops, over the ideology of

[28] *AP* ix. 36–8.   [29] *AP* x. 520.
[30] Scott, *Response of the Royal Army*, 156.
[31] *AP* x. 556.
[32] *AP* ix. 38; x. 522, 557–8.

citizenship, over national pride, and over financial considerations.

The *constitution militaire* of 28 February 1790 did, however, stipulate that the king could not introduce any foreign troops into France without the permission of the legislature.[33] This compromise reflected the Assembly's desire to retain a competent regular army, to maintain good diplomatic relations, but also to ensure that control over foreign troops was not exclusively in the hands of the king. The deputies soon used their powers vested by this arrangement and fixed the number of foreign troops allowed in the French army. On 13 July, Noailles proposed, with impressive if unfeasible precision, that the number be fixed at 24,581. He repeated Maurice de Saxe's rationale: foreign regiments saved French manpower for more productive activities and, for as long as they were in French service, they could not be used by enemy powers. He recognized the counter-revolutionary potential of foreign soldiers 'in these times of trouble and turmoil' and so recommended fixed ratios of foreigners to French citizens in the army: in peacetime, one foreigner to every $8\frac{3}{5}$ Frenchmen and, in wartime, one to every $4\frac{3}{5}$. On 18 August the Assembly produced its definitive decree, which was actually more generous. In 1791, the entire army would stand at 150,848 men, of which foreign troops would not number more than 26,000.[34] In other words, while de Noailles anticipated a fighting force in which up to 12 per cent of the troops were foreigners, the Constituent permitted 17 per cent. In practical terms, the decree signalled no change in the numbers of foreign troops.

As long as the revolutionaries recognized the need to retain such soldiers, the main problem became one of how to ensure their loyalty, while also reforming the military in general. The problem was not merely one of ideology: deputies and the people alike worried that, in retaining foreigners, the authorities were actually nourishing those who might become the stormtroopers of counter-revolution. The first solution proposed applied to the entire army. The Constituent decreed on 10 August 1789 that all soldiers would take an oath 'to the Nation, the Law and the King, head of the Nation'. The comte d'Affry, colonel of the Swiss Guards and colonel-general of all Swiss and Grison troops

---

[33] *AP* xi. 739–42.   [34] *AP* xii. 699–700; xvii. 74–6; xviii. 142.

in France, was told by the minister of war, La Tour-du-Pin, on 23 August that 'the foreign regiments, like nationals, must submit to it'.[35] The problem was that the oath demanded fidelity not only to the monarch, but also to the nation and the law, which ran contrary to the traditional oaths of Swiss troops in French service. It did not take long for their officers to protest to the cantons about this infringement of their treaties and privileges. A week later, the cantons permitted the Swiss to take the oath, but along with a carefully worded protest that this concession must not be taken as permission for the French to legislate over other conditions of service.[36]

The safe retention of foreign regiments required a period of stability, in which it could be shown that they could exist within the national order. Yet relations between foreign soldiers and local people, delicate at the best of times, became strained because of the association of the former with counter-revolution. Their very isolation against the hostility of the populace brought the troops to close ranks and thus maintain their discipline, which in turn reinforced the popular prejudice of foreign troops being obedient servants of reactionary officers.[37] In fact, it was the National Assembly itself which sanctioned the use of the military in restoring order, although it appeared to recognize that it was a dangerous card to play. Foreign units were used because, as general François de Bouillé recognized, they were less susceptible than French troops to the blandishments of 'patriots'. He estimated that of ninety infantry battalions in Paris and north-eastern France, he could depend on only twenty, all German or Swiss. Of 104 cavalry squadrons, he had confidence in sixty, a third of which were German-speaking.[38] In 1790, against the background of municipal upheavals in cities such as Marseille and Lyon, in which foreign regiments played a policing role against the 'patriots',[39] a number of deputies in the

[35] P. de Zurich, 'Les Derniers Serments des troupes suisses au service de France sous l'ancien régime', *Zeitschrift für Schweizerische Geschichte*, 22 (1942), 228.

[36] Ibid. 222–4, 230, 236.

[37] Scott, *Response of the Royal Army*, 61; S. F. Scott, 'The French Revolution and the Irish Regiments in France', in Dickson & Gough, *Ireland and the French Revolution*, 18–19.

[38] Scott, *Response of the Royal Army*, 91.

[39] Ibid. 139–44; AN, F/7/4401; W. Scott, *Terror and Repression in Revolutionary Marseilles* (London, 1973), 21–6; Haas, *Régiment suisse*, 18–20.

Constituent once again questioned the loyalty of foreign troops to the Revolution.

On 5 May, Peyssonnel demanded that foreign regiments be placed under the same terms and conditions as French units. With a strong dose of germanophobia, he warned of the malign potential of eight German regiments which were garrisoned in Alsace and Lorraine, as was customary, and of the dangers of allowing German princes to retain their influence over them. Brushing aside the diplomatic arguments, he argued that France's relations with Germany did not depend solely on the retention of these troops. The diplomatic fallout from disbanding or merging them with the French regiments was a small price to pay for the elimination of these sources of domestic instability. He conceded that the Swiss regiments ought to be left alone because of the French alliance with the cantons, but proposed that all other foreign regiments be subsumed into their French counterparts, with the same pay, discipline, and uniforms. They were to be obliged to swear the civic oath—individually, not collectively as before—which would also act as a naturalization ceremony. Those who wished to leave French service could do so and henceforth the formerly foreign regiments would recruit only French citizens. The foreign contingent would be steadily diluted and would finally disappear altogether.[40]

Not all foreign regiments were written off as the workhorses of counter-revolution. Peyssonnel's phobia over German troops ought to have been abated somewhat when in July the Salm-Salm infantry regiment mutinied in Metz over the management of regimental funds. In this affair, the mutineers had the support of local people and they returned to barracks only when persuaded by the mayor.[41] In Nancy, the mutiny of the Swiss Châteauvieux regiment, along with French troops, occurred in similar circumstances. Despite the opposition of their officers, the Swiss soldiers had celebrated the local feast of the federation, and some had joined the Jacobin club and socialized with the National Guard. Disorder broke out on 9 August among the French troops in the garrison and the Swiss joined them the next day. After Bouillé put down the mutiny, on 4 September one of the Swiss ringleaders was broken on the wheel, twenty-two others were hanged, forty-one condemned to thirty years in the galleys, and seventy-four punished within the regiment.[42]

The mutiny at Nancy seemed to show that not all foreign troops were immune to radical propaganda, even though there was no evidence to suggest that the Châteauvieux Swiss were acting on anything but strictly regimental grievances.[43] If it still feared the counter-revolutionary potential of foreign units, the Constituent was now equally worried that, should they become a source of widespread insubordination, among the most reliable troops in the French army would be disabled. The answer, it seemed, was to insulate all units, French and foreign alike, from radical influences such as political clubs. In September, the Constituent accordingly banned all soldiers from attending political meetings and societies. The Swiss cantons, in particular, welcomed this prohibition, as they feared the contagion of revolutionary propaganda among their subjects. Their fears had been confirmed by the Nancy affair and by the activities of the *club helvétique* in Paris. This society petitioned the National Assembly on 2 September on behalf of the Châteauvieux regiment. Worse, the club had some success in attracting Swiss Guards to its meetings. In fact, by the time the National Assembly banned soldiers from attending political clubs, the numbers of soldiers at the Swiss society had already begun to slump. Many of them had been intimidated by their officers, who had issued stern warnings against participation in radical politics. The cantons lent their authority to the ban by declaring membership of the *club helvétique* punishable as high treason in Switzerland.[44]

The reverberations of Nancy did little to abate popular hostility, not least because foreign regiments were used to crush the mutiny. The Royal-Liégeois infantry and the Lauzun hussars, both involved in the suppression, fired the hostility of the populace of Belfort when officers held a banquet on 21 October, hailing 'the victors of Nancy'. Outside the café, an alcohol-breathed major of the Royal-Liégeois loutishly slurred,

[42] Ibid. 92–5; Fieffé, *Histoire des troupes étrangères*, i. 357–64.

[43] Fieffé, *Histoire des troupes étrangères*, i. 358–9 n.

[44] A. Méautis, *Le Club helvétique de Paris (1790–1791) et la diffusion des idées révolutionnaires en Suisse* (Neuchâtel, 1969), 52–3, 67; Maradan, 'L'Échec de la propagande', 256; Zurich, 'Derniers Serments', 240.

'We are the masters, let's hack up the *bourgeois*!' Other officers joined in the fun, careering through the streets, yelling 'Vive le roi! Vivent les aristocrates!' and, even worse, 'The nation to the devil!' They waved white handkerchiefs tied at the end of their swords, insulting and even wounding some of the locals.[45] Involvement in the repression at Nancy also haunted the Vigier regiment. In March 1791, these Swiss could spend only a few hours in Nancy, because of the 'insults and outrages' which they suffered. Vigier, the proprietary colonel, approached the French envoy to the cantons, de Vérac, who proved to be sympathetic and took the issue to Montmorin, the foreign minister in Paris.[46]

The reputation of a foreign unit among the people depended upon its behaviour: if it proved sympathetic to the Revolution, then it rose in popular esteem. If its politics were dictated by devotion to officers and to duty, then it reinforced popular prejudices. In turn, hostility from the population simply increased cohesion and discipline within the regiment. With the highly publicized exception of the Châteauvieux Swiss, foreign units seemed to lean towards loyalty to their evidently aristocratic officers.

The cloud which hung heavily over the foreign regiments was darkened still further by the royal flight to Varennes on 20–1 June 1791. De Bouillé was charged with providing military cover for the royal family as they rolled ponderously towards the frontier in their Berline coach. Of the ten cavalry regiments selected to provide detachments, half were German-speaking, including the notorious Royal-Allemand. The infantry to be used were two Swiss and four German regiments.[47] After the flight, the German Nassau regiment was forced to march from one hostile town to another, until the municipal officials of Metz finally found it in their hearts to billet the footsore soldiers. They were to regret this hospitality, because French and Nassau troops soon grappled with each other in a running battle through the streets. When this riot was reported in the National Assembly on 21 July, it was remarked that not only had the Nassau regiment been involved with de Bouillé's machinations a

---

[45] Scott, *Response of the Royal Army*, 145–6; Fieffé, *Histoire des troupes étrangères*, i. 369–70.

[46] AN, F/7/4400. [47] Scott, *Response of the Royal Army*, 103.

month previously, but the hostility of the population might also be explained by its presence at Versailles in July 1789.[48]

The uncertainty and fear stirred by the royal flight to Varennes intensified hostility towards foreign troops. On 21 June, the very moment of the crisis, the Constituent hastily decided that soldiers had to renew their commitment to the Revolution through a new oath which made no mention of the king.[49] The new formula provoked a wave of emigrations among the officers in the French army, who considered their last commitment severed. Among these recalcitrant officers were thirty-one from the Irish Berwick regiment, twenty-seven of whom left France between 3 and 25 July, with a few of the rank-and-file trailing after them. By the end of the year, thirty officers had left the Dillon regiment.[50]

For the Swiss, the new oath had a similar meaning, but they could not act without the guidance of the cantons. The revolutionaries considered Swiss grumbling over the oath to be a minor inconvenience next to their own belief that they now faced the serious possibility of invasion. While foreign regiments seemed particularly susceptible to counter-revolutionary suggestion, France needed to be sure that troops deployed against the potential threat of war would be loyal. So, on 25 June, the National Assembly ordered d'Affry to have all Swiss regiments take the new oath. D'Affry obliged that same day, warning his officers that the emergency had made this order absolutely necessary. Between 28 June and 14 July, each Swiss regiment accordingly swore the oath, but a storm of anger erupted in the Swiss Diet at Frauenfeld when this news arrived. Letters were quickly dispatched, reprimanding d'Affry and protesting to de Vérac, the French envoy, over the way in which the Swiss troops were being treated in France. The oath was eventually approved by all cantons except those of Fribourg, Zurich, Basle, and Berne.[51] In the end, it was the French who, on 17 September, softened their attitude with a new oath, in which the king resumed his place alongside the nation and the law. The change, applicable to the whole army, was less in response to the diplomatic furore than the fact that Louis XVI had accepted

---

[48] *AP* xxviii. 471–2.　　　　　　[49] Zurich, 'Derniers Serments', 245.
[50] Scott, *Response of the Royal Army*, 106, 159–60; Scott, 'Irish Regiments', 19.
[51] AN, F/7/4400; Zurich, 'Derniers Serments', 246–7, 249–58, 264–6.

the Constitution and it was aimed at stemming the haemorrhage of officers through emigration.

The Diet's complaints were not restricted to the oath, how- ever: two other revolutionary measures also stirred its bile. One was the payment of soldiers in *assignats*, effectively paper money introduced by the National Assembly. The Steiner regiment appealed to the state of Zurich over this, prompting an official complaint to Montmorin on 22 June 1791.[52] The Diet supported this protest on 7 July on the grounds that the capitulations with France 'demand that the salaries of officers and soldiers are paid in coin'.[53]

This was compounded by the second of the 'onerous innova- tions', the decree of 1 May 1791, whereby the decision to forbid soldiers attending political meetings was rescinded. Almost immediately, a conflict blew up between the desires of the Swiss officers and those of the Constituent. D'Affry tried gingerly to balance obedience to the cantons with respect for French law. On 10 May, he sent an order to all Swiss regiments, explaining that the new decree was aimed only at the civic education of French troops, but that Swiss soldiers would be allowed to attend political meetings in order to learn about the laws of an 'allied power and a friend of their sovereigns'.[54]

His compromise was too mild for the Diet, which on 7 July voted unanimously to send the Swiss troops a letter forbidding them from frequenting the 'So-called Patriotic Clubs' or face 'the harshest and most irremissable penalties'.[55] This order rammed headlong into the National Assembly's decree. On 9 August 1791, the department of the Bas-Rhin heard that the Vigier regiment in Strasbourg had received a copy of the Diet's command. The administration sharply reminded the Swiss officers that, while they were in France, the rights and liberties of the soldiers 'cannot be infringed or repudiated by the arbitrary orders of a foreign sovereign'. Two days later, the Vigier officers defied this ruling, referring to their capitulations, which gave them jurisdiction over their soldiers. The stakes were raised when an outspoken soldier stubbornly persisted in attending the Jacobin club and was flung into the guardhouse by his angry officers. In response, the departmental administration declared

---

[52] AN, F/7/4400.   [53] Ibid.   [54] Ibid.   [55] Ibid.

that this arrest was a 'usurpation' of French law by the Swiss: 'the French Nation is and remains the only Sovereign in the French Empire'. On 19 August, a redfaced d'Affry tried to explain the conduct of the Vigier officers, making an about-turn explicable by his own reprimand from the Diet. If Swiss troops were allowed to attend political meetings, he now argued, they would be led to disobey their officers and their government. He reminded Montmorin of the diplomatic consequences of any poor treatment of the Swiss.[56] In this affair, the department was asserting the absolute sovereignty of the nation against treaties which dated from the Ancien Régime. Also implicit was the egalitarian idea that there could be no privileged groups above the law.

Those such as Peyssonnel who assailed the privileges of foreign troops won a victory from the unlikely quarter of one of the units itself. After its odyssey around north-eastern France and the riot in Metz in July 1791, the Nassau regiment had finally had enough. Four or five hundred soldiers tore off their buttons and insignia, refusing to serve 'for as long as they wear a foreign uniform and are considered a foreign regiment, that they are French and want to serve as Frenchmen'. Many of these troops were, after all, French citizens, German-speakers from Alsace and Lorraine, and were fed up with being reviled as foreigners. It was their officers who, by virtue of their original capitulations, were truly German and, they claimed, 'aristocratic'. To press their point, these soldiers had participated in the festivities on Bastille Day in Metz, taking the civic oath.[57]

The patriotic example of a foreign regiment renouncing its privileged ways probably appealed to an Assembly which, in light of the recent role of foreign troops in the flight to Varennes, had come around to Peyssonnel's radical thinking. On 21 July 1791, the National Assembly decreed that, apart from the Swiss regiments, all foreign units would wear French uniforms and receive the same pay and regulations.[58] Apart from the obvious financial advantages from the reduction of pay, the National Assembly had adopted, it thought, a further means of ensuring the loyalty of well-disciplined troops at a time when it appeared that they would be desperately needed. The Assembly hoped to

[56] Ibid.　　[57] AN, F/7/4399; *AP* xxviii. 472.　　[58] *AP* xxviii. 472.

replace separateness with a new source of identity: that of belonging to a national army in which the virtues of equality and patriotism would rise above unit pride.

Owners of foreign regiments were naturally alarmed by the implications, and no one more than the proprietor of the Nassau regiment itself. De Crolboy, envoy of the duke of Nassau-Saarbrucken, dashed off a memorandum to the Constituent's *comité diplomatique*, reminding its members that the duke was one of France's 'allies and . . . most faithful and zealous neighbours'. He fretted that the destruction of the regiment's separateness would precipitate a collapse in discipline. Soon, the regiment 'would be merely an assembly of vagabonds, recruited from all countries and divided by their customs, having no more relations either with their sovereigns or, consequently, with their homelands'. The duke regarded the troops' loyalty to himself as a cement which bound the unit together. To reform the regiment without his consent would also be to attack its original convention of 1777.[59] De Crolboy's protests were in vain: the men of any regiment other than the Swiss were henceforth not the possession of any individual, nor subject to special privileges, but were to be treated like any other soldiers in the French army. They were expected to be patriotic defenders of the constitution, faithful to the nation, the law, and the king.

The Constituent Assembly had resisted calls for the suppression of foreign units for two years, despite its own nationalizing principles, because of diplomatic concerns and the need to keep the regular army intact. In the various crises of the period 1789–91, however, the foreign regiments, with one or two exceptions, appeared to be prone to counter-revolutionary activity, justifying the worst fears even of moderate revolutionaries. Many of these fears were self-fulfilling: often treated with hostility by the local population, the soldiers naturally sought refuge within their own regiment, which usually meant that they were likely to retain their cohesiveness. This in turn meant that the politics of the foreign troops were dictated by their obedience to their officers.[60] Yet at the same time, the apparently hostile gestures of Prussia and Austria over the summer of 1791 made it

---

[59] AN, F/7/4399.   [60] Scott, *Response of the Royal Army*, 145.

clear to the revolutionaries that a well-trained and disciplined regular army was needed urgently. To dismiss the foreign regiments would be foolish, but it was politically dangerous to keep them as they were. This dilemma led the Constituent to dispense with diplomatic niceties and to risk relatively minor disputes by taking measures which breached French international commitments in the name of ensuring, or perhaps testing, their loyalty. In these actions was the application of the nationalizing, egalitarian logic of the Constituent's own principles. This logic, however, was let loose by the desire to ensure the internal security of the Revolution on the one hand and the strength of its military defences on the other.

III

The existence of the foreign clergy presented a smaller, but still rocky, obstacle against the tide of revolutionary reforms. They were not protected by treaties, strategic, or political concerns, but they actually survived in their original state for longer. Revolutionary legislation concerned directly with them was protective rather than reforming: it sheltered them from most of the measures which affected their French counterparts.

When the Constituent passed its decrees nationalizing church lands (3 November 1789), dissolving monasteries and convents and forbidding religious vows (13 February 1790), understandably no one considered the complex problems which the relatively small number of foreigners might pose. Yet the foreigners had reasons to be anxious over their place in the new order, as some revolutionaries had argued ominously since early August that all ecclesiastical property belonged to the nation. As the National Assembly began to tackle this controversial question, some of the Irish clergy seized the initiative. On 8 October 1789, the deputy Lally-Tollendal, himself of Irish descent, presented a donation of silver from the Irish College chapel in Paris. While the priests and students declared that they were bound to the French by their religious faith, they also swore 'the same sentiments to the new *patrie* and to the prince who has adopted us'.[61]

---

[61] *AP* ix. 385.

The loyalty of the Irish may have been sincere, but the Constituent did not take the hint. Less than a month later, the Assembly nationalized church property which, for the foreign clergy, presented a double-headed threat. They were to lose their most important source of income and they faced redundancy. With the loss of their land, the French clergy were to be salaried by the state, a provision of the Civil Constitution of the Clergy, voted on 12 July 1790. It was not at all clear that foreigners would be eligible for ecclesiastical office under these new structures. On 9 November, the abbé Grégoire deplored the appointment of foreigners as curates, a well-established practice in dioceses such as those of Bordeaux and Bazas.[62] Grégoire requested that 'to possess a benefice . . . one must be French, or naturalized and resident for at least ten years'.[63]

This demand was in keeping with the nationalizing tendencies of revolutionary ideology, but it was brushed aside without a debate. Until the revolutionaries had worked out the broader issues, they could not fiddle with the finer points. In fact, it would be a year before the fate of the foreign clergy would be resolved, if only temporarily. For the foreign seminaries, there was an additional layer of uncertainty: the reorganization of French education caused ripples of panic among the staff. John Farquharson, rector of the Scots College at Douai, wrote gloomily of the anticipated suppression of French universities: 'if no mercy be shown to National Foundations what have not foreign ones to dread?'[64] Faced with a precarious future, the foreign clergy mobilized. On 20 December 1789, the English Clarists of Gravelines, Aire, Rouen, and Dunkirk drew up a petition in response to calls for the complete suppression of religious orders. While they did appeal to traditional principles, such as the '*droit des gens* and that of hospitality', they engaged the issue within the same frame of references used by the Constituent. The French *nation* had granted them the 'right of asylum'. To the argument that ecclesiastical property had merely been held in trust by the church on behalf of the people, the Clarists replied that their

---

[62] Loupès, 'Irish Clergy', 29; Loupès, 'Ecclésiastiques irlandais', 88.
[63] *AP* ix. 729.
[64] C. Johnson, *Developments in the Roman Catholic Church in Scotland 1789–1829* (Edinburgh, 1983), 92.

property and investments came not from French, but from English sources, so however urgent the needs of the nation, there could be no legal justification for its nationalization. The nuns were appealing to the inalienable and sacred right of property. They also emphasized their utility as an educational and charitable order. As proof of their civic virtue, they offered the nation a quarter of their revenue: 'they have French hearts when the State needs help'.[65]

Other foreign establishments repeated the arguments made by the Clarists, stressing, above all, the foreign origins of their property. Addresses to the Constituent or its *comité ecclésiastique* all sought to adopt the revolutionaries' own terms, particularly the rights of property and usefulness to the state. They combined this with references to Ancien Régime notions such as the *droit des gens* and the *droit d'azile*. They often substituted the term 'nation', for 'king' or 'state', as if to underline the idea that the Constituent ought to honour commitments made before 1789.[66]

If the Clarist nuns had French hearts, their petition, and those of the other orders, still stressed their separateness from the French clergy in order to show that the National Assembly's decrees could not apply to them. Of all the arguments, this one was the most likely to grate against the abolition of privilege. Despite the number of petitions which made similar points—at least seven were delivered by the English, Irish, and Scottish establishments—the uncertainty over their future remained until October 1790. Until then, local authorities and *notaires* made inventories of the property and revenue of foreign establishments, apparently prior to their appropriation by the state, beginning in February 1790.[67] What forced the revolutionaries to tread more carefully was the intervention of the British government.

Alexander Gordon, the principal of the Scots College in Paris, had written to the British Prime Minister, William Pitt, in October 1789 seeking the British government's protection over the college.[68] Lord Robert Fitzgerald, British *chargé d'affaires* in Paris until May 1790, eventually presented a petition on behalf of the college and made similar efforts for

[65] AN, D/XIX/30.
[66] AN, S//4616; D/XIX/30.
[67] AN, D/XIX/30; S//4616; S//4619.
[68] Black, 'Archives', 53, 56.

its Irish counterparts.[69] The interest of the British government led Fréteau de Saint-Just subtly to advise his colleagues in the Constituent that the status of the British and Irish houses 'presents delicate considerations from the point of view of foreign powers'. The Assembly was given cause to think, but still made no definitive decision.[70] Further petitions from the foreign clergy became more frantic, including requests to be allowed to sell their property if their institutions were suppressed.[71]

Finally, on 14 September, the *comité ecclésiastique* agreed to exempt the Irish College of Paris from the nationalization of church lands. The Irish priests urged the committee to formalize this decision with a decree. Ironically, the priests also argued that the preservation of the Irish colleges would attract many Irish investors in *biens nationaux* 'because individuals will believe in the inviolability of their property'.[72] This last point carried great weight in the revolutionaries' final decision on 4 October. The Constituent's decree designating which lands were to be sold as *biens nationaux* excluded all foreign religious establishments, for as long as their own governments respected the property of French citizens abroad.[73] To have done otherwise would have cast doubt on the Revolution's commitment to foreigners' property rights, which would have emitted severe commercial and diplomatic fallout. The importance of this decree, adopted gradually over the period 6–15 October, was not only that all foreign clerical establishments were assured of an income from their lands, but also that the revolutionaries implicitly confirmed the legitimacy of their existence in France. It was not long before the ecclesiastic and diplomatic committees made this explicit. They were acutely aware, however, of the anomaly which these foreigners presented to the spirit of reform. On 28 October, the two committees agreed that the continued existence of foreign orders in France would be both 'opposed to the constitutional laws' and contrary to the law of 13 February, which suppressed contemplative orders. Yet, adopting the foreigners' own arguments, they urged that their property had been legally acquired

---

[69] Scottish Catholic Archives (SCA), CA1/25/1–8; AN, D/XIX/30.
[70] *AP* xix. 241.
[71] AN, D/XIX/30; SCA, CA1/25/1–8; *AP* xvi. 109.
[72] AN, D/XIX/30.   [73] *AP* xix. 436.

and so their establishments 'will continue to exist, as in the past'.[74]

There was a price to be paid for this survival. Any privileges which had been granted to the foreign clerics were naturally abolished. For the English Benedictines of the *faubourg* Saint-Jacques, this was financially disastrous. The *comité ecclésiastique* estimated that the fourteen benefices held by these clerics brought in an annual income of 72,388 *livres*. The Civil Constitution of the Clergy nationalized these posts, making them elective like any other. Those deprived of an income were to be given a pension in compensation, backdated to 1 January 1790, but the pensions, alms, and donations granted to the foreigners by the crown were to be reconsidered by the Assembly. Moreover, any tax exemptions enjoyed by the establishments disappeared.[75]

The foreign secular clergy ministered to French citizens, and so were subject to the law in common with their French counterparts. They therefore faced the oath of loyalty to the Civil Constitution, decreed on 27 November 1790. The response of foreign priests did not mirror exactly that of their French colleagues. In the Gironde, for example, the eighteen Irish priests who held parishes or cures were split evenly between jurors and non-jurors. This was different from the figures for all priests across the Bordeaux region, where 59 per cent of the clergy were jurors. Memories of persecution in Ireland may have made the Irish priests more dogmatic in their attachment to the 'old' church. Still, half of the Irish priests were initially willing to compromise with the new order. James Burke, parish priest of the Bec d'Ambès, was even an enthusiast for the French Revolution, buying, as *biens nationaux*, the lands of the Ursuline convent at Ambès with two French merchants in March 1791, employing sixty labourers to work the fields. For some of the Irish jurors, however, the oath was a painful step, even before the pope spoke out against the Civil Constitution. Two Irish priests, François Loebardy and Matthew O'Leyn, retracted in the early months of 1791.[76]

Yet the very fact of persecution in Ireland pushed some clergy

---

[74] *AP* xx. 67–8.   [75] *AP* xx. 68–70.
[76] Loupès, 'Irish Clergy', 30, 32, 35–7.

into the arms of the Revolution. The priests of the Irish College in Paris certainly showed revolutionary sympathies, arguing in one of their petitions that the French Revolution would inspire the Catholic majority in Ireland to throw off the yoke of British rule. The Irish Colleges, they argued, had their part to play in instilling the principles of the rights of man in their students.[77] Crucially, they had identified the importance of loyalty to the new order as a factor in their survival as an institution. These priests were more than just Irish exiles, however: they were Catholic clergymen. If the oath was a test of loyalty, some of the college staff still refused it. For the refractories, their place in the church overrode all other considerations. This was especially true when congregations encouraged opposition. In January 1791, the English students at Douai provoked a violent confrontation with the civil authorities when they tried to administer the oath.[78]

Such resistance implied hostility towards the Revolution and would mark out the clergy for suspicion. Over the next two years, acts of loyalty to the Revolution—or a lack of them—would determine the fate of foreign clerics in France. When popular hostility did break out, it was primarily because they were clergy, not because they were outsiders. In Douai, from May to July 1790, soldiers intimidated and roughed up French and British clerics and students indiscriminately.[79] Yet the fact that the foreigners remained a privileged group did provoke resentment. After Robert Fitzgerald's intervention on behalf of the Scots College in Paris, the *Moniteur* fumed that the institution was 'opposed to the Decrees of the National Assembly, when the French Clergy . . . is destroyed as a Body, annihilated as an Order, and now consists merely of Citizens and public officials!'[80]

It was the schism over the clerical oath which brought aggression bubbling to the surface. Cornered in the *faubourg* Saint-Marcel, one of the heartlands of Parisian radicalism, the English Benedictine convent was a target for popular resentment towards the clergy in 1791. The house was mobbed by a crowd 'consisting of the worst sort of people'.[81] By 26 June, Richard Marsh, superior of the English Benedictines at Dieulouard, had

---

[77] AN, D/XIX/30.   [78] AN, S//4619.
[79] Johnson, *Developments*, 92.   [80] SCA, CA1/25/1–8.
[81] Alger, *Englishmen*, 301.

asked Rome 'whether we may carry secular [clothes], since the religious habit is so ill look'd upon in France'.[82] Even the Irish College in Paris, for all the priests' protests of their revolutionary sympathies, was not left unmolested. In the disturbances surrounding the oath in 1791, a crowd tried to break into the college and were only prevented from doing so by a pistol-brandishing student. In September, however, the demonstrations turned violent because the Irish College chapel was being used by French people who sought mass from a refractory priest. On leaving, the congregation was mobbed and a woman was flogged by the vigilantes.[83] The Irish priests were seen to be abusing French hospitality by harbouring non-jurors and their congregations.

In this period, however, the main problem facing these foreigners was financial, which was partly the result of the ecclesiastical reforms, but which also had long-term roots. The Revolution was financially disastrous for the foreign clergy. Anxieties over their prospects, at least until the decree of 28 October 1790, ensured that recruitment of students and novices—and the fees and dowries which came with them— was reduced to a trickle. The English Augustinian nuns claimed on 22 September 1790 that, while they had nineteen pupils, 'at the time of the Revolution there were even more'.[84]

The novelty of taxation on the clergy proved to be another grave problem. On 9 September 1791, Marsh complained that taxes due since Easter amounted to 800 *livres*.[85] For many houses, however, taxation merely compounded financial problems which predated the Revolution. In June 1791, another friar at Dieulouard, Fisher, blamed the monastery's financial embarrassment only partially on the Revolution, frankly admitting to long-term debts and mismanagement.[86] The English Benedictine Order now considered drastic steps for the monks at Dieulouard. They contemplated an offer to take over the English Carthusian house at Nieuport in the Austrian Netherlands. This meant leaving France for good, so they deferred their decision in favour of other measures. In vain, Marsh tried to prevail on Bennett, superior of the apparently money-soaked English

---

[82] AN, S//4619.   [83] Alger, *Englishmen*, 163.   [84] AN, D/XIX/30.
[85] AN, S//4619.   [86] Ibid.

College at Douai, to transfer some of the wealth to its poorer relative in Lorraine.[87]

Dieulouard's tribulations under the Constituent Assembly reveal the complexity of the problems faced by the foreign clergy in France. At first they suffered from uncertainty over their place within the new regime, but even when the Constituent recognized their legitimacy, their troubles were far from over. They were not integrated into the new order, but merely coexisted with it, their foreign status protecting them from most of the reforms which affected the rest of the Church in France. This in itself caused some resentment. For as long as they remained a special case, their existence would sit awkwardly with the new state-sponsored ecclesiastical settlement.

Against any nationalizing urge to storm these survivals of clerical privilege stood an equally strong respect for the rights of property. The foreign clergy successfully convinced the revolutionaries that theirs had been legitimately purchased with their own funds. The revolutionaries realized that to nationalize it would be to discourage foreign investment in the French economy and to cause diplomatic ripples. There was no ideological dynamic which made the eventual abolition of the foreign clergy inevitable. Rather, their survival was officially guaranteed by the revolutionaries' own respect for property, which was as much, perhaps more, a part of their ideology as egalitarianism.

The threat to this balance came from anticlericalism which stirred and expressed itself in ever more violent ways in the wake of the controversy over the ecclesiastical oath. Although they could not have known it at the time, many foreign clerics compromised their long-term prospects in France by refusing to swear. Their foreign status already placed them outside the structures of the new order and their refractory status made them more so. The violence and the popular hostility towards the refractory clergy were still not officially sanctioned by the authorities, however, so the single most important threat remained their financial problems. Taxation and worries for their long-term future were often compounded with financial

[87] AN, S//4619.

difficulties which predated the Revolution. These problems were serious, but this did not drive out the foreign clergy—nor did the revolutionaries seek to do this. It would take a dramatic shift in political opinion to bring that about.

IV

The fate even of those who were enthusiasts for the French Revolution was also anchored in the precariously shifting sands of revolutionary politics. These people were foreign radicals, political refugees, and sympathizers of the Revolution. Certain groups, such as the Dutch, Swiss, and Genevans, had been in France prior to 1789, not through any ideological affinity with the Ancien Régime, but because they lived in hope that *raison d'état* might induce the monarchy to encourage them in their projects. With the Revolution, the collapse of censorship, and the rise to prominence of the very people with whom these foreigners had hob-nobbed in previous years, seemed to show that political and moral regeneration was possible anywhere. Paris was no longer simply a centre of the Enlightenment, but was now showing the way to a new era. The exiles were given hope that a new regime based on radical principles might be more easily persuaded to lend active assistance to their cause.

France therefore attracted more radicals and intellectuals, some into long-term residence, others for brief, inspirational visits. The Germans Cloots, Bitaubé, Karl von Hesse, Karl Reinhard, and the Dutch feminist Etta Palm d'Aelders were all already in France and now stayed on, to immerse themselves in the liberating atmosphere. Others made the trip specifically to witness the fall of 'despotism' in France. In July 1789, Wilhelm von Humboldt arrived with his tutor, Campe. Later, other German arrivals included Gerard von Halem, Johann von Archenholz, Konrad Oelsner, and Gustav von Schlabrendorff. For many German exiles fleeing the political reaction in the Rhenish states in 1791, an obvious place to settle was Strasbourg, where Johann-Georg ('Eulogius') Schneider became vicar to the constitutional bishop of the Bas-Rhin and rose to the leadership of the city's Jacobin club. He was joined by Anton Dorsch and

Jean-Jacques Kaemmerer.[88] The Russian prince Paul Stroganov
was accompanied to Paris in July 1789 by a tutor, the future
conventionnel Gilbert Romme. The young Nikolai Karamzin was
also present as the old regime tumbled.[89] The Scottish Unitarian
Thomas Christie made two visits to Paris during 1789–91.
William Priestley from Birmingham, son of Christie's co-
religionist Joseph, scribbled an excited letter home from Paris
with news of the fall of the Bastille. Other Channel-crossers
included Helen Maria Williams, Thomas Paine, Benjamin
Vaughan, John Oswald, Robert Pigott, and, most famous of all
the Britons, William Wordsworth.[90] From Savoy came François-
Amédée Doppet, who embarked on a military career.[91] The
founder of the US navy, John Paul Jones, arrived from Warsaw,
seeking a new post. He died of dropsy in France in July 1792.[92]
The Italian poet Victor Alfieri d'Asti lived in Paris, writing
advice to Louis XVI, although by May 1790 he had condemned
the Revolution. Louis Pio, secretary to the Neapolitan ambassador, was faced with his own resignation letter after he had
gushed over-enthusiastically about the changes in France. On
11 March 1790, at the instigation of the abbé Fauchet, the Paris
Commune decreed his naturalization as a French citizen.[93]

These foreigners shared, to varying degrees, the cosmopolitan
view that the French Revolution was the dawn of a new era in

[88] J. H. Campe, *Été 1789: Lettres d'un Allemand à Paris*, tr. J. Ruffet (Paris, 1989),
26; A. Ruiz, 'Un regard sur le jacobinisme allemand: Idéologie et activités de certains
de ses représentants notoires en France pendant la Révolution', in F. Furet and
M. Ozouf (eds.), *The French Revolution and the Creation of Modern Political Culture*,
iii. *The Transformation of Political Culture 1789–1848* (Oxford, 1989), 257–9, 261–2,
264; Gooch, *Germany*, 321–2, 326–7, 332, 335, 338, 341, 348–50; H. Gough, 'Politics
and Power: The Triumph of Jacobinism in Strasbourg, 1791–1793', *Historical
Journal*, 23 (1980), 335; G. Kates, *The Cercle Social, the Girondins, and the French
Revolution* (Princeton, 1985), 122.

[89] Godechot, *Grande Nation*, 98.

[90] T. Christie, *Letters on the Revolution of France* (London, 1791), 58–9; Alger,
Englishmen, 14, 39–44, 69, 91–2; J. Keane, *Tom Paine: A Political Life* (London,
1995), 284–5; M. Philp, *Paine* (Oxford, 1989), 12, 14, 15; Woodward, *Une Anglaise*,
41–2; D. V. Erdman, *Commerce des Lumières: John Oswald and the British in Paris,
1790–1793* (Columbia, Mo., 1986), 82, 114.

[91] F.-A. Doppet, *Mémoires politiques et militaires du général Doppet* (Carouge,
1797), 20–1.

[92] G. Morris, *A Diary of the French Revolution 1789–1793*, ed. B. C. Davenport, 2
vols. (London, 1939), i. 440; ii. 468.

[93] Mathiez, *La Révolution et les étrangers*, 26, 29–30; A. Dupuy, 'Voyageurs italiens
à la découverte de la France (1789–1848)', *Revue d'histoire moderne et contemporaine*,
9 (1962), 269.

which old religious and national prejudices would be swept aside as people recognized their common rights. The Revolution was a moral as well as a political transformation which would affect all humanity. Decrees such as the renunciation of wars of conquest and aggression in May 1790 caused a sensation in radical and intellectual circles in Europe. Revolutionary journalists like Marat and Desmoulins invited foreigners to share in the fruits of France's regeneration.[94]

For some French revolutionaries, the main advantage of France's openness to foreign radicals was the moral and intellectual cross-pollination which would result. Some revolutionary politicians actually made practical use of these exiles. Mirabeau gathered around him the four leading Genevans as a 'think-tank'. Since January 1789, Lafayette had submitted his drafts for a Declaration of Rights to Thomas Jefferson, then United States ambassador to France, who made his own suggestions. Such was the American's reputation that Champion de Cicé, archbishop of Bordeaux and member of the Constitution Committee, asked him for an 'audience' on 20 July, because his colleagues wished 'to turn the light of Your reason and Your experience to France's profit'. Such behaviour merely served to confirm that the Revolution was the property of humanity in general, open to all who cared to participate. As the archbishop himself put it, 'For you, foreigners no longer exist when it is a matter of the happiness of mankind'. Jefferson, however, politely declined to intervene in French domestic affairs.[95]

Through their writings and influence, such foreigners had intellectual or political influence beyond their small numbers. Of greater numerical importance were those who fled the upheavals which were crushed after 1789, the revolutions in the Austrian Netherlands and the bishopric of Liège. Lille was one of the main towns in which the Belgian exiles congregated after they were beaten. The first to arrive in 1790 were the radical Vonckists, supporters of Jean-François Vonck, who had sought political reform in an independent Belgium. Expelled by their conservative rivals, the Statists, hundreds of fugitives, including Vonck himself and the banker Edouard de Walckiers, fled to

[94] J.-P. Marat, *L'Ami du peuple*, 96 (13 Jan. 1790); C. Desmoulins, *Révolutions de France et de Brabant*, 1/8. (18 Jan. 1790).
[95] Jefferson, *Papers*, xv. 165–8, 230–1, 249, 255, 291, 298.

France over the spring and summer. When the Statists in their own turn were ousted by the returning Austrians in November, they also fled to France, congregating around the duc de Béthune-Charost at Douai.[96]

The Liégeois fared little better than their Brabançon counterparts. The reformed municipal council, led by *bourgmestre* A. Donceel, scrambled to the safety of Givet in the French Ardennes when Austrian troops restored the prince-bishop in January 1791. Hundreds of soldiers led by General Ransonnet trailed behind them. While Donceel succumbed to illness in February, Jean-Nicolas Bassenge and Jacques-Joseph Fabry made their way to Paris, where they sought to influence French policy. There they joined others such as Jean-Joseph Fyon, P. Henkart, and Pierre Lebrun-Tondu, a French-born journalist who had lived in Liège since 1785.[97]

Foreign exiles quickly understood that they were more likely to win the support of the French revolutionaries if they echoed their principles and aspirations. They did not, however, blindly adopt French ideology and language. As foreign patriots, they viewed the Revolution in the light of their own aspirations. This standpoint is echoed in the works of foreign visitors such as Christie and Paine, for whom the Revolution offered a new standard by which the British constitution could be examined and judged. Exiles, whose experience had already involved open resistance to their sovereigns, were likely to adopt French forms more directly in order to secure sympathy. In May 1790, Swiss exiles from the Fribourg uprising of 1781 campaigned for the release of two political prisoners from the galleys at Brest. These activities led to the formation of the *club helvétique*, which coaxed to Paris a leader of the uprising, Jean-Nicolas-André Castella, who had been lurking timidly in Savoy. In its May address, the society stressed its loyalty to the new order in France and referred to the Revolution as an example to follow. When Castella took over leadership of the *club helvétique* with François Roullier, a new petition described the Fribourg uprising of 1781

---

[96] O. Lee, *Les Comités et les clubs des patriotes belges et liégeois (1791–An III)* (Paris, 1931), 45–6.

[97] L. Delange-Janson, *Ambroise: Chronique d'un Liégeois de France* (Brussels, 1959), 24–5; P. Raxhon, 'Les Réfugiés liégeois à Paris: Un état de la question', in Vovelle, *Paris et la Révolution*, 215.

as a precursor to 1789.[98] The Fribourgeois petitions show how foreign radicals in France sought to adopt the French Revolution to further their own, specific ends. They did not abandon appeals to their own political traditions, but tried to push them into the whirlwind of the French Revolution, by explaining it as part of a chain of events which included their own struggle.

For this reason, the whole course of relations between the revolutionaries and foreign radicals in France was based on expediency accompanied by cosmopolitan flourishes. Obviously, where unadulterated cosmopolitanism could do no harm to French interests, the revolutionaries were willing to accept and encourage even its more eccentric expressions. On 19 June 1790, Anacharsis Cloots styled himself 'the Orator of the Human Race' and led before the National Assembly a delegation of people claiming to be from all over the world. He asked that they be allowed to join the *fête de la fédération* on 14 July, which, he suggested, was not only a festival for the French, but for the human race. The president, Menou, agreed, but he chose his words carefully when he called on the foreigners to ask their rulers to follow the example of Louis XVI, 'restorer of French liberty'.[99] This message was not a call for international revolution, as the initiative was left up to the governments. For their part, the deputies in the National Assembly either laughed the affair off as harmless lunacy, or they saw no harm in accepting the flattery of the deputation. Bizarre as Cloots's deputation may have seemed, it gave the revolutionaries the opportunity to express their often sincere cosmopolitan aspirations without offending neighbouring sovereigns.

For all the cosmopolitan implications of revolutionary ideology, the relationship between the French and foreign patriots was governed by practical politics. Both sides had concrete problems and aspirations of their own. Many foreign radicals, having tasted the bitterness of defeat and persecution, sought revenge and, like most exiles, a safe return home. Meanwhile, the French had no desire to alienate people who were manifestly their admirers and friends, but they did not want to encourage the radicals so far that they provoked a diplomatic incident, just when the country needed peace and stability in its foreign

---

[98] Méautis, *Club helvétique*, 34–5, 227–9.   [99] *AP* xvi. 373.

relations. Consequently, beneath the veneer of international fraternity lay a tug-of-war in which the foreigners tried to pull the revolutionaries further than their political concerns would allow.

The Constituent released the two Fribourgeois *forçats* in Brest on 20 May 1790 and then, in October, refused a request by the Fribourg government to extradite nine members of the *club helvétique* in October.[100] This was not because it put the rights of man over French international interests. There were other principles at stake which outweighed the risk of diplomatic fallout. Much as some deputies deployed the rhetoric of the rights of man in the process, the National Assembly was determined to show that, within its own territory, the sovereignty of the French nation was immutable. They would have no part in executing the sentences handed down by foreign courts.[101] Here, the revolutionaries' perceptions of national interest and their universalist pretensions coincided happily and allowed them to brave the potential diplomatic difficulties.

The apparent encouragement offered by the French to the Swiss exiles did unsettle the cantons, already angry at the treatment of the Swiss regiments. From Soleure, the French ambassador, de Vérac, who was no sympathizer to political radicalism, darkly warned that the behaviour of Swiss patriots in France could 'infinitely damage our political and military interests'. On 22 July 1791, the envoy of the prince-bishop of Basle claimed that four of his subjects were 'the principal authors of the troubles which have, up to now, desolated the Bishopric'.[102] To these complaints, Montmorin could do little more than press the *comité diplomatique* to persuade the National Assembly to take measures against the Swiss exiles, while assuring the Swiss government that France wished to satisfy its allies. At the same time he warned the cantons that he was obliged to tread with caution because, as he told de Vérac, 'it is a question of attacking personal liberty'.[103] Montmorin was in effect quietly reminding the ambassador of the fine balance between diplomatic necessity and the principles of the French Revolution.

---

[100] *AP* xv. 630; AN, F/7/4400.   [101] Méautis, *Club helvétique*, 35.
[102] AN, F/7/4400.   [103] Ibid.

The revolutionaries themselves trod this balance gingerly when they were dealing with more influential powers, like Austria. On two occasions, 10 December 1789 and 17 March 1790, both the Constituent and the foreign ministry refused to receive the manifesto issued by the Statists, the emperor's rebellious Belgian subjects. Lafayette explained that the Statists 'do not appear to have all the characteristics which emanate from the sovereign power of the people', but there was a diplomatic dimension to the rebuff. The French revolutionaries could not be seen to support any subversive initiatives for fear of the diplomatic repercussions with Austria. The Statists, however, were persistent in seeking more than just platitudes from the French. From Lille in November 1789, the 20-year-old count Béthune-Charost proposed to raise a legion of Belgian patriots, with himself as proprietary colonel. At the time, however, the French were extremely reluctant to allow this. It would take a change in domestic and international politics to make them more receptive to such ideas.[104]

Caution dictated the reluctance of the revolutionaries to go much beyond the limits set by the absolute monarchy in its assistance to foreign patriots in exile. On 28 November 1789, the Constituent's *comité des finances* allocated 120,000 *livres* for a two-month period to be paid to the Dutch refugees, but, a year later, the Patriots complained that the French ambassador to the United Provinces had not answered their request to grant asylum to a new wave of their countrymen. In January 1791, the foreign minister, Antoine Delessart, suggested that new arrivals might be allowed to take over the pensions of those refugees who had died in France, but this implied that no extra funding would be available to them.[105] On 26 July 1790, a petition drawn up by the Valckenisten did coax 829,000 *livres* from the Constituent, to go towards the establishment of manufactures and workshops, including a fishery at Gravelines.[106] This, however, was the furthest departure by the revolutionaries from the aid first offered to the Dutch fugitives in 1788. The very nature of the innovation showed that the revolutionaries believed that the Patriots would be in France for a considerable amount of time,

[104] Lee, *Comités et les clubs*, 85–7; *AP* x. 493; xii. 205.
[105] AN, D/X/1; *AP* xvii. 353, 378.
[106] *AP* x. 321–2; xvii. 377; Schama, *Patriots and Liberators*, 148.

with the implication that the French would offer no political support in the short term.

The treatment of the Dutch Patriots in France showed that the revolutionaries were willing to accept the responsibilities bequeathed to them by the Ancien Régime, but that they were unable, for both financial and diplomatic reasons, to increase such assistance. Outside the National Assembly, revolutionary opinion on the whole echoed this caution. The Jacobins, for example, were unwilling to promise anything to the Dutch Patriots other than moral support. On 15 May 1791, they politely rebutted a Patriot appeal for a French invasion of the Netherlands.[107]

The Liégeois's bitter taste of defeat also led them to run ahead of events in France and they declared themselves in favour of nothing less than French annexation of their bishopric. On 7 July 1791, admittedly in the ferment which followed the flight to Varennes, Fabry baldly told Tarbé, the finance minister, that, regardless of what the French might think, the Liégeois wanted to be France's eighty-fourth department.[108] Like Béthune-Charost earlier, he proposed the formation of a legion which would be sent to the frontier in preparation for an invasion. On 5 August, undeterred by Tarbé's tactful silence, Fabry approached Aoust, a deputy to the Constituent, who also prevaricated.

The revolutionaries placed diplomatic concerns—in other words, the interests of France—far above cosmopolitan idealism. Revolutionary support for foreign radicals was limited to public rhetorical flourishes which signified moral support and little else. The revolutionaries were usually moved to take concrete measures or to snub foreign governments only when other principles, such as French sovereignty, were at stake. Should the foreign radicals themselves have done anything to upset French interests, the revolutionaries were willing to act vigorously. On 14 September 1790, François Roullier's son was arrested while trying to distribute the *club helvétique*'s propaganda among the Swiss Guards, which resulted in the ban on soldiers from participating in political societies.[109]

---

[107] Mathiez, *La Révolution et les étrangers*, 59–60; Schama, *Patriots and Liberators*, 150.

[108] Lee, *Comités et les clubs*, 82–3; Raxhon, 'Réfugiés liégeois', 217.

[109] *AP* xix. 67; Méautis, *Club helvétique*, 68.

Foreign refugees learnt quickly that the best means of gaining French sympathy was to attach themselves as closely as possible to already existing political currents in the French Revolution. The Genevans had developed a symbiotic relationship with the comte de Mirabeau, whose fire as an orator in the National Assembly they hoped to harness for their own aims. In return, Mirabeau tapped the financial expertise of Clavière in order to attack Necker, while Dumont, Du Roveray, and, occasionally, Reybaz, wrote both his speeches and in his journal, *Le Courrier de Provence*.[110] Such meddling in French affairs evoked hostility from some revolutionaries, who resented their enthusiasm for British ideas, namely those emanating from Lord Lansdowne's Bowood set, including Jeremy Bentham and Samuel Romilly.[111] The association of the Swiss patriots with the French Revolution was split along ideological lines, aggravated by clashes of personality. Roullier, *père et fils*, were both considered too extreme in their methods by other leading members of the Swiss club, such as Castella. The older Roullier was a friend to Marat and was accused of setting the entire right wing of the Constituent against the *club helvétique* after his son's arrest in September 1790. Roullier's radical connections led him and his supporters to join the Cordelier Club. On top of financial problems, these divisions contributed to the club's early demise in August 1791.[112]

The problem for the Dutch Patriots was to identify which political colouring it was best to assume. Personal political conscience undoubtedly played a part in their choice, but they tended to associate with those currents best suited to their aims and methods. This was complicated by personal rivalries within the Patriot camp, particularly between Valckenaer and van Beijma. Their supporters would make conflicting choices in French revolutionary politics, although this situation did not become fratricidal until the Terror.[113] The Valckenisten had taken the initiative in binding their cause to the French Revolution. While van Beijma continued to defy the

[110] Dumont, *Souvenirs sur Mirabeau*, 60–1; Bénétruy, *L'Atelier de Mirabeau*, 186–8.
[111] *Courrier de Provence*, 137 (suite, 28–9 Apr. 1790).
[112] Méautis, *Club helvétique*, 47, 49, 54.
[113] Schama, *Patriots and Liberators*, 145–6.

French government's demands for inspection of the cash registers until 1790, Valckenaer recognized that there would be no success in the United Provinces for the Patriots without the help—diplomatic or otherwise—of the new people running France. He also realized that the French were unlikely to aid the Dutch if their principles, like those of the Liégeois, were too far astray from the needs and aspirations of the French revolutionaries. Valckenaer therefore proposed that the Dutch immerse themselves in the political life of the Revolution. In 1790, besides joining the National Guard at Watten and encouraging his compatriots to follow suit, Valckenaer founded the local Jacobin club, becoming its first president. The Dutch Patriot press endorsed the French constitutional monarchy in journals and pamphlets published in places such as Dunkirk, Gravelines, and Arras, rejecting republicanism, but demanding an elected legislature for the Netherlands.[114] In the petition of 26 July 1790, the Valckenisten tailored their language to suit the principles and interests of the revolutionaries, rejecting the past as a precedent (formerly a trusty weapon in Dutch Patriot politics) and speaking in terms of inalienable rights, meritocracy, opposition to aristocracy, and the abolition of 'feudalism'.[115] Their French hosts could reject wilder schemes for a war of liberation, but they could not easily brush aside foreign radicals who seemed to speak their own political language.

The problem with affiliating with the French Revolution, however, was that the shifting sands of political alignments stranded those not adept enough to move with the tide, or who were too doctrinaire to do so. When political orthodoxy became necessary for actual as well as political survival in 1793–4, fluidity in political allegiances would be literally vital for foreign radicals. No one could have predicted such developments, and at the end of the Constituent Assembly, it looked as if the orthodoxy might be swinging rightwards rather than leftwards, in the wake of the Champ de Mars massacre on 17 July 1791. This trend threatened to soil some foreign patriots with republicanism. French revolutionaries and foreign radicals alike were suddenly faced with hard political choices. Some, like Cloots, hesitated: the self-styled orator of the human race was

114 Schama, *Patriots and Liberators*, 142, 147–8, 152.
115 *AP* xvii. 374–7.

not yet committed to a republic. After the flight to Varennes on 21 June, he distanced himself from the moderate Barnave, but he was not yet ready to follow the likes of Condorcet and Brissot. He refused to sign the Champ de Mars petition on the grounds that it was politically dangerous to do so.[116] Cloots, later seen as eccentric if not actually insane for his utopian vision of a universal republic, had more than a grain of political shrewdness. For those who were evidently Cordeliers, such as Roullier and his followers, there was little question that they would take the republican line. After 17 July, they were watched closely by the authorities. So, too, was James Rutledge, the son of a Jacobite exile who had joined the Cordeliers and who, in an obvious rejection of his father's political conservatism, had supported the admission of inactive citizens to the militia.[117] Paine was a founding member of the Société Républicaine which placarded Paris on 1 July, declaring that the king's flight was nothing less than abdication. When this provoked a sharp rebuke from Sieyès in the *Moniteur*, Paine countered that he had declared war 'against the *whole hell of monarchy*'. In the Constituent, Malouet demanded his arrest and prosecution. As the smoke cleared from the Champ de Mars, Paine and other foreigners with republican sympathies such as John Oswald and Etta Palm d'Aelders were now suspect. Paine had left for Britain on 8 July, so missed the political reverberations, but d'Aelders and Oswald remained in Paris, to see their radical society, the Cercle Social, close down after the massacre. D'Aelders was arrested on 19 July.[118] The wake of the slaughter on the Champ de Mars was the first time in which foreigners' political attachments left them open to attack when political orthodoxy became narrower. As it turned out, those beached for the time being would be rescued when the revolutionary tide resumed its leftward course, but not all foreigners had declared for a republic.

The Dutch Patriot Daverhoult and the Prussian von Archenholz (now naturalized) joined Lafayette in the Feuillants,

---

[116] A. Soboul, 'Anacharsis Cloots: L'Orateur du genre humain', *AhRf* 52 (1980), 33.

[117] *Journal du Club des Cordeliers*, 2; Alger, *Englishmen*, 19.

[118] Keane, *Tom Paine*, 315–19; M. D. Conway, *The Life of Thomas Paine with a History of his Literary, Political and Religious Career in America, France, and England*, 2 vols. (New York, 1892), i. 308–10; Philp, *Paine*, 15; Kates, *Cercle Social*, 162–3, 170; Erdman, *Commerce des Lumières*, 124–5.

conservative Jacobins who had broken away in disgust at the club's brief and timid flirtation with republicanism. On the other hand, Oelsner and his friend, Schlabrendorff, remained with the Jacobins, as did Clavière, Cloots, and others.[119] In Bordeaux, Karl Reinhard enrolled in the National Guard on hearing the news of the king's flight: 'I recorded my resolve to live and die a Frenchman.'[120]

For as long as a relative freedom of political debate was allowed in France, the activities of foreign radicals were rarely threatened by the authorities. The existence of political societies such as the *club helvétique*, the Dutch-led Jacobin club at Watten, the communities of foreign exiles and their production of propaganda suggests that, if foreigners were excluded from the formal political rights of citizenship, they could still organize themselves politically. The new regime gave them ample space to do so. The authorities may not always have been happy with their attempts to influence policy, but foreign patriots did not exist cocooned from French politics. In petitioning and in distributing propaganda, they entered the very arenas of public debate. While foreign patriots pursued their own agendas, they could not help but engage in revolutionary politics. In trying to make themselves heard, they went beyond their own organizations and joined French political clubs, enlisted in the National Guard, and worked as assistants and advisers to French politicians. Foreign radicals therefore made good use of the room left by the Revolution for engagement in French politics, obscuring, although not breaching, the boundaries of citizenship. What closed this space down was not the nationalizing tendencies in revolutionary ideology, but a change in the political climate. If the surveillance of those caught out in the reaction after the Champ de Mars massacre was brief, it was an ominous sign that orthodoxy in political language and behaviour was not merely a means of obtaining French sympathy, but that it could also be a matter of political and personal survival.

---

[119] Mathiez, *La Révolution et les étrangers*, 45; Schama, *Patriots and Liberators*, 151; Ruiz, 'Jacobinisme allemand', 258.
[120] Gooch, *Germany and the French Revolution*, 328.

V

Such vacillations in politics also faced those foreign financiers who were embroiled in the Revolution. Some foreigners had already plunged into the poisonous cauldron of French state finance, while their opponents stirred the spectre of the self-interested foreign speculator leeching off French indebtedness. The image was a familiar one to those who had taken an interest in Ancien Régime finance. *Agiotage*, or speculation on the markets, was a theme which had recurred (with some justice) in the pamphlet wars between different interests in the 1780s. Fear of the entanglement of foreigners in the business affairs of the French state became a weapon in the hands of politicians in the debates on finance in the Constituent Assembly. Perhaps because they did not want to frighten away capital, however, the revolutionaries did little to protect private French interests against the might of international finance and trade.

This was not, however, for lack of effort by some revolutionaries. Some complained that the lifetime, interest-bearing bonds, or *rentes viagères*, held by foreigners were an unproductive expense, depleting advantages in the balance of trade and representing both a loss of hard currency and a form of 'tribute' to foreign powers. It was estimated on 21 November 1789 that *rentes viagères* ate up between 20 to 25 million *livres* in interest a year, which provoked a proposal to repay the capital on all such bonds.[121] It is possible that the ulterior targets of this suggestion were the two rival Genevans, Étienne Clavière and Jacques Necker. Necker had been one of those responsible for establishing the *rentes viagères*, which a group of shrewd Genevan moneymen had bought and attributed to thirty young Genevan girls who had survived smallpox. Dupont de Nemours sarcastically spoke of 'those immortal *demoiselles* of Geneva' whose youth and resistance to illness ensured a long return on the investment.[122] Clavière had been a major investor in these *rentes viagères* himself and, as such, was thought to be linked to the same consortium of Genevan financiers. Necker, meanwhile, proposed to repay the capital on the bonds by offering the Genevans nationalized church lands as payment. Opponents of

---

[121] *AP* ix. 282–3; x. 172.   [122] Bénétruy, *L'Atelier de Mirabeau*, 115.

either Necker or Clavière (and, through him, his protector Mirabeau) could therefore choose their ammunition from this arsenal of apparent sell-outs to foreigners. On 25 June 1790, abbé Maury ground his own clerical axe and, using the scandal to denounce the sale of *biens nationaux*, took bitter delight in verbally chopping at Necker and the foreign Protestant 'usurers'.[123]

It is little wonder that some deputies sought to exclude foreign investors from certain opportunities in France. In the long debate on Necker's suggestion to promote the *caisse d'escompte* to the status of a National Bank, Custine reminded the Assembly on 20 November 1789 that foreigners had already profited from France's financial misfortune, through speculation in the very paper money which the *caisse* had created. He proposed stringent conditions and regulations for anyone who wished to make deposits with the National Bank. They aimed specifically at excluding all but naturalized foreigners, who even then would not receive interest payments until fifteen years after their initial deposit.[124] The Assembly was not convinced about the commercial or financial wisdom of these suggestions, not least because two notable financiers involved in the debate were Genevan.

The clash between Necker and Clavière showed how foreign financiers could influence French reform at the highest level. The two protagonists' origins meant that supporters of either had to argue that the confidence of foreign financiers was a crucial factor in stemming the flight of capital and specie from the kingdom. The difference between the two sides was how to remedy this faltering confidence. Ultimately, it was Necker who lost the argument, when the decrees of 19–21 December 1789 rejected the plan to create a National Bank.[125] The course of this long debate was peppered with references to foreigners. Clavière made sure that on 6 November Mirabeau drove home the point that it was Necker's beloved *caisse d'escompte* which had frightened them off. Eight days later, Necker retorted that the crisis of confidence among foreigners was explicable by the civil unrest in France.[126] Not nine months after the decrees of 19–21 Decem-

[123] *AP* xvi. 457.
[125] Bénétruy, *L'Atelier de Mirabeau*, 233–46.
[124] *AP* x. 146, 153, 154.
[126] *AP* ix. 705; *AP* x. 57.

ber, Mirabeau was pressing for Necker's dismissal and the appointment in his place of none other than Clavière. By that time, however, Mirabeau was collaborating with the Court, and he regarded his Genevan protégé as a malleable and expendable tool who was a 'victim of no importance if he does not succeed', tolerated by the Jacobins, but not devoted to them. He also recommended him as the man who invented the *assignats*.[127] On 3 September 1790, two days after this secret communication with the Court, Necker resigned, his credibility destroyed by his clashes with the double-dealing Mirabeau and by his failure to staunch the mounting tide of debt. He left in disgrace for Geneva.

The revolutionaries, however, resisted the strong temptation to exclude foreigners from French finance. No one in the Constituent would have opposed efforts to relieve France of the burden of indebtedness to foreign creditors, but many could not accept the means proposed. They were aware that a France isolated from the main sources of international banking would do long-term damage to the economy. Consequently, the Dutch banker and Patriot Balthasar-Elie Abbema could quietly take over the Parisian bank of the English Catholic John-Francis Lambert in 1788 and go happily about his business as the absolute monarchy collapsed. Since 1778, Jean-Baptiste Vande-nyver, another Dutchman, had been closely associated with both Necker and Calonne, with the royal treasury, and with the *caisse d'escompte*. He avoided embroilment in high politics and his bank, one of the largest in Paris, hummed with business under the Constituent. He was appointed an administrator of the new Compagnie des Indes in 1790.[128] Still, the image of foreign adventurers out to make a fast profit, without any sense of civic obligation, was potent and persistent and would re-emerge dangerously a few years later.

Foreign manufacturers and merchants, like their French counterparts, tended to avoid politics. Oberkampf was an exception, being elected mayor of Jouy in February 1790. His nephew took command of the local National Guard.[129] Oberkampf believed that entering politics was a means of protecting his business

---

[127] Bénétruy, *L'Atelier de Mirabeau*, 294, 304.
[128] Lüthy, *Banque Protestante*, ii. 320–2.
[129] Chapman and Chassagne, *European Textile Printers*, 121–2, 190–1.

interests from the uncertain tides of the Revolution. His status in the community accounted for his political success. In November 1789, he wrote to his former collaborator, Maraise, that he was going to give 50,000 *livres* to the *contribution patriotique* because 'my interests dictate that I pay [this] to the municipality'.[130] Yet, tellingly, he also wrote to his sister that he sincerely wanted to be relieved of his public duties. Some foreign entrepreneurs saw opportunities in the Revolution itself. The aptly named Christopher Potter, a British porcelain manufacturer, moved to France in 1789 after a brief and unsuccessful career in politics in East Anglia. The decline in the demand for luxury goods in the economic crisis of the late 1780s had forced the closure of the prince de Condé's porcelain manufacture at Chantilly. Potter reopened the works and, by January 1791, was employing fifty workers in experiments with new methods of colouring.[131] Later that year, an aged John Badger petitioned the National Assembly. His Lyon works, now run by his two sons, monopolized the watered silk industry in France. He asked that the ecclesiastical buildings which his machines occupied be declared, not *biens nationaux*, but his property outright.[132]

The French remained painfully aware that they still lagged behind the British in industrial technology. In 1790, a foreign ministry memorandum declared that, if France's global influence was not to be eclipsed by her old rival, she would need to have an 'industrial revolution' (possibly the first recorded use of this term) on top of the political one.[133] Attempts to recruit foreign skills through the tried and trusted methods therefore continued, both by the *bureau de commerce* and on private initiative. The *bureau* continued the work, begun by Calonne, of settling Philemon Pickford in France. This Manchester machine-maker had offered to bring over a manual spinning mule and had arrived in 1788, but it was only in May 1790 that his first machine was produced. Then, with a salary and other inducements from the *bureau de commerce*, he transferred his operations from Brive to Paris, where he was given premises in the old

---

[130] Chassagne, *Oberkampf*, 155–6.

[131] *AP* xxii. 279; Alger, *Englishmen*, 56–7.

[132] Harris, *Industrial Espionage*, 104.

[133] J. R. Harris, 'The Transfer of Technology between Britain and France and the French Revolution', in C. Crossley and I. Small (eds.), *The French Revolution and British Culture* (Oxford, 1989), 182.

hospital of Quinze-Vingts.[134] In 1790, the Toulouse entrepreneur François Boyer-Fonfrède recruited ten British artisans in order to establish a mechanized spinning mill. In December the next year, his agent, Charles Albert, was arrested, fined, and gaoled in Britain for trying to lure further recruits and to pilfer more technology.[135]

Foreign businessmen also sought to exploit opportunities offered by the Revolution. The American colonel James Swan used his contacts with Lafayette to win lucrative government contracts for naval supplies and salted meat.[136] Some of these entrepreneurs were more scrupulous than others. From 1788, agents of American speculators began to arrive in Paris to sell frontier land to French investors who were too nervous to keep their funds in their own country. In 1789, Colonel Blackden was in Paris pressing 50,000 acres of Kentucky on a jittery French market. Joel Barlow had also appeared in Paris in June 1788, to represent the Scioto Associates who, led by Colonel William Duer, had obtained the pre-emptive right to three and a half million acres of wilderness. Joining with a Scot named William Playfair to form the Compagnie de Scioto, Barlow sought to sell off this land to French settlers, issuing a seductive prospectus with dubious promises. By January 1790, purchasers included French nobility (understandably) and, more inauspiciously, members of the National Assembly. Yet Duer had only bought a reservation for the land, not the land outright, and, from November 1789, Barlow, duped himself by his slippery associate, began to implore the colonel to arrange for the actual transfer of the land to the French settlers. When the first thousand emigrants arrived in America in the summer of 1790, they found that they had been sold not the title-deeds, but merely the right of first refusal.[137]

In France, meanwhile, Playfair chose not to live up to his name and absconded with the company's money, leaving Barlow to face not so much the music as the cacophony. Gouverneur

[134] Harris, *Industrial Espionage*, 380.

[135] C. Ballot, *L'Introduction du machinisme dans l'industrie française* (Paris, 1923), 92; Henderson, *Britain and Industrial Europe*, 25, 46.

[136] D. Echeverria, *Mirage in the West: A History of the French Image of American Society to 1815* (Princeton, 1957), 118.

[137] Ibid. 134–5; R. F. Durden, 'Joel Barlow in the French Revolution', *William and Mary Quarterly*, 3rd ser. 8 (1951), 328–31.

Morris, the United States ambassador to France, found him unable to honour any of the bills drawn on his credit. Although he was cleared of any wrongdoing, it was a chastened Barlow who crept off to London in the spring of 1791 to escape embarrassment. Morris had little sympathy for Barlow, probably because he had initiated a similar scheme with his brother, Robert, by selling New York lands to would-be French emigrants. On 16 November 1790, Gouverneur wrote to Robert that 'if I do not realize your Expectations and Wishes, you may place it to the Account of this same [Scioto] Company, against whose Deceptions the Cry is general here'.[138] Besides damaging the prospects of these large-scale estate agents, however, the Scioto scandal also severely hurt the image of America in France.

With happier results, the Revolution seems to have encouraged a dramatic increase in the numbers of Nantucket whalers established at Dunkirk. By 1790, there were six or seven owners, all with largely foreign crews, mainly from Nantucket and Boston, but also from other maritime cities in the United States and from Britain and Scandinavia.[139] There was mutual economic benefit to be reaped from this settlement. American sperm-whale oil was subject to heavy import duties in France and, to protect French whaling, the Constituent's committee of commerce was disposed to ban all imports of such oil altogether. It may have been the Nantucket whalers at Dunkirk themselves who, seeking to monopolize the French market, encouraged this tendency. William Short, secretary to Thomas Jefferson, wrote to Morris on 13 February 1791, claiming that the Nantucketers had 'besieged the committee day and night and persuaded them that by this means they would come in great numbers to settle in France and thus transplant that art to that Kingdom and at the same time deprive us of it—they saw immediately their national fisheries surpassing those of England—and no rivalship to fear from us'. While Short managed to persuade the committee not to recommend a ban on imports of whale oil, the Assembly doubled the committee's proposed duty on it.[140]

In the south, long-standing tensions between Spanish and French fishermen in Marseille erupted shrilly. Both the

[138] Morris, *Diary*, i. 558, 581, 584; ii. 50, 60.
[139] Pfister-Langanay, *Ports, navires et négociants*, 270–2.
[140] Morris, *Diary*, ii. 128–30.

prud'hommes, the people responsible for the commercial life of the city, and the fishing-boat owners, the *patrons-pêcheurs*, voiced their complaints, presenting the National Assembly with long and detailed petitions, received on 28 October 1790. The Catalans, said the Marseillais, had long refused to pay the same dues as French fishermen, they were not liable to service in the navy, and their fishing methods destroyed stocks to such a degree that they could barely reproduce themselves. The *prud'hommes* demanded that the National Assembly either submit the Catalans to the same dues, practices, and jurisdiction as the Marseillais, or expel them from the port. The *patrons-pêcheurs* claimed that when Spanish fishermen arrived in Marseille, they rarely bothered to declare themselves to the *bureau de santé*, throwing 'the scourge of plague into the kingdom'. While the Catalans 'offer the State neither hope nor resources', the French fishermen, of course, provided 'the nursery and permanent school of sailors' for the navy and mounted guard at Marseille free of charge. The *patrons* demanded 'equality of rights, equality of obligation'. They solicited a decree by which no one could run a fishing boat without French citizenship, without registering all their crew at the relevant *bureaux*, and without both the owner and the crew declaring their intention to remain in France as French citizens. The Catalans retorted that they merely provided healthy competition for the French, which kept prices low, and that they supported the local economy by spending most of their profits in Marseille.[141]

The French fishermen expressed a combination of patriotic and egalitarian language and xenophobia. The master-fishermen presented the Catalans as a privileged group who undermined the French fishing industry while their French counterparts both fulfilled their civic obligations and struggled against unfair competition. As ever, the Constituent Assembly compromised. On 8 December 1790, the Spanish were permitted to fish along the French coast, to sell their fish in French ports, and to harbour there. They were also eligible for the same representation in the council of *prud'hommes*. The condition attached to these concessions was that they follow the same rules as their French rivals and pay the same fees.[142] There were diplomatic motives behind

---

[141] *AP* xxi. 323–4, 327, 330, 334.   [142] *AP* xxi. 324.

this decision, as the Assembly had, in the wake of the Nootka Sound crisis, renamed the *pacte de famille* of 1761 with Spain as the *pacte nationale*. The alliance had guaranteed the reciprocal rights of French and Spanish fishermen in each others' waters, provided that they submitted to the same regulations and statutes. By imposing parity on both parties, the revolutionaries were simply enforcing the terms of the Spanish alliance.

For the poorest foreigners, the Revolution meant little more than business as usual. The seasonal migration of Savoyards continued and even intensified owing to the economic crisis which had caused so much misery in 1789. The rumours of hordes of foreign vagrants were not new, but the complaints were sometimes expressed in terms of national exclusion. On 15 April 1790, the *curé* of Chaillot led a deputation from the Paris Commune to the National Assembly, complaining about the vagrants teeming in the capital, including 'a multitude of foreign beggars emboldened by their numbers'. The vicar asked that the National Assembly expel such foreigners from the country, on the grounds that it was not for the city to bear the cost of their upkeep. The president agreed. While he expressed sympathy for the indigents, saying that 'enlightened charity is the only remedy', he agreed that French resources should be applied only to French people in need.[143] No measures were taken, but this reply suggests that the cosmopolitan, assimilationist view of nationality was limited in its application to those who could contribute something to the economic or political well-being of the state. Citizenship was being cited as a means of social closure, by which, for the benefit of nationals, the welfare resources of the country were denied to migrant foreigners.

VI

Foreign enthusiasts saw in the French Revolution an event for all humanity, from which to draw inspiration, from which to learn, and in which all people, regardless of nationality, were able to participate. The revolutionaries themselves did little to discourage this impression, partly because they sincerely believed it

[143] *AP* xiii. 67–8.

themselves and because they were encouraged by the flattery of their admirers. As politicians, however, the revolutionaries were faced with the reality of the financial crisis, the breakdown of French institutions, and diplomatic uncertainty. In trying to resolve these problems, the revolutionaries had to take hard, political facts into consideration, which often meant shelving or compromising their principles. Sometimes, this meant retaining the privileges enjoyed by foreigners, even within institutions which were to be restructured along national lines, like the army and the clergy. On other occasions, it meant reining in their cosmopolitan impulses, as in their dealings with foreign patriots. Their decisions may have been couched in the cosmopolitan terms of universal rights or in the nationalizing terms of an order based on citizenship, but beneath the rhetoric there was always a careful calculation of what the circumstances implied for French needs.

The revolutionaries were not insincere in their expressions of cosmopolitanism. The enthusiasm with which they abolished the *droit d'aubaine* seems genuine enough. But they were also patriots, which meant putting the interests of the nation as a whole above those of individuals and groups. An egalitarian civic order implied the levelling of all privileges—including those of foreigners. The apparent conflict between, on the one hand, the desire to allow foreigners to participate in the life of the nation and, on the other, the impulse to abolish privilege was resolved by the same careful balancing of the practical factors involved. In general, the revolutionaries seem to have been able to strike a balance between conflicting interests. Although there were variations, an equilibrium was reached whereby foreigners could serve in the army and the clergy, they could fish in French waters, run banks and manufactures, provided they played by the new rules and accepted the new order. Occasionally, diplomatic, political, or economic considerations led the revolutionaries to reserve special treatment for certain categories. The Swiss regiments remained as they were, even after other foreign regiments were ordered to take French pay and regulations. The foreign clergy kept all their religious houses even though French contemplative orders were abolished. In some cases, however, the revolutionaries were often driven by circumstances to follow the implications of their ideology through, as with the abolition of distinct foreign regiments (except the Swiss) in July 1791. The balance which emerged in each specific case evolved from a weighing of diplomatic, economic, political, and financial considerations.

The Revolution made the rights and duties of citizenship dependent on nationality, but, if foreigners were excluded from formal political rights, they could still make their voices heard and their influence felt. The retention of foreign troops and the involvement of some foreigners in French politics, if only in informal capacities, suggests that the Constituent Assembly never entirely nationalized either the state or the broader political arena in which citizens were meant to participate. Foreign patriots and financiers alike advised French politicians and thereby engaged in the debates over the reform of France. Groups of foreign patriots sought to influence French policy through their own political organizations, by distributing propaganda, and by joining French institutions such as the National Guard and political clubs. Such activities brought foreigners to interact with French political institutions and even to work within them. The precise limits of citizenship, therefore, while clearly staked out by the Constitution in terms of formal political rights, were informally challenged by activities which had an impact on the state. The revolutionaries themselves recognized the role which some foreigners played in French politics and this informed their thinking over naturalization. Foreigners could spur a reaction from the authorities when their behaviour appeared to jeopardize French interests, but this is very different to silencing them because they were foreign. The backlash against republicanism, first signalled by the red flag of martial law and by the volleys fired into the crowd at the Champ de Mars on 17 July 1791, narrowed the channels of political activity, not along lines of nationality, but along those of political allegiance.

Until that event, under the Constituent Assembly, there was no political orthodoxy except a willingness to accept the reforms and to live under the law. Circumstances were such in the period that most foreigners found ample scope for their social, economic, and political activities within the conditions laid down by the reforms of the Revolution. It was only in the wake of the Champ de Mars massacre that the net of political orthodoxy was pulled in tighter and a number of foreigners found themselves outside it. Although the reaction was brief, it was a taste of what was to come during the Terror. It had little to do with any retreat from cosmopolitanism, but the rules as to what was legitimate behaviour became more restrictive. Whenever political orthodoxy became more exclusive, it became easier for foreigners in pursuit of their own special aspirations to fall foul of the revolutionaries.

3

Foreigners, War, and the Republic

At 7 o'clock in the evening, 9 March 1793, a well-organized band of forty men, armed with pistols and sabres, swept into the rue Tiquetonne. The first to arrive at the printshop at number 7 burst through the doors and seized the porter before he could call out for help. The rest filed in behind and set about smashing the presses. They scattered the typesets over the floor. Pages of the journal, the *Courrier des 83 Départements*, were still drying on lines strung across the workshop. As their accomplices continued their destructive work on the machinery, others tore the lines down, ripped up the sheets, and littered the street outside with the fragments. The editor of the journal was Antoine-Joseph Gorsas, a Girondin deputy to the Convention, who was still in the building as the crowd invaded the premises. He seized his pistol and fled through the back into the small garden. Vaulting over the rear wall, he ran to the safety of the local authorities, the *section* du Contrat-Social. Their work complete at Gorsas's newspaper, the crowd poured back out into the street, releasing the porter, and turned down the rue Saint-Denis, heading southwards to cross the Seine in order to mete out similar punishment to another journalist.[1]

The next day, the militants, their numbers swelled, besieged the homes of Girondin ministers and demanded a purge of the Convention. Some politicians believed that the masterminds behind these operations were shady characters who gathered at the café Corazza to give their instructions to the popular leaders. Among them were two foreigners, a Belgian financier named Pierre Proli, thought to be the illegitimate son of Kaunitz, the Austrian chancellor, and Andrès Maria de Guzman, a Spanish businessman. On 12 March, the Girondin Marie-David Lasource claimed that those responsible were 'the

[1] *AP* lx. 23–4, 54.

agents of Pitt, of William or Francis . . . fugitives from Savoy, Mainz and Belgium who are flooding Paris only to conspire'.[2] Three days later, Duquesnoy, a Montagnard or left-winger, agreed, speaking of a *comité d'insurrection* in Paris led by foreign agents.

There was no doubt that the riots were part of an attempt to remove the Girondins from government. Those responsible, however, were not foreign agents, but popular militants. Frustrated by the economic crisis, stirred by military defeat, by fear of treachery at the front, and by the reluctance of the politicians to deal with these problems, the Parisian sections challenged the authority of the Convention in the insurrection on 9–10 March. They were well-organized, directed by a central committee which since October 1792 had met in the *Évêché*, the archbishop's palace adjacent to Notre-Dame. This assembly was composed of the delegates of the forty-eight sections of Paris and its ability to rally and direct the *sans-culottes* made it potentially as powerful as the formal organs of authority, the Commune and the Convention. Their uprising collapsed on the evening of 10 March because of the resistance of the Jacobin club and the refusal of the Commune to support it.[3]

Hysterical as the accusations of Lasource and Duquesnoy may have been, the crisis of the spring of 1793 stirred xenophobia which would help to drive the demand for surveillance of French and foreign suspects alike. This impulse came from both the politicians in the Convention and the militants from the sections, as they all feared the insidious influence of aristocrats, foreigners, and others behind both their immediate political opponents and the counter-revolution. Within a fortnight, the Convention gave legal recognition to the *comités de surveillance*, which the sections had set up spontaneously since August, and extended the system across all of the Republic. Their remit was to watch suspects and hear denunciations. Foreigners were named as people to look out for. While the revolutionaries were no strangers to xenophobia, such fears had now been given an official channel, which, because it was locally based, would make nationality an almost daily legal and personal concern.

[2] Mathiez, *La Révolution et les étrangers*, 122–3.
[3] R. B. Rose, *The Enragés: Socialists of the French Revolution?* (London, 1965), 18–21.

The period between the dissolution of the Constituent Assembly and the crisis of March 1793 was therefore a transitional time for foreigners living in France. The frictions between the political needs of the revolutionaries and the aspirations of the foreigners began to heat up in a bellicose atmosphere charged by fear or panic. These rapidly changing circumstances ensured that the relatively broad net of political orthodoxy familiar under the Constituent would begin to shrink. Although there was still room for dissent, it was becoming easier to appear as an enemy to the Revolution. This was especially true of foreigners. Those who retained any special privileges, such as the Swiss regiments and the foreign clergy, looked increasingly like survivals from the Ancien Régime, and therefore suspect. On the other hand, the revolutionaries abandoned the caution of the Constituent and loudly proclaimed their support for foreign patriots, as allies in the war against European 'despotism'. As the overriding concerns of the revolutionaries no longer entailed the retention of peaceful diplomatic relations with other powers, so new factors emerged which dictated their policies towards foreigners. By March 1793, the conditions were critical. The political attitudes of foreigners and the role they played in French society became the most important determinants of their fate.

I

Despite the war fever which broke out in the wake of the flight to Varennes, the general conditions in which foreigners lived changed little until the actual outbreak of conflict and, more importantly, the second wave of defeats early in 1793. Until then, and even afterwards, it was hoped that foreigners who shared the Revolution's aspirations would associate with the struggle. This attitude can be seen in the revolutionaries' approach to citizenship, naturalization, and the political rights of foreigners. Their underlying concern was not nationality alone, but an adherence to the principles of the Revolution, particularly after the overthrow of the monarchy. Indeed, there were some suggestions that foreigners devoted to 'humanity' were honorary French citizens. The first military defeats in the summer of 1792 led the revolutionaries to impose restrictions on the movement of foreigners through passports, but it was only when the international situation of the French Republic deteriorated by March 1793 that the revolutionaries seriously considered concerted measures of surveillance.

In the last year of the constitutional monarchy, naturalized foreigners engaged in revolutionary politics at the highest level, emphasizing in the process both the success and the problems of the assimilationist notion of citizenship. The naturalized Dutch Patriot refugee Daverhoult sat in the Legislative Assembly. The Genevan Clavière obtained French nationality and served as finance minister in the Brissotin government between 10 March and 13 June 1792. Yet such people, although legally French, did not shed all their concerns for their mother countries, as the assimilationist view of nationality demanded. Clavière associated with the Brissotins because their policies seemed the most likely to achieve political change in Geneva.[4] In May 1792, Daverhoult joined the Fayettists in the Legislative,[5] due to the possibility that Lafayette would be the most useful ally in any 'liberation' of the United Provinces. The influence of such naturalized foreigners would later raise anxieties about the ease with which political rights could be obtained. When, on 26 August 1792, the Legislative voted to give honorary citizenship—and, with it, eligibility for office—to a list of notable foreigners, it was over the objections of Claude Basire and Jacques Thuriot. Basire warned against the ease with which these foreigners might infiltrate French politics and 'then betray the public interest'.[6] Thuriot questioned whether such new citizens would willingly acquiesce in measures taken by the Convention against their countries of origin.[7]

For the time being, the majority in the Legislative brushed aside such worries. French citizenship was not only to remain open to all foreigners who fulfilled the conditions laid down by the Constitution of 1791, but it was also a propaganda tool. In the first months of the war, denied the easy victory which they had been led to expect, the revolutionaries took solace in demonstrating that the French cause was that of all humanity. Empowered by the Constitution to naturalize any foreigner it saw fit, on 8 June 1792 the Legislative Assembly granted French

---

[4] Bénétruy, *L'Atelier de Mirabeau*, 392, 415–19, 421–2.
[5] Schama, *Patriots and Liberators*, 151.
[6] *AP* xlviii. 689–90.   [7] *AP* xlviii. 691.

citizenship to Joseph Priestley's son, William, in recognition of his father's sacrifices in the name of liberty.[8]

A sense of diplomatic isolation after the overthrow of the monarchy on 10 August led the revolutionaries to seek a further morale-boosting endorsement of their actions by adopting foreign thinkers and radicals as French citizens. The acceptance of the honour by such luminaries, it was hoped, would provide proof that the most enlightened figures accepted the Revolution and joined its struggle. So the decree of 26 August 1792, which naturalized eighteen prominent publicists, politicians, reformers, and radicals, was both an expression of the universalist principles of the rights of man and a nationalist statement of France as their fountainhead. Those honoured were Joseph Priestley, Paine, Bentham, Wilberforce, Thomas Clarkson, James Mackintosh, David Williams, Gorani, Cloots, Cornelius Pauw, Joachim-Heinrich Campe, Pestalozzi, Washington, Hamilton, Madison, Klopstock, Schiller, and Kościuszko. A further group of foreigners were added on 25 September, including Thomas Cooper, John Horne Tooke, John Oswald, Thomas Christie, Joseph Warner, and Joel Barlow.[9] Chabot neatly expressed the sense of the universality of the French people when he described Priestley as 'cosmopolitan *and therefore* French'. This implied that the 'family of free men' (to use Guadet's phrase) was French in spirit. Nationality was not a matter of birth or culture, but a state of mind. On the other hand, such a proposal had its risks, as Lasource pointed out: if acceptance of French citizenship could be interpreted as an endorsement of the Revolution, then what did a refusal mean? To give the title of French citizen to those who had not asked for it was to risk humiliation in the case of a rebuttal.[10] In the event, none of those named actually turned down the offer,[11] although some, such as Wilberforce, who was politically conservative, prudently failed to reply. The revolutionaries were unfortunate enough to have their measure upstaged by the September massacres less than a week later. Joseph Priestley, while endorsing

[8] Mathiez, *La Révolution et les étrangers*, 73–4.
[9] *AP* xlix. 10; Woodward, *Une Anglaise*, 6.
[10] *AP* xlviii. 689–91.
[11] Mathiez, *La Révolution et les étrangers*, 77.

the Revolution in general, took the opportunity to condemn the atrocities as an aberration.[12]

The collapse of the constitutional monarchy raised the question as to whether or not the usual provisions for naturalization in the Constitution of 1791 still applied. Petitions for French citizenship were forwarded to the Convention's *comités de législation et de féodalité*. On 8 November 1792, these committees insisted that 'it is impolitic to refuse admission to foreigners, who are friends of liberty, into our society'.[13] When the new constitution was finally discussed, the revolutionaries' own militant cosmopolitanism, as well as the extension of the suffrage to almost all adult males, encouraged a lowering of the formal barriers to naturalization. 'Cosmopolitanism' in the old sense, of fitting chameleon-like into élite society across Europe, was, however, becoming increasingly unacceptable. Lally-Tollendal's claims to Irish and French 'dual nationality' were rebuffed by the Legislative Assembly on 22 August 1792.[14] For a Frenchman to claim foreign nationality implied a rejection of the new order. For a foreigner to request French nationality was an endorsement of it, particularly if the foreigner then used his acquired political rights in the service of the nation. Joel Barlow, however, was sharply critical of the notion that an individual could only be a citizen in one country. In his critique of the Constitution of 1791, presented to the Convention on 7 November 1792, he appealed for citizenship to be detached from nationality, on the grounds that human rights are universal. The idea that one owed exclusive loyalty to one nation was 'an old, feudal idea of loyalty, based on the supposition that fidelity owed to one country is incompatible with our duties towards another'.[15] After all, did the gift of honorary citizenship deprive the foreigners of their original nationality?

The constitutional committee wavered over this issue of basing citizenship either on universal, natural rights or on nationality. Condorcet accepted Barlow's view that, once a foreigner had arrived in France, a simple declaration of intent to stay there was sufficient to obtain political rights. Political rights were to be detached from nationality, which meant that citizenship was to be dependent only on one's presence on the

[12] *Moniteur* (30 Sept. 1792).   [13] AN, D/III/368–70.
[14] *AP* xlviii. 616.   [15] Wahnich, *L'Impossible Citoyen*, 73.

country's territory. The first Girondin proposals for a constitution, presented on 15–16 February 1793, therefore brought the residence requirement down from five years to one for the acquisition of political rights, the year being officially a 'civic noviciate', during which foreigners would not so much become French nationals as learn the practices of citizenship. Eventually, with the darker atmosphere in the spring of 1793, the Convention rejected the notion that citizenship was merely a natural right, open to all men who came to live on the territory of the Republic. On 29 April, Lanjuinais demanded that foreign residents declare their desire to become part of the French nation before they could be admitted to political rights, because, he argued, too many foreigners had abused their political and administrative positions in order to foment disorder. Consequently, the new Girondin proposals insisted that political rights be given only to people of French nationality.[16]

This issue had been injected with a new urgency, because the execution of Louis XVI had brought the legitimacy of the Revolution into question as never before. To assume French nationality meant an implicit acceptance of the new Republic, symbolized by the civic oath. Naturalization in France remained assimilationist, but limited by the narrowing boundaries of political orthodoxy. The inclusive dimension of French citizenship is illustrated by the elections to the Convention of the newly naturalized citizens, Paine, and Cloots. Once he had taken up his seat, Paine was appointed to the constitutional committee on 29 September and Cloots was elected to the Convention's *comité diplomatique* on 15 October 1792.[17] Joel Barlow was entrusted with a mission to Savoy in November to oversee the inauguration of the French republican administration.[18] Priestley was elected to the Convention, but turned down his seat because of his broken French (a problem which did not dissuade Paine).[19] Yet the fact that foreigners could be given citizenship and then immediately entrusted with weighty political responsibilities suggests that, if only for a brief period, the revolutionaries rejected concerns over split loyalties when the commitment of

---

[16] Wahnich, *L'Impossible Citoyen*, 74–6; Portemer, 'L'Étranger', 544.
[17] Keane, *Tom Paine*, 356; Soboul, 'Anacharsis Cloots', 39.
[18] Durden, 'Joel Barlow', 341–4.
[19] *Moniteur* (30 Sept. 1792).

the new citizens to the Republic did not seem to be in doubt. It was the demand for such commitment, rather than nationality, which excluded foreigners from citizenship.

Even more than their adherence to revolutionary principles, Priestley, Paine, and Cloots arguably owed their election to their connections with the Brissotins. While Cloots soon attacked them in his writings, his advocacy of war had brought him into an alliance with them in late 1791 and early 1792. Paine, meanwhile, had long been associated with Brissot and Condorcet. Priestley was a scientific correspondent of the latter. Significantly, his candidature for Paris was vociferously opposed by Marat and it was the Puy-de-Dôme which eventually elected him.[20] That such elections may have been a partisan move to enhance the profile of the Girondins is also suggested by the experience of David Williams, who was on friendly terms with Brissot and Pétion. On being naturalized, he was approached by a Brissotin agent in London, prior to the nomination of candidates for the Convention. They discussed 'the consequences of my being nominated and elected . . . if I checked the rapidity of the revolution or commenced hostilities on the Jacobin Club'. As it was, Williams refused to stand because he felt he had little knowledge of French affairs.[21] Barlow was urged by the abbé Grégoire to stand for the new department of Mont-Blanc in recently annexed Savoy, when elections were held there on 17 February 1793. The American radical, poet, and luckless entrepreneur had obviously re-established enough of a good reputation in France, if not as a salesman, then as a patriot. At this late date, however, he suffered for his Girondin connections and was defeated.[22]

Non-naturalized foreigners could play a part in French politics. Doppet, the exile from Savoy, was briefly employed as a secretary by Aubert de Bayet, deputy to the Legislative for the Isère. In Paris, he joined the National Guard, the Jacobins, and the Cordeliers.[23] Karl Reinhard accompanied his friends Vergniaud and Ducos from Bordeaux when they took their seats in the Legislative Assembly. He joined the Jacobin club and was

[20] O. Coquard, 'Le Paris de Marat', in Vovelle, *Paris et la Révolution*, 179.

[21] D. Williams, *Incidents in my Own Life which have been Thought of Some Importance*, ed. P. France (Brighton, 1980), 26–7.

[22] Durden, 'Joel Barlow', 345–6.　　　　　　　　　[23] Doppet, *Mémoires*, 23, 34.

secretary to the French embassy in London until the outbreak of war with Britain, when he was transferred to Naples.[24] The French sometimes used foreigners, or people with foreign background, on diplomatic missions because of their local connections. It was for this reason that early in March 1792, Talleyrand specifically requested Du Roveray for his mission to ensure British neutrality in the coming war. In September, as the Genevan's political allegiances looked increasingly suspect, the nominal leader of the French legation in London, Chauvelin, pleaded with Lebrun, the foreign minister, to let him stay with the mission for 'his talents, his enlightenment, and his deep knowledge of this country'.[25] When the French sought to avoid a final breach with Britain after the execution of Louis XVI, David Williams was sent over the Channel, although by the time he arrived in London it was too late.[26] Foreigners could still find outlets for their political energies and could therefore exercise influence in revolutionary politics. The revolutionaries accepted these efforts provided they coincided with French interests and for as long as the foreigners concerned were ideologically committed to the Revolution.

Most of this period would, however, be darkened by measures which were intended as temporary expedients. The imminence of war in early 1792 and then the course of the conflict itself brought restrictions to foreigners' freedom of movement. On 31 January 1792, the Legislative reintroduced passports for those crossing the frontiers. While passports were nothing new for travel within France, they were now needed to *enter* the country. Deputies of the left stressed the dangers of allowing foreigners to enter at will, while others argued that passports represented an assault on individual liberty.[27] In these final months before the war, few other precautions were taken against the possibility that some foreigners might genuinely attempt to subvert the Revolution.

Yet ominous signs emerged in the military and political crisis of the summer. When, on 4 July 1792, the death penalty was demanded for those who wore any cockade other than the

[24] Gooch, *Germany*, 328, 330.
[25] MAE, CP, Angleterre, 582; Bénétruy, *L'Atelier de Mirabeau*, 406.
[26] Williams, *Incidents*, 29–30.
[27] Mathiez, *La Révolution et les étrangers*, 72.

tricolore, only foreign ambassadors were exempt. Discussing the *patrie en danger* decree, the revolutionaries were in no mood to respect the individual rights of foreigners. When a lone deputy courageously insisted that foreigners could wear their own countries' colours, he was silenced by murmurs on the left.[28]

Circumstances soon drove the revolutionaries to impose more restrictions. The day after the overthrow of the monarchy, all people were forbidden to leave Paris without a passport, and these could only be obtained with a *certificat de civisme* from the local sections. In these fraught weeks, panicking foreigners tried to negotiate the labyrinth of Parisian bureaucracy. Gouverneur Morris was besieged by people of all nationalities, begging for the precious documents. John Moore recognized on 21 August that: 'it is difficult at this time to obtain passports: they have been refused to many strangers'. The predicament of British subjects was more difficult because Lord Gower, the British ambassador, had been recalled by London. While Pétion, the mayor of Paris, refused to issue Moore and Lauderdale with passports, on the grounds that such a refusal was temporary and for their own safety, it was Moore's own letter of introduction from Du Roveray to Clavière which secured them.[29]

On 23 August, the Assembly ordered the foreign ministry to issue passports only to foreign diplomatic personnel. This represented the greatest restriction on the movement of foreigners since the beginning of the Revolution. While it was mainly aimed at preventing emigration from France, the deputies were under no illusions that it would also prevent foreigners from crossing the frontier. Guyton-Morveau of the *comité diplomatique* provoked widespread murmurs when he objected that the French could not reasonably force foreigners 'to share the dangers of a homeland which is not theirs'. Thuriot rejoined by insisting that the suspension of passports was a temporary expedient: 'this situation ought not to last long enough to become a state of oppression for foreigners'.[30] If it is possible to trace the rhetoric of the Terror to before 1793, the revolutionaries' own familiarity with concepts such as *droit des gens* and

---

[28] *AP* xlvi. 116.
[29] Morris, *Diary*, ii. 490; J. Moore, *A Journal during a Residence in France from the Beginning of August to the Middle of December, 1792*, 2 vols. (London, 1793), i. 127–37.   [30] *AP* xlviii. 661–2.

their ideals of individual liberty exerted a force in the opposite direction. Foreigners still succeeded in procuring passports, despite the legislation. Heinrich Meister, the Swiss tutor and writer, understandably feared for his safety after the slaughter of his compatriots on 10 August. He sweated for more than twenty days until news of the September massacres spread like a dark shroud over Paris. Meister managed to persuade Commune officials to issue a passport and he made his way out of the city.[31] There were still wide loopholes which the law of 23 August had left open. If the issue of passports by the foreign ministry had been forbidden, it did not explicitly rescind the authority of the Commune to do so.

Despite such omissions, it was becoming clear that hostile attitudes towards foreigners were running ahead of legislation, which was evolving piecemeal. Foreigners were merely being subjected to the same laws on passports and mobility as French citizens. The structures of surveillance and control associated with the Terror were, however, beginning to take shape. From 11 August, Parisian sections had elected *comités de surveillance*, whose duties included hearing reports on suspect individuals and foreigners. From 19 September, foreigners arriving in Paris were required to make themselves known at the local section.[32] Above all, these measures represented the early growth of an apparatus which would eventually make nationality a criterion for discrimination in the legal treatment of individuals.

For the time being, however, neither the Legislative nor the Convention officially recognized the *comités de surveillance* and the legal measures aimed at both French citizens and foreigners were regarded as temporary. Like the 'Patrie en Danger' proclamation itself, they were to remain in force only during the crisis. Foreigners were regarded with increasing suspicion in the autumn of 1792, as befits the period known as the 'First Terror', but the revolutionaries still trod carefully in their legislation. When the Convention declared war on Britain and the United Provinces on 1 February 1793, the issue of how the *droit des gens* related to the treatment of enemy subjects was raised. Fabre d'Églantine secured considerable support for a

---

[31] H. Meister, *Souvenirs de mon dernier voyage à Paris (1795)*, ed. P. Usteri and E. Ritter (Paris, 1910), 209–12.

[32] Portemer, 'L'Étranger', 546.

proclamation which would have placed British and Dutch subjects in France 'under the protection of the law'. While this measure was not voted, the Convention did name a commission, which included Thomas Paine, to draw up an address to the British people and dismissed a further call, by Marat, to prohibit all foreigners from staying in maritime towns.[33] Further measures against foreigners were not, however, long in coming. On 26 February, the Convention ordered all landlords, hoteliers, and hosts to appear before their local section or commune and declare within twenty-four hours, under pain of three months' imprisonment, any foreigners who were staying with them. Once those declarations were made, they were to be posted up at the door of the local section or municipality, with an invitation to all citizens to denounce any omissions.[34] For the first time, foreigners were being targeted on a national scale. The spark for this decree was an immediate crisis, as food riots swept the capital the day before. The xenophobic manner in which the unrest was interpreted can be explained by the war, in which the Revolution was beginning to sustain renewed military strain.[35] The law of 26 February was a knee-jerk response to a domestic upheaval, behind which the revolutionaries saw the machinations of foreign agents. When the news from the front became worse in March and was compounded with the worsening situation in the interior, rumours of foreign complicity rang truer and would lead to more intense surveillance of foreigners.

The pattern of 25–6 February was repeated in the insurrection of 9–10 March. Although the targets of the uprising were the Girondins, it was the Montagnard Duquesnoy who, agreeing that foreign agents had organized the troubles, proposed that foreigners be ordered to leave Paris in twenty-four hours, unless they were vouched for by 'two good citizens'. This went too far for the Convention: Prieur de la Marne reminded his colleagues that the Alien Act was one of France's official motives for declaring war on Britain in the first place. He insisted that those who loved liberty 'should come to France to enjoy its happy revolution'. The Convention's reluctance to go beyond the surveillance of foreigners implies that it did not wish to follow the traditional path of the *droit de représailles*, which paid

---

[33] *AP* lviii. 120–2.   [34] *AP* lix. 283–4.
[35] Mathiez, *La Révolution et les étrangers*, 122.

no regard to the universal rights of man. Such a refusal was a propaganda coup, showing France to be the true land of liberty. Prieur merely identified 'those men whom it is useful to put under the gaze of their fellow citizens', who were as likely to be French as they were to be foreign.[36] The Manichaean struggle between the Republic and despotism still cut across lines of nationality, but, alongside this, the erratic pulse of xenophobia quickened and slowed with the passing of each new crisis. The Convention was not consistent in its concern for vigilance.

For as long as the war exerted its weight on the economic crisis and the political opposition it provoked, so xenophobia would continue to rear its ugly head. On 18 March, Barère appeared before the Convention on behalf of the Committee of Public Safety and proposed that the Republic expel 'those disreputable men who live only by foreign gold, who have relations with our enemies, who feed troubles and conspiracies'. Barère's proposal was greeted enthusiastically and the Convention adopted the proposal to 'chase from the Republic' foreigners who could not prove a reputable livelihood.[37] In fact, the revolutionaries may have recognized specific individuals in Barère's description. Proli and Guzman did frequent the haunt of the militant sectional leaders in Paris, the café Corazza, and both men were involved in radical politics. Guzman would later be dubbed *Tocsinos* by his Girondin foes, after the bells sounded for the insurrection of 31 May.[38] The expulsion of such people, it was hoped, would weaken the militant Parisian movement which had sorely tested the authority of the Convention. This law was not yet a general measure aimed at all foreigners, but only those *sans aveu*, who could not satisfactorily explain their purpose in France.

The identification of such foreigners, however, required discriminatory surveillance against foreigners in general. It required the official bureaucracy by which strangers could be identified, watched, and acted against. When it came, this machinery legitimized xenophobia by giving it an official channel. It made all foreigners legal targets of suspicion and denunciation. The implications of this logic were not lost when, the

---

[36] *AP* lx. 222–3.   [37] *AP* lx. 294.

[38] Mathiez, *La Révolution et les étrangers*, 105, 111, 123; L.-S. Mercier, *Paris pendant la Révolution (1789–1798), ou Le Nouveau Paris*, 2 vols. (Paris, 1862), ii. 268.

next day, the Convention discussed the Vendée uprising. Cambon warned of the dangers of allowing France's external enemies to correspond with those in the interior and demanded that all foreigners be ordered to leave the country. Only six days previously, the Convention had heard a report on the expulsion from Spain of French citizens, so Cambon based his proposal on the old *droit de représailles*. The motion therefore drew vocal support, but while the Convention agreed in broad terms that something had to be done with potentially hostile foreigners, it did not go so far as to expel them all. Lasource and Boyer-Fonfrède argued that there were plenty of foreigners who were useful to the Republic and took up Prieur de la Marne's notion that it would be wrong for the Republic to imitate its enemies. Boyer-Fonfrède proposed that, instead of expulsion, surveillance committees should watch over foreigners.[39]

Two days later, the decree 'on foreigners' gave legal recognition to the *comités de surveillance*. They were charged with receiving the declarations of all foreigners within their jurisdiction, both residents and new arrivals, who would register within eight days. Those who failed to do so would be expelled from the commune immediately and from France within eight days. Significantly, these rules applied to all foreigners, including neutrals. Those from enemy countries also had to prove either that they had a useful occupation or property in France, or that they had 'civic sentiments', confirmed by six citizens. Those who failed to show such commitment were to be cast out. Foreigners who passed the test were granted a *certificat d'autorisation de résidence*, which has a worryingly modern, bureaucratic ring to it. In Paris, from 26 March, such *cartes de sûreté* were to be red for foreigners and white for French citizens.[40] A foreigner who received such a certificate only on the basis of his *civisme* was also bound to furnish a deposit of half his presumed wealth. The most draconian clause stemmed from the 'lessons' of 25 February and 10 March: 'any foreigner arrested during a riot, or who is convicted of having provoked or entertained it, by money or suggestion, will be punished with death'.[41]

All French citizens aged 18 or over were also meant to make

---

[39] *AP* lx. 318–19; Mathiez, *La Révolution et les étrangers*, 124.
[40] AN, F/7/4779.
[41] *AP* lx. 389–90; Mathiez, *La Révolution et les étrangers*, 126.

declarations similar to those of foreigners before the *comités de surveillance*.[42] The law, in short, may have reserved its harshest measures for enemy subjects, but its basic provisions applied equally to French citizens. Onerous and sinister as the procedure must have been for people almost unaccustomed to such bureaucracy, it fell far short of the general expulsion committed by the Spanish government and proposed by Cambon. While the revolutionaries would watch enemy subjects, they were still unwilling to punish with expulsion or arrest those who had committed no obvious crime. Xenophobic outbursts reached very shrill notes, however, when the law was enforced sluggishly. On 27 March, Duquesnoy rose to the tribune, urging the Convention to apply the law. 'Every day foreigners arrive in Paris', he cried, melodramatically adding that he himself had narrowly missed assassination.[43] Yet not all foreigners were harassed by the new legislation. Those who were actually arrested had long been suspected of links either with the recent Paris riots, or with the counter-revolution. The Commune put seals on the papers of certain foreigners and arrested those who were deemed to be highly suspect, including Guzman and the Italian poet, Alfieri. Guzman was believed to have been behind the disturbances of February and March. Alfieri's poetic sympathies were increasingly with the counter-revolution (and the experience of arrest would more than confirm him in these views[44]). Grace Dalrymple Elliott was also taken from her home in the dead of night and interrogated by the Committee of General Security. The section visited her not simply because she was British, but because of her ties with d'Orléans. Her papers included a letter addressed to Charles James Fox, which was enough to incriminate her as an enemy courier. She was released within a few days after the Fox letter was found to be full of praise for the French.[45] Such cases suggest that it was not enough at this stage simply to be foreign to be harassed by the authorities. While such treatment did not say much for the revolutionaries' tolerance of opposition, the authorities did

---

[42] *AP* lx. 390.   [43] *AP* lx. 603.

[44] Mathiez, *La Révolution et les étrangers*, 125.

[45] G. D. Elliott, *Journal of My Life during the French Revolution* (n.pl., 1955), 97–108; P. Gerbod, 'Visiteurs et résidents britanniques dans le Paris révolutionnaire de 1789 à 1799', in Vovelle, *Paris et la Révolution*, 139.

release the prisoners once they were reassured that they posed no great threat. Moreover, the vast majority of foreigners remained at liberty.

The surveillance and arrests were due as much to a desire to weaken the domestic opposition as it was a product of xenophobia. Fear was strengthened by military defeat, but it was the unrest in the interior of France which provoked its expression in legislation. The fact that suspicion was institutionalized in the form of *comités de surveillance* and *cartes de sûreté* was ominous for both French and foreigners alike. In this bureaucratization of xenophobia, it is possible to discern the early negative, discriminatory legislation against foreigners. Enemy subjects were targeted by additional clauses in the law of 21 March, while foreigners carried a different coloured identity card from French citizens. Moreover, the registers of foreigners drawn up by the revolutionary committees provided the information required for the enforcement of further police measures. When, in August 1793, the arrest of all enemy subjects was decreed for the first time, the *section* de l'Unité in Paris took as its point of departure the registers compiled in execution of the law of 21 March.[46]

Revolutionary cosmopolitanism had been irretrievably damaged by the combination of defeat and civil unrest, and hostility to foreigners intensified in this period, but some revolutionaries did not relinquish the vision of a Manichaean struggle which cut across nationality. While foreigners were singled out for particular attention by the revolutionaries, in practice the authorities were reluctant to do much more than interrogate and, if necessary, detain for a few days at the most. Political loyalties mattered more than nationality. For now, it was the radicalization of revolutionary politics which excluded foreigners from France, as much as the response to military defeat. The foundation of the Republic made both the Revolution less acceptable to many foreigners and the activities of certain foreigners less acceptable to the revolutionaries.

The extent to which foreigners were affected by these developments depended to a great degree on their specific role in French life. An ability to contribute to the war effort through military service, economic activity, or propaganda might have

[46] AN, F/7/4779.

helped, but very often political orthodoxy and usefulness were not mutually inclusive. The revolutionaries were sometimes faced with the awkward choice of either keeping in France those foreigners who provided useful services, but whose political commitment was suspect, or of expelling them, and then losing their skills.

II

Among no other group of foreigners was this dilemma more pressing than with foreign soldiers. This period saw the demise of the Swiss infantry, but the rise of new foreign units, the legions. The difference was that the Swiss regiments were survivals of the Ancien Régime whose political commitment was questionable, while the legions were made up of foreigners who were, in theory, ideologically devoted to the Revolution. The fall of the former and the rise of latter show that the revolutionaries, albeit with some misgivings, were still willing to accept foreigners within the armed branch of the French state, but that conformity to a narrowing set of political values was increasingly important. Yet there still remained the expediency which had dictated the maintenance of foreign regiments under the Constituent. Unwilling to lose trained and seasoned troops, the revolutionaries quietly permitted some of the soldiers from the disbanded foreign regiments to join the legions or French regular units.

Even as war approached, and despite the assumption by most foreign regiments of French pay and regulations, relations between French civilians and foreign soldiers were still strained. At Neuchâtel in January 1792, seven or eight officers of the 87th (Dillon) Infantry seized a billiard cue from a café and beat the *limonadier*'s dog. Officers and soldiers were also accused of damaging hotel property. In March, the 77th (La Marck) regiment supported the royalist *Chiffonistes* against the radical *Monnediers* in Arles, with the blessing both of the municipality and of Louis Narbonne, the Fayettist minister of war.[47] Next month, the 77th was in Lyon *en route* from Avignon to Brest

[47] Scott, *Response of the Royal Army*, 146; Scott, 'Irish Regiments', 20.

when their colonel, described by one of his men as 'un aristo-crate', provoked a mutiny because he had failed to issue the regiment with French uniforms.[48] The reluctance of officers to forsake their foreign identity naturally aroused suspicion. It was the Swiss regiments, however, who were the most despised for their discipline and for their almost exclusively foreign member-ship. Fights broke out between soldiers of the Courten regiment and French soldiers in Douai in January 1792, over allegations that the Swiss were counter-revolutionaries. The worst incident before the outbreak of war involved the Ernst regiment in Marseille. Isolated since 1790 in a sea of popular hostility, these Swiss were increasingly loathed for their policing role. In February 1792, when the regiment's barracks was besieged by a seething crowd, the commander was persuaded to pull out of the city. The canton of Berne recalled the regiment to Switzerland on 16 March and the chastened Swiss left France on 26 May.[49]

The affair had diplomatic repercussions. The senate of Berne protested against the shoddy treatment of the soldiers and the failure of the authorities to respect the treaties signed under the Ancien Régime.[50] For their part, the revolutionaries realized that the predicament of the Swiss sorely tried the alliance with the cantons. A memorandum to the Legislative Assembly's *comité diplomatique*, dated 3 April 1792, warned that the 'unhappy affair' in Marseille would lead to a break with Switzerland. With war against Austria now imminent, such a situation would simply compound France's difficulties. The author urged that other Swiss regiments be treated with special care.[51]

The revolutionaries in the Legislative, however, were in less accommodating mood than their Constituent predecessors. The Swiss Guards were denied their traditional role of guarding the king on 13 November 1791. The decree stated that, while the regiment's regulations would otherwise be unaffected, the role of royal bodyguard would be taken up by a French force. When the constitutional guard finally took up its duties on 16 March 1792, the élite *Cent-Suisses* company was made obsolete and was

---

[48] P. de Pardiellan, *Mémoires d'un vieux déserteur: Aventures de J. Steininger* (Paris, 1898), 181.

[49] Haas, *Régiment suisse*, 18–20; Scott, *Response of the Royal Army*, 141; Bodin, *Suisses*, 257–8; Fieffé, *Histoire des troupes étrangères*, i. 388.

[50] Haas, *Régiment suisse*, 19; Fieffé, *Histoire des troupes étrangères*, i. 388.

[51] AN, F/7/4401.

disbanded. These changes were dictated by a need to ensure that the king would be guarded by troops who were not bound by loyalty to him alone. Yet it contradicted the Swiss capitulations and this grievance was compounded by the arrears in pay since January.[52]

The approach of war and the slave rebellion in Haiti, however, required every ounce of military muscle and the more seasoned the better. Successive ministries up to August 1792 therefore favoured the retention of foreign units. They sent the former Irish regiments to the colonies, which was a continuation of an Ancien Régime tradition.[53] The Swiss regiments, meanwhile, were deployed mostly along the frontiers or in major provincial towns.[54] The revolutionaries were determined not to fritter away military strength under the pressure of popular hostility to foreign troops. There were always other countries willing to pay for their services, maybe against France.[55]

The possibility of war therefore encouraged the Legislative Assembly to make gestures to consolidate the loyalty of foreign soldiers, as against the dubious faith of their officers. This policy brought new sources of tension between France and the Swiss cantons. While the forty-one Swiss soldiers imprisoned since the Nancy mutiny were regarded increasingly by the revolutionaries as the victims of aristocratic oppression, the cantons saw them as insubordinate embarrassments and as subversives. On 26 December 1791, the cantons refused to consent to their release from the galleys. In March 1792, they were freed anyway.[56] The revolutionaries had swept aside Swiss objections and enforced the policy which they considered to be in the national interest. Revolutionary faith in the loyalty of the Châteauvieux soldiers was severely misplaced. Days after the disbandment of the Swiss regiments in August, its men considered desertion to the *émigré* army.[57]

The war presented a new test of loyalty to the Revolution: foreign troops had to choose to fight for or against the new regime. The hostility of the French population ensured, in some

---

[52] AN, F/7/4401; Bodin, *Suisses*, 258.
[53] Scott, 'Irish Regiments', 20.
[54] Bodin, *Suisses*, 257.   [55] AN, F/7/4401.
[56] Fieffé, *Histoire des troupes étrangères*, i. 365–8.
[57] AN, F/7/4401.

regiments, a cohesion between officers and the ranks lacking in many other units in the French army. Such solidarity meant that when their officers chose to emigrate, their men followed, as was the case with the 15th (Royal-Allemand) Cavalry regiment, the 1st (Berchény), and 4th (Saxe) Hussars in May 1792. Only in the Berchény regiment was opinion seriously divided. A bitter nocturnal fight erupted between the cavalrymen when it became clear that their officers were leading them across the frontier into Germany. Eighty hussars then followed most of the officers to join the enemy. Sixteen officers of the 92nd (Walsh) regiment deserted in the same month.[58] On 28 May, the Legislative Assembly heard that Swiss Guards barracked in Neuilly were sporting Bourbon-white cockades.[59]

Despite such ominous signals, foreign troops were too good an asset to lose in wartime. In July, a worried French envoy to Switzerland reported that the Spanish were trying to raise a Swiss regiment.[60] As conditions for the Swiss worsened in France, so Spanish gold would seem to glisten more brightly. On 15 July, the Legislative decreed that all regular troops remain at least $36\frac{1}{2}$ miles from Paris. Colonel d'Affry protested to Lajard, the minister of war, claiming that, according to its conditions of service, a third of the regiment should remain close to the king. Although Lajard urged the Legislative to allow no exceptions, the Assembly demurred, perhaps thinking of further diplomatic repercussions, and allowed a battalion to remain in the Paris area.[61] Most of these soldiers would perish with the monarchy.

The Swiss insistence on old regime regulations and a privileged status within the French army, their deference to orders from the cantons, and their loyalty to the king all jarred with the growing revolutionary vision of a citizen army dedicated to the national cause. The French ambassador to Switzerland, Barthélemy, warned that, when the capitulations were renewed, the cantons would insist on the regiments' old privileges, rather than adjust to the new order.[62] Such issues were merely aggravated by the more militant, egalitarian atmosphere of the summer of 1792. With relations between the French authorities and the Swiss regiments already strained, they finally snapped on 10 August.

[58] Scott, *Response of the Royal Army*, 114–16; Scott, 'Irish Regiments', 21.
[59] *AP* xliv. 190–1. [60] AN, F/7/4401.
[61] Ibid.; *AP* xlvi. 574–6. [62] AN, F/7/4401.

On that day, the 900 Swiss Guards defending the Tuileries were overwhelmed by Parisian National Guards and *fédérés* from the provinces. The king they had sworn to defend slipped out through the gardens, kicking up fallen leaves as he went, to seek refuge with the Legislative Assembly. When the palace was taken, popular hostility boiled over with the claims that the Swiss had fired on the patriots after luring them into negotiations. As the Swiss soldiers fled in panic through the Tuileries gardens, they were torn to pieces by crowds of enraged Parisians, using axes and knives. That night all but one of seven terrified Swiss captured on the Champs-Elysées were shot by the orders of the committee of the *section* du Roule. The next day, the nervous municipal authorities in Neuilly were confronted by a mob demanding that two Swiss being held prisoner be handed over to the 'people'. When the Swiss prisoners were locked up in the Abbaye, it was promptly attacked by a crowd.[63] When the blood-letting of 10 August was over, 650 Swiss were dead, 100 wounded, and in all 250 officers and men were eventually imprisoned in the Abbaye, La Force, and the Conciergerie. A further 200 were killed in the carnage of September.[64]

Official treatment of the Swiss Guards, while less bloodthirsty than that of the sections and the mob, was no less dictated by hostility. On 11 August, the National Assembly imprisoned the officers and ordered their immediate trial. The jury was chosen from delegates of the forty-eight sections, which would hardly guarantee a fair hearing. Major Bachmann was condemned to death and guillotined on 3 September for his role, but d'Affry was acquitted in October because he was at home ill on the fateful day. At the end of the year, he returned to Switzerland, where he died soon after on his estate.[65] On the other hand, both the American merchant James Price and John Moore witnessed on 11 August revolutionaries such as Pétion and Gorsas haranguing the crowds to prevent them from indulging in the further slaughter of the now defenceless Swiss. Their imprisonment was as much for their own protection as it was to prevent their escape. The Commune sent National Guards to defend those Swiss held at the Feuillants. Danton personally led fifty Swiss from the Legislative to the Abbaye; the *fédérés*, declaring that

---

[63] AN, F/7/4401; *AP* xlviii. 2, 15, 16.   [64] Bodin, *Suisses*, 269, 270.
[65] *AP* xlviii. 1, 15, 134; Bodin, *Suisses*, 270, 272–3.

they no longer saw the Swiss as enemies (and perhaps trying to ease their own consciences) offered to carry out similar duties.[66]

The slaughter eliminated what little confidence the revolutionaries had left in the Swiss regiments. All of them were unofficially charged with complicity in the sinister projects of the king and the Swiss Guards. Rumours of a broader conspiracy involving Louis and his loyal foreign troops appeared to have been believed by some deputies and were reinforced by the 'unpatriotic' behaviour, understandable in the circumstances, of officers of the Salis-Samade regiment in Rouen.[67]

Despite the diplomatic ramifications, the Legislative disbanded the Swiss regiments on 20 August. Brissot, who presented the decree for the new provisional government, stated that 10 August had made renewal of the capitulations impossible. The old treaties with the cantons, he argued, were intended as much to defend the king against the French as to ensure the defence of the nation. French blood had been spilt by the iron of the Swiss Guards. The misplaced loyalties of the Swiss regiments now weighed more heavily against them. Well-trained and seasoned they may have been, but they were now too much of a danger to remain in France. This fear made the arguments for a citizen army more compelling. 'The army of a free people', Brissot declared, 'is itself.'[68]

Brissot admitted that he and Servan, the new minister of war, were worried about the possible collapse of the alliance with Switzerland.[69] Yet the decree of 20 August insisted that Swiss returning home could only do so without arms and in detachments of no more than twenty men. Palavicini, lieutenant-colonel of the Vigier regiment, was outraged, likening this clause to the treatment given to criminals. The Swiss Diet defiantly ordered their regiments to ignore the law and to return with their arms and their colours, in a style compatible with 'military honour'. Lebrun replied on 14 September, insisting that the blame for the slaughter lay with the Swiss officers and so the privileges of their regiments could no longer apply.[70] On 17 October, Servan

---

[66] W. J. Chew, *A Bostonian Merchant Witnesses the Second French Revolution: James Price, a Voyage and a Visit to France in 1792* (Brussels, 1992), 29, 32; Moore, *Journal*, i. 63, 66–7; *AP* xlviii. 2, 14, 16, 17, 24, 25, 40.

[67] *AP* xlviii. 103–4, 121.

[68] *AP* xlviii. 417–18.

[69] *AP* xlviii. 418–19.

[70] AN, F/7/4401.

warned General Biron, commanding the army of the Rhine, to be very sensitive to the manner in which the Swiss regiments were allowed to return home, so that their treatment could not be cited as a cause for hostility by the cantons.[71]

Some Swiss rebelled. A hundred Swiss Guards who had been sent to Dieppe only days before 10 August eventually enrolled in the rebel army in the Vendée under a non-commissioned officer named Keller.[72] Officers of the Châteauvieux regiment flirted with the attentions of the comte d'Artois, who was attempting to seduce them into joining the *émigré* army. On 25 August, the regiment crossed the frontier into the duchy of Zweibrücken to do just that, but on 3 September the Basle government angrily ordered its subjects to return home without delay.[73]

Now that the capitulations were broken and the diplomatic furore was unleashed, the revolutionaries had more freedom for manœuvre over the way they treated the Swiss troops, short of doing anything which might provoke open war with the cantons. In his letter to the Swiss Diet, Lebrun could now explicitly place the sovereign rights and interests of the French nation over the privileges of the Swiss regiments. To the complaint that the imprisonment of the Swiss Guards had been a breach of their special judicial rights, he replied curtly that 'a nation's right to arrest and judge foreigners accused of conspiracy against her can never be questioned'. The diplomatic dispute did not amount to much beyond the straining of relations between France and Switzerland. Servan believed that the Swiss Diet was as worried about incurring French wrath as the revolutionaries were about the military and diplomatic consequences of the loss of the Swiss troops. Such optimism proved well-founded, because in November Barthélemy reported the failure of Spanish efforts to recruit a new Swiss regiment.[74]

The details of the disbandment continued to dog the French authorities in the autumn and the presence of hundreds of disgruntled Swiss troops in towns across France was naturally a cause of concern.[75] By the end of October all those who had chosen to return to Switzerland had done so and were eligible for

---

[71] Service Historique de l'Armée de Terre (SHAT), X^{g}30.
[72] Bodin, *Suisses*, 270–1.   [73] AN, F/7/4401.
[74] AN, F/7/4400; SHAT, X^{g}30.
[75] SHAT, X^{g}30; AN, F/7/4401.

French pensions. The loose ends, such as the return of regimental papers and funds, were still being tied well into 1793.[76]
On the other hand, the revolutionaries were reluctant to lose
such good soldiers and tried to retain their services, provided
they could be assured of their loyalty to the new order. Some
Swiss provided evidence of that loyalty. As early as 11 August,
some bedraggled Swiss Guards were greeted with applause in
the Legislative when they offered to fight on the frontiers.
That same month in the Seine-Inférieure, soldiers and non-
commissioned officers of the Salis-Samade regiment deserted
rather than return to Switzerland because they 'intend to
continue their service in France'.[77]

The decree of 20 August accordingly offered a bounty of 150–
300 *livres* to any Swiss soldier who joined a regular French unit.
Naturally, the soldiers were required to take the new civic oath of
10 August. Even before the precise regulations were published,
however, Dumouriez indulged in some freelancing and formed
compagnies franches out of the Swiss Diesbach regiment.[78] On 12
September, the Swiss were allowed to join any of the fourteen
light infantry battalions under the same conditions as their
French counterparts.[79] Sixty-seven Swiss enlisted with a
French regiment in Strasbourg, just a fraction of the 3,000–
4,000 Swiss soldiers who joined the French army between 20
August and the beginning of October.[80] By November, Barthélemy was proposing the recruitment of *compagnies franches* in
Switzerland from officers and men who were dedicated to the
principles of the French Revolution. Nothing came of this idea
and no Swiss units were to be raised for French service until
November 1798.[81]

The Swiss regiments were not the only foreign units to suffer
from the crisis of the summer of 1792. With the fall of the
monarchy, the 6th (Lauzun) Hussars lost seventy horsemen who
followed some of their officers into emigration. The entire 92nd
(Walsh) Infantry was arrested by a battalion of *gendarmes* after
the capitulation of Verdun in September and were held until

[76] SHAT, X^g30; Bodin, *Suisses*, 271.
[77] *AP* xlviii. 25; SHAT, X^g30.
[78] *AP* xlviii. 419; Mathiez, *La Révolution et les étrangers*, 69.
[79] *AP* xlviii. 677–8.
[80] SHAT, X^g30; Scott, *Response of the Royal Army*, 166–7.
[81] AN, F/7/4400; Fieffé, *Histoire des troupes étrangères*, ii. 36.

their patriotic credentials were verified. On 9 September, the 101st (Royal-Liégeois) regiment was disbanded after general Montesquiou complained of its 'bad attitude' and 'uncivic conduct'. The dismissal of the Royal-Liégeois brought to twelve the number of foreign regiments disbanded in 1792, a strength of 12,000 men in all.[82]

The year was not a good one for the retention of foreign military muscle. The revolutionaries, however, allowed those who remained to join French units. Although they would have preferred not to lose their manpower, by August 1792 the revolutionaries could afford to dismiss foreign regiments because what they lost in quality and experience could be made up in numbers, with the enrolment of French volunteers. The recruitment of large numbers of French citizens together with the dismissal and emigration of foreign troops diluted the importance of the latter. In the surviving foreign regiments such as the Irish, death, desertion, and emigration further reduced their number. By February 1793 only 4 per cent of the manpower in the line army was foreign, a substantial reduction from the 15 per cent in 1789.[83]

The dilution of the foreign element in the regular army was enhanced by the creation of separate legions for foreign 'patriots' and deserters who sought to fight for the Revolution. The idea of foreign legions predated the outbreak of war. As early as December 1791, Liégeois, Belgian, and Dutch patriots made separate requests to form military units. The issue was adjourned, but the Liégeois and the Belgians began to organize anyway, with the unofficial compliance of the Brissotin ministry appointed in March 1792. Dumouriez, as foreign minister, released secret funds to arm and equip both a Liégeois legion, which was ready a mere eight days after the declaration of war, and a Belgian *corps franc*. Both legions, numbering 1,150 men in all, were formally recognized with the decrees of 20 July, providing equipment, and 28 July, granting half a million *livres* for their expenses.[84] A Dutch legion was also decreed on 26 July.

---

[82] *AP* xlix. 492–3; Scott, 'Irish Regiments', 21; Scott, *Response of the Royal Army*, 114–16, 148.

[83] Scott, *Response of the Royal Army*, 185; Scott, 'Irish Regiments', 23.

[84] Fieffé, *Histoire des troupes étrangères*, ii. 10; Mathiez, *La Révolution et les étrangers*, 64; Delange-Janson, *Ambroise*, 27.

Dumouriez had already released 700,000 *livres* from his minis-
terial funds to a *comité hollandais* charged with its organization.
The decree now provided additional funds from the treasury to
pay for its first year of recruitment, equipment, and upkeep.[85]
The first Dutch legion was joined by a second seven months later,
when Dumouriez was engaged in his doomed invasion of the
Netherlands. This other *légion batave*, officially known as the
chasseurs-tirailleurs nationaux bataves, was established on 5 March
1793, under the command of the Dutch Patriot, Makketros.[86]

These first legions were all initially recruited from those
groups of political refugees who had substantial reserves of
men with military experience and who had tasted the bitterness
of defeat. These groups would naturally be the first to respond to
the crusading rhetoric aired by bellicose revolutionaries, but their
links to Dumouriez raised doubts among some revolutionaries.
When the Batavian legion was made public on 8 July, Brissot
expressed astonishment that the general should have raised
troops without consulting the National Assembly. Marat, of
course, explained that Dumouriez wished to become the duke
of Brabant.[87] About a month later, the government's agent to
Belgium, Rutteau, proposed an investigation into the funding of
the legions.[88]

Despite these suspicions, the notion of foreign legions spread.
The *club des patriotes étrangers*, organized in the first days of 1792
from both Swiss and Savoyards in Paris, sought to recruit their
compatriots as well as Piedmontese for a *légion des allobroges*. It
was decreed and provided with funds on 1 August. There were
plenty of willing Savoyard migrant workers in Paris. The legion
fought alongside the *fédérés* on 10 August, but this did not deter
some of the despised Swiss soldiers from joining the unit, which
left for Grenoble on 22 August.[89] In July 1792, Anacharsis
Cloots and the Saxon doctor, Freymuth Saiffert, mooted the
idea of the *légion prussienne* for German and Austrian patriots
and deserters. They organized a steering committee which
included themselves, Dambach, a Prussian colonel who had

[85] *AP* xlvii. 147–52; Mathiez, *La Révolution et les étrangers*, 64–5.
[86] Fieffé, *Histoire des troupes étrangères*, ii. 20.
[87] *AP* xlvi. 246; Schama, *Patriots and Liberators*, 151.
[88] M. Robespierre, *Œuvres de Maximilien Robespierre*, ed. M. Bouloiseau,
G. Lefebvre, and A. Soboul, 10 vols. (Paris, 1939–67), iv. 339.
[89] Doppet, *Mémoires*, 48–52; *AP* xlvii. 376–7.

fought under Frederick the Great, an Austrian named Schwartz, and two others.[90] On 12 August, Cloots petitioned the Assembly for a German legion, which was finally decreed on 4 September.[91] Unlike the others, the *légion germanique* did not have the same pool of refugees or immigrants from which to draw recruits, which meant that it reluctantly made up its numbers with Frenchmen. By 17 December 1792 it had 1,071 men under arms, many of whom appeared to have been French, but it did enlist career soldiers who had served in the former German regiments, or in the armies of the Holy Roman Empire.[92]

Legions did have some appeal among the French revolutionaries. The declaration of war on 20 April 1792 included an invitation to foreign sympathizers to range themselves under French banners. On 27 August, Lasource supported Cloots's request for a German legion, drawing parallels with the previous day's decree on honorary French citizenship. Just as foreign philosophers fought tyranny with reason, so foreign soldiers fought it with bayonets.[93] There were equally practical reasons behind this appeal. On 8 July, the war minister Lajard stressed 'the urgent necessity to increase our forces' and the advantages 'of new recruitment at the expense of a foreign power'. These arguments were identical to those employed by Ancien Régime generals. This time, however, there would be no question of the loyalty of these men, because they had fled persecution in their own countries.[94]

Foreign legions raised some diplomatic problems. When Lajard proposed recognizing the first Batavian legion on 8 July, Brissot poured cold water on his enthusiasm. The United Provinces were still neutral and, he said in a masterful understatement, it would be 'very impolitic' for the French to foster the Dutch legion.[95] Besides the obvious threat such troops would pose to the Stadholder, the revolutionaries were also aware that to raise them would be to make a statement of intent towards the Low Countries.[96] The proposal was still voted in its entirety by the National Assembly when it was re-presented on 26 July. With the *patrie* being declared *en danger* only four days pre-

[90] SHAT, X^{k}3; Mathiez, *La Révolution et les étrangers*, 67.
[91] *AP* xlviii. 72; xlix. 349–50.
[92] SHAT, X^{k}3.   [93] *AP* xlix. 41.
[94] *AP* xlvi. 246.   [95] *AP* xlvi. 246.
[96] A. Sorel, *L'Europe et la Révolution française*, 8 vols. (Paris, 1885–1904), ii. 454.

viously, the deputies were quite ready to ignore the international ramifications and plug the widening holes in the French army with any available troops. The only concession to diplomatic sensibilities was the change of name from *légion des bataves* to the *légion franche étrangère*. The *conseil d'administration* of the legion, however, left no doubt as to who was intended to fill its ranks: its leaders were the Dutch Patriots Abbema, de Witt, de Boetzelaer, Huber, de Kock, and van Hoey.[97] The persistent diplomatic embarrassment of recruiting Dutch Patriots was such that at the end of August the executive council told François Noël, its agent newly dispatched to London, to lie to the British government by assuring them that 'the Batavian Legion, which might have caused some offence, . . . has just been dissolved'. A squirming Noël was to explain that the legion was only established because of 'a trap set against the good faith of the National Assembly'.[98]

Beyond diplomatic difficulties, there was still much hostility to the recruitment of foreigners in the French army. It seemed foolish, as Carnot objected on 21 April, to make the task of 'nationalizing' the army still more difficult by recruiting yet more foreigners.[99] There was also a suspicion that foreigners would not be the most dedicated of soldiers. When, on 29 May, Coustard supported four foreign officers who requested permission to raise a corps of British soldiers, Servan cautiously suggested that these officers be permitted to recruit only French citizens.[100] On 29 January 1793, Bréard bitterly remarked that '*émigrés* have enlisted; you paid, dressed and equipped them, and then they deserted'.[101] There were attempts to forestall these problems. Recruits to the German legion were screened for ideological suitability. All officers had to have 'good references' and were subject to approval by the minister of war, who could propose people 'whom he believes worthy of National confidence'.[102] The objections, however, breathed life into the questions first raised in the *cahiers de doléances*: should those who were not French seriously be asked to defend a nation which was not theirs? Could non-citizens defend the *patrie*, when they did not have the same stake as citizens?

For the time being, the foreign legions, with their apparent

[97] *AP* xlvii. 146–52. [98] MAE, CP, Angleterre, 582.
[99] *AP* xlii. 256. [100] *AP* xliv. 47.
[101] *AP* lviii. 10–11. [102] SHAT, $X^k 3$.

ideological commitment, were accepted as propaganda tools and as welcome additions to the hard-pressed French forces. The problem was that their aspirations led them to associate with particular political groups. In the unpredictable currents of revolutionary politics, such ties could be perilous. The Batavian, Belgian, and Liégeois legions were closely associated with Dumouriez, as his personal ambitions made him their most sympathetic protector.[103] Having been established with his considerable assistance, however, the legions were polluted with suspicion when Dumouriez deserted early in April 1793. Furthermore, all legions relied on the continuing faith of French politicians in the revolutionary potential of France's European neighbours. Once both Dumouriez and the 'crusade for universal liberty' were discredited, so the whole purpose and even the good faith of the legions were called into question. Most of the legions were to be disbanded under a cloud of suspicion during the Terror. Exceptions were the Belgians and Liégeois, who were subsumed into the French army on 26 January 1793 in anticipation of the absorption of Belgium by the French Republic.[104]

A further difficulty was that, although destined for specific nationalities, the legions often found that to make up numbers they had to draw on others, including Frenchmen. The German legion included Dutch and Frenchmen, among whom was Charles Augereau, who would later become one of Napoleon's marshals.[105] Such a mix of nationalities could cause problems. A government agent claimed at the end of July 1792 that the 'aristocratic' members of the Belgian committee in Lille imposed 'an atrocious despotism' on the Belgian legion, barracked at Los, 'notably against the French who have enlisted'.[106] On 10 December 1792, Dambach angrily wrote to Pache, saying that among the cavalry officers 'almost all are French, while the capitulation says expressly that the officers are to be foreign, or to have a foreign father'.[107]

This recruitment of French officers into the *légion germanique*

---

[103] Schama, *Patriots and Liberators*, 153–4.
[104] Fieffé, *Histoire des troupes étrangères*, ii. 13.
[105] Ibid. ii. 21.
[106] Robespierre, *Œuvres*, iv. 339.
[107] SHAT, X^k3.

may have been the cause of internal divisions. In the spring of
1793, Saiffert claimed that French officers sought to seize control
of the legion by encouraging insubordination in the ranks. He
accused Marat of encouraging two French officers to denounce
their comrades as aristocrats.[108] The two French officers in
question told a different story, complaining of financial corruption in the *conseil d'administration*.[109] That the rift followed lines
of nationality is suggested by the rejoinder to this accusation,
signed by thirty-one officers, mostly German and far from a
majority of the officer corps.[110] The dispute continued into the
spring and summer of 1793, when the legion was disbanded. It
appears, therefore, that this schism played an important part in
the early demise of the *légion germanique*.

The cosmopolitan rhetoric applied to the adoption of foreign
soldiers was also used when the revolutionaries discussed the
treatment of foreign deserters and prisoners of war. On 4 May
1792, the decree on prisoners of war stressed the human rights of
those captured and the 'principles of justice and humanity'.
Prisoners would live in district *chefs-lieux* and fortresses at least
20 miles from the frontier. There, they would receive the same
pay as their French counterparts in the army. They would be
entitled to take an *engagement d'honneur* before the municipal
officers, whereby they 'will have the town as their prison', but
would be submitted to roll-calls three times a day. Such prisoners would enjoy 'the same laws as the French', including, as the
decree said pointedly, those applied against revolt, but it also
meant that they could engage in any profession.[111]

Such relatively liberal terms had causes other than cosmopolitan ideals. First of all, they reproduced eighteenth-century
habits. Secondly, they were intended to undermine the discipline
and strength of enemy forces. Thirdly, they were meant to show
that the French fought for humane principles. The Brunswick
manifesto provided the revolutionaries with a coup in this
respect. When the duke's declaration had been read to the
Assembly on 1 August, the principles behind the law voted on
4 May were reasserted by the deputies, but with one exception.

---

[108] Ibid.; Gooch, *Germany*, 334.   [109] SHAT, X^{k}3.
[110] Ibid.   [111] *AP* xlii. 743–4; xlvii. 412–14.

The new decree added that while enemy soldiers from the ranks would always be well-treated, whenever the enemy violated the 'ordinary laws of war', captured nobles and officers would be treated in kind.[112] The decree served as a warning to the coalition not to carry out the threats in Brunswick's declaration, but it would also, the revolutionaries desperately hoped, reassure the invading Austrian and Prussian phalanxes that it would still be safe to surrender to the French.

To stress this last point, and to encourage desertion, the Legislative put into practice an idea which had been mooted immediately after the outbreak of war.[113] On 2 August, enemy soldiers and NCOs—but not commissioned officers—who defected to the French would receive a tricolour cockade as a symbol of adoption. On declaring their intention 'to embrace the cause of liberty', they would immediately receive a bounty of 50 *livres*, followed by a life pension worth 100 *livres* a year.[114] The decree was translated into German and Latin to seduce the Prussians, Austrians, and Hungarians and was posted on walls and trees along the Rhine and on roads near the frontier.[115] The cosmopolitan rhetoric was not always applied in the field. The officers of the Mauconseil battalion of Parisian volunteers reported that, on 15 September 1792, some of their men at Château-Thierry 'wanted to slaughter five prisoners'.[116] On 5 October, that very same battalion was implicated in the massacre of four deserters from the imperial army, who had just enlisted in the 10th Dragoon regiment at Rethel.[117]

Just before Valmy, the revolutionaries resorted to the traditional practice of exchanging prisoners of war.[118] The unfavourable tide of the conflict and the failure to persuade hordes of Austrians and Prussians to embrace their French brethren stood behind this change of direction. Besides, keeping prisoners cost money, an expense which could be eliminated by trading them for French captives. The decision to enact such exchanges also shows that, despite the revolutionaries' claims of a war based on new principles, the old practices persisted. The revolutionaries

---

[112] *AP* xlvii. 359–60.
[113] Mathiez, *La Révolution et les étrangers*, 63.
[114] *AP* xlvii. 395–6.
[115] *AP* xlix. 336; Mathiez, *La Révolution et les étrangers*, 63–4.
[116] AN, F/7/4445–4550[1].
[117] Ibid.   [118] *AP* l. 139–40.

apparently still believed that the enemy would keep to their word and would not return their freed prisoners to the front. Eighteenth-century rules of warfare were yet to mutate beyond recognition, whatever the rhetoric suggested.

The first exchanges also resurrected another Ancien Régime concept, the *droit de représailles*. On 5 January 1793, the Convention heard complaints of bad treatment from returned French prisoners. Bréard argued that there should be retaliation, but limited to enemy officers. Even now, however, the Convention was reluctant to condone the practice. Instead, the issue was exploited for propaganda purposes. The complaint of the soldiers was printed and Pache seized the opportunity to show that the French stood on moral high ground. He told the Convention that he would write to the generals asking them to remind the enemy to follow the French example and to remember that 'their own interests demand that they show our prisoners the same humanity'.[119]

The approach and outbreak of war put the French army under pressure to increase its strength and to stop the haemorrhaging of its best troops through emigration. Despite any desire to the contrary, the revolutionaries found that these new considerations demanded initially that they retain the foreign regiments. On the other hand, it became increasingly hard to justify these units as they failed to meet the tests of loyalty posed by the war and the fall of the monarchy. Exactly four months into the conflict, the revolutionaries dismissed by far the largest foreign contribution to the French army, the Swiss regiments. Fear of their counter-revolutionary potential now outweighed reluctance to upset diplomatic relations with Switzerland. The demise of the foreign regiments came not from any impulse to nationalize the army, potent as it may have been, but rather because at last the revolutionaries decided that, whatever the advantages, they were now outweighed by the threat which foreign troops posed to the internal safety of the Revolution.

If they could not tolerate foreigners who were clearly hostile to their cause, such was the need for troops that the revolutionaries overcame their misgivings about creating new foreign units. The

---

[119] *AP* lvi. 223–4.

establishment of legions sat uneasily with the protests, heard since 1789, that the French nation should only be defended by French citizens. The adoption of foreign patriots to fight for the Revolution could be justified in cosmopolitan terms: the ideological commitment of the recruits showed that the French cause was universal. Moreover, they had a practical use as the spearhead when revolutionary forces began to liberate France's neighbours. The problem with such a justification was that when the crusade for universal liberty was discredited, so the desirability of foreign legions was open to question. The legions of foreign patriots were therefore as vulnerable to shifts in revolutionary politics as were the older foreign regiments. In other respects, the revolutionaries' adoption of foreign legions had similarities with the practices of the Ancien Régime. Ideological differences aside, the revolutionaries shared the opinion with their predecessors that such recruitment increased French strength at the expense of foreign powers. This continuity was disguised by the cosmopolitan claims of the Revolution.

III

Animosity against those clerics whose commitment to the Revolution was already suspect sharpened in this period of upheaval and anticlericalism would find greater resonance in official circles. The privileged position of the English, Scottish, and Irish clergy made that hostility still more acute. Until official measures were actually taken against their institutions, or against British subjects, the question of legal survival still remained uncertain, but not hopeless. What undermined them was the climate of fear.

Seething anticlericalism darkened the lives of the foreign clergy, but it is hard to tell whether the antagonism in their case was due more to their profession or to their nationality. In March 1792, John Naylor, confessor to the English Benedictine nuns in Paris, complained of harassment by the inhabitants of the *faubourg* Saint-Marcel.[120] With the outbreak of war, it was even more pressing to appear to be on the right side. John

[120] AN, S//4619.

Farquharson, rector of the Scots College in Douai, wrote in July 1792 that 'I have been obliged to change the dress of my boys; none dare stir without doors but in secular Cloaths and with a flying tricolour cockade to his hat.'[121] The situation only got worse when the main obstacle to legislation against refractory clergy, the king, was overthrown in August. With the decree against non-jurors and the arrests of priests by Parisian militants, the foreign clergy felt very vulnerable. Their structures and activities had remained almost immune from the reforms of the Constituent, which merely sharpened their appearance as privileged Ancien Régime survivals. MacSheehy, an Irish student at the college in Paris, later recalled that after 10 August 'all the pupils were obliged to leave their houses furtively, because public indignation had targeted them for the Vengeance of the people'.[122] In the fear which enveloped Paris towards September, a quivering English Conceptionist nun in Paris fretted that 'our Nuns . . . are affraid they will soon be killed'.[123] The September massacres ensured that this terror would linger. On 3 October, the same nun proposed to visit Naylor, saying that she could 'put on a coulourd Peticoat, and a Capote over our Habit' when treading cautiously through the streets. She soon considered fleeing France for good.[124]

Until the overthrow of the monarchy, the relevant ecclesiastical authorities were unsympathetic to plans for flight. In an acrimonious meeting in February 1792, the Scottish bishops Geddes and Hay and some leading French clergymen reviewed Alexander Gordon's suggestion that the Scots College in Paris sell all its property and move to another country. Far from accepting the need to flee, the meeting admonished the bishops to send as many students to the college as its finances allowed.[125] In the spring, Mary Kirby, an English Benedictine in Paris, applied to a sister convent in Ypres for a refuge 'in these dismal times of persecution', but from the relative safety of the Low Countries the abbess coldly rejected her request, explaining that such a refuge 'can only be sought for in the last extremity'.[126]

Such extremity was not far off, with the first harsh measures against the refractory clergy coming after 10 August. In the surge

---

[121] Johnson, *Developments*, 93. [122] AN, BB/3/70.
[123] AN, S//4619. [124] AN, S//4619.
[125] SCA, CA1/24. [126] AN, S//4619.

of anticlericalism which accompanied the establishment of the Republic, the local authorities began to act more aggressively. The Scots College in Paris was twice invaded by an armed crowd at the end of August. Alexander Gordon was marched off by four National Guards to the local revolutionary committee in order to be confronted with the new clerical oath. He refused, but, shaken, he also applied for a passport to leave France. The prefect of studies, Alexander Innes, courageously refused to go, so Gordon left alone in September.[127] In October, Maher, the procurator of the Irish College in Paris, complained to Lebrun about the behaviour of the Commune's commissioners. They were investigating complaints of the bad political faith among the staff. Despite the earlier decrees to the contrary, the officials acted 'as if the property of this House belonged to the nation', by placing seals on the superior's papers and demanding to see the seminary's accounts.[128] These intrusions continued, supported by some of the students who appear to have drunk from the revolutionary chalice. On the morning of 29 October, seven Irish students, maybe embittered by a dispute with the college priests over bursaries, joined three Paris commissioners in a coup. Kearney was removed as the superior and replaced by a priest named Madgett. This time Lebrun was stung into action and wrote to the minister of the interior, Roland, asking him to protect the establishments from such illegal incursions.[129]

For the foreigners among the secular clergy, the decree against refractory priests on 26 August 1792 signalled the end of their ecclesiastical career in France, as it did for French non-jurors. The law ordered that refractories would have to leave the country within a fortnight, or else face deportation to fever-ridden Guiana. Foreigners responded in the same way as French priests. At Dieulouard, Richard Marsh pragmatically decided of the new oath that 'in my opinion it has nothing at all against Religion'.[130] In Bordeaux, however, Irish refractories fled either to Spain, like their French colleagues, or to Ireland. Martin Glynn risked his stubborn neck by staying in Bordeaux, where he was eventually caught and executed. For the time being, those

---

[127] Halloran, *Scots College*, 174; Johnson, *Developments*, 98.
[128] MAE, CP, Angleterre, 582.
[129] MAE, CP, Angleterre, 583.
[130] AN, S//4619.

who did take the oath developed their careers: by 1793 George Jennings was the constitutional curate at Saint-Seurin; Baptiste O'Hennessy became the constitutional priest of Saint-Germain du Puch and Myler Prendergast received the prestigious parish of Saint-Dominique in Bordeaux.[131]

The approach of war with Britain intensified fears of persecution. Daniel O'Connell and his brother, attending the English College at Douai, were called home by their uncle in late January 1793, after Daniel had worried him sufficiently with reports that reprisals would be 'almost inevitable' should conflict break out between the two countries.[132] With war declared, flight became a more attractive option. Naylor wrote to his agent in Britain, asking him to find him a suitable position.[133] Until any measures were actually taken specifically against British subjects, however, the foreign orders were allowed to subsist in a manner denied to their French counterparts since 1790. They were only subject to the whole panoply of laws regarding the clergy if they wished to minister to French citizens. This, at least, is what the municipality of Bordeaux advised Everard, the vice-rector of the Irish seminary, on 12 February 1792.[134]

While fear was beginning to drive clerics and students away, the institutions themselves were subsiding under financial pressures. The Revolution itself certainly contributed to the difficulties. On 22 February 1792, Gordon complained that there were only two students at the Scots College in Paris, severely affecting its revenue.[135] Eleven days later, Richard Marsh fretted that it was almost impossible to get people to make donations because 'they seem afraid of the consequences of the Revolution'. He also complained of the *imposition foncière* on the land held by the English Benedictines at Dieulouard. No tax relief could be granted, because the local commune had a quota to fulfil. By the time war had broken out between Britain and France, inflation had wiped out any economies made by the clerics. The Scots College at Douai also suffered because rents

---

[131] Loupès, 'Ecclésiastiques irlandais', 95; 'Irish Clergy', 32–3, 38 n. 12.

[132] D. O'Connell, *The Private Correspondence of Daniel O'Connell*, ed. W. J. Fitzpatrick, 2 vols. (London, 1888), 7.

[133] AN, S//4619.

[134] C. Preston, 'Le Collège irlandais de Bordeaux', in Hayes, Preston, and Weygand, *Les Irlandais en Aquitaine*, 24.   [135] SCA, CA1/24.

payable to the institution were settled in *assignats*, devalued by inflation.[136]

The response of some houses to these ever-increasing difficulties soon involved measures which, to Catholic clergymen, were unpalatable. Initially the administrators tried to tap existing resources, but this was not enough to keep their establishments afloat.[137] Some clerics began to think about buying nationalized church lands, a step which they were loath to take. Marsh was aware of their potential value, but knew full well that 'the purchasers are look'd upon with an evil eye'. By December, he had overcome his scruples, hungrily eyeing a small farm which would consolidate the monastery's holdings. The plan brought little fruit because the Benedictines were easily outbid in the sale of the *biens nationaux*. They managed to salvage something from the set-back when the successful buyer immediately sold off the farm in smaller parcels, some of which were snapped up by the monastery.[138]

Despite the war between Britain and France from February 1793, initially no measures were taken against British or Irish subjects, so, precariously, their institutions remained. The revolutionaries were reluctant to close houses which might yet have been of some public use. On 9 February 1793, Fouché's report on education suggested that the law suppressing secular orders should not include those involved in education. On 14 February, the Convention adopted this proposal.[139] This decision applied to the foreign institutions, because the Convention also decreed that all English, Irish, and Scots colleges would continue to receive the revenues due to them for the first six months of 1793.[140] The decrees of 8–12 March 1793 confirmed the foreign colleges in the possession of their property, with management remaining in the hands of the college administrators.[141] For some, this law came too late. If the Convention was still reluctant to seize foreign property, this did not stop local authorities from illegally confiscating what they could. On 18 February, the municipality of Douai seized all British property and placed the foreign clergy and students under house arrest.

---

[136] AN, S//4619; Johnson, *Developments*, 93.   [137] AN, S//4619.
[138] Ibid.   [139] *AP* lviii. 395–6, 522–3.
[140] *AP* lviii. 523.   [141] AN, H/3/2561/A.

Officials swooped on the English College and grabbed the silver. Stung by this behaviour, John Farquharson of the Scots College applied for passports for himself and his students to travel back to Britain. At the end of March, eight Scottish students sailed across the Channel.[142]

The position of the foreign clergy was undercut in this period. On paper, their foreign status ensured the existence of their institutions long after French houses had been closed down. The main condition for the authorities' tolerance was that they restricted their activities to people of their own nationality. Legally, if not in practice, their property was protected, but they were severely threatened by their financial problems, which admittedly emanated in large part, but not exclusively, from the Revolution. For secular priests, on the other hand, it was their status as clergy, rather than as foreigners, which mattered. Like their French colleagues, the legislation of 26 August 1792 forced them to choose between abandoning their careers, submitting to the oath, or defying the revolutionary authorities. Yet if the foreign colleges, convents, and monasteries were protected from such choices, the anticlerical measures and the violence in general discouraged recruitment and investment. By the spring of 1793, the Convention had recognized the legitimacy of their property and activities, but the war with Britain created an atmosphere which made their position increasingly precarious. It was, above all, the conflict which began to dissolve the uneasy coexistence between the foreign ecclesiastics and the French Revolution.

IV

Foreign radicals faced new challenges in republicanism and the leftward march of revolutionary politics. Some who were attached to specific French political groupings could find themselves stranded once the revolutionary tide had passed over them. For the revolutionaries, foreign patriots could be of some use in their diplomatic and propaganda efforts, but in

---

[142] *Correspondence of Daniel O'Connell*, 7–8; Johnson, *Developments*, 94.

some instances they proved to be more of a liability than a help. The period saw new arrivals, or the return, of foreign radicals, some driven out of their own countries for their activities. The Lausanne patriots, Karpe de Gers, J. Cart, and Ferdinand Rosset, the Spanish radical José Marchena, the cosmopolitan Thomas Paine, and the British journalist Sampson Perry all fled prosecution for their views.[143] Meanwhile, the British radicals Mary Wollstonecraft and John Hurford Stone were lured by the early promise of the French Republic and, in Stone's case, by the business opportunities which he perceived there.[144] Joel Barlow had recovered sufficiently from his embarrassment over the Scioto affair to return to France in November 1792.[145] In January 1793, Tadeusz Kościuszko arrived in Paris from his refuge in Saxony as the Second Partition of Poland was being signed. Leader of the more radical wing of Polish resistance, his mission was to prompt French assistance. Georg Forster, the librarian of the elector of Mainz, arrived in Paris in March 1793 with Adam Lux, not as refugees, but as the delegates from the Rhineland Convention which requested annexation by France. They were stranded when the coalition forces drove the French from Germany.[146]

The first major development to affect foreign patriots in this period was the radicalization of revolutionary politics. Opposition to the monarchy was only temporarily suppressed after Varennes and, when it re-emerged as war approached, the aspirations of some foreign patriots looked distinctly conservative. Since 14 December 1791, unarmed bands of Belgians had flooded Lille and Douai in order to form a new Statist army, which was to be reviewed by Béthune-Charost. Soon, there were 4,000 exiles assembled in this northern corner of France. Such an alarming gathering at a diplomatically sensitive time stung the department of the Nord into acting harshly. All those who failed

[143] AN, F/7/4400; MAE, CP, Espagne, 634; R. Herr, *The Eighteenth Century Revolution in Spain* (Princeton, 1958), 273–4; Conway, *Life of Thomas Paine*, i. 350–1; Keane, *Tom Paine*, 344; Alger, *Englishmen*, 97–8.

[144] C. Tomalin, *The Life and Death of Mary Wollstonecraft* (London, 1974), 120; Woodward, *Une Anglaise*, 66–9; Erdman, *Commerce des Lumières*, 237; M. B. Stern, 'The English Press in Paris and its Successors', *Papers of the Bibliographical Society of America*, 74 (1980), 311.

[145] Durden, 'Joel Barlow', 338–9; A. Goodwin, *The Friends of Liberty: The English Democratic Movement in the Age of the French Revolution* (London, 1979), 253.

[146] Gooch, *Germany*, 312.

to appear before the municipality and obtain a certificate were to be marched to the frontier and expelled. Patrols were mounted to enforce the regulations. The local authorities acted from fear of disorder fomented by large groups of alienated foreign rebels. Nationally, however, the revolutionaries had other concerns: the Feuillant ministry desperately wanted peace with Austria, in order to provide the domestic stability needed to make the constitutional monarchy work. Dealing strictly with Belgian rebels sent a clear message of the government's intentions. On 21 December, the government issued orders to the Statists to disperse. Béthune-Charost was reduced to begging for scraps of support from the unlikely quarter of the Lille Jacobins.[147] Parisian radicals were particularly hostile to the young aristocrat's enterprise. While Camille Desmouslins had supported the Statists in 1789 and 1790, by the end of 1791 they were considered unworthy of such backing, composed as they were, in the words of Robespierre in May 1792, 'of the clergy, the nobility and the *bourgeoisie aristocratique*'. French principles corresponded more, Robespierre argued, with those of the rival Vonckist party.[148] Over the course of 1792, most of those exiles who had gathered around Béthune-Charost recognized that, for their own well-being, they were better off serving in the more radical Belgian legions.[149]

The outbreak of war provided the next challenge. For the Liégeois, the conflict was an opportunity to achieve their aims of a democratic republic, either through absorption by France or the formation of an independent state under French protection. The Vonckist Belgians began to think in the latter terms and they entered into negotiations with the Liégeois to find a common goal. Together, they formed the *comité des belges et liégeois unis*. As they sought to be treated as equals by the French, they realized that they would have to play an active part in their own liberation. The French-born Liégeois Pierre Lebrun therefore embarked on a political career in Paris in order to influence policy. On 18 December 1791, he led a deputation to the Legislative Assembly to muster support for a Liégeois legion.

---

[147] Lee, *Comités et les clubs*, 92–5; Sorel, *L'Europe et la Révolution Française*, ii. 312–13; Palmer, *Age of the Democratic Revolution*, ii. 75; Wahnich, *L'Impossible Citoyen*, 86–97.

[148] Robespierre, *Œuvres*, iv. 17.   [149] Lee, *Comités et les clubs*, 96.

He finished with a stirring, Brissotin-style call for universal liberty, but the revolutionaries were publicly reluctant. Eventually, the Liégeois and the Brabançons alike would raise their own legions to march in the vanguard of the French armies.[150] For those German radicals who accepted the crusading rhetoric, the war was the trumpet call for a general uprising. Saiffert, Schneider, Friedrich Cotta, and the Prussian lawyer Karl Clauer all launched propaganda tracts, pamphlets, leaflets, songs, and poems from Alsace into Germany.[151]

A few of the Genevan exiles also saw the war as a chance to bring the blessings of the French Revolution to their city, but they were a minority. After the fall of the monarchy, Clavière and Jacques Grenus were almost alone in envisaging the annexation of Geneva by France. This plan put them at odds with others, such as Reybaz. Clavière's political career in France offered more possibilities than his native city ever could and he lost sight of the original goals of his compatriots.[152] In contrast, for Clavière's Genevan critic, the outspoken monarchist Mallet du Pan, Paris was now a dangerous place and he toyed with moving the production of the *Mercure* to Brussels. Instead, the *monarchien* Pierre Malouet and the foreign minister Montmorin offered him a role as special emissary for Louis XVI to the courts of Vienna, Berlin, and the *émigrés* at Koblenz. He accepted this mission and never returned to France.[153]

Radicals from the Swiss cantons anticipated opportunities in the war ahead. If the original *club helvétique* had collapsed, they found willing allies among the Savoyards, whose energy was infectious. The Savoyard club was founded by Doppet and Desaix, an editor of the *Correspondance des Nations*, early in 1792. Originally called the *club de propagande des Alpes*, the society's aim was 'to bring liberty to Savoy'. Before long, Swiss patriots were admitted and so the group then called itself the *club des patriotes étrangers*. The title was sufficiently vague not to give the French authorities yet another diplomatic headache. It was from this society that sprang the *légion des*

[150] P. Harsin, *La Révolution liégeoise de 1789* (Brussels, 1954), 150–2; Lee, *Comités et les clubs*, 98–101; Raxhon, 'Réfugiés liégeois', 218.

[151] Ruiz, 'Jacobinisme allemand', 260–2.

[152] Bénétruy, *L'Atelier de Mirabeau*, 415, 418–19, 421–4.

[153] Acomb, *Mallet du Pan*, 249–53.

allobroges and propaganda aimed at Savoy. With the downfall of the monarchy and the first victories of the French Republic, times seemed auspicious enough to merit a more explicit name and the society became known as the *club des allobroges*.[154]

Despite the onset of the 'crusade for universal liberty', the revolutionaries were still cautious towards neutral powers. On 4 June 1792, the Paris Jacobins resisted the alarmist blandishments of John Oswald. This Scottish member of the club claimed that Thomas Cooper, a leading light of the Manchester Constitutional Society, had been arrested in Britain. Cooper had recently visited Paris and, along with James Watt, son of the steam innovator, had been given honorary membership of the Jacobins. In a blistering attack on the British government, Oswald demanded, in vain, an address of support for the Manchester Constitutional Society.[155]

The Jacobins cast aside their caution, first with the overthrow of the monarchy and then with the triumph of the French armies in the autumn of 1792. The first event further radicalized revolutionary politics and challenged the basis of foreign patriots' loyalty to the Revolution. This change is illustrated by the warmer reception given by the Jacobins to another of Oswald's proposals. On 22 August, the Jacobins agreed to send all British radical societies an address explaining 'the conspiracy of the traitor Louis XVI, and all the outrages which provoked the sacred insurrection of 10 August'.[156]

For some foreign radicals, the transition to a republic was smoothly made. Thomas Paine's republican credentials were already well-established and on 11 October he joined the Convention's constitutional committee, while David Williams presented his observations in January 1793.[157] Helen Maria Williams (no relation to David) and Mary Wollstonecraft both had personal ties to the Girondins, so accepted the Republic, but were horrified by the execution of the king.[158] Oswald and

---

[154] Doppet, *Mémoires*, 48–50, 57; Mathiez, *La Révolution et les étrangers*, 35–7.

[155] F.-A. Aulard, *La Société des Jacobins: Recueil de documents pour l'histoire de club des Jacobins de Paris*, 6 vols. (Paris, 1889–97), iii. 496, 499–502, 653–5; Erdman, *Commerce des Lumières*, 162.

[156] Aulard, *Jacobins*, iv. 230–1, 356–9.

[157] Conway, *Life of Thomas Paine*, i. 357; Williams, *Incidents*, 27, 119.

[158] Woodward, *Une Anglaise*, 58–9; R. M. Wardle, *Collected Letters of Mary Wollstonecraft* (Ithaca, NY, 1979), 227.

William Maxwell were among the pikemen who escorted Louis Capet to the scaffold. Wordsworth, living in Blois in 1792, attended the local Jacobin club and met the abbé Grégoire, the constitutional bishop of the department who was elected to the Convention. The poet wrote a defence of the democratic republic in his 'Letter to the Bishop of Llandaff', signing it 'a Republican'.[159]

The *comité des belges et liégeois unis* had thought in terms of a united Belgian republic since January 1792. Lebrun had attacked hereditary monarchy in his *Manifeste*, penned for the committee, which eventually drafted a Belgian constitution which anticipated the French 'Jacobin' version of 1793 by over fifteen months. It provided for universal manhood suffrage, the recall of deputies by the people, progressive taxation, and the *duty* of a people to rebel against oppression.[160] Among the Genevan exiles, Clavière was one of the few who did not appear to undergo any soul-searching as Louis XVI teetered on the brink of a second revolution in 1792.[161] The German Oelsner had long believed that Louis's flight in 1791 made the monarchy irreconcilable to the Revolution. As early as April 1792, he declared for a republic as the only alternative to anarchy, even though he withdrew from the Jacobin club a month later out of revulsion for Robespierre. Like Oelsner, Reinhard was repulsed by what he saw as Jacobin rabble-rousing, but since the flight to Varennes had made little secret of his desire to see the throne overturned.[162] Cloots had abandoned his wariness of republicanism on 21 April 1792, with the publication of his internationalist clarion call, *La République universelle*. Elected to the Convention, he voted for the death of the king.[163]

Those foreign patriots who failed to adopt the new political orthodoxy were forced out of revolutionary politics. Du Roveray had been reintegrated into the Genevan Council of Two Hundred in November 1790, from where he vehemently opposed Grenus's *égalisateurs*. Talleyrand secured Du Roveray's services in the French diplomatic mission to London in March

[159] Erdman, *Commerce des Lumières*, 245–9.
[160] Raxhon, 'Réfugiés liégeois', 217–18.
[161] Bénétruy, *L'Atelier de Mirabeau*, 420.
[162] Gooch, *Germany*, 328, 338–9; Ruiz, 'Jacobinisme allemand', 258–60.
[163] Soboul, 'Anacharsis Cloots', 34, 38.

1792, but the Genevan was recalled on 12 October, because of 'very pressing observations and denunciations', which came 'from every quarter'. According to Lebrun, however, it was Du Roveray's compatriot, Clavière, who was the source. Étienne Dumont also fell out of step with the Revolution, despite his friendship with republicans such as Brissot, because of 10 August and the September massacres. After a brief return to Geneva, he settled in Britain in March 1793.[164] In November 1792, the Lausanne patriot Cart inadvertently exposed the painful discrepancy between the aims of his colleagues and the ideology of the French Republic. While Cart and his friends wanted to restore the Estates as a legal barrier to the aristocracy of Lausanne, the French would not even countenance the existence of such a traditional institution.[165]

Archenholz of the Paris *Minerva* was a supporter of Lafayette, became affiliated to the Feuillants, and made no secret of his dislike of the Jacobins. After the overthrow of the monarchy, he was persecuted by Cloots, who denounced him as a counter-revolutionary agent and he scrambled to safety in Hamburg.[166] Dutch exiles with Feuillant or Fayettist sympathies such as Daverhoult and Marie-Antoine Cérisier likewise found their revolutionary careers abruptly cut short.[167] Daverhoult fought with the palace guard on 10 August and shot himself when he was arrested.[168] A German supporter of the constitutional monarchy, Georg Kerner flew to the Tuileries on 10 August in order to defend the king. Escaping unscathed, he was further shaken by the September massacres and the execution of Louis. Yet he managed to separate the ideals of 1789 from the violence which twisted and abused them. For that reason, he could not renounce the French Revolution altogether, choosing to remain loyal to its principles, even if the power to implement them was in the hands of those he detested.[169]

Those radicals who survived the shock from the tumbling

---

[164] MAE, CP, Angleterre, 583; Bénétruy, *L'Atelier de Mirabeau*, 380–99, 406–12, 427–31.

[165] AN, F/7/4400.

[166] Ruiz, 'Jacobinisme allemand', 259.

[167] Mathiez, *La Révolution et les étrangers*, 44.

[168] Schama, *Patriots and Liberators*, 151; J. Rosendaal, 'Qui était l'être suprême pour les réfugiés bataves?', *AhRf* 61 (1989), 201.

[169] Gooch, *Germany*, 340–2.

edifice of the monarchy and the September massacres were rapidly confronted with new choices with the apparently complete victories of the revolutionary armies. The 'First Propagandist Decree', or the 'Edict of Fraternity', of 19 November 1792 promised 'fraternity and help' to all peoples who 'wished to recover their liberty', but it soon became clear by the decree which followed, the 'Second Propagandist Decree' of 15 December, that this meant bowing to the needs of the French occupiers. Not all patriots from Brabant and Liège sought annexation by the French Republic, but the French feared that an independent Belgium would be too vulnerable to counterattack from Austria. The patriots therefore faced the uncomfortable choice between either submitting to French strategic interests or turning their backs on the Republic. Liégeois patriots persuaded their fellow-citizens to vote for *réunion* with France, but the Brabançons were less keen. The Vonckist Walckiers, for example, envisaged an independent federal republic of Belgium and Liège.[170] Those who sought independence had to yield to the superior strength of the French and go along with the votes for annexation. The representatives from the Rhine Convention, Forster, Lux, and Potocki, had fewer doubts. Although Forster knew that the vast majority of his fellow-countrymen resented the French invaders, he and his colleagues rejected the goal of independence on the grounds that a small state could not defend itself. At the end of March 1793, Forster presented the Convention with the request for annexation.[171]

Although their government was still at peace with France, British and Irish radicals established in Paris were inspired by the French victories and the Propagandist Decrees. On 24 November, fifty-two of these radicals signed an address which was presented to the Convention four days later. In the wake of the Edict of Fraternity, its ambiguous language could have been read as an invitation to the French to provide 'fraternity and help' to their neighbours across the Channel.[172] The impact of these radicals on French revolutionary policy was out of all proportion to their scanty numbers. Along with other addresses from

[170] Raxhon, 'Réfugiés liégeois', 217–19.

[171] Gooch, *Germany*, 312.

[172] J. G. Alger, 'The British Colony in Paris, 1792–1793', *English Historical Review*, 13 (1898), 673–4.

societies in Britain, the French were given the impression that the British people were quivering near the abyss of insurrection. Such an interpretation erroneously strengthened the case for a declaration of war on Britain.[173]

José Marchena did for Spain what the British exiles did for their country. The deterioration of French relations with their southern neighbour, which followed the overthrow of the monarchy, encouraged the French government to listen to Marchena's idea to organize 'some establishment to prepare [Spain] for revolution'. With his colleague, Joseph Hevia, and encouraged by Brissot, Marchena mooted the idea for a revolutionary committee on the Spanish frontier. As with foreign patriots of other nationalities, however, Marchena's aspirations for his country rested on traditional institutions, such as the Cortes, albeit in a more democratic form, rather than on any radical overhaul of the system of government. Such moderate goals were to leave him open to attack. Meanwhile, it was not until the Convention actually declared war on Spain on 7 March 1793 that Lebrun set the organization of *comités espagnols* into motion.[174]

The further test of loyalty to the Revolution in this period was the execution of Louis XVI, particularly for the British radicals in Paris, for whom the problem was compounded by the outbreak of war between France and Britain. Captain George Monro, an unofficial British agent, reported to the Foreign Office on 27 December that many of the exiles had become 'friends of royalty', which meant that they were opposed to the execution of Louis XVI. Paine and Helen Maria Williams both exerted themselves in trying to save Louis's life. The Scottish radical Thomas Muir, who was facing a charge of treason in Edinburgh, skipped bail to go to France specifically to persuade the Convention to spare the king. Although a republican, he was convinced that the execution would irreparably damage the cause of reform in Scotland. He arrived in France on 15 January, too late to add much weight to the efforts of other expatriates.[175] Meanwhile, the British community was breaking up under the pressure of events. On 11 January, Paine and John Frost came to

---

[173] Goodwin, *Friends of Liberty*, 244–52.
[174] MAE, CP, Espagne, 634; Herr, *Eighteenth Century Revolution*, 282–3.
[175] C. Bewley, *Muir of Huntershill* (Oxford, 1981), 56.

blows over the question of sending a second address to the Convention. Paine was in favour, Frost passionately against.[176]

For the majority of the British radicals, the watershed was the outbreak of war on 1 February. Most were fearful of appearing as traitors, particularly when, for all their support of the French Revolution, their main concern was the cause of reform at home. Among those who suffered from such divided loyalties were those forty radicals who sailed back across the Channel, including John Hurford Stone.[177] Some were willing to stay in France, risking accusations of treason. Stone himself would be back in France by April. Mary Wollstonecraft turned down a place in a carriage bound for the coast, explaining to Ruth Barlow in February that 'all the affection I have for the French is for the whole nation' and that she was 'writing a plan of education' for the Convention's *comité d'instruction publique*.[178]

Despite their claims of unity of purpose with the Revolution, all foreign patriots had their own agenda to follow, which meant that they would fall in with those revolutionaries whose interests or aims would best serve their own. Relationships developed between groups of foreign radicals and French politicians, which by 1793 mirrored the Girondin–Montagnard divide. Early in 1792, tensions within the Belgian and Liégeois committee had already led to a split between moderates, such as Lebrun, Bassenge, Fabry, and Walckiers, who forged ties with the Brissotins, and radicals who, after the fall of the monarchy, would associate closely with the Montagnards.[179] Those Dutch Patriots who sought French military might to rid the United Provinces of the Stadholder also made associations similar to the Liégeois moderates. Joannes de Kock, for example, cultivated links with Lebrun and Dumouriez.[180] Such associations would put these patriots under suspicion during the Terror.

With exceptions such as Oswald who supported the Mountain, those British radicals who remained in Paris gravitated towards the Girondins. Drawing on a tradition of constitution-

---

[176] *Moniteur* (22 Nov. 1792); Tomalin, *Mary Wollstonecraft*, 132–3; Erdman, *Commerce des Lumières*, 242; Alger, 'British Colony', 675.

[177] Alger, *Englishmen*, 65; Alger, 'British Colony', 675–6.

[178] Woodward, *Une Anglaise amie*, 79–80; Wardle, *Collected Letters of Mary Wollstonecraft*, 230.

[179] Delange-Janson, *Ambroise*, 25–6; Godechot, *Grande Nation*, 213.

[180] Mathiez, *La Révolution et les étrangers*, 45; Rosendaal, 'L'Être suprême', 201–2.

alism, the British admired this political grouping because they appeared to be less willing than the left, or the Mountain, to appeal to the mob.[181] Among the Germans, Karl Reinhard had known Vergniaud, Guadet, and Ducos since his days in Bordeaux. Ultimately, Georg Kerner supported the Girondins, because, compared with the Jacobins, he saw them as the lesser of two evils.[182] The Genevan Clavière unambiguously associated with the Girondins, being the Brissotin finance minister between March and June 1792 and again after the fall of the monarchy. On 8 September, he was a target of the venomous Marat, who spat that he was 'devoted to Brissot's faction, which put him in his post'.[183] From his arrival in Paris in January 1793, Kościuszko made overtures to the Girondins, but found them ill-informed about Poland. He received no help from the Mountain, either. In the spring, Danton, as the Committee of Public Safety's first spokesman for foreign affairs, was worried that French help, even if it were possible in the military crisis, would merely draw the coalition forces closer together in their determination to crush revolution in Europe.[184]

Some foreign radicals associated with the Mountain. The Savoyard Doppet hedged his bets as member of both the Jacobin and Cordelier clubs. While serving as president of the former, he praised Dumouriez when the general was appointed foreign minister in March 1792. Yet just before 10 August, he was accused by the Jacobins of extremism, of being overly influenced by the Cordeliers, and of preaching 'democracy'.[185] The defeat of the French in the Alps in December led him to believe that the Girondins were incapable of protecting the Republic, which by now included his native Savoy, and he became a Montagnard. It was to prove a wise choice for his military career.[186] Cloots did not think of himself as a Girondin, but initially those who heard him describe the war in his expansive, internationalist excitement

[181] Gerbod, 'Résidents britanniques', 344–5.

[182] Gooch, *Germany*, 328, 342.

[183] Marat, J.-P., 'L'Ami du Peuple, aux Bons Français', in *Les Pamphlets de Marat*, ed. C. Vellay (Paris, 1911), 322.

[184] S. Meller, '"Pour notre liberté et pour la vôtre": 200ᵉ anniversaire des légions polonaises qui combattirent aux côtés de l'armée française sous le commandement du général Bonaparte', *AhRf* 70 (1998), 313.

[185] Doppet, *Mémoires*, 45–6, 48.

[186] Mathiez, *La Révolution et les étrangers*, 47.

made the association. In his newspaper, Gorsas recommended him as trustworthy during the elections to the Convention. Marat acidly warned his readers on 30 August 1792 that Cloots was an 'informer for Berlin', who sought to 'serve . . . the enemies of liberty'.[187] Cloots, however, read the lie of the immediate political landscape well and dramatically broke with the Girondins. Either impressed or alarmed by the brutal, destructive power of the Parisian crowd, he moved leftwards in an attempt to seduce the sympathy of the militants. In a speech to the Jacobin club on 17 November, he attacked Brissot and his friends and sat with the Mountain in the Convention.[188]

The defeats of early 1793 and the hostility with which 'liberated' peoples met the French invaders discredited Brissot's 'crusade for universal liberty'. For the time being, the foreign radicals who remained in France were not yet treated with the same disdain as their indifferent countrymen. They were the enlightened spirits who might still spread the gospel. Between October 1791 and March 1793, foreign patriots were faced with a series of rapid political changes which presented them with some stark choices. While the judgements they made in the face of the outbreak of war, the overthrow of the monarchy, the first French victories, and the execution of Louis XVI were determined in a large part by their own principles, interests, and aspirations, they were also aware that their decisions might affect their political survival. As the net of political orthodoxy was pulled tighter, foreign patriots could not remain aloof from the internal political battles in France. Yet, despite the establishment of a Republic which demanded purer political credentials, foreigners could still organize politically and were encouraged to do so, particularly under the Brissotin or Girondin ministries. While not formally citizens, they therefore tried to engage in the political process, entering into relationships with those politicians who seemed to suit their interests best. Revolutionary politics, however, were still in flux. The choices made in this period would return to stalk foreign radicals during the Terror.

---

[187] Marat, J.-P., 'Marat, L'Ami du Peuple, aux amis de la Patrie', in *Les Pamphlets de Marat*, 310–11.

[188] G. Avenel, *Anacharsis Cloots: L'Orateur du genre humain* (Paris, 1976), 290–1; Soboul, 'Anacharsis Cloots', 36–8.

V

For those foreigners who participated in French economic life, the greatest challenge was the war. Merchants of all nationalities found that, even if they were not enemy subjects, it disrupted their livelihood. This was particularly the case when France fought the two major maritime powers of Europe, Britain and the United Provinces. It was not until the autumn of 1793 that the Convention decreed the confiscation of enemy property and a navigation act against enemy shipping, but the conflict could present other problems. The maritime tradition of arming corsairs which would seize enemy shipping persisted, even if the war was meant to be fought on new principles. The rules of maritime prizes still applied and this feature of warfare was used against the British and the Dutch as it had been in conflicts before 1789.

Privateering on British and Dutch goods began early in the war. On 1 March 1793, the Convention received from the Jacobins in Bordeaux a donation from British and Dutch merchants in gratitude for the exemptions on grain and other vital commodities.[189] British and Dutch ships carrying other cargo were, however, seen as fair game. At the *tribunal de commerce* at Dunkirk later that month, the proprietors of four British vessels, apparently used for smuggling French goods across the Channel, unsuccessfully brought legal action against the Gravelines corsair who had captured them.[190]

The prosperity of foreign merchants was not only jeopardized by the behaviour of the revolutionaries, but also by the response of foreign governments. Britain, Spain, and Russia each made proclamations and laws which, while intended as prophylactics against the contagion of revolutionary propaganda, also made commerce between their subjects and French citizens suspect, if not actually illegal. The loyalties of merchants whose governments were hostile to France were tested.

While foreign merchants could relocate with relative ease by finding new ports and new trading partners, manufacturers, with their workshops, factories, and labour forces, were more inert. Besides his political radicalism, John Hurford Stone's

---

[189] *AP* lix. 500–1.   [190] *AP* lx. 223–4.

investment in his French enterprises, including, among others, a sal-ammoniac factory, might explain his decision to return to France in the spring of 1793, risking a charge of treason in Britain. The French government itself remained conscious of the need to acquire and retain foreign expertise, particularly in textiles, if France was to fight off cheap imports of British cotton. The state therefore remained active in coaxing foreigners either to come to or to remain in France. By January 1792, Philemon Pickford was being paid a bounty of 300 *livres* for each mule built in his Paris workshop, along with a salary of 48 *livres* a week for developing a machine which might spin finer cloth. By the end of the year, the *bureau de commerce* had induced John McCloude, who had been working in France since before the Revolution, to set up twenty-three fly-shuttle looms at Auguste and Jacques Périer's works and fifty more at Evreux.[191]

The radicalization of revolutionary politics, the war, and the economic crisis still presented foreign manufacturers with extraordinary pressures. Oberkampf, for example, was faced with growing militancy among his workers. While an organized action by his workforce in March 1792 had purely economic roots, as owner of a former *manufacture royale* with foreign origins and with 9 per cent of his workers recruited from abroad, Oberkampf was understandably keen to preclude any insinuations about his patriotism, both as a foreigner and as a one-time beneficiary of royal favour. The difficulties of balancing these pressures with his private business interests are made clear by his response to the decree of the *patrie en danger*. When ten of his workers enrolled as volunteers, Oberkampf gave them 300 *livres* each and promised them as much again on their return. By September 1792, however, he was grumbling privately that the war was making labour scarce.[192]

Unlike Oberkampf, the Dutch banker Vandenyver and his two sons showed an unfortunate lack of political tact in running their business. When Madame du Barry visited London between 1791 and 1793, the Vandenyvers underwrote the letters of credit which ensured her a comfortable stay. They would come to regret this generosity.[193] This family was not alone among

---

[191] Harris, *Industrial Espionage*, 380–1, 392.

[192] Chassagne, *Oberkampf*, 171; Chapman and Chassagne, *European Textile Printers*, 122–3, 178. [193] Lüthy, *Banque Protestante*, ii. 323.

foreign bankers to draw poisonous attacks from revolutionaries who feared the influence of foreign money. On 15 December 1792, taking up an attack which first flowed from Marat's bitter pen, Carra wrote in his *Annales patriotiques* that the Belgian financier Walckiers was an agent of Austria. Nine days later, he accused him of handling the money and gold 'which Marie-Antoinette stole from the French nation' and alleged that, while pretending to be a Belgian patriot, he was using Austrian funds to ensure that Brabant would be returned to the Habsburgs.[194] In the following year, such attacks on foreign bankers would have lethal consequences. It is noticeable, however, that while the revolutionary leadership was quick to blame foreign merchants and bankers for the Republic's woes, the popular movement itself focused its ire on distinctly French targets. In the spring of 1793, with the value of the *assignat* falling from 50 per cent of its face value in February, popular anger was directed not against foreigners, but against more obvious enemies. They were the Girondins and those considered guilty of economic crimes: hoarders, *l'aristocratie marchande*, monopolists, military contractors, bankers, and financial speculators.[195] Over the course of the summer, however, the *sans-culottes* proved more open to the suggestion that foreigners were to blame for the hardship.

While foreign merchants could respond to the difficult conditions with some flexibility, manufacturers and bankers could not. If they were to protect their investments and businesses in France, they, like other types of foreigners, had to show increasingly that their patriotic credentials were sound. While Oberkampf, long established in the community of Jouy, immersed himself in local politics to protect his livelihood, bankers such as Vandenyver and Walckiers did so less easily. As the Revolution and the war intensified, they found it hard to explain their relations with some of their more embarrassing clients and their financial ties with foreign banking houses, some of which had dealings with enemy governments. With the deepening political crisis in 1793, such associations would become extremely dangerous.

---

[194] Mathiez, *La Révolution et les étrangers*, 109–10.
[195] A. Mathiez, *La Vie chère et le mouvement social sous la terreur*, 2 vols. (Paris, 1973), i. 162–3, 209.

VI

Revolutionary cosmopolitanism became more militant between October 1791 and March 1793, because of the war, but the period also saw the emergence of the more exclusive implications of patriotism. The former encouraged foreigners to participate in the political life of the Revolution through naturalization, membership of political societies, consultation on the new republican constitution, employment in diplomatic missions, in government departments, and even in the Convention. It also permitted foreigners to fight alongside their French brothers in specially organized legions and encouraged foreign patriots to take on a propaganda role in the war which, by the end of March 1793, had set western Europe aflame. In their stridency, the revolutionaries abandoned the diplomatic caution shown by the Constituent, but this was due less to the revolutionaries' attachment to abstract, universalist principles than an assessment of their own political interests. In 1792, it was originally hoped that French military success would be assisted by peoples who would welcome the French as liberators. For those like the Girondins and Dumouriez, who pinned their personal aspirations on such a triumph, the use of foreigners in most branches of the revolutionary state was not only a propaganda tool, but also a viable means of achieving their aims.

As the Revolution became increasingly radical, however, the political credentials of those foreigners had to be screened if their contribution to the cause was not to be counter-productive, if not actually malignant. The Swiss troops were finally cast aside, because after 10 August the benefits of their discipline and experience were offset by the apparent threat they posed to the internal safety of the nation. Such political failings, and not foreign nationality, were becoming the criteria for exclusion from the life of the Revolution. As the revolutionaries alienated more strands of political opinion, and as the fortunes of war fluctuated, so they became increasingly worried about domestic security. Such concerns began to override diplomatic considerations in the treatment of foreigners. The imposition of passports and surveillance reflected this shift and gave xenophobia both legal form and official channels through which it could be expressed. French citizens were subjected to similar infringements on their civil liberties and, for now, it was political associations and behaviour, rather than nationality, which was the primary consideration. If this does not say much for the revolutionaries' tolerance of dissent, it does suggest that they did not regard civic virtue as an exclusively French trait.

This period did, however, witness the early development of discriminatory legislation against foreigners. Attempts to watch and control their activities meant that nationality was becoming a matter of daily concern. By the end of March 1793, passports and the surveillance committees represented the lengthening reach of the state, touching the movements of foreigners and French people alike. By explicitly referring to foreigners in the law of 21 March, the state was trying to make French citizens more aware that certain people were outsiders. Citizens were beginning to be encouraged to keep an eye open and, if necessary, to denounce foreigners. Foreign status would be felt more keenly than before. Legal differences between citizens and non-citizens were sharpening and there were the first signs that nationality might become a criterion for exclusion from French social life. This development was, however, only just beginning and, for the time being, relatively few foreigners were seriously affected by these early, if sinister, signals.

If the revolutionaries' concern for domestic stability made them more willing to err both from their libertarian impulses and from the earlier diplomatic caution, they were not yet ready to repudiate measures taken by the Constituent Assembly if there was no urgent need to do so. While the dismissal of the Swiss regiments was dictated by fears of their counter-revolutionary potential, the foreign clergy remained a privileged if beleaguered group, with their property and their institutions remaining independent of state control. Their status as foreigners still protected them from revolutionary legislation out of diplomatic necessity, until Britain entered the war, and because the revolutionaries recognized their property rights. Infringements were the product of local initiative rather than the result of legal policy.

The fate of foreigners in France was increasingly linked to their political reliability, which meant that they would be at the mercy of the sweeping political tides which were gathering strength. Not only were revolutionary politics still fluid at the end of March 1793, but, for fifteen months thereafter, the Republic would be fighting for its very life. Patriotism was to become increasingly focused on the survival of France itself and many foreigners had already become associated with politicians whose ideas and behaviour were to be discredited by crisis and betrayal. These foreigners would themselves reek of defeat and treason and would be excluded from the life of the Republic.

4

The Terror

On 28 December 1793, at 3 o'clock in the morning, Thomas Paine was disturbed in White's Hotel in the passage des Petits-Pères. Two commissioners from the Committee of General Security had come to arrest him in the cold night. Behind them, three officials and a witness from the Guillaume Tell section filed through the door, escorted by a squad of five National Guardsmen. Paine had been expecting them and had been scribbling desperately only six hours before in his permanent lodgings in the *faubourg* Saint-Denis, finishing the final forty-four pages of part one of the *Age of Reason*. He had already entrusted the rest of the manuscript to Joel Barlow, for fear that it would otherwise be destroyed. After he put down his pen, he had walked to the passage des Petits-Pères, because that was still his address listed in the Convention's almanach, where he waited for his impending arrest. Now that they had arrived, the officials searched White's Hotel before leading Paine out. The morning was already well advanced by the time this alarming group of people clattered up to 63, rue du faubourg Saint-Denis, where the exhausted commissioners finished their inspection of Paine's papers at 4 o'clock in the afternoon. Nothing suspicious was found, although the officials scrutinized the pages which Paine had just written. One congratulated him on his work and he was allowed to add these last sheets to the rest of the manuscript already in Barlow's hands. After this gruelling process, Paine was marched through the darkening and cluttered streets to the Luxembourg prison. There he stayed incarcerated for over ten months. The guillotine did not kill him, but the illness contracted in the squalor almost did. He was finally released on 4 November 1794.[1]

Thomas Paine's predicament symbolizes that of many foreigners during the Terror. The legal motive for his arrest was

[1] Keane, *Tom Paine*, 401–2; Conway, *Life of Thomas Paine*, ii. 101–10.

that his original British nationality made him an enemy subject. He himself was certain that it was because he was a foreigner, despite his honorary naturalization as a French citizen. Significantly, Paine was only released when the American ambassador to Paris, James Monroe, recognized him as a United States citizen, rather than as a British subject.[2] On 5 August 1793, he had also been denounced in the Jacobins for 'very great correspondence with England' and for being among the 'agents of Pitt'.[3] Paine may, therefore, have suffered from the retreat of the Revolution from its earlier cosmopolitanism and the development of a xenophobic, exclusive patriotism. The Thermidorians certainly explained that Paine had aroused Robespierre's hostility because 'he had worked to establish liberty in the old and new worlds'.[4] Historians have also suggested that foreigners like Paine suffered during the Terror because the cosmopolitanism which they represented was now suspect.[5]

Yet the statements of the revolutionaries themselves suggest that two political motives lay behind the arrest. First, he had been close to the Girondins. Paine had rushed to the Convention on 2 June in order to lend his intellectual weight against the coup, but was warned off by Danton, who told him that to assist his Girondin friends might have meant adding his own name to the proscription list. Paine had then sensibly avoided politics altogether, living quietly in the *faubourg* Saint-Denis for almost seven weeks.[6] Still, on 18 June 1793, the Convention had received a letter from the citizens of Arras, which amounted to a timely renunciation of the 'Girondin' deputies for the Pas-de-Calais, among whom was Thomas Paine. The instigator of this move may well have been Joseph Lebon, who was Paine's substitute.[7] The charges of *girondisme* mounted. On 25 December, Bourdon de l'Oise remarked that Paine had not set foot in the Convention since the Brissotins had been expelled. The next

---

[2] Conway, *Life of Thomas Paine*, ii. 136–8.

[3] AN, BB/3/72.

[4] E. B. Courtois, *Rapport fait au nom de la commission chargée de l'examen des papiers trouvés chez Robespierre et ses complices* (Paris, An III), 39.

[5] Mathiez, *La Révolution et les étrangers*, 137; Soboul, *Les Sans-Culottes*, 208; R. Cobb, *The Police and the People: French Popular Protest 1789–1820* (Oxford, 1970), 130.

[6] Keane, *Tom Paine*, 380, 383.

[7] *AP* lxvi. 664; Conway, *Life of Thomas Paine*, ii. 79–80.

day, Thuriot cited Paine's opposition to the death penalty for Louis XVI and the fact that he always voted 'with men recognized as traitors to the *patrie*'. When a deputation of Americans led by Joel Barlow sought his freedom in the Convention on 27 January, the president, Vadier, paid tribute to Paine's achievements, but added that 'his genius has not perceived that which has regenerated France', seeing the French Revolution only through the 'illusions' conjured up by 'the false friends of our revolution'. It was not his nationality which mattered, but the fact that his conformity to the current political orthodoxy was suspect.[8]

Bourdon also let slip a second political motive. On 25 December he stated, 'I know that he is intriguing with a former agent of the office of foreign affairs.'[9] This hinted at the hidden but probably the most potent reason behind Paine's arrest. It was a misguided attempt by the government to control any damage which Paine might have caused to French relations with the United States. The ministry of foreign affairs had used Paine in September in the hope that he could help procure desperately needed flour from the Americans.[10] Yet this work simply stoked more suspicion. Among those responsible for fanning the flames was the American ambassador to Paris, Gouverneur Morris, who was hostile to Paine's democratic republicanism. He suggested that Paine supported the efforts of France's wayward envoy to the United States, Edmond Genêt, to 'revolutionize' the Mississippi valley. Genêt was the agent referred to by Bourdon, implying that Paine was severely damaging relations with France's only ally.[11] After Paine had been locked up, Robespierre wrote in his notebook, 'Ask that Thomas Payne be indicted, for the interests of America as much as those of France.'[12] Paine's removal from public life was apparently expedient for French diplomatic relations.

The period from April 1793 to July 1794 witnessed the most acute measures taken against foreigners. They can be explained by a decline of revolutionary cosmopolitanism and the heated

---

[8] *AP* lxxxii. 303, 339; *Moniteur*, 130 (An II).
[9] *AP* lxxxii. 303.
[10] Keane, *Tom Paine*, 384–5.
[11] Conway, *Life of Thomas Paine*, ii. 80–96.
[12] Courtois, *Papiers trouvés chez Robespierre*, 211.

expansion of xenophobic patriotism, but these were not the only ingredients in the poisoned pot. Paine's experience suggests that the revolutionaries' treatment of foreigners was not always dictated by xenophobia, but, first, by considerations of their loyalty to an increasingly demanding political regime and, secondly, by concerns about the benefits or damage they could bring to the Republic. If Paine's arrest seems to have been dictated by political motives, the revolutionaries were practical enough to protect foreigners who did not appear to threaten the government and whose skills and services might be of use.

I

The renunciation of the two Propagandist Decrees on 13 April and the overthrow of the Girondins on 2 June had potentially sinister implications for foreigners in France. The first represented a retreat from the militant cosmopolitanism of the previous year and a patriotism focused more exclusively on the nation itself. The second narrowed the scope of what was regarded by the revolutionaries as legitimate political opinion.

Initially, foreigners were still encouraged to adopt France as their *patrie*. The fundamental principles which defined citizens as French and which permitted the assimilation of foreigners into the national community remained almost unaltered. The Montagnard constitution, voted through on 24 June 1793, reduced the residence requirement from five years to one, like its Girondin predecessor. Economic barriers to naturalization were lowered, with the stipulation that a foreigner must simply live in France by the fruits of his own labour, in marked contrast to the more demanding provisions of the Constitution of 1791. Broader social contributions were also encouraged, with such additional options as the adoption of a child or the support of an elderly citizen. The cosmopolitan claims attached to French nationality were retained in a clause which would allow the legislature to grant citizenship to any foreigner 'worthy of humanity'. It also offered 'asylum to foreigners banished from their countries for the cause of liberty'.[13] There was some

---

[13] *AP* lxvii. 145, 150.

opposition from Mazoyer, who sneeringly urged his colleagues not to 'degrade the dignity of the French name by lavishing it out haphazardly, by granting it, without any investigation, to that crowd of adventurers who are nothing but the muck and filth of nations'. He was also anxious about the role of foreigners within the French state 'at the head of the armies, in every administration, in every office'.[14] Such fears over foreign influence were widely shared, but this was partly why the revolutionaries sought to encourage the assimilation of those foreigners who could serve the state. The Constitution of 1793 provided the most generous conditions for naturalization France had seen since 1789.[15]

Those who failed to take the opportunity to assimilate might, however, be excluded from state structures. In the wake of the coup of 2 June, foreigners who worked at the *assignat* administration were sacked, on the grounds that they no longer had the right to work in the bureaucracy, although no law had been passed to this effect. On 19 June, the eighteen foreigners, from Germany, Belgium, Switzerland, and elsewhere, issued an emotional appeal to the deputies. Denouncing 'a great attack on the rights of man', they protested that, while they did not have 'the advantage of being born French', their unwavering patriotism had brought them to dedicate 'all their energies to the maintenance and strengthening of the one and indivisible French Republic, their adoptive *patrie*'.[16] Their plight exposed the central ideological contradiction of the French Revolution. On the one hand, the rights of man were universal, which implied that men could enjoy their rights anywhere. On the other, the principle of national sovereignty suggested that people could only assert their political rights in the society of which they were explicitly members. Foreigners who wished to serve the cause of humanity could do so in their own countries, but not in France, unless they were naturalized. Those who refused to abandon their original, foreign identity could not be fully assimilated and could not enjoy the rights of citizenship.

[14] Mathiez, *La Révolution et les étrangers*, 135–6; Wahnich, *L'Impossible Citoyen*, 77.
[15] B. Schnapper, 'La Naturalisation française au XIXe siècle: Les Variations d'une politique', in *La Condition juridique de l'étranger hier et aujourd'hui: Actes du colloque, 1988* (Nijmegen, 1988), 209–21; J. Gaudemet, 'L'Étranger: De l'image au statut', in Lequin, *Histoire des étrangers*, 47–53.
[16] Wahnich, *L'Impossible Citoyen*, 122–4; *AP* lxvi. 729.

It was not clear, however, that this meant that foreigners could not assume salaried positions within the French state. Collot d'Herbois, president of the Convention, promised the petitioners that his colleagues would examine their situation and passed their protests to the Committee of General Security. The Committee reported back on 11 August, but the Convention referred the question to the *comité des assignats*.[17] Such delays in tackling the question certainly did not help the foreigners involved, but it does suggest that the revolutionaries were hesitant over expelling useful and politically loyal people from state service simply because of foreign birth. On 14 June, the Convention asked the Committee of Public Safety to find military and administrative offices for foreign political refugees.[18] Foreigners continued to perform bureaucratic duties and take political action at local level, in some cases retaining their posts for the duration of the Year II. The purge of the Girondins on 2 June, however, had expelled from the scope of republican orthodoxy a substantial body of opinion. The demand for vigilance and surveillance was now more acute, to distinguish between who could be trusted and who could not. At first, the Convention was uncertain about how to proceed. On 6 June, the deputies discussed a general law against foreigners, but the proposal was sent to the Committee of Public Safety for further consideration.[19] Most revolutionaries still believed that foreigners responsible for disorders in France were a minority identifiable through the existing system of surveillance and that a general expulsion would be counterproductive.

They had already resurrected the Ancien Régime practice of holding 'hostages', but this was in response to the capture of French commissioners by the allies. Certain prisoners of war were to guarantee their safety. On 8 September, a dozen 'women of distinction' from Mainz were also taken hostage until the wives of Rhenish political exiles were allowed to join their husbands.[20] The broadest measure of hostage-taking came after the surrender of Toulon to the British. From 9 September, all British subjects arrested in France were to answer for the

[17] *AP* lxxii. 29–30.
[18] *AP* lxvi. 516; lxix. 143–4.
[19] *AP* lxvi. 109–12, 173–9.
[20] *AP* lxiv. 707; lxxiii. 526.

conduct of Admiral Hood. Workers, artists, 'and other useful citizens' would be exempt from this law.[21]

The Convention was finally persuaded to overcome its initial squeamishness about overstepping traditional practices by the mysterious activities of an alleged British agent in Lille in the summer of 1793. The Convention voted on 1 August to arrest all subjects of enemy powers who had arrived in France since 1789.[22] The law went beyond the reprisals traditionally accepted as part of the *droit des gens*. Only days after it had been voted, therefore, doubts were raised about its applicability. Such back-pedalling was not popular with some deputies,[23] but local authorities, while implementing the law, nodded to the objections expressed in the Convention. Between 3 August and 21 October, the *comité de surveillance* of the Observatoire section in Paris arrested twenty-four foreigners and left five at large. Of those arrested, three were subsequently released. Leniency was shown to enemy subjects who did not appear to pose any serious threat to domestic security, such as an Irish cleric from Douai, who was vouched for locally, and two pain-wracked Piedmontese residents of a *hospice venérien*. The section proved even more reluctant to arrest foreign patriots, allowing seven British subjects to live under house arrest because an inspection of their papers 'has yielded proof only of the purest civic virtue [*civisme*]'.[24]

The efficiency of the local authorities in executing the law could not be taken for granted. The Unité section in Paris sent out nineteen commissioners, who investigated 269 names.[25] Forty-nine of these were crossed from the lists, either because some appeared more than once, or because the foreigners in question had presumably left the section. Even so, of the 220 remaining entries, twenty-one were still repetitions of the same name, leaving a total of 199 people listed as foreign in the section, representing a tiny fraction of the population of around 21,600. In fact, the number of foreigners in the section was undoubtedly larger, as those mentioned were all men, reflecting the prevalent assumption that women and children assumed the nationality of the husband or father.[26] The officials

[21] *AP* lxxiii. 573, 600.
[22] *AP* lxx. 90–109.
[23] Mathiez, *La Révolution et les étrangers*, 145–6.
[24] AN, F/7*/2514.
[25] AN, F/7/4779.
[26] R. Monnier and A. Soboul, *Répertoire du personnel sectionnaire parisien en l'an II* (Paris, 1985), 439.

failed to establish the nationalities of forty-six of the 199. Two of those described as foreign were actually French citizens, coming from Alsace. Of the 151 remaining, the vast majority (123 if one excludes the sixteen Belgians and the Liègeois) were enemy subjects. Most, therefore, would be affected by the legislation against foreigners in the coming months. The commissioners undoubtedly missed a large number of transients and migrant workers, but the machinery of the Terror equated foreigners with a danger out of all proportion to their numbers.

The fact that there was repetition on the lists suggests that, when it came to implementing the legislation, some local authorities were not always effective. The appearance of some names more than once shows that the commissioners duplicated each other's work, with several officials visiting the same street at different times verifying the names and addresses of the same foreigners. Nineteen foreigners were checked on at least twice. The unfortunate Hackermann, a seamster from Frankfurt, had his details checked by no less than three different commissioners. It was not, however, only the relatively few repetitions which suggest either a lack of organization or, possibly, reluctance on the part of the commissioners. The rue de Buci and the other main thoroughfares of the section, such as the rues de Seine, Jacob, Mazarine, and Boucheries, were the most frequently tramped by the officials. An intrepid few strayed into the darker alleys such as the cour du Cardinal, to discover a Polish cobbler quietly plying his trade, or the fantastically named rue Cour du Dragon, where a Prussian broommaker lived in the shadow of the Abbaye prison. Such people were only visited once.

The sketchiness of some of the details suggests that the section was dependent on the co-operation of local citizens and foreigners alike. While inevitably some Parisians had scores to settle and willingly helped, it is likely that others were resistant, and refused to divulge too much information on those foreign neighbours whom they liked, or upon whom they were dependent for goods, services, or employment. The sectional authorities of the Unité may also have had their own reasons to drag their feet. Some of those who appear on the list of foreigners were themselves involved in sectional politics, which may have provided reason enough for the officials to tread carefully. Christian Dimpré, from Nassau in Germany, served on the civil committee. The cobbler Jean-Baptiste Coppin, from Liège, was involved in the *société populaire* and would later join the Parisian *armée révolutionnaire*.[27] When the section appealed for volunteers to act as guardians of the seals placed on the papers of those foreigners who were actually arrested, the first name on the list was a German named Lock.[28] The section was not twitching with indiscriminate suspicion against all foreigners.

The Genevan Louis David Sandoz was not even mentioned. Unlike most of those foreigners listed, he was well-to-do, as a printer and engraver, and politically influential, as a member of the section's revolutionary committee and National Guard detachment.[29] He was therefore in a position to ensure his own security from harassment. Most of the foreigners named were typical of poor, migrant workers of the time. As seamsters, pin-makers, cobblers, and the like, they may not have been in Paris for very long and did not enjoy Sandoz's influence. Yet much of the revolutionary bile spat at foreigners was aimed precisely at those who had money or power, as they were more likely to be able to inflict damage. Sandoz's protection was probably as much due to his political credentials as to his position in the section. The humbler, poorer foreigners were certainly more vulnerable to harassment from the authorities, but their day-to-day struggle to live at least meant that they kept a low political profile. This anonymity may have protected them from the treacherous tides of revolutionary politics.

Other sections or communes may have been more efficient than the Unité. The officials may have become more practised with time, or as the pressure to conform to the will of the central government intensified. Still, when the Convention reviewed its measures with the decree of 6 September, Garnier-Saintes persuaded his colleagues to except foreign workers useful to the war effort.[30] Foreigners in France for their education were also exempt, as one of Jacques-Louis David's pupils found early in October, provided their landlords vouched for their *civisme*.[31]

---

[27] Monnier and Soboul, *Répertoire*, 441; R. Cobb, *The People's Armies. The Armées révolutionnaires: Instrument of the Terror in the Departments, April 1793 to Floréal Year II*, tr. M. Elliott (New Haven, Conn., 1987), 106–7.

[28] AN, F/7/4779.   [29] Cobb, *People's Armies*, 106.
[30] *AP* lxxiii. 462–3.   [31] *AP* lxxvi. 131–2.

The law also protected any foreigner who could provide evidence of 'civic virtue and attachment to the French Revolution'. These wide loopholes were remarkable in the fraught atmosphere charged by the news of Toulon's surrender to the British.

Many as the exemptions were, in other respects the new law went further than that of 1 August, as neutral subjects were also required to prove their *civisme*. Those who did so received a *certificat d'hospitalité*, while those who failed were to be expelled as suspects. In practice, some were imprisoned, because on 7 June 1794 the Committee of Public Safety had to order the release of neutrals who had been arrested, on the grounds that they should have been expelled instead.[32] Institutionalized suspicion was now aimed at foreigners of all nationalities, and not just at enemy subjects. The law of 6 September also permitted French citizens to denounce suspicious foreigners. The decree encapsulated both a recognition that many foreigners were useful to the war effort and a growing phobia of foreign subversion.

Even so, the first measure aimed at a specific nationality was less a step towards 'nationalizing' the war than a resort to *représailles*. The first seizures of property were inflicted on the Spanish in retaliation for the behaviour of their government. The expulsion of French citizens from Spain and the confiscation and sale of their property were bad enough. The stories of the relentlessness with which Spanish creditors were pursuing their expelled French debtors put the icing on this bitter cake. These complaints were merely the shrill crescendo of often justifiable moaning which had arisen since the autumn of 1792. From then until France went to war with Spain in March, the French plenipotentiary minister to Madrid, Bourgoing, sent dispatches back to Paris listing cases of official harassment of French people.[33] Even before hostilities had officially opened, Lebrun had received news from the French *chargé d'affaires*, d'Urtubrise, that Spanish edicts against French citizens were being executed to their fullest extent.[34] All this combined to persuade the revolutionaries to overcome their reluctance to seize Spanish property. Expulsion of enemy subjects and the confiscation of their wealth were employed in wars prior to the Revolution. The

---

[32] MAE, ADP, France, Carton 8.   [33] MAE, CP, Espagne, 634.
[34] Ibid. 635.

revolutionaries, however, believed (perhaps rightly) that the coalition powers took such measures with more abandon than they might have done if they were waging war against a 'legitimate' European sovereign. The French response on 16 August 1793 was a delayed, but deliberate, mirroring of the Spanish measures. Property belonging to Spanish subjects in France would be seized and sold for the benefit of those French citizens who had been expelled from Spain. Debts owed to Spanish creditors would be frozen until further notice.[35] What followed, however, was certainly a departure from past practice. On 7 September, sequestration was extended to include the property of all enemy subjects. Still, the revolutionaries were uncertain about the legitimacy and consequences of this measure. It was repealed on 13 September, only to be reimposed the next day after howls of protest from the Paris Jacobins.[36] Despite the confusion, the law was certainly applied: from his refuge in Brussels, an Irish peer, Kerry, sent a letter to Deforgues, the foreign minister, politely protesting against the seizure and sale of his property in Paris.[37]

The contrast between the revolutionaries' resolve over the decree of 16 August and their wavering over that of 7 September is revealing. While the one could be justified on the traditional basis of *représailles* and had a clear goal as retaliation against Spain, the other was more novel. The revolutionaries were reluctant to take unprecedented measures when they were unsure of the commercial and political consequences. When Delaunay d'Angers of the Convention's finance commission reported back on the confiscation of property on 20 September, he said that the committees of finance, commerce, and Public Safety were reluctant to implement the law because it would be contrary to the Revolution's own principles of the sanctity of property. British and Dutch subjects who had acquired property in France tended to be 'true friends of our revolution'. The Convention was clearly given food for thought, as it delayed discussion for three days.[38]

By the time they reconsidered, however, events had outpaced the finance commission's scruples. Frustration at British tactics

---

[35] *AP* lxxii. 249–50.   [36] *AP* lxxiii. 491; lxxiv. 46; lxxiv. 106–8.
[37] MAE, CP, Angleterre, 588.   [38] *AP* lxxv. 362–5.

in the war had been mounting since the summer when, on 8 June, the British government's Orders in Council allowed the Royal Navy to seize any ship bound for France. On 9 October, news arrived in Paris that Beauvais, the captured *représentant en mission* to Toulon, had been executed. The rumour was false, but it hardened attitudes. The Convention decreed the arrest of British and Hanoverian subjects and the seizure of their property in France.[39] The fact that both measures had already been decreed on 1 August and 6–7 September suggests that the earlier decrees had been only partially enforced and that, this time, the Convention wanted no exceptions to the law. Among the victims was Walter Boyd, the banker, who had fled the country and whose estate at Boulogne outside Paris was searched on 19 October.[40] The underlying motive behind the decree of 9 October, besides vengeance, was the destruction of British commercial might. Thomas Clarke, from Limerick, saw his trading establishment at Bordeaux seized by the authorities, as did merchants like James MacCulloch at Roscoff and the Galway brothers at Nantes. The Irish peer Lord Trimbleton had his house in Toulouse and land in the Haute-Garonne and the Lot confiscated.[41]

Arrests began promptly, too. In Paris at least 160 and perhaps as many as 250 British people were arrested by virtue of the law of 9 October. In Le Havre on 12 October, *représentants en mission* supervised armed citizens scouring the city for British subjects. The next day the *comité de surveillance* of Boulogne, near Paris, arrested all Britons living in the commune. William Codrington sarcastically explained that he was arrested because 'it was taken much amiss that my countrymen should accept of a town that was very kindly offered to them'. Students were no longer protected. In the Observatoire section of Paris, nine students, a doctor, and a tutor of the Irish College were arrested on 10 October.[42] Accident of birth became more important than political virtues, as even those Britons whose politics had previously protected them were now exposed. The seven British 'patriots' in the Observatoire section were now taken from house arrest

[39] *AP* lxxvi. 286–8.   [40] AN, BB/3/72.

[41] J. Vidalenc, 'Quelques cas particuliers du cosmopolitisme en France au XVIIIe siècle', *AhRf* 35 (1963), 203–4.

[42] AN, F/7*/2514; BB/3/72; *AP* lxxvi. 286–8, 318–19, 599; Gerbod, 'Visiteurs et résidents britanniques', 339; Alger, *Englishmen*, 292, 334–49.

and put in prison.[43] On 11 October, Helen Maria Williams was led off to the Luxembourg with her mother, her sister, and two other British subjects. Her lover John Hurford Stone was also arrested with his long-suffering wife, Rachel Coope. Predictably, however, artisans who had been working in France for at least six months were protected.

Some voices were raised in opposition to the persecution of British subjects for the fact of their nationality. Pons de Verdun suggested on 13 October that the British were ready to over-throw their government and so the measure would be counter-productive.[44] The tenacious Saint-Just returned three days later to defend government policy. Rather than revoke the law, he proposed to extend the arrests to all enemy aliens, but at least restricted the sequestration of property to the Spanish and British. The government sought to maintain commercial rela-tions with all except Britain and Spain, because France would otherwise have been dangerously isolated. Numerous demands to shield foreign patriots from arrest were however brushed aside by Robespierre and Barère. The latter thundered that 'many foreigners have come wearing precisely the mask of persecuted patriots, the better to fool us and thereby be admitted every-where. So, no exceptions!' The Convention still charged the Committee of Public Safety with considering just that.[45]

The government's determination might have stemmed from a deep-seated fear of subversion which had been aroused by Fabre d'Églantine's denunciation of a 'foreign plot' on 12 October. As with the law of 1 August, however, the way in which the new measures were applied suggested that, in practice, the authorities both nationally and locally were reluctant to apply the measure fully. This was perhaps less out of compassion than for fear of the economic consequences. Both the government and local officials could apply the rule exempting workers and artisans very loosely. John Hurford Stone and his wife were freed, officially because they both worked as printers. James White, who was working on navigation methods for river boats, was also released.[46] On 17 October, a Dutch shipbuilder, Matther,

[43] AN, F/7*/2514.
[44] *AP* lxxvi. 491; Mathiez, *La Révolution et les étrangers*, 156.
[45] *AP* lxxvi. 638–9; Mathiez, *La Révolution et les étrangers*, 157–9.
[46] *AP* lxxxi. 704; lxxxiii. 48.

successfully protested his patriotism and his usefulness to the Republic.[47] On 3 November, Desmoulins persuaded the Convention that doctors, 'as health workers' were not liable to arrest.[48] The Observatoire section therefore freed an Irish doctor named MacSheehy, who was given a *carte d'hospitalité*.[49] Such initiatives reflect the lethargy with which the Committee of Public Safety approached its task of considering general exemptions to the law. The Convention issued it with a reminder on 10 December, which went unheeded.[50]

Foreigners with the right political credentials were sometimes treated more leniently than the letter of the law demanded. The Observatoire section lent its support to the petition of MacSheehy's son, Roland, and Bartholomew Murray, both students at the Irish College, for their release in order to join the French navy.[51] However, that foreigners may have been increasingly regarded as incapable of the kind of patriotic virtue required to serve the Republic is suggested by the decree of 25 December (or 5 Nivôse). This law excluded all foreigners from the right to 'represent the French people', which sealed the fate of Thomas Paine and Anacharsis Cloots.[52] Denied their immunity as deputies, they were arrested soon afterwards. More important than an exclusive patriotism may have been an urge to reduce to impotence those whose political views and associations were regarded as dangerous. Cloots's presence in the Jacobins had also provoked the expulsion of foreigners, bankers, priests, and nobles from the Paris club on 12 December. Robespierre instigated what appeared to be a general measure, but the real target was Cloots for his role in the militant dechristianization movement and for his links to the Hébertists.[53] The foreign nationality of Paine and Cloots was arguably an excuse for the exclusion of two potentially damaging opponents of the revolutionary government.

Symbolically, the law of 25 December represented a step in the nationalization of citizenship, where the government 'drew a new political frontier which truly became . . . the frontier of national sovereignty'.[54] In practice, however, foreigners retained

---

[47] AN, AF/II/61.   [48] *AP* lxxviii. 223.

[49] AN, AF/II/61; F/7*/2514.   [50] Mathiez, *La Révolution et les étrangers*, 160.

[51] AN, AF/II/61; AN, F/7*/2514.   [52] *AP* lxxxii. 303.

[53] Robespierre, *Œuvres*, x. 247–50.   [54] Wahnich, *L'Impossible Citoyen*, 146.

positions in French administration and participated in politics at lower levels. In Paris, a Neapolitan teacher of Italian named Joseph Tosi was president of the *comité révolutionnaire* of the Bonnet-Rouge section, on which the Milanese Piccini also served. Italians were still more numerous on the committee of the La Fontaine-de-Grenelle section. The Genevan Sandoz was politically active in the *section* de l'Unité, while the Swede Lindberg, from the Bonnet-Rouge section, was closely associated with Vincent and Momoro.[55] The Irishman Nicholas Madgett headed the government's *bureau de traduction*.[56] When the popular *armées révolutionnaires* were activated on 5 September, Albert Mazuel, the Parisian army's cavalry commander, openly flouted the ban on recruiting foreigners for this essentially political, militant wing of the Terror. He took on an unnamed Belgian 'dashing young revolutionary' and a Hungarian hussar named Georgius Kenessey, who wrote his application in Latin declaring that he was a 'bonus Respublicanus'. Pierre Cardinaux, a Swiss from Neuchâtel, was active in the establishment of the Parisian *armée* and then served as an officer.[57] These individuals would lose their positions not because of their nationality, but because the Convention abolished the revolutionary armies on 27 March 1794, as creatures pulsating with extreme militancy.

The final, apparent step in the expulsion of foreigners from the political arena was the law of 26–7 Germinal (15–16 April 1794). Once it had killed off its Hébertist and Dantonist opponents, the Committee of Public Safety presented this decree on law and order to consolidate its hold on the country. Among its main targets were foreigners and the ex-nobility. The new law ordered the expulsion of enemy subjects from Paris, frontier towns, and ports for the duration of the war. They were forbidden to attend political clubs, to sit on *comités de surveillance*, or in the assemblies of communes and sections. The latter rule appears as the final step in making political participation the preserve of French nationals, by denying foreigners access to

[55] R. Cobb, 'Quelques aspects de la mentalité révolutionnaire (avril 1793–thermidor an II)', *Revue d'histoire moderne et contemporaine*, 6 (1959), 109.

[56] M. Elliott, *Partners in Revolution: The United Irishmen and France* (New Haven, Conn., 1982), 60.

[57] Cobb, *People's Armies*, 115, 121.

those very institutions where popular sovereignty was expressed at the grassroots. The fact that the foreigners exempted from this clause were those who had been in France for more than twenty years, or who had been married to a French citizen for six, may also suggest that citizenship was no longer simply a matter of choice, but also the result of long-term social and cultural assimilation.[58]

Yet not all foreigners lost their positions. There were, of course, those who had been in France long enough to be exempt from the law, like the Germans Jean Schwerdfeger and Mathias Halm, the Bohemian Jean-Ferdinand Krubert and the Swiss Cardinaux. All were actively engaged in sectional politics in the Year II, variously holding positions in the National Guard and the local civil and revolutionary committees. Cardinaux also worked as an agent for the Committee of General Security.[59]

More revealing of the limits to the law in practice were those foreigners who did not fulfil the demanding residence requirement, yet who still managed to remain active in the section or commune. Foreigners who had the backing of their sections could make a strong case, as the Italian Piccini found when his colleagues on the *comité de surveillance* of the Bonnet-Rouge section defended him as 'a *sans-culotte* republican'.[60] A reputation for civic virtue and sound political credentials ensured a continued career in local politics. Recent arrivals, since 1790 and some only in the Year II, who clung to their posts included the Belgians Pierre Chanorier and Joseph Biot, the Germans Christophe Plug, Joseph Klaine, Martin Vichterich, and Jean Heimen, and the Italian Joseph Tosi. These individuals served variously on their local *comité révolutionnaire*, as civil commissioners, or remained otherwise engaged in militant politics. Vichterich was a member of the Paris Commune until the fall of Robespierre.

In some cases, foreigners may have been too militant for the central government, which had just triumphed over its extremist adversaries. The Genevan-born Sandoz presided over the Cordeliers club when its Hébertist champions were executed. He was denounced as a member of this faction, but he tactfully

---

[58] Wahnich, *L'Impossible Citoyen*, 223–5, 231–2.
[59] Monnier and Soboul, *Répertoire*, 278, 354, 431, 491; Cobb, *People's Armies*, 58, 79–80, 115.
[60] AN, AF/II/61.

penned an address to the Convention, renouncing the extremists as conspirators. He survived and retained his position on the Unité's surveillance committee.[61] Outside Paris, the *commissaire de subsistances* of Saint-Denis was an Englishman named Devonshire and, in Cahors, the mayor who held office throughout the Year II was Swedish.[62]

For most foreigners, however, the real worry was not expulsion from politics and administration, but their physical exclusion from the capital, from frontier towns, and from seaports. This clause would destroy their very livelihood, by tearing them away from their work and business. While justified as a security precaution, the law of 26–7 Germinal therefore represented an attempt, on paper, to deny foreigners admission not only to the political rights and duties of citizens, but also to the most important centres of French social and commercial life. In practice, the government sought to limit the economic dislocation which full implementation would have caused. Workers employed in the manufacture of arms, foreign retailers, foreigners aged below 15 and above 70 years old and women who had married French patriots were excepted. The Committee of Public Safety was empowered to 'requisition' whomever it saw fit, which entailed exemptions from the rules. Immediately, the Committee used this power to shield all soldiers from the law. On 25 April, the Committee informed the Convention that it had also requisitioned patriot refugees from Belgium, Liège, Mainz, and the United Provinces. The next day, it bowed to commercial motives and exempted citizens of all Hanseatic towns. It also forbade officials from separating women and children from their husbands and fathers and waived the law for pregnant women.[63]

The Committee quietly used its powers to requisition a wider range of foreigners. There were entrepreneurs and artisans who were not engaged in the manufacture of arms, as the strict letter of the law required, but others, such as sail-makers. Even those whose role in the war economy was indirect at best were sheltered, including any merchant or manufacturer who had practised their trade for at least six months in a list of ports and

---

[61] Monnier and Soboul, *Répertoire*, 153, 352, 368, 410, 445, 472, 508; Cobb, *People's Armies*, 61, 106, 584.

[62] Cobb, 'Quelques aspects', 109.

[63] *AP* lxxxviii. 649, 711; lxxxix. 347, 401–2.

frontier towns from Saint-Omer and Sedan in the north to Agde and Marseille in the south.[64] Far from any direct involvement in the war effort were the Italian and German musicians of the Théâtre du Lycée des Arts and Lazzari, the Italian owner of the Théâtre des Variétés Amusantes on the boulevard du Temple, whose petition was supported by eighty-seven signatures.[65] Other individuals were given special dispensation to live in Paris for a limited period while they concluded their affairs.[66]

The exemptions suggest that the decree of 26–7 Germinal was not applied as widely as its sweeping provisions at first suggest.[67] It certainly did not create the exclusively French, republican 'city' demanded by Saint-Just when he presented the law to the Convention. In its exclusion of foreigners from political activity and from the social and economic life of the nation, the decree was limited in effect by two factors. First, foreigners who showed a clear commitment to the Revolution and, more precisely, to the government, were shielded. Secondly, the revolutionaries were reluctant to expel from its main centres of manufacturing and commerce all those foreigners who could contribute, even indirectly, to the war effort.

The legislation aimed at foreigners during the Terror cannot be explained only by a retreat from cosmopolitanism. The decree of 1 August 1793, placing all enemy subjects under arrest, went beyond traditions of *représailles*, certainly suggesting that the war was being waged against whole peoples, and not just against their governments. The 'nationalization' of the war therefore owed much to the evolution of a more exclusive patriotism. This seemed to be confirmed by the still more uncompromising law of 16 October, which admitted no exceptions except for artisans, and by the expulsion of foreigners from France's major towns by the law of 26–7 Germinal. Foreigners were also progressively excluded from the practice of citizenship, first by their expulsion from state administration, then from the Convention, and finally, on paper, from political life at the most local level.

This development might be explained by the evolution of revolutionary ideology, which, focusing increasingly on the

[64] AN, AF/II/61.
[65] Ibid.   [66] Ibid.
[67] Mathiez, *La Révolution et les étrangers*, 181.

survival of France itself, implied that patriotism could only be the reserve of French people. Yet, if ideology gave novel expression to xenophobia, it did not create these anxieties. What brought them to a new pitch was the unprecedented intensity and adversity of the war, combined with internal political conflict and civil strife. These circumstances brought out some of the exclusive tendencies in revolutionary ideology. The measures against foreigners were therefore a response to the political and military crisis, albeit a response conditioned by ideological developments.

Serious as the implications of a retreat from cosmopolitanism were, some revolutionaries were reluctant to abandon altogether the universalist claims of their ideology. If only for purposes of motivation and propaganda, some revolutionaries still implied that the rights of man—and therefore patriotism—were not the reserve of any specific nationality. So foreign individuals and groups who demonstrated loyalty to the government were protected from the laws. The problem was that such demands for loyalty made the circle of true patriots, French or foreign, an increasingly exclusive club. The number of foreigners acceptable to the government was in danger of becoming so small that patriotism might just as well have been the exclusive preserve of French citizens. Few as they were, however, foreigners did persist in the *armées révolutionnaires*, the various sectional or communal committees, and in the National Guard detachments. While this was less likely to have been due to any residual cosmopolitanism than to human sociability, it does suggest that foreigners still had narrow space in which to flex some political sinew, if only locally. At times, the government even appeared to collude in this persistence, where the political allegiance of individual foreigners was above reproach. Yet there can be little doubt that, as the current of legislation flowed powerfully against foreign participation in revolutionary politics, in general such activity by foreigners was regarded unfavourably. As the government's primary concern was the war effort, it was far more generous in its protection of foreigners on grounds of their social or economic contributions, rather than for their political action.

Far more important, therefore, than politically motivated exemptions were those based on more material concerns. Most revolutionaries were not blind ideologues led only by their principles or prejudices. The Terror was increasingly justified by an appeal to unbending revolutionary ideals, but the government, in particular, was painfully aware of the scale of the difficulties which it faced. In need of the skills and commerce which foreigners offered, the authorities at all levels sought to protect those who were of some use to the war effort. A similar expediency ensured that the confiscation of property was limited to a reprisal against the Spanish and to economic warfare against the British. As in every regime since 1789, their appraisal of the realities ensured that the revolutionaries did not always live up to their rhetoric.

II

The same suspicions which had confronted regular foreign regiments in 1789 now shadowed foreign generals and legions in the Republic's service. Generals as a whole had long been considered warily by civilian politicians in Paris. In March 1793, Robespierre demanded the expulsion from the Jacobins of all foreign generals 'to whom we have imprudently confided command of our armies'.[68] It did not take long for respectability to be lent to Robespierre's suggestions. When Dumouriez slipped away into the night and across the lines to the Austrians on 6 April 1793, two foreigners were implicated. Count Joseph Miaczinsky, who had fled Poland in the summer of 1792, was charged with complicity. Francisco del Miranda was accused of misconduct during the entire campaign in the Low Countries. Miaczinsky was executed on 22 May 1793.[69]

Miranda was more fortunate. Paine, Barlow, Christie, and Stone testified in his favour before the revolutionary tribunal and he was acquitted on 16 May. He tried to live quietly in Belleville, then a village outside Paris, but was placed under house arrest on 5 July, in common with other generals who had been dismissed.[70] His close friendship with the Girondin Pétion, how-

---

[68] Mathiez, *La Révolution et les étrangers*, 127.

[69] Robespierre, *Œuvres*, x. 63.

[70] C. Parra-Pérez, *Miranda et la Révolution française* (Paris, 1925), 227–53; W. S. Robertson, *The Life of Miranda*, 2 vols. (New York, 1969), i. 134–8, 143.

ever, returned to haunt him later. In one of his letters to 'my worthy and dear friend', dated 26 October 1792, he wrote that he was happy to see 'the Demagogue Robespierre' fall into neglect, and he raged against Marat and Charette, 'even more loathsome'. When, between 27 May and 6 June 1794, the Committee of General Security finally got around to rifling through Pétion's papers, it discovered this letter and one of its members boldly underlined this particular passage. With proof of his hatred for the Mountain's dearest icons, the Committee had Miranda locked up in La Force, where he remained until January 1795.[71]

In the spring of 1794, he was accused of complicity in a 'prison conspiracy' to free the Dantonists, allegedly hatched by Arthur Dillon, for which that Berkshire-born general was executed on 14 April. At the other end of the political spectrum, Karl von Hesse, who boasted the title 'General Marat' during the siege of Lyon, was relieved of his command on 13 October 1793 for his aristocratic background. It was his ties with the Hébertists, however, which brought him to prison on 11 November. He remained there for more than a year.[72]

Miaczinsky, Miranda, Dillon, and Hesse all fell foul of the government for their failure to keep in step with the narrowing political orthodoxy. It was this, rather than their foreign origins, which condemned them to death or imprisonment. In the desperate climate of the Terror, military failure could also be defined as treason, as Miranda was not alone in discovering. Military reverses brought a long spell in prison for Dublin-born General Charles Kilmaine and his wife, between August 1793 and July 1795. The aged Marshal Luckner was executed at the end of 1793 and General James O'Moran from Elphin trod wearily in his footsteps on 6 March 1794.[73] Foreign generals suffered primarily for the same failings as their French counterparts, such as alleged betrayal, their lack of zeal, and their simple bad luck on the battlefield.

Xenophobia was only one of many factors which led to the demise of foreign legions. These troops, like their Ancien Régime

[71] AN, F/7/4774[70]; Parra-Pérez, *Miranda*, 266–7.

[72] AN, T//754; Mathiez, *La Révolution et les étrangers*, 174; Gooch, *Germany*, 332.

[73] Robespierre, *Œuvres*, x. 62; Alger, *Englishmen*, 152–3, 177; Weygand, 'Le Régiment de Dillon', in Hayes, Preston, and Weygand, *Les Irlandais en Aquitaine*, 53; Gooch, *Germany*, 331.

predecessors, suffered tense relations with the French citizenry. They were increasingly believed to lack political zeal, even to the extent of having outright counter-revolutionary intent. These problems, piled on top of logistical issues such as recruitment and desertion, led the revolutionaries to believe, as they had done with the Swiss not a year before, that having foreigners in separate units was more of a liability than an advantage. Besides, they were made obsolete when the Propagandist Decrees were revoked on 13 April 1793. The stormclouds thickened with the fall of the Girondins. After 2 June, the legions were not only irrelevant to the defensive war now being fought, but highly suspect because in both their conception and their purpose, they could be regarded as the creatures of the discredited Dumouriez, the Girondins, and the damaging policies which they pursued.

These suspicions were promptly acted upon, even before the Convention was purged of the legions' protectors. Marat supported a campaign by French officers serving in the *légion germanique* against the commanders and twenty-four other officers who were duly arrested and imprisoned in Tours on 1 May. The official reason was that they had creamed off the legion's funds into their own pockets, but it was not long before political elements were added to the charges.[74] The German officers were accused of persecuting 'patriot' soldiers and the Jacobins of Troyes and Montargis joined the chorus by accusing them of *incivisme*. Prieur de la Marne, the war commissioner at Tours, added his voice to this ugly chant by saying that the legion recruited German-speaking prisoners of war: 'Can the French rest on agreements made with men captured fighting the Republic?' The Convention decreed an investigation into the legion's recruitment and finances.[75] The crescendo came when the Vendéans took Saumur on 9 June and footsoldiers in the legion deserted to the rebels.[76] On 26 June, the brigade commander, General Fabrefond, was ordered to disband the *légion germanique*.[77]

Their lack of faith in the legions' political commitment led the revolutionaries to imply that they did not have the patriotic fervour required to fight for the *patrie*. On 10 November 1793, Gossuin, speaking for the military committee, advised that

[74] SHAT, X^k3.   [75] *AP* lxiv. 64–6.
[76] Gooch, *Germany*, 334.   [77] SHAT, X^k3.

henceforth they be used solely in the interior 'to make desertion more difficult'.[78] What was left unsaid was equally important: as foreigners, they were unlikely to be squeamish about being deployed against the French population. In fact, since the summer most legions had been used not at the front, but in the provinces. The Liégeois, Savoyard, Dutch, and German legions requisitioned grain, repressed the Federalist revolts in Lyon, Marseille, and Toulon, and fought bitterly in the Vendée.[79] Use of foreign troops in a counter-insurgency and policing role led to accusations of brutality towards the French population. Immediately after Prieur had made his damning report on the *légion germanique* on 3 May, Couthon came and denounced the *légion Kellermann*, 'in which there are precious few Frenchmen', for murder and pillage. The Convention ordered the Committee of Public Safety to gather information on all foreign legions, with a view to taking relevant security measures.[80] The legions were rapidly stimulating the same hostility and distrust as the old foreign regiments.

Besides the questions of loyalty and discipline, the foreign legions were incapable of recruiting enough men of the correct nationality to be viable fighting units. The second *légion batave*, when lined up for review at Saint-Omer on 31 May 1793, had an unimpressive total strength of ninety-nine men, of whom six were absent without leave. For this reason, however, it was overlooked and was not disbanded until after the Terror.[81] Makketros's *chasseurs-tirailleurs nationaux bataves* were not so fortunate and were dismissed on 12 October. When the Convention abolished the first *légion batave* on 6 November, there were precious few Dutch Patriots swelling its ranks, but substantial numbers of French, Prussians, Austrians, and Britons.[82] Four days later, Gossuin told the Convention that a regular Belgian regiment raised during the French invasion of the Low Countries could only muster thirteen men.[83]

The revolutionaries were suspicious of the legions as autonomous units, but they were reluctant to get rid of soldiers

[78] *AP* lxxviii. 702.

[79] Delange-Janson, *Ambroise*, 39, 41, 46–7; Doppet, *Mémoires*, 110–41, 164–80; SHAT, X^k46; X^k3.

[80] *AP* lxiv. 66–7.

[81] SHAT, X^k46.

[82] *AP* lxxviii. 455.

[83] *AP* lxxviii. 702.

whose experience and numbers, however small, might still prove useful. A decree of 1 August 1793 had already provided for the incorporation of depleted Belgian regiments into regular French corps. Now the law was implemented. On 10 November, all separate Belgian, and Liégeois units were suppressed, but the soldiers were ordered to assemble at Péronne by 25 November to be reorganized into new *bataillons de tirailleurs*. These new units would be identified only by numbers, so there would be no references to their foreign origin. The Belgian element would be gradually diluted by French recruits.[84] In the event, five battalions were raised, each commanded by a Belgian or a Liégeois and composed of Dutch, Belgian and Liégeois troops.[85] The revolutionaries did not even scrub the disgraced *légion germanique* from their hands. The infantry were redesignated as the 22nd Light Infantry and the cavalry as the 11th Hussars, but they were no longer to recruit only Germans.

As the Terror progressed, so the demands for the right political loyalties became more urgent. Any officer whose political orthodoxy was in doubt was refused a position. Since its disbandment in June, those officers of the German legion who were not actually arrested were dismissed and found it difficult to obtain new posts.[86] When, on 4 October 1793, Makketros presented a list of seventeen officers to be approved by the ministry of war for commands in the Dutch *chasseurs-tirailleurs*, every one of them was rejected, possibly because Jean Bouchotte, the minister of war with Hébertist sympathies, saw in them the protégés of Dumouriez and the Girondins. Eight days before the legion was actually suppressed, the officers were still protesting their 'purest patriotism'.[87] A few days after the disbandment, Makketros was suspended, eliciting protests from nine loyal officers.[88] He had already been damned by the surveillance committee of the Paris Bonconseil section on 16 September. These citizens scribbled a note to the Committee of General Security that the Dutchman was a 'man of bad faith' because he had shown no zeal in suppressing brigandage in the Meaux area.[89]

Yet a good republican to the Hébertist war ministry was not

---

[84] *AP* lxx. 82; lxxviii. 702.
[85] Fieffé, *Histoire des troupes étrangères*, ii. 14–15.   [86] SHAT, X^{k}3.
[87] SHAT, X^{k}46.   [88] Ibid.   [89] AN, BB/3/70.

likely to coincide with the government's ideas, particularly when Robespierre and his allies began to lash out against extremism towards the end of 1793. Those who survived the ideological screening by the ministry were less likely to meet with the same success once the government had decided to curb the Hébertists. On 20 January, two of the leading officers of the 11th Hussars, Avice and Haindel, were dismissed by the Committee of Public Safety. Charles Haindel went so far in his efforts to ingratiate himself to the government that he testified against the Hébertists at their trial on 23 March. More than two and a half months after his patron Ronsin was guillotined along with the other Hébertists on 24 March, Avice was still asking the Committee for his position back.[90]

As with the regular foreign regiments, the revolutionaries were concerned less about the foreign nationality of the legions than about their loyalty to the cause. The revolutionaries certainly believed that foreign troops were incapable of the patriotism required of French soldiers, but the deployment of foreign legions in the interior and their redistribution into new units shows that the revolutionaries were still not opposed to their use, provided they were organized in a manageable, secure way. The Convention naturally remained reluctant to shed experienced troops and the French army was always in need of numbers. The government was also willing to retain foreign officers and foreign soldiers when their revolutionary credentials remained unimpeachable. The foreign legions were disbanded because their leadership and their purpose were associated with the Girondins. Their credibility as independent units was shattered by their inability to recruit enough foreigners of the relevant nationality. With the war of propaganda repudiated, their main function as the vanguard of the liberating French armies was irrelevant. The war now focused on the defence of the *patrie* and, to ensure that the remaining foreign troops identified with that struggle, they were denied their separate identity.

The suppression of foreign legions raised the question as to what to do with foreign deserters. They had been allowed to join the French army, and the legions in particular. It was becoming clear, however, that many had crossed the lines less from love of

[90] SHAT, X^{k}3; Slavin, *The Hébertistes*, 213.

the French Revolution than from an understandable desire to escape military discipline, mutilation, and death. German and Austrian deserters sent to fight in the *légion de la Moselle* were accused of indiscipline and bad behaviour by General Custine in May 1793.[91] The ever-imaginative Robespierre went so far as to suggest that deserters were planted by the enemy in France as spies and saboteurs. On 29 July, he persuaded the Jacobins to reject the appeal of an Austrian officer to obtain permission for him and his comrades to march on the Vendée.[92]

Reports about the behaviour of deserters ensured that the bounties they were offered to join the French army began to grate, when French volunteers were given no such enticement. On 2 December, Gossuin reported on the daily abuses caused by the 'throngs of deserters in our armies, and the advantages which they are granted'. The Convention not only withdrew the bounties, but also denied deserters the right to enrol in the French army. Instead, they were to be employed in other useful tasks.[93]

Accordingly, on 20 December, the Executive Council issued instructions to the commanders of each army to march the foreign deserters serving at the front to the rear, disarmed and under escort if necessary. There, departmental and municipal authorities were to maintain and police them.[94] Conditions varied from place to place because of the latitude given to local authorities. In Poligny in the Jura, they were simply locked up in a *maison d'arrêt* on 21 December and were still there twenty months later. Even if deserters were allowed to wander freely in their allocated town, there is clear evidence of hardening attitudes. Before the law of 2 December, only two Spanish deserters had been imprisoned in Quigney in the Doubs, and they were only held overnight. Between 24 January and 22 September 1794, however, no less than 105 deserters were shut away, before being driven elsewhere.[95]

Deserters were to be employed in public or private works, because this would 'defray the cost of their upkeep'.[96] Work was not always found, however, especially when they were sent to

---

[91] *AP* lxv. 53–4.   [92] Robespierre, *Œuvres*, x. 43–5.   [93] *AP* lxxx. 562.
[94] A. Cochin, *Les Actes du Gouvernement Révolutionnaire (23 août 1793–27 juillet 1794)*, 3 vols. (Paris, 1935), ii. 71–6.
[95] AN, F/9/137.   [96] Cochin, *Actes*, ii. 76.

live in small villages. Two deserters who arrived in the commune of Villedommange near Rheims on 19 July 1794 did not find jobs until the grape harvest began on 22 September. Still, the Committee of Public Safety ordered on 17 July 1794 that those deserters or prisoners of war who refused to work would be imprisoned until the end of the war.[97] Those who could not fend for themselves through illness, wounds, or want of opportunities were, however, to be given 10 *sous* a day for their subsistence, and a 24 ounce ration of bread, which was the standard issue for the French army.[98] The freedom allowed to foreign deserters since 1792 had certainly been reduced by the beginning of 1794, but the order of 17 July 1794 meant that in monetary terms deserters who could not work were actually better off than before, as the daily allowance amounted to 182 *livres*, 10 *sous*, a year. The conditions in which they lived, however, converged increasingly with those of prisoners of war.

The original freedoms offered to prisoners of war were truncated. They were now held in buildings chosen by the local authorities and penned in by National Guardsmen or the *gendarmerie*. They still received subsistence money according to rank and were offered the same rations of bread as soldiers in the French army.[99] In some localities, they were allowed some freedom to roam. In Moulins, the *comité de surveillance* gratefully paid some Prussian prisoners who played music during local *bals patriotiques*. The authorities at Montpellier may have screamed that Spanish prisoners were sowing the seeds of 'fanaticism' amongst local women, and at Valence a British captive may have got into hot water for making suggestions 'aimed at sowing terror and discouragement', but these accusations are no less an indication of the freedom allowed to prisoners of war in the Year II.[100]

Exchanges of prisoners continued as before and new guidelines for French commanders were set down on 25 May 1793. The honour system for officers persisted, suggesting that, despite their rhetoric, the revolutionaries still retained a belief—at least until the summer of 1794—that certain rules of war would be followed by the enemy. The cost of keeping prisoners, as Merlin de Thionville complained on 2 December,

[97] AN, F/9/137. [98] Ibid.
[99] *AP* lxv. 297–9. [100] Cobb, 'Quelques aspects', 110.

took its toll on the war effort. The administration of the Seine-et-Marne had complained of these 'numerous slaves' near Paris 'who ate up supplies which are vital to the *défenseurs de la patrie*'. This, Merlin argued, gave the exchanges special urgency.[101]

The idea that enemy troops were 'slaves' lay behind the terrible decree of 7 Prairial II (26 May 1794) which ordered that 'no British or Hanoverian prisoners will be taken'.[102] The British had often been accused of violating the conventions of eighteenth-century warfare—and sometimes with good reason. They had been the first to forge French currency and to prevent food from reaching French ports. The Convention had heard stories of British atrocities: on 11 September 1793, after the first French victory of the year at Hondschoote, Bentabole, the commissioner attached to the army of the Nord, wrote to his colleagues of the massacre of French prisoners of war by the British and of the killing of a child near Lille. 'So', exhorted Bentabole, 'let us employ all means to exterminate those barbarians unworthy of the name of men.'[103] Such rhetoric attempted to dehumanize the enemy by placing them outside the human race and therefore beyond the rules of normal warfare. Similarly, political opposition in France was regarded by some revolutionaries as outside the nation and therefore not protected by the usual legal guarantees. The law of 7 Prairial sprang from the same logic as that of the equally notorious law of 22 Prairial, which permitted no defence to those arraigned before the revolutionary tribunal.[104]

There was not, however, an inevitable line of development from Bentabole's letter of September 1793 and the decree ordering the murder of British and Hanoverian prisoners, for two reasons. First, in September, many revolutionaries still clung to the belief that the British people were mostly opposed to Pitt and to the war. This changed in February 1794 when Robespierre brought the Jacobins to their feet by condemning the British people as well as their government. He did this to divert the Jacobins from their fratricidal feuding between moderates

---

[101] *AP* lxxx. 525.   [102] *AP* xci. 41.
[103] Hampson, 'Idea of the Nation', 18; *AP* lxxiv. 225.
[104] Hampson, *Saint-Just* (Oxford, 1991), 85–6; Hampson, 'Idea of the Nation', 19–20; Wahnich, *L'Impossible Citoyen*, 237–327.

and extremists and, for a brief period, the 'crimes' of the British united them in the face of the common enemy. Conformity now demanded the use of similar xenophobic language from all revolutionaries, although the rapturous response of the Jacobins also suggests that a deep-rooted anglophobia was being tapped.[105] From then on, the sort of language employed by Bentabole months earlier was given more respectability. Secondly, anglophobia was turned from words into deeds with the assassination attempts on Collot d'Herbois and Robespierre on 20 and 23 May. These were committed by French people, but on 26 May Barère traced these attempts to the old enemy and drove the Convention into a frenzy by listing atrocity after atrocity committed by the British government and armed forces. Some deputies began to rage 'War to the death against every British and Hanoverian soldier!' Barère had no difficulty in having the decree voted through.[106] The hate-filled law was not only produced by the anti-British rhetoric employed by revolutionaries like Bentabole, Robespierre, and Barère, but stemmed also from the poisonous, internecine struggles within revolutionary politics.

The enthusiasm with which civilians received the order is, however, no indication as to how far it was actually carried out. Fear of reprisals no doubt weighed on the troops in the field, but so too did a revulsion at killing men who had thrown down their arms. The effectiveness of the decree was limited, therefore, among troops who ignored it. The law was certainly carried out at least once, when the frigate *La Boudeuse* captured a British merchantman, a civilian vessel. The captain reported that he had transferred the crew to his ship and had them shot.[107] This appears to have been the only recorded instance of the law being executed.

During the Terror, official revolutionary attitudes towards foreign troops swayed between pragmatism and the depths of nihilistic xenophobia. The cosmopolitan appeal of 20 April 1792 for foreigners to range themselves under the banners of the French Revolution had been all but forgotten. The repudiation of the Edict of Fraternity rendered foreign legions obsolete

---

[105] Robespierre, *Œuvres*, x. 348–9; *Moniteur*, 136 (An II).
[106] *AP* xci. 32–41.
[107] Hampson, 'Idea of the Nation', 25.

and problems of recruitment and desertion underscored their impracticality. Some revolutionaries suggested that foreign troops were not capable of the ideological commitment to the *patrie* which was demanded in such trying times. Yet, while the political loyalties of the officers were closely monitored, that some were retained implied that patriotism, meaning loyalty to a particular republican orthodoxy, was still not an exclusively French virtue. Even so, it was restricted to a very select few. At one and the same time, such surveillance allowed the revolutionaries to calm their own fears about foreign counter-revolutionaries in the army, while justifying the retention of some foreign troops and officers on the grounds that they were politically reliable. Expediency underlay this logic, as the war demanded supplies of cannon-fodder as well as experienced troops.

The revolutionaries did not, therefore, dogmatically exclude foreigners from service in the French army simply because they were foreign. Even after they disbanded the legions, they distributed the remaining troops among regular units. Officers, however, needed political credentials tailored to the exacting demands of the government. It was this last factor, more than the ideological retreat from the universal pretensions of revolutionary principles, which determined the fate of many foreign troops. If it was not incompetence or failure, what doomed certain foreign soldiers to death, imprisonment, or inactivity was their apparent lack of zeal or loyalty. Those officers and units who were tied too closely to patrons such as Dumouriez, the Girondins, and then the Hébertists were cast under suspicion.

On the other hand, the revolutionaries gave more expression to xenophobia when they dealt with foreign deserters and prisoners of war. The dangers of disorder in the countryside and in frontier towns lay behind the decision to demobilize foreign deserters and to guard them closely in the interior. The law of 7 Prairial suggests that xenophobia was not the exclusive product of revolutionary ideology, but ideology gave it an expression peculiar to the Revolution. The tendency to regard the war as a Manichaean conflict between reason and darkness suggested that those who ought to have known better—the relatively enlightened British—were guilty of betraying the legitimate aspirations of the human race. However, xenophobia, and particularly anglophobia, also grew from more traditional attitudes dating to long before 1789.[108] If revolutionary ideology lay behind the law of 7 Prairial, the power behind the logic (if it can be called that in this context) was provided by anglophobia which stemmed from deeper cultural and political roots. Whatever its origins, the law of 7 Prairial was the negation of revolutionary cosmopolitanism.

III

Before any laws changed their increasingly isolated status as aberrant remnants of the old regime, the foreign clergy remained in an uneasy state of uncertainty. While, as clerics, they were targets for hostility and harassment, it was their nationality which finally determined their fate. The irony was that it was precisely this factor which had protected them from the reforms imposed on the French clergy since 1789. Certain clergymen and seminary students could still escape imprisonment and persecution if they had the right political credentials. For the revolutionaries, even a very rare foreign ecclesiastic might have been capable of patriotism.

The arrest of enemy subjects, decreed on 6 September 1793, exempted all students under 16 years old, which naturally applied to the British and Irish seminarians. Those over that age had to prove their *civisme* by the testimony of one good citizen.[109] The pressure was not off, however, because when the Convention decreed the confiscation of enemy property the next day, Rühl (who would later lead anticlerical festivities in Rheims) suggested that the property of the foreign clergy in France be included in the order.[110] The proposal was sent to the Committee of Public Safety for consideration, but any relief at this brief respite was shortlived: on 15 September the department of the Seine launched a bitter assault on the University of

---

[108] N. Hampson, *The Perfidy of Albion: French Perceptions of England during the French Revolution* (Basingstoke, 1998); F. Acomb, *Anglophobia in France 1763–1789: An Essay in the History of Constitutionalism and Nationalism* (Durham, NC, 1950); Wahnich, *L'Impossible Citoyen*, 282.

[109] *AP* lxxiii. 463.　　　　　　　　　　　　　　[110] *AP* lxxiii. 497.

Paris. While it did not name the Irish or Scottish institutions, both of which were affiliated to the university, all the Parisian colleges were castigated as barbaric remnants of the Middle Ages, 'the refuge of prejudices amassed for centuries'.[111] More positively, the department demanded that the Convention implement a national system of public education. Both elements of the petition came close to a direct attack on the foreign colleges in the capital. They sent students to study in the university and they were religious establishments with no place in a secular, state education system.

Ultimately, it was not their clerical status which destroyed the foreign houses, but their nationality. With the law of 9 October, ordering the arrest of all British and Irish subjects and the confiscation of their wealth, many of the foreign clergy were simply placed under guard in their own buildings, like the students of the Irish College, the English Augustinian, Conceptionist, and Benedictine nuns and the intrepid Alexander Innes, now the sole occupant of the Scots College, in Paris. The more fortunate Scottish students of Douai, meanwhile, had long been sent to a safe haven in a Bruges convent.[112] When they were not kept under house arrest, the clerics and students lived in dark squalor. The English Benedictines of Cambrai suffered the deaths of four nuns and their confessor in January 1794 while in prison at Compiègne.[113] The students and staff of the English College of Saint-Omer, which was closed down on 10 October 1793, joined their colleagues from Douai in the citadel of Doullens in May 1794, where they lived without fuel, sleeping on straw and eating the daily ration of bread provided by the authorities. Some died in this state.[114] The Irish clergy were treated with more leniency by the authorities, possibly because they were thought to be hostile to the British government. The Irish students and clerics from the Bordeaux college were not arrested until December 1793, while those from Nantes were repatriated. On 24 April 1794, ten of the remaining Irish students from the college in Paris were released from custody and given 500 *livres* each to defray the cost of their journey home. When they arrived at Dunkirk, however, the government had second thoughts and they were imprisoned in Arras for five months instead.[115]

It was no longer enough to be a constitutional priest to be protected from arrest as a British or Irish subject. In the diocese of Bordeaux, the decree of 9 October hurt even those who had taken the oath, which was now only a loose guarantee of loyalty to an ever more demanding regime. Nationality was increasingly the prime determinant of their fate. Jurors among the foreign clergy were, however, better off than the refractories when they fell foul of the authorities. Alexander MacDonald, a juror from the parish of Audenge, tried to find anonymity in Bordeaux to avoid arrest, but was captured and deported. The fact that he had been a constitutional cleric probably saved his life. In contrast, Martin Glynn was a refractory who also went into hiding, only to be arrested and brought before the military commission of Bordeaux. On 7 July 1794, he was sentenced to death and decapitated.[116]

James Burke had not only taken the ecclesiastical oath, but had publicly expressed enthusiasm for the Republic, buying a farm in the sale of *biens nationaux* near Bordeaux. No amount of political commitment could wash away his original birth as an Irish subject and he was duly arrested on 19 October 1793. He was released twelve days later by the *comité de surveillance*, probably for two reasons: his economic importance as a farmer, who employed local labourers, and his civic virtue. Burke was shrewd enough, and perhaps sincere enough, to strike up a friendship with the *représentant en mission*, Ysabeau, and he was not rearrested until after 9 Thermidor.[117] Two Irish students in Paris were released on 13 October 1793 so that they could join the French navy. The local surveillance committee had shuffled through their papers and concluded that 'there can be no doubting the Patriotism and the Republicanism of these young Citizens'. It probably helped that one of the students in question, Roland MacSheehy, had denounced his own superiors to the Parisian authorities.[118] Therefore even priests and

[115] Ibid.; AN, H/3/2561/A; Simms, 'The Irish', 652; *AP* lxxxix. 339–40.
[116] Loupès, 'Irish Clergy', 34–5.
[117] Ibid. 35–6.
[118] AN, F/7*/2514; BB/3/70.

seminary students who were enemy subjects could sometimes remain at liberty, if they showed enough political orthodoxy and had some luck with the authorities. To escape persecution, it was no longer enough, however, merely to have taken the clerical oath: the priests and students had to demonstrate active enthusiasm for the Republic.

The arrests and imprisonment of foreign clergy provided the human drama of persecution and suffering, but the real threat to the long-term survival of their institutions was the confiscation and sale of their property. In Paris, the first steps towards the seizure coincided with 'dechristianization', which feverishly gripped the popular movement, the Commune, and the extremist Hébertists. In October and November 1793, the Commune sent commissioners to inventory the property and *rentes* of the foreign establishments and they duly reported back to the Parisian administration of *biens nationaux*.[119] Actual confiscation followed. Movable property as well as real estate was seized. In November 1793, sometime after their convent had been converted into a prison, the English Benedictine nuns in the *faubourg* Saint-Marcel had their *rentes* frozen and could only watch as their silverware was removed. At the end of the month, their copper and brass followed and the church was stripped of its fittings and furnishings. Apparently infected by the dechristianization virus, the militia 'with joy mixed with fury . . . kicked up and down the church what they threw down'.[120] Much of the Scots College library was confiscated in two raids by the Commune in January and June 1794; its buildings in Paris and its farm at Grisy were seized.[121] At Saint-Omer, the English College saw all its property, including its buildings, *rentes*, furniture, silver, and linen confiscated on 10 October 1793.[122] In December 1793, the buildings of the Irish College of Bordeaux were taken over by the president of the military commission, Jean-Baptiste Lacombe, for use as his offices and home. The right wing became a boarding school for children.[123]

[119] AN, M/250/18; S//4616.

[120] Alger, *Englishmen*, 305, 309.

[121] A. Cherry, 'The Scots College Books in Paris', *Innes Review*, 44 (1993), 70; P. A. Moran, 'Grisy, the Scots College Farm near Paris', *Innes Review*, 43 (1992), 62; Halloran, *Scots College*, 187.

[122] MAE, ADP, France, 10.   [123] AN, H/3/2561/A.

The next phase was the sale of these *biens nationaux*, decreed on 1 February 1794. The principals of both the Irish and Scots Colleges protested and for the time being the sale did not go ahead.[124] Instrumental in this delay was the fact that the authorities themselves were often already using the buildings concerned as prisons and offices, so were unable and unwilling to auction them. Yet once the sales did go ahead, as they certainly did after Thermidor, the re-establishment of the institutions was a frustrating and often thankless struggle.

The fate of the foreign clergy under the Terror was determined by their nationality. As British and Irish subjects, they were liable to arrest and the confiscation of their property. The same factor which had sheltered them from the blast of revolutionary legislation now ironically condemned them doubly to imprisonment and to penury. Their indelible origins meant that, as far as most revolutionaries were concerned, the fact of being a juror or non-juror was almost irrelevant. To avoid imprisonment, it was no longer sufficient simply to have taken the clerical oath. To win their freedom, foreign clerics had to contribute actively to the political, economic, or even military life of the Republic. These were the proofs of civic virtue which purchased liberty for a rare number of foreign clergy and students. Otherwise, the experience of imprisonment and the loss of their property led these foreigners to feel an acute sense of alienation from a country which had formerly offered them asylum, but which now snapped angrily at them. Such an experience certainly contributed to the failure of the foreign clergy to reopen their institutions in France, but even those who attempted to salvage something from the debris failed, with a few exceptions. Dramatic and terrible as the Terror was for the foreign clergy, what actually destroyed their establishments was the confiscation of their property. In the Year II, this sequestration was still reversible, because most of the buildings were used by the revolutionaries for official purposes and so could not be sold. Once the Terror was dismantled, and with it the localized bureaucracy and *maisons d'arrêt*, there was less need for these buildings and so their sale as *biens nationaux* became more

---

[124] Ibid.

likely. For the survival of their houses in France, the worst was
yet to come for the foreign clergy.

IV

On 13 April 1793, the Convention revoked its Propagandist
Decrees and on 17 November, Robespierre spoke on behalf of
the Committee of Public Safety to outline its foreign policy. He
confirmed the renunciation of revolutionary expansion and wars
of liberation. The period between the end of March 1793 and 9
Thermidor II, therefore, has been characterized as a time when
foreign patriots were persecuted by a hostile government, which
was scrambling back from cosmopolitanism towards an exclusive nationalism.[125]

It was certainly a dark time for the exiles. Lebrun had only just
organized two 'Spanish committees' at Bayonne and Perpignan,
when the Convention renounced revolutionary proselytism in
April. A foreign ministry report suggested that French defeats in
Belgium and failure to foment revolt in Spain 'have shown us
how illusory the activities of these Committees are among people
who cannot appreciate liberty'. The committees limped on in the
face of waning official support. By 27 April, there only appears
to have been one Spanish subject among their membership,
Carles, recently secretary to the French embassy in Madrid.
Marchena and Hevia were absent. In August, with Spanish
troops still encamped on French soil, Lebrun's Montagnard
successor at the foreign ministry, Deforgues, agreed that the
committees should abandon any propaganda role and concen-
trate on providing supplies to the French army.[126]

The nature of this official hostility begs the question as to
whether foreign patriots suffered because of the retreat from
cosmopolitanism or because of their political loyalties. Behind
the rhetoric, the revolutionaries took a practical approach. While
publicly disavowing the policies in which foreigners had set so
much store, both the Convention and the government seemed to
recognize some obligation to foreign refugees and envisaged a

[125] Mathiez, *La Révolution et les étrangers*, 162, 177; Godechot, *Grande Nation*, 78.
[126] MAE, CP, Espagne, 636; Herr, *Eighteenth Century Revolution*, 285–6.

future use for them. Foreign patriots certainly suffered imprisonment and even execution, but usually for the same reasons as French citizens. They fell out of the ever-tightening net of political orthodoxy because they failed to scrape low enough before the revolutionary government. Those who had associated with the Girondins, with Dumouriez, and later with the Hébertists were in trouble if they failed to renounce them in time. Even then, some were defended by powerful figures, including Robespierre. Despite the snarling xenophobia unleashed by the war, loyalty or usefulness to the government could ensure such protection.

The political environment was becoming increasingly hostile. The arrest of British subjects decreed on 9 October 1793, extended to all enemy subjects a week later, made no exception of foreign radicals. Nationality now threatened to cut across considerations of attachment to the Revolution. On 21 October, the British patriots under house arrest in the Observatoire section of Paris were transferred to the English Benedictine convent, now a prison.[127] Among other British radicals, Sampson Perry and Helen Maria Williams were incarcerated. Authorship of the politically correct *Crimes des rois d'Angleterre* could not protect Henry Stevens.[128] Mary Wollstonecraft escaped imprisonment. She was wise enough to make herself scarce after the fall of her Girondin friends, moving from the capital to a small cottage at Neuilly-sur-Seine. She was later protected when, at Le Havre, her American lover, Gilbert Imlay, registered her as his wife and, therefore, as an American citizen.[129]

When the law was extended to include all enemy subjects on 16 October, Robespierre admitted bluntly that 'it could strike several philosophers and friends of humanity; but they are so rare that the number of victims will not be great'.[130] In practice, the revolutionaries backpedalled from the nationalization of the war, even if the rhetoric and the law suggested otherwise. On 18 February 1794—only two weeks after Robespierre had expressed his ferocious hatred for the British people in the

[127] AN, F/7*/2514.
[128] H. M. Williams, *Letters Containing a Sketch of the Politics of France from 31 May 1793 till 28 July 1794*, 2 vols. (London, 1795), i. 6–13, 204–5; Alger, *Englishmen*, 71–2, 97–8, 150–2, 347–9.
[129] Tomalin, *Mary Wollstonecraft*, 165; Wardle, *Collected Letters*, 233.
[130] Robespierre, *Œuvres*, x. 155.

Jacobins—the Committee of Public Safety ordered the intercep-
tion of the ship transporting the Scottish radicals Thomas Muir,
Thomas Fysche Palmer, and their English colleague Maurice
Margarot to exile in Botany Bay. The order, in Saint-Just's
handwriting, declared that the constitution 'offers an asylum in
France to men persecuted for the cause of liberty'.[131] Such a
rescue would have been a remarkable propaganda coup.

The authorities protected some foreign radicals inside France,
too, particularly those whose sympathies were not obviously with
opponents of the revolutionary government. Helen Williams was
released after two months on the orders of Chaumette, *procureur*
of the Paris Commune, despite her known Girondin sympathies.
The fact that she had been allowed to destroy potentially
compromising papers probably helped her.[132] Like Paine and
Wollstonecraft, Williams and her family tried to live quietly on
the outskirts of Paris. In the spring, she left for Switzerland.[133]
Her lover Stone was also arrested as a British subject on 13
October. He was released with his wife after only seventeen days,
which suggests that political celebrity of the right kind could still
ensure some Britons their freedom.

Foreign radicals from the continent seem to have been treated
with less rigour than the British. Throughout the Terror, many
German, Belgian, and Dutch patriots were at large. While the
Belgians and Rhinelanders were theoretically French citizens by
virtue of the annexations decreed earlier that year, that Dutch
Patriots such as Joannes de Kock and Johann Valckenaer should
remain at liberty for months after the decree of 16 October
shows that even radicals of unequivocally enemy nationality
were not harassed simply because of their national origins.

Despite the letter of the law, the government was willing to
harbour foreign exiles provided they were dependable and of
some use. This meant, however, that the foreigners had to match
up to the increasingly stringent demands of political conformity,
above all by washing out the stains left by past associations. It
was failure to meet this challenge, rather than their nationality,

---

[131] F.-A. Aulard, *Recueil des Actes du Comité du Salut Public*, 28 vols. (Paris, 1889–
1951), xi. 242.
[132] Mme de Genlis, *Mémoires inédits de Madame la Comtesse de Genlis*, 8 vols.
(Paris, 1825–6), iv. 130–1; v. 275; Woodward, *Une Anglaise*, 84–6.
[133] Williams, *Letters Containing a Sketch*, i. 205; Woodward, *Une Anglaise*, 91–9.

which brought the harshest penalties onto certain foreign patriots. The revolutionary government did not persecute them on
principle. In fact, throughout the Year II the authorities provided
subsidies or employment for 6,000–7,000 Belgian and Liégeois
refugees and for 600 German patriots, while honouring the
Dutch subsidies paid since before 1789.[134] Far from being
reduced as the Terror developed, subsistence payments were
systematized on 4 March 1794. The Convention gave 20 million
livres to the *commission des secours* for those patriots forced out of
communes invaded by the allies.[135] Most of the handouts were
given to French refugees, but from 15 March until 9 Thermidor,
Liégeois, Belgian, and Rhenish exiles received a total of 220,620
livres, of which the vast majority (just under 98 per cent) were
given to Belgians and Liégeois, with the remainder going to the
numerically smaller Germans.[136]

The exiles were also encouraged to find positions in the
French civil administration or the military. On 14 June 1793,
the Convention asked the Committee of Public Safety to provide
a list of civil or military posts which the refugees might usefully
fill.[137] In September, the department of the Meurthe gave several
Mainz patriots jobs as guards in a *maison nationale* in Nancy.[138]
Georg Forster was appointed a commissioner overseeing the
exchange of prisoners of war.[139] On 25 December 1793, foreigners were excluded from representing the French people, but
Robespierre reminded the Convention that 'you have here
Belgians and Liégeois who exercise public functions honourably,
so perhaps it would be unjust to remove them'.[140] The salaries
for the administrators of the Belgian department of Jemappes,
taking refuge in Paris, were drawn from the subsidies voted on 4
March 1794.[141]

Despite the repudiation of the Propagandist Decrees, the
French still felt a lingering obligation to those foreigners who
had stood up and welcomed their armies in 1792. Both the exiles
and the Convention's own committees claimed that the foreign
patriots remained victims of their enthusiastic response to the

---

[134] *AP* lxvi. 516; lxix. 143–4; lxxiv. 33–4, 230; lxxx. 88; Raxhon, 'Réfugiés
liégeois', 220.
[135] AN, F/15*/17.   [136] *AP* lxxxvi. 509; AN, F/15*/17.
[137] *AP* lxvi. 516; lxix. 143–4.   [138] *AP* lxxiv. 33–4.
[139] MAE, CP, Angleterre, 588.   [140] Robespierre, *Œuvres*, x. 283.
[141] AN, F/15*/17.

French promise of fraternity, even if now that promise had been rescinded.[142] The government kept paying the subsidies up to 9 Thermidor and beyond. Such support also implies that the government envisaged some future use for the foreign radicals. 'Robespierrist' foreign policy publicly jettisoned plans to liberate other peoples, but this may have been because it was forced upon the government by defeat. The revolutionaries retained the hope that fresh victories might bring, if not a return of the overzealous crusade for universal liberty, at least tremors within the political structures of enemy powers.[143] Once the French reoccupied neighbouring territories, the foreign radicals who had found shelter in France might provide a core of administrators and suppliers, who knew the locality better than the invading French, but who might also be suitably grateful for their refuge during their exile. The government made use of foreign patriots in this way long before Thermidor. The Pisan radical Filippo Buonarroti met Robespierre and Saint-Just in Paris in March 1793. On 22 April 1794, he was appointed commissioner to Oneglia by the representatives on mission, Augustin Robespierre and Saliceti. Oneglia, where Piedmont had its outlet on the Mediterranean, had been conquered by the French on 9 April and Buonarroti was chosen primarily for his knowledge of Italian affairs. He was also politically reliable. He warmly supported Robespierre's cult of the Supreme Being, which he enthusiastically celebrated in Oneglia on 8 June.[144] The Irish republican William Jackson was employed by the Committee of Public Safety in February 1794 to glean information on the likely reaction of the British and Irish populations to a French invasion. The Committee of General Security protected him, calling him an 'American' and declaring him to be an 'irreproachable patriot'.[145]

The revolutionary government did not, therefore, persecute foreign patriots as such, but rather struck at those whom it deemed suspect, which was admittedly an increasingly broad category. Foreigners like Buonarroti, Jackson, Stone, and others

---

[142] *AP* lxix. 143–4.   [143] Godechot, *Grande Nation*, 78.
[144] J. Godechot, 'Les Jacobins italiens et Robespierre', *AhRf* 30 (1958), 67–9; Godechot, *Grande Nation*, 220–1; T. C. W. Blanning, *The French Revolutionary Wars 1787–1802* (London, 1996), 171.
[145] Woodward, *Une Anglaise*, 107–12.

owed their freedom either to their utility or to the fact that their politics did not appear to challenge the government. The government's urge to impose orthodoxy in turn engendered a need on the part of the foreign patriots to conform, a need which had been developing since the spring of 1793 with the defection of Dumouriez. The Dutch Patriot Jan van Hooff had defied Dumouriez's orders to surrender at Breda in March 1793, but he was still arrested when he returned to France. He was suspected for his ties to the traitorous general and was not released until 9 Thermidor.[146] The pressure of conformity became more acute when the Girondins were purged. On 17 July 1793, Georg Forster penned a petition from the *Convention rhéno-germanique*, asking for 'reunion' with France. He stressed the republican orthodoxy of the Mainz patriots by promising that, when the Prussians were driven back, the *mayençais* would send a deputation to Paris to celebrate the first anniversary of the overthrow of the monarchy.[147] Although his sympathies lay with the Girondins, he showed enough acumen to run missions to the provinces for the new government between August and November 1793. He died in Paris, disillusioned, on 10 January 1794.[148] Adam Lux, another member of the Mainz delegation, was less circumspect. His horrified friends dissuaded him from committing suicide at the bar of the Convention as a means of shocking some sense into it. Finally, brushing off Forster's advice, he refused to destroy his manuscript eulogizing Charlotte Corday, Marat's assassin. The offending papers were found when Lux was arrested and he was executed early in November 1793.[149]

Prior flirtation with the Girondins aroused the ire of the Montagnard Convention and the government, with Paine being among the high-profile victims. Almost immediately after the *journée* of 2 June, Joel Barlow, although an American citizen and therefore a neutral, moved out of Paris to the suburbs, possibly because his revolutionary career had been interwoven too much with the Girondins for comfort.[150] Count von Schlabrendorff and Paul-Jeremie Bitaubé, both

[146] Schama, *Patriots and Liberators*, 159–60.
[147] *AP* lxix. 175–6.
[148] Gooch, *Germany*, 313–14; Ruiz, 'Jacobinisme allemand', 263.
[149] Gooch, *Germany*, 343–4.
[150] Durden, 'Joel Barlow', 350–2.

known for their friendships with leading Girondins, were arrested and held until after 9 Thermidor. Karl Reinhard, who owed his position in the ministry of foreign affairs to the Girondins, was either fortunate enough to have been overlooked or had powerful protectors. He was only imprisoned days before the fall of Robespierre and his associates.[151] With malicious glee, Camille Desmoulins used Anacharsis Cloots's earlier Girondin connections to attack his bitterest enemies, the Hébertists, to whom Cloots was now bound. In the *Vieux Cordelier* on 10 December 1793, Desmoulins displayed Cloots's linen, which, he claimed, was heavily soiled with Girondism: 'It was Guadet and Vergniaud who were his godfathers, and who had him naturalized a French citizen.'[152] Two days later, Robespierre used this devastating attack in his own assault on Cloots in the Jacobins, which led to the expulsion of this colourful character from that citadel of political orthodoxy. Étienne Clavière, the Girondin minister of finance, was among those arrested by order of the *comité insurrectionnel* in the coup of 2 June. He remained in the Conciergerie until 8 December, when he was formally accused of financial corruption. That night, he used a knife to commit suicide.[153] The few Spanish patriots in France, including Marchena, Hevia, and Vicente María Santiváñez, had benefited too much from Girondin help to be left unmolested. Denounced by their compatriot Carles, they spent time in French prisons, where Santiváñez died. Carles had warned the Girondin foreign minister Lebrun that Marchena could not be trusted because he was a monarchist, while Hevia was 'devoid of good sense and reflection'. Lebrun insisted that their civic virtue was well-proven, protection which labelled the Spanish radicals as Girondins.[154]

The larger groups of foreign radicals mirrored the Montagnard–Girondin divide. Despite the natural gravitation of the Liégeois towards the expansive Girondin foreign policy, twenty-three exiles from Franchimont were more radical—and had been since 1789. When Lebrun was purged on 2 June 1793, the Franchimontois minority in Paris celebrated by declaring

[151] Ruiz, 'Jacobinisme allemand', 271 n. 42.
[152] *Vieux Cordelier*, 2.
[153] Bénétruy, *L'Atelier de Mirabeau*, 436–9, 442–3.
[154] MAE, CP, Espagne, 636; Herr, *Eighteenth Century Revolution*, 283.

their 'entire adhesion to the revolutionary principles of the Mountain'. The moderate Henkart wrote a letter protesting against Lebrun's arrest, but from 6 June, the Liégeois renounced their Girondin ties. Those who had courageously if tactlessly supported Lebrun were expelled from their assembly. Now led by the radicals, the Liégeois reconciled with the Franchimontois in July, creating the *assemblée générale populaire des ci-devants pays de Liège, Franchimont, Stavelot et Logne*. Determined not to omit any epithets, they chastized 'the Brissotins, Rolandins, girondins-Liégeois, burning partisans of the ex-minister Lebrun' for 'their perfidious, uncivic and anti-republican sentiments'. The thirty-eight strong *Gironde liégeoise*, as the moderates were known, were denied allocations of French subsidies. As if to underline their personal commitment to the Jacobins, individual Liégeois exiles promised to denounce their more moderate compatriots. In August, Briart promised the Unité section 'information on the aristocrats from his country who are in Paris'. Henkart, the Fabrys, and Lesoinne felt threatened enough to leave the city with other moderates, leaving only Bassenge to soldier on.[155]

Like most of their Liégeois counterparts, the Brabançons sought to wash their hands of the Girondins. On 18 July 1793, the *assemblée des belges* in Paris declared its 'solemn adherence . . . to the Sacred insurrection of 31 May'. On 9 August, it declared its hatred for aristocracy and federalism, swore to defend to the death the new constitution, and, for good measure, wept 'Sincere Tears at the memory of Lepelletier and Marat'. Between 19 October and 17 December, the assembly held a *scrutin épuratoire*, in which four of ninety-five members were arrested, one expelled, and two suspended. Six others understandably declined to attend. The eighty-two orthodox members and eighteen new recruits received *certificats de capacité*, which tactfully followed a format suggested by the ministry of the interior. The club was also obliged to submit its list of members to the municipality's police department.[156] The Belgians were not only striving to conform to the dominant orthodoxy, but were being encouraged to do so by the authorities.

---

[155] AN, BB/3/72; F/7/4779; Harsin, *Révolution liégeoise*, 173; Raxhon, 'Réfugiés liégeois', 219–22; Delange-Janson, *Ambroise*, 36–7.
[156] AN, F/7/4420.

The radicals and moderates among the Dutch Patriots were literally miles apart. The *société populaire des sans-culottes hollandais* at Saint-Omer denounced the *comité révolutionnaire batave* at Boulogne to Deforgues colourfully as 'moderates, statesmen and chameleons' on 27 October 1793. Deforgues's sympathies seemed to lie with the *sans-culottes hollandais*, for when approached by the Boulogne moderates on 6 November, he claimed icily that he had not even heard of the *comité révolutionnaire batave*. Its trembling secretary, Dumont-Pigalle, warned his colleagues that it was dangerous for them to meet when the government did not even recognize their existence.[157] It was fear, as much as arrest and execution, which paralysed the activities of foreign patriots. On 26 January 1794, the *club des allobroges* announced its own dissolution. Yet it is significant that other groups of foreign patriots could still organize, even if they were boxed in tightly by government interference, hostility, or indifference. Grudgingly, foreigners were still left space in which they could pursue their own political activities. That room was, however, far smaller than it was previously and it shrunk further as the Year II progressed, as over the summer of 1794 the Terror developed into a weapon to enforce political uniformity.

Clinging to the net of political orthodoxy was not easy, as the treacherous tides of revolutionary politics remained strong. Foreign patriots were left trying to anticipate where the current might flow. Some foreigners, in their zeal to shed the blemishes left by relations with Dumouriez or the Girondins, went to extremes. The *assemblée des belges* was affiliated to the *comité central des sociétés populaires*, one of the nerve centres of the popular movement in Paris. The Belgian assembly therefore placed itself on the knife-edge of militant politics. On 29 October it warmed to the fiery blast of dechristianization which was blowing through the capital. By acclamation, it adopted the order of the *comité central* which expelled all priests unless they formally retracted 'the errors which they have taught up to now'.[158] As a founder of the *comité révolutionnaire batave*, Joannes de Kock had maintained close relations with Dumouriez and Lebrun. After 2 June, he swung all the way over to the

---

[157] Mathiez, *La Révolution et les étrangers*, 38; Godechot, *Grande Nation*, 79.
[158] AN, F/7/4420.

extreme left, lavishly entertaining Hébert, Cloots, Vincent, and Ronsin in his Passy home. The Belgian Proli, who had been close to Danton and Dumouriez until the spring of 1793, was also seduced by extreme left-wing politics. By the time the Girondins were purged, he was cavorting with Hébert.[159]

Associations with critics of the government were increasingly difficult to sustain safely. Leading elements in the governing committees, and Robespierre in particular, twitched nervously at the rabid demands of the extremists. From January 1794, the government also recoiled from the moderates (or 'Indulgents'), when it became clear that some of them were implicated in the East India Company scandal, or 'foreign plot'. Fear of conspiracy lurked in revolutionary rhetoric as early as 1789 and even pre-existed the upheaval,[160] but it was the intensity of the war and of revolutionary politics, both of which were life-and-death struggles in the Year II, which made the revolutionaries so ready to believe—and to use—the allegations of a 'foreign plot' which emerged in the autumn of 1793. The conspiracy was denounced on separate occasions by two deputies: by Fabre d'Églantine around 12 October 1793, and by the sleazy former monk, François Chabot, a month later. It was probably little more than a financial scandal, in which Fabre and Chabot, along with three other politicians, attempted to blackmail the East India Company, but it stirred some of the most caustic feuding among the revolutionaries during the Terror. The involvement of such colourful figures as the counter-revolutionary baron de Batz suggested that there may have been a political dimension, but its face remained cloaked.[161] Fabre and Chabot probably made their denunciations to deflect suspicion and to save their own lives, but even Fabre may have been framed.[162] Both men accused their personal enemies, who were mainly extremists, of complicity in a financial and political conspiracy, funded by foreign powers, to destroy the Convention and the Republic.

---

[159] Rosendaal, 'L'Être suprême', 202; Mathiez, *La Révolution et les étrangers*, 101–6; Hampson, *Danton*, 101–3.

[160] Hunt, *Politics, Culture, and Class*, 39–42.

[161] A. Mathiez, 'Le Comité de Salut Public et le Complot de l'Étranger (octobre–novembre 1793)', *AhRf* 3 (1926), 318; N. Hampson, 'François Chabot and his Plot', *Transactions of the Royal Historical Society*, 5th ser. 26 (1976), 13–14.

[162] M. Eude, 'Une interprétation "non-Mathiézienne" de l'affaire de la Compagnie des Indes', *AhRf* 53 (1981).

The intricate webs which these two men wove as they spun their stories eventually provided the revolutionary government, and Robespierre and Saint-Just in particular, with the spurious evidence necessary to condemn the opposition. The involvement of the Hébertists in dechristianization merely confirmed, in Robespierre's eyes, the suspicion that they were paid by foreign agents to discredit the Revolution. Yet the evidence of Chabot's and Fabre's own shady behaviour towards the East India Company suggested that they and their Indulgent friends were also seeking to corrupt the people's representatives for darkly obscure reasons. Both extremists and moderates were therefore implicated in a largely fictitious plot, allegedly inspired and funded by Austria and Britain.

This fracture of revolutionary politics culminated in the government asserting its authority against both Hébertists and Indulgents in a double bout of political trials and executions in March and early April 1794. Those associated, however tentatively, with one or other faction were exposed to persecution. Foreign radicals were particularly vulnerable, because the government linked the factional struggle to the mysterious foreign conspiracy. The first foreign victim of the backlash was Eulogius Schneider, a leading member of the Strasbourg Jacobin club and now the public prosecutor at the local revolutionary tribunal. Adopting Hébertist-style politics, he embraced dechristianization and abjured the priesthood in Strasbourg cathedral on 20 November. When the government condemned dechristianization, Saint-Just and his colleague Lebas, on mission together in Alsace, had Schneider arrested, publicly displayed on the scaffold next to the guillotine, and dispatched to the revolutionary tribunal in Paris, where he was executed on 1 April 1794. He was accused by Robespierre of being 'the soul of the foreign conspiracy' in Alsace. One of Schneider's followers, Johann Butenschön from Holstein, followed him to the Conciergerie in July, but was saved by the coup of 9 Thermidor.[163]

Cloots, of course, was also compromised in the government reaction. Wounded by the blistering attacks by Robespierre and Desmoulins, he was expelled from the Convention as a foreigner along with Paine, arrested on 28 December 1793, and shut up in

[163] Mathiez, 'Les Citra et les Ultra', *AhRf* 3 (1926), 515; Hampson, *Saint-Just*, 155–7; Ruiz, 'Jacobinisme allemand', 264–5.

the Luxembourg, before being transferred to the Saint-Lazare. When the government ordered the arrest of the Hébertists, it consciously bound Cloots to their fate in order to give some substance to the charge of foreign conspiracy. It added two others whose behaviour made the accusation stick: de Kock and Proli, who was discovered hiding in the village of Vanderlen, near Gonesse, on 18 February 1794. These three foreigners were indicted, tried, and then guillotined with the Hébertists on 24 March 1794. When the turn of Danton and the Indulgents came on 5 April, they were accompanied to the scaffold by other foreigners who had been involved in revolutionary politics, including the Moravian Frey brothers, their Danish secretary Diederichsen, and the Spanish adventurer Guzman, all of whom had also been implicated in the myth of the 'foreign plot'.[164]

It was never more dangerous to be a foreigner involved in revolutionary politics. Those who were killed, however, died because they were too deeply implicated in opposition to the government. Yet the xenophobic language engendered by the 'foreign plot' certainly contributed greatly to the sense of unease among foreign radicals. After her release, Helen Maria Williams was plagued by a fear of rearrest. Early in July 1794 she left for Switzerland with John Hurford Stone, returning only after 9 Thermidor.[165] Those who had connections with the two 'factions' scrambled to disavow them. On 18 March, five days after the arrest of the Hébertists, the Liégeois grovelled before the Convention, congratulating it for having 'once more saved the *patrie*'. They protested their 'republican hearts' and expelled the extremist leadership from their assembly.[166] The Brabançons had also indulged in their own factional struggles and were silenced by the arrests.[167]

With the destruction of the opposition, the pressure on foreign patriots to appear as orthodox supporters of the government was heavier. In June, the Dutch *société des Montagnards* organized a Festival of the Supreme Being, despite the misgivings of the Dutch Patriots. Johann Valckenaer, who had fled Paris to Bièvres

---

[164] Soboul, 'Anacharsis Cloots', 36, 52–5; Mathiez, *La Révolution et les étrangers*, 179.

[165] Williams, *Letters Containing a Sketch*, i. 174–5, 206.

[166] *AP* lxxxvi. 627; Raxhon, 'Réfugiés liégeois', 221.

[167] AN, F/7/4420.

to avoid the harsh surveillance in the capital, tactfully withdrew from the Jacobin club when the law of 26–7 Germinal forbade foreigners from attending political societies. He still obtained a testimony to his *civisme* from the same club, which applauded his manufacture of saltpetre and stated that his speeches had been 'full of the most ardent patriotism and the soundest morality' and had urged 'adoration of a Supreme Being'.[168] There were some who could not keep up the appearance of loyalty. The Dutch Patriots Abbema and Jan Bicker scrambled out to Hamburg and Switzerland respectively.[169] In May 1794, Oelsner bolted from Paris after a tip-off that he had been denounced. Georg Kerner, whose Girondin sympathies earned him a place on a proscription list in the summer of 1794, escaped to Switzerland with a passport issued through the sympathetic offices of Karl Reinhard at the foreign ministry.[170]

With its authority consolidated, however, the government could protect those foreign patriots whose credentials were not impeccable, but for whom the government may have had some use. The Liégeois generals Jean-Joseph Fyon and Ransonnet were released from captivity in January and February respectively and remained at large throughout the spring and into the summer. When Fyon was accused by the Liégeois extremist Briart of *modératisme*, it was Robespierre who rose to Fyon's defence in the Jacobins on 7 April.[171] On 25 April, the Committee of Public Safety exempted Belgian, Liégeois, and Mainz patriots from the law of 26–7 Germinal. That same date, Dutch Patriots were given a similar exception, provided they had arrived in France before 1790.[172] The United Irishman Archibald Hamilton Rowan escaped from prison in Dublin and sailed into Roscoff in Brittany on 7 May, where he was promptly arrested. Imprisoned as a spy in Brest, he was eventually released in June on the orders of the Committee of Public Safety. Conducted to Paris, he was lodged at public expense while being questioned on the political state of the British Isles.[173]

---

[168] Rosendaal, 'L'Être suprême', 203–5; Schama, *Patriots and Liberators*, 160.

[169] Schama, *Patriots and Liberators*, 160.   [170] Gooch, *Germany*, 339, 342.

[171] Robespierre, *Œuvres*, x. 430; Raxhon, 'Réfugiés liégeois', 222; Mathiez, *La Révolution et les étrangers*, 40–1.

[172] AN, AF/II/61; *AP* lxxxix. 347.

[173] A. H. Rowan, *The Autobiography of Archibald Hamilton Rowan*, ed. W. H. Drummond (Shannon, 1972), 218–36.

John Hurford Stone, who had remained free since the end of October 1793, was rearrested on 24 April 1794. He had been denounced by a compatriot named Arthur, for alleged contacts with two British agents called Milne and Robert Smith. The authorities had second thoughts and he was released two days later, on condition that he obeyed the decree of 26–7 Germinal and left Paris. He and Helen Williams were on the verge of leaving for Switzerland when the government requisitioned him as a printer. When the couple were finally allowed to leave early in July, it was the Committee of Public Safety which granted the passports, which were endorsed to 'assure their return'. By the time Stone was denounced again for being a British agent on 15 July, he was safely in Basle.[174] When Benjamin Vaughan, a former Member of Parliament, fled Britain after he was implicated during the treason trial of Stone's brother, William, he assumed the pseudonym of Jean Martin. He arrived in Paris on 2 June. His identity was initially protected by a handful of revolutionaries and he was held in secret at the Carmes prison. When the Committee of Public Safety discovered his true identity, he was twice interrogated by Armand Herman, head of the Civil and Judicial Commission, who accepted that Vaughan was threatened with a charge of high treason in Britain and recommended his release. Vaughan was freed on 28 June and was provided with a passport for Switzerland on 1 July.[175] It was not only British fugitives who benefited from such unpredictable protection in this period. The Piedmontese lawyer Gedeon Muzio fled persecution in his own country on 8 June. He was allowed to settle in France and was employed as an agent for the departmental administration of the Alpes-Maritimes, where several months later he married before moving to Paris.[176]

As news from the front at last became brighter in the summer, some members of the government may have been more convinced of the usefulness of foreign patriots. While Fyon was rearrested on 18 July 1794, Bassenge, who was imprisoned in June, was released after pressure from Robespierre, who agreed

[174] AN, W//47; Mathiez, *La Révolution et les étrangers*, 182; Woodward, *Une Anglaise*, 117–20.

[175] A. Mathiez, *La Conspiration de l'étranger* (Paris, 1918), 262–4; Woodward, *Une Anglaise*, 118–19.

[176] AN, F/15/3511.

to meet with him on 8 Thermidor to discuss the French liberation of Liège and Belgium. After the victory at Fleurus, members of the Committee of Public Safety actually opened discussions with Dutch Patriots, whose committee the government had refused to recognize only six months previously.[177] Yet when the French finally entered this dialogue, it was very clear that they had their own national concerns in mind rather than any principles of international fraternity. While the Belgians, Liégeois, and Dutch might offer the French territorial concessions and an enhanced strategic position in western Europe, the Poles, who were actually engaged in their own uprising against the Russians, were dismissed by Saint-Just and Robespierre at a meeting of the Committee of Public Safety in July. The former cast doubt on the 'revolutionary' character of the Polish struggle, while Robespierre described it as 'an affair of the nobility'.[178] The dictates of national interest were to remain the guiding principle for successive French governments in their relations with foreign patriots.

The retreat of revolutionary cosmopolitanism and the corresponding nationalization of the war certainly led to the harassment, imprisonment, and expulsion of foreign patriots for the simple fact of their nationality. Some, however, were subsequently released and large numbers remained at liberty throughout the entire period. Those who did suffer on the scaffold were not executed because they were foreign, but because of their compromising political connections.

While the rhetoric made all enemy subjects suspect, the revolutionary government remained surprisingly pragmatic in its approach to foreign patriots. The authorities supported foreign refugees throughout the Terror, granting subsidies and positions in the administration and army. Despite the uncompromising terms of the law of 16 October, a large number of foreign radicals were left at large. They were explicitly exempted from the decree of 26–7 Germinal. The government itself seems to have realized that, once the French armies triumphed again, they would need these people to help in the supervision of the newly occupied territories. The main condition for their freedom

---

[177] Raxhon, 'Réfugiés liégeois', 222; Godechot, *Grande Nation*, 79.
[178] Meller, '"Pour notre liberté et pour la vôtre"', 314.

and for financial support was that their loyalties focused on the government alone. Those who successfully disavowed their former connections with discredited revolutionaries remained at liberty. Foreign political societies in France had to tread carefully and performed embarrassing ideological pirouettes to keep in with political developments. Yet their very persistence through the Terror suggests at worst government indifference and at best a tolerance on the grounds that they might some day have a use. Such official attitudes gave foreigners a confined space in which to organize politically and to pursue their own aspirations. Shortly before Thermidor, when the situation on the frontiers had developed into renewed victories, they were even able to resume discussions with the French government and so had potential influence on French policy. Those foreign chameleons who successfully changed political colour apace with political developments, however, stored up problems for the future. If their politics had to conform strictly to the demands of the Paris government, then foreign patriots were now more distant than ever from their native political culture and traditions. When they returned home, they might be aliens in their own land.

V

While the revolutionaries regarded the war as one of the French people against despotic governments, foreigners who engaged in economic activity in France would remain unmolested. The Convention was reluctant to sever economic lifelines to the outside world. A declaration of 1 February 1793, placing British and Dutch people and property under the protection of the law, was, however, rejected and gradually the revolutionaries overcame their misgivings about disrupting trade. By the late summer of 1793, the suspicion spread in the Convention that foreign merchants and bankers were profiting from the decline in value of the *assignats*, were speculating on exchange rates, and were exporting primary produce, either to make money or to destroy the French economy. The government was spurred into taking measures to restrict their activities. Among the people who found their livelihood most disrupted were foreign merchants.

For much of the summer of 1793, the plunging value of the *assignat* encouraged foreign merchants to head for French ports to acquire cheap exports. As the vast majority of deputies to the Convention believed in the freedom of commerce, a controlled economy emerged only gradually, in response to the crisis and under pressure from the Paris crowd.[179] The revolutionaries had to decide: if war was still one of peoples against tyrannic governments, they could not make foreign merchants suffer for their nationality. If, however, the conflict was one of nation against nation, the Convention had to judge whether or not disruption of trade was economically viable and beneficial to the war effort.

Initially, the revolutionaries sought to distinguish themselves from their enemies by stressing freedom of commerce.[180] When a British merchant named William Trollope was grabbed by a French corsair and carried off to La Rochelle, the municipality released him on 20 March 1793 and, on 8 April, the Convention gave him a passport. On 4 May, the Convention ordered the return of three Dutch vessels seized by the *Sans-Culotte de Jemappe*. The revolutionaries were particularly sensitive towards neutral merchants. When, ten days later, a Danish ship was boarded, the Convention agreed to 'compensate and punish any attack on the *droit des gens* by French citizens' and proclaimed its respect for the neutral trade and 'the rights of peoples'. On 10 April, the tribunal of Le Havre decided that the American merchantman *Lawrence* had been wrongly captured by a French corsair and ordered the transgressors to pay compensation and a fine of 3,000 *livres*.[181]

The increasing scale of the war led the revolutionaries to consider measures which slowly embraced economic warfare. When the French losers in the *Lawrence* case appealed to the Convention's naval committee, the deputies wavered on 9 May and permitted French corsairs to seize neutral ships which carried enemy cargo. American vessels were exempted from this provision on 1 July, but only after vehement protests by

---

[179] G. Lefebvre, 'Le Commerce extérieur en l'an II', in *Études sur la Révolution française* (Paris, 1954), 241–2.

[180] G. Lefebvre, *The French Revolution from 1793 to 1799*, tr. J. Friguglietti and J. H. Stewart (New York, 1964), 21–5.   [181] *AP* lxi. 421; lxv. 238; lxx. 69.

Morris, the United States ambassador.[182] Still, that autumn forty-five American ships were detained at Bordeaux, a sore point both with Morris and with Thomas Paine, who raised the issue with the foreign ministry in September.[183]

The revolutionaries were unclear as to how far they wanted to restrict overseas trade. They understood that rough handling of neutral merchants was both politically and economically damaging, but French trade was being hurt by the embargo imposed by the British on war materials. On 8 June, the British extended their blockade to include foodstuffs and other essential produce. She received the support of Russia and Prussia, and put neutral powers such as Denmark and Genoa under pressure to conform.[184] Moreover, with exchange rates favourable to exports, merchants and manufacturers in enemy countries might benefit from the purchase, resale, or finishing of cheap French merchandise. As the war and the economic crisis bit deeper over the summer, the popular militants became more willing to believe that foreigners were responsible for their troubles. Their self-proclaimed leaders, particularly Hébert in his *Père Duchesne*, thundered against foreign merchants, including neutrals, who were exporting food from France while good *sans-culottes* went hungry.[185]

In this high temperature, foreign merchants were sometimes unable to do business without falling under suspicion. In August 1793, three Belgian merchants in Paris were interrogated after being denounced for 'correspondence with our enemies'. One of them was further 'suspected of being their spy'. They were arrested and sent to the Sainte-Pélagie. These three men had been suppliers to the French army and were in Paris to claim payment from the government. As subjects of the Austrian emperor who were not political refugees, they could easily be pictured as enemy agents. While suspicion of this kind was not enough for them to be arrested, the discovery of a blank passport was.[186] In this intense atmosphere, what might have been normal behaviour in peacetime now seemed highly suspicious.

---

[182] *AP* lxv. 238, 489; lxxxv. 155–6.
[183] Morris, *Diary*, ii. 602; Keane, *Tom Paine*, 385.
[184] Lefebvre, 'Commerce extérieur', 244.
[185] Cobb, 'Quelques aspects', 104.
[186] AN, BB/3/70.

The Convention, however, had no wish to stifle trade when foreign vessels were carrying vital goods into French ports. The revolutionaries tried to restrict enemy shipping, prevent the export of necessary produce, but keep channels open for imports. On 1 August, the Convention revoked its order releasing the three Dutch ships taken by the *Sans-Culotte de Jemappe* and a fortnight later banned foreign merchants from exporting basic foodstuffs, fuels, and fabrics. It also sought to encourage neutral shipping, however, provided it was to the benefit of the French. On 3 September, the Convention allowed neutral ships to leave with certain cargoes originally banned from export, provided they had first imported essential goods. A Navigation Act was adopted on 21 September, which permitted foreign vessels only to import cargo which came from the ship's country of origin. The law was strictly applied, even to neutrals. On 9 October, the Convention heard a complaint from foreign merchants who had chartered a Danish ship to deliver wine and olive oil—clearly not Danish products—to a French trading company in Cette. It was seized by a French ship which disregarded its neutral status. The cargo was declared *bonne prise* and confiscated.[187]

While the seizure of Spanish property decreed on 16 August was intended mainly as a reprisal, a similar measure aimed against the British on 9 October was also motivated by a desire to stifle British trade. A week later, Saint-Just defended these measures, pointing out that the British had already imposed a food blockade and were printing forged *assignats* to force a French economic collapse. Yet while recommending an embargo on Spanish and British goods, he rejected the extension of property seizures to other enemy subjects. Good republicans had no need of British fripperies, while an embargo on them would protect French industry. Trade with the rest of Europe, however, provided essential materials for the war and ought to be encouraged.[188]

Much as the revolutionaries hoped to maintain the flow of vital imports, in practice the combined effect of French restrictions on exports, the seizure of enemy property, and the British

[187] *AP* lxx. 69; lxxii. 350; lxxiii. 263–4; lxxvi. 265; Portemer, 'L'Étranger', 548.
[188] Hampson, *Saint-Just*, 137–9; Lefebvre, 'Commerce extérieur', 245; *AP* lxxvi. 638–9.

naval blockade scared off foreign merchants, who envisaged little gain for high risk. The General Maximum of 29 September 1793, which fixed prices on a variety of goods, including food, drink, fuel, clothing, and tobacco, destroyed any incentive for foreign merchants to import produce into France, as they could not sell at a profit.[189] At Bordeaux, neutral merchants never seemed to be in short supply, but at Marseille, Italians were understandably reluctant to run the British blockade, especially when the enemy held Toulon and Corsica. Pious neutral merchants from southern Europe also appear to have been scared off by the horror stories of dechristianization.[190] Up to 9 October 1793, merchants had been exempted from decrees against foreigners, but now British merchandise was barred and British merchants were liable to arrest. Thomas Collow, a Scot who had moved to Le Havre in 1785 to set up a trading company, was arrested despite his record over recent years for importing desperately needed foreign grain. The municipal officers signed his petition to the Convention for his release on 24 November. They remarked pointedly that a law as sweeping as that of 9 October meant that there were plenty of British people 'whose civic virtue is generally recognized', yet who languished in irons.[191] Similarly, a Dutch timber merchant from Delft named Matther petitioned the Committee of Public Safety for an exemption to the law of 16 October ordering the arrest of all enemy subjects. His Parisian section vouched for his conduct.[192]

Ultimately, foreign merchants were too useful to be excluded from French commerce. Those based in French ports proved to be one of the most important means by which imports still flowed into the country. In Bordeaux towards the end of October, a provisioning and commercial commission was established, fifteen members of which had German names. The German mercantile community in the city had maintained an important hold on its commercial activity throughout the Terror. Their ties with northern Europe were invaluable to Tallien and Ysabeau, the two *représentants en mission*, who sent German

[189] Lefebvre, 'Commerce extérieur', 245.
[190] Cobb, 'Quelques aspects', 104; Lefebvre, 'Commerce extérieur', 261, 264–5.
[191] T. Collow, *Le Citoyen Thomas Collow à la Convention Nationale* (Paris, An II).
[192] AN, AF/II/61.

merchants as contacts with neutral powers. One Zimmermann was sent to Paris to obtain the blessing and collaboration of the *commission des subsistances* in the search for imports of prime necessity. Another, Pohls, was dispatched to Hamburg. Merchants with English names were also used, including the American Jonas Jones, who accompanied Zimmermann to Paris, and his compatriot Gernon, who was sent to the United States. The authorities in Bordeaux were using foreign merchants to exploit existing commercial networks which had been closed off to French traders by the war. Nantes and Le Havre followed this example.

Such localized initiatives did not last long, as the Committee of Public Safety was alarmed at their lack of co-ordination. On 18 November, it forbade any such missions without its permission, but this centralization of commercial initiative simply meant that foreign merchants thus employed were now accredited by the Committee rather than the municipality. Pohls continued his work in Hamburg and was given money on 11 January 1794 to make his purchases on behalf of the government. On 5 December, Tallien and Ysabeau established a 'committee of neutrals' in Bordeaux, with the blessing of the subsistence commission in Paris. With three merchants representing the neutrals, the committee was to deal with foreign merchants willing to import food and raw materials into France. Marseille appointed a similar committee on 4 May 1794.[193]

The important role of foreign merchants, and particularly neutrals, was recognized by the Convention in a series of decisions which protected their interests. On 17 January 1794, a deputation of Americans claimed compensation for losses during the embargo and were promised an investigation. Indemnities for all neutral merchants who had suffered confiscation of their cargoes were decreed on 3 April. Meanwhile, the curtain of restrictions on exports was lifted slightly. On 26 February, neutral consuls succeeded in having the embargo on exports raised at Bordeaux. On 11 March, the Convention decreed that all merchandise which the subsistence commission had decided was not of prime necessity could be exported by neutrals. The Commission accordingly revised its list of primary goods and

---

[193] Lefebvre, 'Commerce extérieur', 247–8, 251, 266.

issued export licences, through commercial agencies established in the major ports. The Bordeaux agency included Zimmermann and Jones. On 17 May, Garnier-Saintes, who had replaced Ysabeau at Bordeaux, established a committee of twelve merchants who would organize exports so that they could be shipped *en masse*. To make its task easier, the committee appointed twenty *chefs d'exportation*, most of whom came from the German colony.[194]

The combined effects of the war, popular hostility, economic laws, and measures against foreigners put foreign merchants under pressure during the Terror. Some suffered because the very nature of their business aroused suspicion. Yet the Convention was reluctant to restrict trade. While enemy merchants were arrested and trade with Britain was ruptured, the revolutionaries tried not to disrupt commerce with other enemy countries and remained sensitive to the needs of neutrals. The latter often provided France's most secure links to the outside world and the Convention was receptive to their complaints. The services and goods which foreign merchants offered prevented the revolutionaries from pursuing the autarky which would have excluded foreigners from French commerce.

Like merchants, bankers and financiers suffered from popular hostility, while being saved from official harassment by the services which they offered the Republic. The flight of capital and the low value of *assignats* brought much suspicion to bear on foreign moneymen.[195] Many were believed to have disproportionate political influence, or to be financing the government's enemies. There was some evidence supporting this last charge: both de Kock and Proli backed the Hébertists, while the Dutch Vandenyvers were bankers to characters as far apart in their politics as Madame du Barry and Anacharsis Cloots. Walckiers and Boyd were both implicated in the 'foreign plot', with the latter having ties to both Chabot and William Pitt. Jean-Frédéric Perregaux from Neuchâtel slipped money to Proli when he fled to Boulogne to escape arrest in November 1793.[196] Bankers and

---

[194] Ibid. 250–4, 260; *AP* lxxxiii. 410.
[195] Lefebvre, 'Commerce extérieur', 244.
[196] N. Hampson, *The Life and Opinions of Maximilien Robespierre* (London, 1974), 239.

financiers were sometimes suspected of speculating with exchange rates on behalf of enemy governments and of being the channels for their subversive funds. Boyd was arrested in June 1793 after being accused of correspondence with Pitt and of distributing money for the counter-revolution, but he was released within a month.[197] Such fears about the machinations of bankers and their international networks were not novel,[198] but during the Terror they were more intense and pervasive.

As with merchants, foreign connections and correspondence were an integral part of the activities of foreign financiers. Boyd was a banker to the British government, while Walckiers, although a Vonckist, had once undertaken missions to London for the Austrians.[199] Perregaux's main operations were in Paris, but for a long time he had lines of credit extending across western Europe, including London banking houses. Swiss and Genevans almost monopolized the role of financial intermediary between London and Paris, with others like Boyd, Kerr, and the Vandenyvers sharing in this lucrative business.[200] In peacetime, most of such transnational relations were considered perfectly legitimate and desirable. By the autumn of 1793, they seemed subversive. They would become increasingly incriminating as the war, the Terror, and the political conflict in Paris gathered pace. Not all of the revolutionaries' suspicions were mere fantasies, for there is evidence to suggest that some foreign bankers, such as Boyd, Kerr, and Perregaux, did use their connections for obscurely sinister purposes.[201]

The evolving obsession with foreign financiers found expression in legislation. On 7 September, during the debate on confiscating enemy property, Danton asked for a measure which would 'strike at those bankers living in France who, by the most criminal manœuvres, have continually conspired against the *patrie* and fomented counter-revolution'.[202] That night, the governing committees placed seals on the papers of all foreign

---

[197] Mathiez, *La Révolution et les étrangers*, 142.
[198] Jarrett, *Begetters of Revolution*, 197, 203, 211–12.
[199] Mathiez, *La Révolution et les étrangers*, 107.
[200] Lüthy, *Banque Protestante*, ii. 318; Mathiez, *La Révolution et les étrangers*, 102.
[201] Hampson, *Perfidy of Albion*, 128–9; Hampson, *Life and Opinions*, 214–15; Hampson, *Danton*, 173; Mathiez, *La Révolution et les étrangers*, 100, 152–3.
[202] *AP* lxxiii. 491.

bankers.[203] Two days later, however, the Convention reversed its decision, lifted the seals, and released the imprisoned bankers into house arrest.[204] This about-turn was based on arguments presented on 8 September by Ramel of the finance commission, who warned that foreign businessmen owed more to French citizens than vice versa. To freeze the accounts held by foreigners in France would be to deprive French manufacturers and merchants of the payment of their debts.[205] This wavering by the Convention was not surprising, because the revolutionaries remained unclear about the economic and political effects of the unprecedented measures they were taking. Suspicion towards foreign financiers was deep-rooted, however, as the Vandenyvers discovered.

On 8 December, Jean-Baptiste Vandenyver was sent to the guillotine with his sons, Edme-Jean-Baptiste and Antoine-Augustin. The most sensational part of the charges was their association with Madame du Barry, once royal mistress to Louis XV, who had been their client since 1771 and to whom they had extended substantial credit for her four journeys to London between 1791 and 1793. Although the Vandenyvers may simply have been doing their job, they were doubly condemned for correspondence with both an *émigrée* and the enemy. They could not control what du Barry did with the money while she was in London. She was entertained by Forth, a British agent known to the French government, she met William Pitt, and lent the *émigré* cardinal de la Rochefoucauld 200,000 *livres*. These indiscretions by their profligate client were enough to condemn the Vandenyvers to death.[206]

Suspicion of bankers finally gelled into more general action on 25 December 1793, when Robespierre persuaded the Convention to put on trial those bankers, many of whom were foreign, who were charged with treason or conspiracy.[207] This was a response to the thickening 'foreign plot', but can also be seen as the outcome of long-festering suspicions towards foreign financiers.

[203] Mathiez, *La Révolution et les étrangers*, 149–50.
[204] *AP* lxxiii. 598.
[205] Mathiez, *La Révolution et les étrangers*, 150.
[206] H. Wallon, *Histoire du Tribunal révolutionnaire de Paris, avec le journal des ses actes*, 6 vols. (Paris, 1880–2), ii. 221–30; Lüthy, *Banque Protestante*, ii. 323; Hampson, *Life and Opinions*, 213–14.
[207] *AP* lxxxii. 299.

It was at this time that Perregaux had his papers seized and inspected.[208]

Foreign bankers whose dealings did not incriminate them were safe from persecution if they could be of service. Lack of foreign exchange dogged the government in the Year II and, on 26 February 1794, all Parisian bankers were obliged to subscribe to a banker's draft which permitted the government to exchange 50 million *livres* for foreign currency. The chairman of the committee overseeing the subscription was Perregaux.[209]

As with merchants, foreign bankers were cast under suspicion for connections and activities which might have been considered uncontroversial outside the extraordinary circumstances of war and Terror, but which now seemed sinister to the revolutionaries. The Vandenyvers paid the ultimate penalty for serving one of their clients. Others, such as de Kock and Proli, were embroiled in revolutionary politics and died because they were on the losing side. Bankers as a whole suffered from the specific animosity which was directed against them in the Year II. This was not particularly new, as *agiotage* and international banking networks had long aroused hostility for their alleged influence in French domestic politics. What was novel were the circumstances, in which the depth of hostility and suspicion could be translated into charges of subversion, and where such charges could lead to the scaffold. The revolutionary government, however, needed money and credit, which dictated a certain pragmatism. For all their shady transactions, Walckiers and Perregaux therefore remained at liberty, as their connections with international money markets were useful to the government.

Practical considerations also ensured that those foreigners employed in manufacturing were the most sheltered from revolutionary legislation. It was not even necessary to have skills which were directly related to the war effort in order to be protected. When, in 1793, a group of clockmakers from Neuchâtel arrived in Besançon, the representatives on mission to the Doubs sold the craftsmen a *maison nationale* and paid

---

[208] Hampson, *Life and Opinions*, 213.
[209] Lefebvre, 'Commerce extérieur', 253, 264.

them indemnities for the travel costs incurred by their apprentices. The hope that these foreign artisans would disseminate clockmaking skills throughout France was shared by the central government. As more foreign workers arrived in Besançon over the course of the Year II, the manufacture was offered 60,000 *livres*, a concession for fifteen years, another *maison nationale* to house fifty artisans rent free, and a three-year promise by the government to buy the clocks at a price set by experts.[210]

A similar effort to attract foreign expertise was made at Annecy, where on 4 June 1794 the Committee of Public Safety established a manufacture of metal files under the management of a Swiss named Goldschmidt. He was charged with attracting his compatriots and was told that the government would pay for their travel, give them a six-year indemnity for their lodging, and reward them with bounties proportionate to the numbers of files produced. Goldschmidt enticed fifteen artisans to Annecy, all of whom brought their own tools. By July 1795, the plant had 110 workers who had made 888 dozen files.[211] In Tarare, an Irish prisoner of war who had once worked in a Glasgow mill, introduced local muslin-weavers to more advanced looms. These machines were gradually adopted in the region.[212] Ancien Régime practices of attracting foreign technology and craftsmen were still being deployed by the Republic of Virtue.

Foreign artisans in France were protected from the worst of the legislation aimed against foreigners. On 19 August 1793, the commissioners to the armies of the Rhine and the Moselle exempted all foreign arms workers from the law of 1 August, which ordered the arrest of all enemy subjects.[213] Of the 199 foreigners listed by the commissioners of the Unité section in Paris that same month, a substantial proportion were likely to have been exempt from much Terrorist legislation against enemy subjects on the basis of their occupation. The occupations of 175 are known. Of these, 136 were in crafts such as tailoring, shoemaking, joining, and masonry. Six were engaged in 'luxury' trades, including a goldsmith, a wig-maker, an engraver, and a piano-maker. Ten were involved in professions

---

[210] *Moniteur* (8 Nivôse III).
[211] Ballot, *L'Introduction du machinisme*, 26.
[212] Henderson, *Britain and Industrial Europe*, 26.
[213] *AP* lxxiii. 119.

or literary pursuits, including teachers or professors, a printer, a bookseller, an apothecary, and an architect. Five were retailers— two shopkeepers, two café owners and a baker, while there was one wholesale merchant. Seven offered their services variously as domestics, clerks, a coachman, and a messenger, while the remaining ten lived as 'citizens', a 'patriot', an official, a military officer, and a *rentier*.[214]

The largest groups among the 136 craftsmen, the seamsters (*tailleurs*, of whom there were sixty-five) and the cobblers (*cordonniers*, of whom there were forty) and many others, such as the locksmiths, broom- and pin-makers, masons, and the solitary tinworker represented the poorest levels of urban society, working long hours for very low wages in menial tasks.[215] Yet much of their labour, and that of the saddlers, curriers, and joiners, could conceivably have been turned to military use. Approximately three-quarters of those foreigners whose jobs are listed therefore stood a plausible chance of being exempted from the various laws against foreigners. Even those who were not engaged in manufacturing, such as those involved in literary pursuits, printing, and the booktrade, may have been given special dispensation because, in practice, the authorities could take a very broad view of usefulness. What the figures do show is that, up to August 1793 at the earliest, a substantial number of workers, artisans, and craftsmen, most of them enemy subjects, had chosen to remain in the section rather than uproot themselves, their families, and their business because of the war. In the case of the poorest workers, they may well not have had a choice. The relatively small proportion of foreigners engaged in luxury trades might be explained by the collapse in demand for their services, brought about by the economic and social crisis of the Revolution and the international conflict.

It does not appear that these foreign artisans and workers suffered from any special venom from the popular militants, even during the economic crisis when, in August, the *assignat* dropped to 22 per cent of its face value. Suspicion and hostility was reserved rather for the rich, the speculators, the hoarders. When economic fears were expressed in xenophobic terms, it was aimed primarily at those thought to be enemy agents. It was

---

[214] AN, F/7/4779.   [215] Hufton, *The Poor*, 42–3, 96.

foreign financiers who were increasingly thought to be paid by enemy powers to discredit the *assignats*, to starve Paris, and to ruin the good *sans-culottes*.[216] While the poorer, migrant labourers almost certainly felt targeted by outbursts of xenophobia, it was usually aimed at the richer foreigner who was embroiled in revolutionary politics.

The law of 6 September exempted from arrest those labouring in workshops and manufactures, provided their sound principles and behaviour were vouched for by two worthy citizens.[217] Among those who benefited were Nicholas Joyce and Christopher White, both merchants and manufacturers of cotton. Reported as British subjects to the *comité de surveillance* of the Paris Observatoire section on 16 September, they were allowed to remain free because of their occupation.[218] Even with the uncompromising decrees of 9 and 16 October, such foreigners had a reasonable chance of being left unharassed. In a memorandum to the Committee of Public Safety, Ramel criticized the decree of 16 October because 'workers occupied in the workshops and living near their work' had not been protected.[219] The law of 9 October exempted those British subjects working in manufactures, which could be loosely or strictly interpreted by local authorities. In Toulouse, the brother of the Girondin deputy, Boyer-Fonfrède, was deprived of his prized Manchester weavers who had been introducing new looms since 1791.[220] On 6 January 1794, however, James White was released by an order of the Convention, because he was employed at Choisy-sur-Seine by two American citizens, who were developing a means of making French rivers more navigable.[221] In Normandy, where small colonies of British textile workers had remained largely unharassed, municipal authorities protected them by citing the exemption clauses.[222] None the less, Meister, returning to Paris in 1795, noticed the change in the capital's working population: there were fewer foreign craftsmen, most of whom had fled in order to escape the possibility of arrest.[223]

[216] Mathiez, *La Vie chère*, i. 262, 265–6, 311; ii. 191.
[217] *AP* lxxiii. 463.
[218] AN, F/7*/2514.
[219] AN, AF/II/61.
[220] M. Lyons, *France under the Directory* (Cambridge, 1975), 187.
[221] *AP* lxxxiii. 48–9.   [222] Cobb, 'Quelques aspects', 110.
[223] Meister, *Souvenirs*, 78–9.

Yet substantial numbers of foreign artisans and manufacturers, even those from countries at war with France, remained at liberty because they were craftsmen. Of 7,810 *cartes de sûreté* issued by three of the four sections of the *faubourg* Saint-Marcel in the Year II, those given to foreigners remained a small proportion of the total, but what is significant is the nationalities represented. Among the most numerous were people of unequivocally enemy nationality, including the Netherlands, Austria, and some of the Italian and imperial states. There was also a heavy presence of Belgians and artisans from neutral countries such as Switzerland.[224]

The law of 26–7 Germinal explicitly excluded from its provisions workers employed in arms manufactures and 'foreign workers living by manual labour', provided they had worked at their trade since before August 1793. Retailers were also shielded, provided they had been established in France since May 1789.[225] The Committee of Public Safety also exempted any foreigner involved in the manufacturing of sails and all 'merchants, manufacturers, heads of manufactures, of workshops, of factories', or people employed in them, in nineteen different towns on the coast and the frontiers, if they had worked there for at least six months. There was, however, one condition attached: representatives on mission were to keep track of their *civisme* and their utility.[226] The committee also placed under its wing individual manufacturers and artisans who provided employment or whose products were of benefit to the public at large. In Calais, such foreigners included a British soap manufacturer named Rush and the Dutch printers charged with publishing the maximum prices. In Paris, the government requisitioned a Dutch or German printer charged with the work emanating from the Committee of Public Safety.[227]

Some foreign manufacturers still thought it prudent to show that they had patriotic credentials. In Jouy-en-Josas, Oberkampf used his money and his position to maintain an image of political orthodoxy. In May 1794, he bought *biens nationaux*. He also gave or loaned large sums of money for the war effort, including

[224] H. Burstin, *Le Faubourg Saint-Marcel à l'époque révolutionnaire: Structure économique et composition sociale* (Paris, 1983), 81–2, 318–19.

[225] *AP* lxxxviii. 649; lxxxix. 29–30.

[226] AN, AF/II/61.   [227] Ibid.

160,000 *livres* to the first forced loan, decreed on 20 May 1793. Late in February 1794, he was summoned by Perregaux's *commission du commerce et des approvisionnements*, where Oberkampf added his signature to those of forty-one merchants and bankers to raise 50 million *livres* for the purchase of foreign exchange. A month later, he presented a full set of equipment for a cavalryman to the local Jacobin club, at a cost of 3,192 *livres* which came from his own pocket. His status as a large employer alone brought him recognition from the revolutionary government. On 23 June 1794, Couthon visited the manufacture and, on behalf of the nation, saluted him for 'having maintained 1,100 workers of both sexes'.[228] The number was an exaggeration, but Oberkampf was not about to argue with the Committee of Public Safety when it was congratulating him.

His engagement with local politics was also a means of protecting himself and his business. He joined the Jacobins of Jouy-en-Josas on 30 December 1793, one month after the club was established. As a large employer, Oberkampf used his patronage to control the society. He and his employees made impressive patriotic contributions at the meetings. His nephew Samuel Widmer used his chemical skills to extract the constituent elements of saltpetre from ferns collected by children in the forests. Every *décade*, Oberkampf funded the club's distribution of 400 *livres*' worth of bread to the town's poor and sick. While such activities might be regarded as paternalism, they also wore a political face. By behaving as a good patriot, Oberkampf effaced the sins of his recent ennoblement and, perhaps, shielded himself and his associates from suspicion over his foreign origins. If it was merely a ploy, it paid off. Christian-Henry Voët, a Prussian engraver who worked at Oberkampf's plant and who was an *agent national*, denounced his employer to the Committee of General Security. It was his reputation, and not that of Oberkampf, which was ruined. The Committee could not believe that he was 'stained with moderatism, with royalism and suspected of hoarding' and in May 1794, Voët was expelled from the Jacobin club. Oberkampf magnaminously gave him his old job back.[229] Some were not as shrewd or as fortunate. Pierre and Louis-Benoît Badger, two silk weavers and sons of the British entrepreneur who

---

[228] Chassagne, *Oberkampf*, 171, 174–6, 184 n. 65.
[229] Ibid. 173–5; Chapman and Chassagne, *European Textile Printers*, 122.

had established their mill in Lyon, were shot in the city on 28 November and 4 December 1793, condemned for their part in the Federalist uprising.[230] As with other foreigners in France, artisans and manufacturers who fell from the net of political orthodoxy could pay the ultimate price.

The treatment of foreign artisans, manufacturers, bankers, and merchants shows that the revolutionaries were cautious when they dealt with the economy during the war. Hostility to foreign merchants and bankers did create an atmosphere in which their activities suddenly seemed suspicious. Some merchants and financiers certainly fell foul of the authorities for no other reason than that their everyday activities involved foreign correspondence, which could be construed as contact with the enemy. For the most part, however, the revolutionaries recognized the importance of foreigners to the French economy and were reluctant to exclude them totally. Just as they developed price and wage controls under pressure and with much reluctance, so the revolutionaries dallied when it came to cutting off commercial and financial ties.

Not only did they adhere to the principles of free trade, but they were also uncertain about the economic and political consequences of protectionism. Foreign merchants brought cargoes which fed, clothed, and supplied the French armed forces and which ensured some social stability in the towns. Networks of foreign bankers opened lines of credit and allowed the purchase of foreign currency. Foreign artisans and manufacturers created employment and produced the equipment needed to wage the war. Reluctance to close the door on these contributions explains the exemptions offered to foreigners and the indecision with which the authorities often approached the role of foreigners in the French economy.

The revolutionaries never entirely excluded foreigners from French commercial and economic life. British and Spanish merchants were prevented from trading in France because they were subjects of an enemy government, but this was the furthest the French economy excluded on the basis of nationality alone. The revolutionaries tried to avoid a breach of commercial

---

[230] Alger, *Englishmen*, 350; Harris, *Industrial Espionage*, 104.

relations with other enemy countries, including the Dutch. Above all, neutral merchants were treated with sensitivity, as the Convention sought to encourage them to import vital supplies. Trade was 'nationalized' in the sense that the government sought to co-ordinate it, but foreign merchants and bankers helped administer this control, because the revolutionaries recognized their potential in attracting goods and capital. Other enemy subjects, including some British, continued their activities as artisans and manufacturers in France. Most of the laws against foreigners exempted them from imprisonment or expulsion because the revolutionaries assumed that they had something to contribute, either to the long-term development of the French economy, or to the war effort. Where the law did not explicitly protect them, local authorities, vouching for their usefulness, sometimes did. The revolutionary government itself used its powers to requisition such foreigners for the Republic.

All this was done, however, on the understanding that foreign merchants, bankers, manufacturers, and artisans did not abuse their freedom. The Badgers were executed for their part in the Federalist revolt in Lyon. The Vandenyvers were unfortunate in having as their client an indiscreet, if generous, former royal mistress. De Kock and Proli died not because they were bankers, but mainly because they were associated with opposition to the revolutionary government. Foreigners with a high profile who failed the test of orthodoxy paid a high price. Oberkampf therefore went out of his way to prove his *civisme* and enjoyed the confidence of the government, but for the vast majority of merchants, manufacturers, and artisans, the safest tactic was to avoid revolutionary politics altogether.

VI

The period of the Terror was marked by xenophobia. Fear of spies and of malign foreign influence producing sweeping measures against foreigners. The hostility and suspicion were certainly produced in part by revolutionary ideology. Some rhetoric did equate patriotism with the exclusion or even the death of certain foreigners. The decree of 7 Prairial, for example, stemmed in part from the logic which placed all opposition to the government beyond humanity. Xenophobia, however, was not the exclusive product of revolutionary ideology. Distrust and scorn of the British, Austrians, and Spanish, in particular, were rooted in prejudices which predated the Revolution. Revolutionary ideology merely gave novel, immediate expression to these hatreds, which in turn were intensified by the unprecedented scale of war and internal crisis.

On paper, the revolutionaries' attempts to regulate and control the movements and activities of foreigners made nationality a matter of almost daily concern. Arguably, even the range of exemptions for certain types of foreigners stressed that they were being tolerated *despite* their nationality. The cause of this development was the expansion of the state, made necessary by the laws providing for the surveillance, imprisonment, and expulsion of foreigners and the confiscation of their property. Such laws made the state, or its representatives at local level, the arbiters of their fate. It was this penetration of state authority which thrust nationality forward as the most important facet of an individual's identity.

Yet if the rhetoric and letter of the law implied the nationalization of the state and even of much of French social life, the practice was very different, for five reasons. First of all, the authorities responsible for executing the law were not always as efficient or as sweeping as the decrees themselves demanded, as the manner in which the Unité section in Paris implemented the law of 1 August 1793 suggests. It is possible that, with experience, the revolutionaries became more practised in imposing surveillance, searching premises, and making arrests. Yet both local and central authorities also explicitly and deliberately limited the impact of the laws by protecting some foreigners, giving them exemptions, and requisitioning them for their services.

Secondly, many of the measures taken against foreigners were dictated less by a nationalizing ideology than by practical concerns. The disbandment of foreign legions may finally have realized Dubois-Crancé's vision of a citizen army, but there were other reasons behind the measure, such as concerns over their loyalty and their viability. Even then, rank-and-file foreigners were allowed to re-enlist in French regiments.

Thirdly, the primary concern of the authorities in their

treatment of foreigners was the domestic security of the Republic. Over the course of the Year II, the revolutionary government came to regard the imposition of political conformity as a necessary condition for stability. Although the Terrorist regime could hardly be commended for tolerance of dissent, this did suggest that foreigners who did conform would be protected. The treatment of foreign radicals, for example, showed that, despite the broad terms of the decrees against enemy subjects, ideological orthodoxy could still cut across nationality. Those foreign troops who were arrested and denied postings fell into that predicament not because they were foreign, but because their political loyalties and competence were suspect. Even a few clergymen and seminary students escaped arrest when there was unequivocal proof of their republican commitment. The numbers of foreigners who benefited from their patriotism was so small, however, that such a virtue came close to being defined in practice as an exclusively French trait.

Fourthly, therefore, a far more important factor than political orthodoxy was utility. Soldiers disbanded from the legions were distributed to regular units rather than sent away, potentially to the enemy. Foreign patriots remained at liberty, unless they were too embroiled with the losing sides in revolutionary politics, because the government envisaged a future role for them once the French armies surged across the frontiers again. If certain foreign bankers and merchants could fall foul of the authorities because of the very nature of their activities, the revolutionaries also realized that they had important potential in supplying the beleaguered Republic with foreign exchange, materials, and food. Above all, artisans were protected from almost every law on foreigners, and these exemptions were sometimes loosely interpreted to include even those whose contributions to the war effort were not immediately apparent. The practical sense of the revolutionaries limited the translation of both xenophobia and ideology into the actual exclusion of foreigners from French social, economic, and military life.

Fifthly, despite legislation to the contrary, even political activity was never entirely nationalized. In the first place, organizations of foreign patriots persisted, despite the publicly expressed hostility of the government to any war of liberation. Official toleration was often grudging and dependent on political conformity, but the very survival of Dutch, Belgian, and Liégeois committees and assemblies in this period meant that some space still existed for foreigners to engage in political activity of their own. The pressures imposed by political orthodoxy turned that room into a narrowly confined space during the Terror, but it enabled foreign radicals to cocoon their own aspirations. When military circumstances looked more auspicious in the summer of 1794 and the government was more receptive to their aims, foreign patriots were ready to negotiate with the French government. In the second place, foreigners were never entirely excluded from participating in the structures of the French state. While they were prohibited from sitting as deputies to the National Convention on 25 December 1793, foreigners continued to join in French political activity at a more localized level, in sectional surveillance committees, popular societies, assemblies, and in the *armées révolutionnaires*. Some retained these positions even after the law of 26–7 Germinal ordered their dismissal. If some did so because they fulfilled the stringent residence requirements, others did not and instead benefited from the support of their French colleagues and even the quiet acquiescence of the ruling committees. Individual foreigners were used by the French authorities in official or semi-official capacities because of special insights or connections which they might have offered. With foreigners serving the French state in various roles, the limits of citizenship did not coincide precisely with the legal boundaries of nationality. If this was due less to any residual cosmopolitanism than to pragmatism on the part of the revolutionaries, it still meant that, in practice, the Republic of Virtue never became Saint-Just's 'city' exclusive to French nationals.

5

Foreigners between Thermidor and Brumaire

To repeal confiscation would be to provide for foreigners, who will give us nothing in return. It would offer our debt-ridden enemies the means of waging the next campaign. During both war and peace there exists a *droit des gens*. They must return a penny for a penny, a prisoner for a prisoner, a million for a million. (Thirion, deputy to the Convention, 29 December 1794.)[1]

Eight days after the law was proclaimed, sixty-two thousand foreigners went before the police bureau and the Directory, in order to secure exemptions and to be permitted to stay in Paris. But, after a severe examination, barely a tenth of these petitioners obtained a favourable response. (Friedrich Meyer, May 1796.)[2]

The period after the Terror has been described as a period in which conditions for foreigners in France improved. Cosmopolitanism flourished once more and the repressive measures against foreigners were steadily repealed. The assumption has been that the more draconian measures against foreigners were related to the system of the Terror. Dismantle the Terror and the laws against foreigners would be lifted.[3] The Thermidorians, however, proved more willing to speak cosmopolitan language than to act on it. Thirion was not an isolated politician in stressing the need for caution. The very fact that he cited older precedents of reciprocity suggests that not all revolutionaries were ready to return to the cosmopolitan ideas associated with the earlier years of the Revolution.

If the Thermidorians repealed the decree confiscating foreigners' property, as well as the laws of 26–7 Germinal and 7 Prairial II, there was no guarantee that they would not re-emerge in a

---

[1] *Moniteur* (11 Nivôse III).

[2] F. J. L. Meyer, *Fragments sur Paris*, 2 vols. (Hamburg, 1798), i. 276.

[3] Mathiez, *La Révolution et les étrangers*, 183.

new form, as Friedrich Meyer, a law professor from Hamburg, discovered in 1796. This was because the measures were bound up less with the Terror than with the same force which had lurked beneath it: the war. The Thermidorians and the Directory retained the same fears about foreign conspiracy and espionage as before. For as long as the war continued, the domestic pressures it aggravated still threatened the stability of the Republic. It was the conflict which encouraged the tendency to see foreign machinations behind each new crisis. With real 'conspiracies' involving foreigners, such as the royalist landings at Quiberon and the Babouvist plot, the reflex of the post-Thermidor regimes was to re-enact measures of control, naturally reverting to the models of the Year II. Ideology conditioned the tendency to see foreign subversion behind the crises, but ideology did not provoke the crises themselves, for they were very real. Meanwhile, the timid emergence of cosmopolitan rhetoric from its hibernation during the dark months of the Terror did not herald the return of the civil freedom which foreigners had enjoyed before the war. Instead, it shrouded expansionist and exploitative policies in attractive packaging.

I

If the measures taken against foreigners in the years 1793–4 were bound to the Terror, then one would expect the laws to have been razed as the Terror itself was dismantled. In fact, most of the laws against foreigners remained in place for longer. The revolutionaries sometimes allowed their residual cosmopolitanism some expression, but the xenophobia which had flourished in the acidic soil of the Terror never disappeared. Politicians were still too likely to see the shadows of foreign agents lurking behind internal upheavals, but at least they seem to have regarded the measures taken against foreigners as temporary. Looking forward to more tranquil times, the Thermidorian civil code guaranteed foreigners the same civil rights as French citizens.[4]

French suspects were released from the beginning of August,

---

[4] *Moniteur* (19 Frimaire III).

but foreigners were freed only in a trickle. William Codrington remarked that so many French prisoners had left his gaol that he was only one of a few remaining inmates. He was freed on 2 December 1794 only because a friend secured him an apprenticeship with a French printer, officially making him an artisan.[5] The three Belgian army suppliers arrested in Paris in August 1793 were not sprung until 30 September 1794.[6] The decrees arresting all enemy subjects were never formally repealed and British subjects, in particular, only gained their freedom on an arbitrary basis, depending upon how much of a threat they seemed to pose. Most seem to have been released between September 1794 and July 1795.[7] Once at liberty, large numbers of British and Irish subjects applied for passports to leave the country.[8]

It was not just British subjects who were affected by Thermidorian reluctance to open the prison doors. Karl von Hesse had to wait until 13 November 1794 for his freedom, while Miranda, despite his former ties to the Girondins, was not allowed to walk out until 16 January 1795, by decree of the Convention.[9] Meanwhile, enemy subjects newly arrived in France could still be incarcerated. Mathieu Ivanovich, a Hungarian, was arrested on 10 June 1795 shortly after his arrival in Paris.[10]

The law of 26–7 Germinal was repealed on 8 December 1794, but, until then, it was rigorously enforced. The Committee of Public Safety reiterated its commitment to executing the law on 19 September, although it still used its requisitioning powers to protect certain foreigners. As before, not all those protected by the government had any direct contribution to make to the war effort. A poverty-stricken and blind foreign musician named Fridzery, who had a family to feed, was exempted from the law after a recommendation from the *comité d'instruction publique*.[11]

The Thermidorians were keener to release property than individuals. The revolutionary belief in free trade motivated the return of wealth to foreigners, because the open market was thought to be more efficient than a controlled economy in

---

[5] Alger, *Englishmen*, 298–9.   [6] AN, BB/3/79.
[7] Alger, *Englishmen*, 334–49.   [8] AN, D/III/368–70.
[9] Mathiez, *La Révolution et les étrangers*, 186–7; Robertson, *Life of Miranda*, i. 148–9; Parra-Pérez, *Miranda*, 293–4.
[10] AN, D/III/368–70.   [11] AN, AF/II/61.

supplying the Republic. On 29 December, the Convention lifted the confiscation on all foreign property save that of enemy princes, but only after intense debate.[12] The way was now open for a shower of claims for compensation from aggrieved foreigners.[13] The repeal was also driven by a belief that French merchants and businessmen were on the whole the creditors, not the debtors, of foreigners. To release foreign property from confiscation could therefore only benefit the Republic's balance of trade. That the revolutionaries were motivated purely by French economic interests is shown by the restoration, on 14 March 1797, of imprisonment for debt in civil cases which, on 23 April 1798, was even extended to commercial debts. The preamble spoke of giving 'the commerce of the Republic the splendor and superiority which it deserves'.[14]

If there were any illusions after Thermidor that the revolutionaries were becoming more lax in their surveillance of foreigners, they were soon shattered in the bitter winter of 1794–5. In the killing cold, food prices spiralled upwards to unprecedented levels, now unfettered with the repeal of the Maximum. Anticipating trouble, Armand warned the Convention on behalf of the Committee of General Security on 16 January 1795 that 'foreigners and intriguers' had obtained *cartes de sûreté*. In response, the Convention decreed the issue of new cards for everyone living or arriving in Paris. Those who arrived henceforth had to go to the *comité civil* of their section within twenty-four hours, where their passports would be given a visa after a brief questioning. If the committee's suspicions were aroused, they could arrest the newcomers. This was not much different from the surveillance imposed on foreigners during the Year II. Some of the Thermidorians objected on grounds of individual liberties, but the Convention chose to put order and stability before such considerations.[15] On his arrival in Paris in 1796, Friedrich Meyer experienced the heavy-handed and arcane bureaucracy involved in complying with the law.[16] In the summer of 1798, Johann Heinzmann, another German more sympathetic to the Revolu-

---

[12] *Moniteur* (5, 9, 11, 12 Nivôse III).
[13] AN, D/III/368–70.
[14] MAE, ADP, France, 7; Portemer, 'L'Étranger', 552.
[15] *Moniteur* (29 Nivôse III).
[16] Meyer, *Fragments*, i. 3–7.

tion, noted that without a *carte de sûreté* a foreigner could be arrested, but that this was necessary because of the possibility of disturbances.[17]

It was this reasoning that led both the Thermidorian Convention and the Directory to enact laws of surveillance and even expulsion against foreigners. The Prairial insurrection in Paris of 20–3 May 1795 and the royalist landing at Quiberon on 27 June combined to stir the old fears of foreign subterfuge. Official jumpiness over foreign involvement in Jacobinism and popular militancy was not merely the product of the fertile revolutionary imagination. Some foreigners were arrested in the wake of the Prairial uprising and had been directly involved in the popular movement, sometimes showing leadership and initiative.[18] Such involvement testifies to the continued immersion of resident foreigners in local, militant politics. Yet the violence of Prairial had stirred a desperate fear in the Thermidorian authorities, who combined this evidence with the international conflict and concluded that the insurrection was the work of more sinister and concerted action by foreign agents.

It was, however, the British-backed royalist landing in Brittany which sparked the most alarm. On 11 July 1795 (23 Messidor III), ten days before the royalist bridgehead at Quiberon was crushed by Hoche, Mariette had the Convention order that all enemy subjects who had arrived in France since 1 January 1792 leave within eight days. Neutrals had to have their passports endorsed by the Committee of General Security on arrival in France, which could mean a long wait, although the decree permitted communes to issue temporary authorizations for merchants. Any foreigner found in a seditious meeting could be executed as a spy. This threat was reiterated after the royalist Vendémiaire uprising on 5 October 1795.[19] When it appeared that the law of 23 Messidor had not been implemented, the Convention decreed that any foreigner found in contravention would also be put to death as an enemy agent.[20] The provisions

---

[17] J. G. Heinzmann, *Voyage d'un Allemand à Paris, et retour par la Suisse* (Lausanne, 1800), 14.

[18] Monnier and Soboul, *Répertoire*, 278, 352, 354, 410, 431, 499

[19] *Moniteur* (19 Vendémiaire IV).

[20] *Procès-Verbal de la Convention Nationale*, 72 vols. (Paris, 1792–An IV), lxv. 85; *Moniteur* (27 Messidor, 20 Thermidor III).

of the law were not relaxed, even with the defeat of the royalists at Quiberon and the apparent triumph of French arms on the continent. The revolutionaries probably regarded the measure as temporary only in the sense that it would be repealed when the Republic had achieved complete victory over all its opponents, foreign and domestic. The war and insurrection continued to disturb the ghost of the Terror, long after its corpse had been buried by the Thermidorians.

The *feuilles de travail* of the minister of police, Cochon de Lapparent, between 27 March and 1 May 1796, reveal the law at work. He issued the district police commissioners and the police *bureau central* of Paris with orders which included the investigation of specific foreigners to see if they had obeyed the decree; the surveillance of those who had done so, but who had aroused suspicion; and the expulsion of others. On 1 May, he 'invited' the *bureau central* 'to redouble its zeal in the execution of laws against foreigners thronging Paris'. Every three days this police bureau addressed to the minister lists of foreigners lodging in hotels. Occasionally, certain hoteliers were reminded of their obligation to inform foreigners of the law. The minister was helped by denunciations. It was said that a large number of British people dined at the *Écu d'Orléans*, situated, appropriately enough, on the rue d'Enfer, 'and who are suspected of being adventurers and enemies of the Republic'. Such surveillance only failed to reach the intensity of the Year II because the institutions were not so localized as they were during the Terror.[21]

The bark of the law was worse than its bite. Passports belonging to neutral or allied citizens were usually endorsed by the ministry with little or no investigation. Only those whose behaviour or reputation aroused suspicion were treated with wariness. Cochon granted exemptions to foreign radicals and refugees (mainly from Italy) and even to British subjects who appeared to be harmless.[22] On 31 July 1795, the Piedmontese Gedeon Muzio was allowed to stay because, according to the Paris police bureau, 'he has taken refuge in France from Sardinian persecution, he has put himself, as a patriot, under the protection of the Republic . . . and at every opportunity he

---

[21] AN, F/7/3081.   [22] Ibid.

has developed the principles of a true Republican'.[23] Republican commitment still ensured that some foreigners escaped the vigour of the laws.

Suspicion of foreigners was carried into the debates on citizenship in the Constitution of the Year III. Pierre Daunou proposed that foreigners over 21 years of age, who had lived in France for seven years, paid direct taxation, and in addition possessed property, a farm, or a commercial establishment could be naturalized once they had declared their intention to spend the rest of their lives in the country.[24] These restrictive conditions owed more to the Constitution of 1791 than to that of 1793. Stress on property ownership showed that the Thermidorians, like the Constituents, were determined that foreigners have a stake in the country before being admitted to citizenship. The only concession to those who owned no property was the alternative of marriage to a French citizen. Moreover, the Thermidorians omitted a clause which allowed the legislature to award citizenship to any foreigner deserving the honour. This decision reflected an absence of the earlier cosmopolitan idealism.

The residence period of seven years was a reaction against the year-long requirement of the Constitution of 1793, but it was still longer than the five-year period prescribed in 1791. Behind this was a will to be absolutely certain that no ill-intentioned foreigner could easily gain access to citizenship. On 14 July 1795, Mailhe, criticizing the new law for not being restrictive enough, said that the Constituent Assembly had made it easy to be naturalized because 'it had not learned to recognize all the perfidy of the governments who surround us'. As for the 'anarchists' who wrote the Constitution of 1793, 'they joined with foreigners to make republican government odious, to vilify it and to dissolve it'. He was especially dismissive of marriage to a citizen as a precondition, as that made the acquisition of French nationality too easy. Lakanal agreed: political rights could only be given to foreigners once 'the republic was entirely certain of their love for it' and when they had acquired a profound knowledge of French laws, customs, and government,

---

[23] AN, F/15/3511.
[24] *Moniteur* (28 Messidor, 10 Fructidor III).

which 'is the fruit of time and experience'.[25] Lakanal was defining nationality not just as a matter of political choice, but also as the fruit of long-term social and cultural immersion. Thermidorian stringency in the extension of French citizenship expressed a wariness of foreigners, who now would have to prove their firm commitment to the Republic before being assimilated. The war, combined with the dual threat of Jacobinism and counter-revolution, ensured that xenophobia still simmered.

The law of 25 February 1796 suggests that legislation against foreigners was linked to political circumstances. Despite the security measures already taken, a resurgence of Jacobinism alarmed the government. Although fed in part by a drift into Paris of French Jacobins fleeing persecution in the provinces, the Directory saw the revival as the product of more sinister, alien forces. Two days before the government closed down the neo-Jacobin *club du Panthéon* on 27 February, a Directorial edict bemoaned the number of foreigners who wandered freely in Paris, despite the decrees against them, and called upon the laws on passports to be implemented fully. It revoked all the resident permits previously issued by the *bureau central* or the *commission de police*. Although foreigners could obtain renewals, they would only be for 'very brief delays'. Those who were refused new permits were to leave Paris. In a reinforcement of surveillance, the *bureau central* was to 'deploy the greatest vigilance over the entire canton of Paris' and was commanded to arrest any foreigners found breaking the law. Without the sectional *comités de surveillance* of old, such a task was probably not as vigorously prosecuted as the Directory may have wished. Moreover, there remained a degree of flexibility, for the edict exempted those who could show 'reasons of utility and justice'.[26]

Even when the *club du Panthéon* was suppressed, the government did not relax, for it had merely pushed opposition underground. The fear of the unseen led the Directory to reinvigorate the laws of surveillance on 1 March. In a message to the lower house, the Council of Five Hundred, the Directors requested a special law to allow the police to keep an eye on foreigners staying in private homes—and not just in inns and *maisons*

---

[25] *Moniteur* (28 Messidor III).   [26] *Moniteur* (16 Ventôse IV).

garnies, whose obligatory registers were already open to official inspection. The government was convinced that 'the most dangerous among them have avoided those residences'.[27] The Directory sought a return to the intrusive vigilance of the Terror. Moreover, no distinction was made between enemy subjects, neutrals, or allies, because foreign Jacobins were unlikely to be only from enemy countries.

On 12 March, the Council of Five Hundred addressed the Directory's concerns by adopting a bill which declared that 'the throng of foreigners in the commune of Paris demands measures which will activate surveillance by the government'. French citizens and foreigners alike, who had arrived in Paris since 1 Fructidor III (18 August 1795), were required to present themselves at their *arrondissement*, to state the address of their lodgings in Paris, and to produce their passports, all within three days. The foreigners' hosts were responsible for making a similar declaration.[28]

Some revolutionaries shared the Directory's fears of foreign influence in Paris, while others suggested that such police measures were not only counter-productive, but a dangerous extension to the powers of central government. The fears inflamed by the Jacobin revival divided the revolutionaries between those who sought to exclude foreigners and those who did not. Both sides of the argument, however, revealed a deep anxiety over popular uprising and Jacobin-inspired Terror. Nervously referring to a combination of hunger and political radicalism, Ludot claimed that foreigners should not be tolerated in France at all, because they were 'useless mouths' when there was a subsistence crisis and depreciation of the *assignats*. He warned that foreigners had always played a part in the Revolution and that 'France resounded with the foreign party'. Cadroy countered that foreigners were not a threat, but brought benefits to the country. To limit their freedom would be to deny France their wealth and skills. If Ludot and Cadroy shared a fear of Jacobinism, the latter was enlisting the cosmopolitan arguments of the early Revolution to support his point. He also suggested that while the government had targeted the *club du Panthéon*, the proposed law was wrong to assume that other, unknown, people

---

[27] Ibid.   [28] *Moniteur* (22, 27 Ventôse IV).

also had hostile intentions. 'In speaking vaguely of foreigners in Paris, of their presumed intentions and of suspicion', he eloquently warned, 'we should beware of chasing mere shadows'. He feared that the extension of police powers over foreigners would not be the end of the story, that the revolutionaries stood once more at the top of the slippery slope which led to the police state of the Terror.[29] The Council of Five Hundred dismissed such reservations and adopted the proposals. They passed through the Council of Elders on 17 March.[30]

Nine days later, the Elders rejected a proposal to oblige neutrals and allies to renew their passport visas every three months, because they believed the law to be inexecutable. They were not opposed to the idea of passports, however, and deputies in both chambers, ever-anxious about Jacobins and royalists around every corner, thought it necessary to watch foreigners. On 21 March, the Five Hundred heard that while circumstances demanded 'greater surveillance over French travellers', it was more important to keep a fixed gaze on foreigners. For the revolutionaries, the continuing conflict also justified such controls. Dumas told the Elders that 'it is only with peace that you can shed your policing laws'. Until then, France must bear these measures which restricted individual freedoms in order to defend liberty. Yet Dumas also gave the first indication that passports and visas might become a permanent part of the irritating bureaucratic paraphernalia which clutter the lives of travellers. Travel documents should become, he suggested, 'a principle of international law . . . you will thus lay the foundations of reciprocal controls between nations'.[31]

Existing legislation proved onerous enough. Friedrich Meyer arrived in Paris in the night of 31 March and early next morning the law-abiding hotelier warned Meyer and his fellow-travellers that, in accordance with the decree of 17 March, their first duty was to exchange their passports for what he called *cartes d'étrangers*. The host accompanied all five guests, including servants, to the committee of the *arrondissement*, where they had to get their visas. Meyer complained about the filth in the offices and grumbled that the law was so vague that the officials

[29] *Moniteur* (26 Ventôse IV).
[30] *Moniteur* (1, 3 Germinal IV).
[31] *Moniteur* (6, 13 Germinal IV).

were confused over its execution. The visitors were passed from one room to another, in the manner still familiar to those who have had occasion to deal with state bureaucracy. They finished up at the *bureau central* at the Palais de Justice, where, over the course of an hour and a half, their documents were stamped, signed, and exchanged in three different offices for the precious cards, 'palladium of the security of Paris'.[32]

Another crisis provoked yet more measures. On 10 May 1796, the police arrested Gracchus Babeuf and his Equals, exploding their conspiracy to overthrow the government and establish an egalitarian social order. In response, the Directory called for the expulsion from Paris of a variety of people. The legislative councils obliged by excluding, among others, all foreigners not attached to consulates and who had arrived in Paris since 1789. The penalty for non-compliance with this, the law of 21 Floréal, was deportation. The inclusion of foreigners in the measure had become a reflex, but it was undoubtedly encouraged by the fact that the Italian Filippo Buonarroti was among the Babouvist leadership, as was the Liégeois General Jean-Joseph Fyon. Also implicated for direct involvement were the Belgian Joseph Biot and the Genevan Sandoz. The Swiss café owner Pierre Cardinaux was interrogated because his establishment was a meeting-place of known Jacobins, while other foreigners were discovered on the Babouvist lists of dependable militants.[33] On 3 September the law was extended to include Vendôme, the seat of the high court of justice specially assembled for the trial of the Babouvists.[34]

When, on 11 May, Meyer confronted Sieyès about this measure, the revolutionary shrugged, 'What can we do . . . several rogues are the cause, and many honest people suffer.' Foreign ambassadors showered the government with complaints. In the wake of the Babeuf conspiracy, the authorities clearly saw order rather than individual liberties as the priority. Using the registers of foreigners collected by the *arrondissements* for the *cartes de sûreté*, those living in the capital were informed of the law. Immediately, the Directory and the ministry of police

---

[32] Meyer, *Fragments*, i. 3–6.
[33] *Moniteur* (27, 28 Floréal IV); Monnier and Soboul, *Répertoire*, 152, 352, 432, 445, 473, 499, 508.
[34] *Moniteur* (21, 23 Fructidor IV).

were besieged by foreigners clamouring for exemptions. Those who were fortunate enough to receive such dispensation still had to renew their *cartes de sûreté*. Meyer secured permission to remain in Paris from the minister of foreign affairs, Charles Delacroix.[35] Thomas Paine's application was accepted by the Directors on 13 May.[36] Theobald Wolfe Tone received permission from the Director Carnot on 20 May.[37] The Jacobin 'uprising' at the military camp at Grenelle, on the outskirts of Paris on 9 September, undoubtedly encouraged the Directory to uphold this law. It was not revoked until 29 June 1797, after the Spanish patriot Marchena, who was no Jacobin or Equal, had complained that he had been harassed on account of his foreign birth.[38] With the Babouvists safely tried and convicted a month earlier, without a tremor in the streets of Paris, the immediate stimulus behind the law had also disappeared. The legislature was also dominated by the right at this period and many of the deputies probably regarded the law as a 'Terrorist' measure.

While the Directory could not feel safe from both its foreign and domestic opponents, it was reluctant to abandon all restrictions against foreigners. This was particularly true after the coup of Fructidor in September 1797, which purged the right from the government and legislature. Peace negotiations with Britain at Lille collapsed and the regime was instilled with a new determination to realign foreign policy on an aggressive course. Britain was the target, but domestically the coup also signalled the revival in persecution of priests and *émigrés* in the 'Fructidorian Terror'.[39] For foreigners, repression in the wake of Fructidor simply illustrates the persistence of the underlying factors which had brought laws against them before, during and after the Year II. It might be concluded that certain categories of people in the period 1793–9 experienced an almost permanent state of potential Terror, a potential which in particular times of crisis erupted in the form of official persecution. Underlying this

[35] Meyer, *Fragments*, i. 275–8.
[36] Keane, *Tom Paine*, 421.
[37] T. W. Tone, *Life of Theobald Wolfe Tone*, ed. W. W. Tone, 2 vols. (Washington DC, 1826), ii. 113.
[38] *Moniteur* (30 Prairial, 19 Messidor V).
[39] D. Woronoff, *La République bourgeoise de Thermidor à Brumaire 1794–1799* (Paris, 1972), 195.

condition was the link which the revolutionaries made between the international conflict and domestic subversion.

During the Fructidorian period, the upsurge of anglophobia led the Directory to resurrect measures against British subjects in France. In particular, security concerns which surrounded the build-up of the *armée de l'Angleterre* in northern French ports led the Directory to order, on 26 February 1798 (8 Ventôse VI), the arrest of all British and Irish subjects in French maritime towns. In particular, all foreigners, without exception, were to be expelled from Brest, Boulogne, Calais, and Dunkirk. The idea, reminiscent of the law of 26–7 Germinal II, came from General Bonaparte, who had written to the Directory that, in preparing for a descent on Britain, it would be essential 'to forbid any foreigner, and above all any Anglo-American', to enter these towns. Suspicion of Americans was based on the sometimes justified belief that the British government used agents with United States citizenship to circumvent French laws against enemy subjects. Recently stony relations between France and the United States no doubt fuelled the impression that American citizens had British sympathies. The Directory did not go so far as to expel or arrest Americans in seaports, but the *arrêté* of 8 Ventôse was phrased in such a way as to allow the interrogation of United States citizens in any French maritime town. It defined as British or Irish 'all individuals speaking the English language, unless they prove with authentic documents that they are Americans'.[40]

The municipality of Le Havre set about the task of arresting 'British' subjects enthusiastically. On 2 March, it placed seals on the papers of ten people who spoke English. Two of them were already known as Americans and one, Nicolas Thierry, was obviously (and later proved to be) French, but was noted as 'speaking the English language'. Only one of the ten was actually British and he had received special permission from the Directory to travel to Paris. By 10 March, the seals were lifted from all the papers.[41] Le Havre's incorrigible zeal still led to the arrest of three more Americans in June, eliciting a protest from the American consul, Fulwar Skipwith, to Talleyrand, the minister of foreign affairs.[42]

[40] AN, F/7/7446; J. E. Howard, *Letters and Documents of Napoleon: The Rise to Power* (London, 1961), 225.

[41] AN, F/7/7446.   [42] Ibid.

The civil authorities at Le Havre, however, appear to have been alone in their aggressive application of the law. As with every piece of prior legislation against foreigners, most local officials were reluctant to be so sweeping. The naval administrators of Le Havre proceeded with more sensitivity than their civilian counterparts. They drew on the law of 23 Messidor III to claim exemptions for those who had been in France before 1792 and they took the view that fulfilment of the conditions for naturalization, particularly seven years residence, entailed exemption from the order. The municipality of Boulogne did apply the law to the letter, but immediately sent a series of queries to the minister of police, Dondeau, about its applicability to certain types of foreigner. Taking up the enquiry, the minister proposed to the Directory that the order apply only to those British and Irish subjects 'convicted of being, or presumed to be, our Enemies and the agents of Britain'. The government should exempt those who 'have given unequivocal proof of their attachment to France', by military service, economic contributions, marriage, or long-term residence. Dondeau accepted the executive's concern for the four ports specifically mentioned and suggested that the proposed exemptions not apply to them. Boulogne's strict adherence to the order was to stand.[43]

The police minister's response suggests that some revolutionaries still sought to judge foreigners not just by their nationality, but by their behaviour. Yet willingness to make concessions to 'patriots' who happened to be enemy subjects had decayed. The second division of the ministry of police was more uncompromising than the minister himself and demanded that no exemptions be made from the Directory's edict.[44] The coups of Fructidor V and Floréal VI showed that the regime still felt threatened by both monarchists and Jacobins. As always, the central government feared that foreign money and foreign intrigue were behind these two groups. The assumed link between enemy powers and domestic subversion ensured that foreigners would be suspect until the Republic was at peace. The same connection had eroded almost to nothing the eighteenth-century notion that wars were matters between governments and ought not to affect personal relations. In July 1798, Lecarlier, the

[43] AN, F/7/7446.   [44] Ibid.

new minister of police, informed Talleyrand of a request from an English lawyer named Matthew Gibson, who wanted permission to visit France as the executor of the affairs of his British clients. 'I do not think', Lecarlier advised, 'that, in the present circumstances, we can allow an individual from that Nation to penetrate the territory of the Republic.'[45]

The end of the Terror did bring an improvement in the conditions of foreigners. Those imprisoned were eventually released and others felt safe enough to return from exile. After Thermidor, neither enemy subjects nor their property were ever sequestered on the same scale as in 1793–4, at least until Bonaparte. When legislation was levelled against foreigners, the authorities used their discretionary powers to exempt those whom they believed to be useful or politically sound, as in the Year II. Yet the demise of the Terror begs the question as to why life for foreigners did not improve more than it actually did, as they were still subject to surveillance, passport controls, expulsion, and even renewed arrest. Some revolutionaries vented their cosmopolitan idealism once more, but this hid the continuities in the treatment of foreigners. To many, foreigners remained potential spies and agents of domestic subversion. Each new crisis, from the royalist landings at Quiberon to the Babouvist conspiracy, provoked laws against them. The Directory itself often created its own problems in seeking security by eliminating its opponents through illegal means. These efforts were also accompanied by laws against foreigners. The Fructidorian Directory was particularly heavy-handed, because it was determined to prosecute the war against Britain and to protect the regime against domestic enemies. In a time of international conflict, it was easy for both the Thermidorians and the Directory to see foreign conspiracy behind domestic instability. In such circumstances, the revolutionaries usually favoured order rather than the individual liberties of foreigners. Opposition to this tendency came from those, still quaking from the experience of the Terror, who feared that laws against foreigners were a prelude to the broader repression of the French population. The war, however, ensured that the revolutionaries would

[45] MAE, CP, Angleterre, 592.

still respond to their internal crises with restrictions against foreigners. This reflex was not bound inextricably to the apparatus of the Terror, or to any ideology *behind* it. It was the war and its attendant crises which repeatedly brought the revolutionaries both to re-enact measures against foreigners, learnt especially during the Year II, and to realize the *exclusive* implications of their ideology.

II

Foreign troops, scattered as they now were among regular French units, no longer gave the revolutionaries real cause for soul-searching. The Thermidorians were well aware of the spectacular lack of success which some foreign legions had met in their recruitment. In December 1794, Bourdon de l'Oise reminded the war ministry that the *deuxième légion batave* was still on the payroll, 'does not amount to a single company', and was a waste of money. Orders were issued for its dismissal on 23 December, and its men were distributed among regular units.[46] The Terror may have been over, but, for a time, the policy towards foreign legions remained the same.

To pre-empt any embarrassment with the recruitment of foreign units, Article 287 of the Constitution of 1795 simply forbade the employment of foreign troops. The French would not, however, dismiss foreigners who were already serving with regular French units. Visiting Paris during the last months of the Convention, Meister noted that the deputies' military guard were drawn from élite line regiments and that 'the greatest number, moreover, are foreign: Swiss, German, Swedish'.[47] On 17 August 1794, Captain H. Nagtglas, a Dutch soldier formerly of the German legion, petitioned the Committee of Public Safety to be allowed to join his comrades in the Nord, where (he had heard) they had been 'requisitioned for an expedition'.[48] Other officers of the former *légion germanique* sought redress for injuries inflicted during the Terror. They secured the support of Tallien for compensation for loss of personal property, horses, equipment, and papers, a claim which

---

[46] SHAT, X^k46.   [47] Meister, *Souvenirs*, 107.   [48] SHAT, X^k3.

they submitted on 12 October 1794 to the Committee of Public Safety. They further demanded their rehabilitation at the same rank and pay as on the day of their arrest. On 21 June 1795, the officers were reintegrated into the army, although they received no pay until then and some were still looking for posts the following February.[49]

It was one thing to assimilate foreign soldiers already serving in France, but another to establish new units. When the Polish generals, Jan Henryk Dabrowski, Wielhorski, and Wyzkowski, submitted their separate plans for the creation of a Polish legion in November 1795, the Directory was cautious. The Poles argued that their legion would deprive the partitioning powers of recruits; would form the nucleus of a Polish republican army; and would nourish the Poles with the principles of the French Revolution. Resting on Article 287, the post-Thermidor regimes remained wary of encouraging foreign ventures which brought no immediate benefit to France. The first seeds of the Polish legion fell on rocky ground.[50]

The Directory seemed to have had fewer reservations about recruiting foreign legions when they were intended to fight the British. In March 1796, the Irish republican Nicholas Madgett was authorized (according to Tone) to 'propagate the faith amongst the Irish soldiers and seamen' among foreign prisoners of war and then to enrol them into French service. Next month, General Humbert was ordered to prepare a force of 1,000 to 1,500 men to be let loose on Cornwall and Wales. On 2 November 1796, the Directory authorized General Lazare Hoche to form a *brigade étrangère* for service in Ireland. These various orders came together when Irish prisoners of war were among the French deserters, mutineers, and convicts who were marched to Brest, some still in irons. They were mustered into the 600-strong *légion noire* under the command of an American, William Tate. Tone described this force ironically as 'very little behind my countrymen, either in appearance or morality'. They were rough—and reluctant—enough to be held in island fortresses off the Breton coast to prevent their escape. Tate's legion eventually set sail on 13 February 1797, after Hoche's Bantry

[49] Ibid.
[50] B. Lešnodorski, *Les Jacobins polonais* (Paris, 1965), 315–20; Godechot, *Grande Nation*, 483.

Bay expedition had already been scattered by the bitter winter winds. The famished, motley band landed on the Pembrokeshire coast and pillaged food and livestock shortly before surrendering.[51]

After the failure of this expedition, French commanders clashed with the civil authorities over the use of foreigners in the build-up of the next invasion force. As the *armée de l'Angleterre* was being assembled in northern France in the spring of 1798, Tone asked General Kilmaine, its commander-in-chief, whether or not Irish refugees would be used. Kilmaine replied frankly that the Directors had insisted that the recruitment of foreigners was illegal. He concluded that 'nothing could be done, the constitution being express against employing foreigners'. He pointed out that only recently, the Directory had been obliged to refuse an offer from the Cisalpine Republic of a regiment of hussars. He still hinted that, once the campaign was under way, no one would complain if Irish patriots were to join the invasion force. Irish exiles did assemble in the build-up, concentrating especially in Dunkirk, from where the advance party was to set sail.[52] Kilmaine's wink to Tone and the actual use of Irishmen in Humbert's army shows how the Directory's loosening grip on the military gave the generals more latitude. This was helped by the withdrawal of civilian commissioners overseeing the army in the spring of 1797.

As the revolutionary armies became more extended across Europe, French strategic needs demanded greater numbers of troops and therefore greater flexibility in recruitment. Annexations and the establishment of sister republics provided the means of circumventing the Constitution of the Year III. Recruits from the annexed territories, first Belgium and then the Rhineland, were no longer constitutionally foreigners, even if in every other sense these people resented the demands of the French state, to the point of revolt in 1798. In countries beyond the annexed territories, troops were levied without controversy by prodding the sister republics into raising their own armies.

[51] Elliott, *Partners in Revolution*, 85, 116–17, 274; M. Elliott, *Wolfe Tone: Prophet of Irish Independence* (New Haven, Conn., 1989), 293; Fieffé, *Histoire des troupes étrangères*, ii. 34–5; Tone, *Life*, ii. 61, 64, 80, 82, 224, 238; E. H. S. Jones, *The Last Invasion of Britain* (Cardiff, 1950), 55.

[52] Tone, *Life*, ii. 502; Elliott, *Partners in Revolution*, 220.

These forces were under the supreme command of the French, used for French strategic interests, and sometimes even paid for by the French government, but were officially the armies of independent, allied powers. By such means, the Poles finally raised their own legion. In September 1796, Dabrowski secured the support of General Kléber, who prevailed on the Directory. On 30 October, Petiet, the minister of war, wrote to Dabrowski informing him that nothing prevented the Poles from 'establishing themselves among peoples with whom the Republic has good relations', and that the French government would be willing to provide 'indirect' help to the Polish patriots working for the 'regeneration' of their homeland. In November, Dabrowski left Paris to join his exiled comrades in northern Italy and, on 9 January 1797, the 2,000 strong Polish legion was raised in Mantua by agreement with the Congress of Lombardy. By June, the Poles had recruited enough men to create a second legion. When the Cisalpine Republic was created, absorbing Lombardy, it had no constitutional ban on foreign troops and, early in 1798, it agreed to maintain an army of 22,000 men at French disposal. With Bonaparte's encouragement, the Polish legions therefore passed into the Cisalpine army.[53]

Such troops raised in the sister republics became mixed up with the French army during the retreat from the resurgent coalition forces in 1799. The Swiss *légion vaudoise*, recruited that same year by the Helvetic Republic as part of its treaty obligations with France, fell back with the French. It certainly helped that by then the Directory itself had shown increasing contempt for the Constitution of the Year III. Cisalpine troops who fled as Suvorov swept through Italy in the spring of 1799 joined the French army as the *demi-brigade cisalpine* on 30 April 1799 and were barracked successively at various places in the south-east of France. The Poles in the Cisalpine army were betrayed, however: the Polish legions had covered the French retreat from Italy, but capitulated at Mantua on 28 July. While their French comrades were allowed to leave, the Polish soldiers were surrendered to the Austrians, who treated them not as prisoners of war, but as deserters. Troops from other sister republics in

---

[53] Meller, '"Pour notre liberté et pour la vôtre"', 315–16; Godechot, *Grande Nation*, 483; Fieffé, *Histoire des troupes étrangères*, ii. 41–4; Palmer, *Age of the Democratic Revolution*, ii. 320.

Italy were, however, incorporated into the French army. The Ligurian, the Roman, and the Parthenopean Republics all made their contributions, involuntary and severely thinned as their ranks may have been.[54]

In the military crisis of 1799, the French legislature finally abandoned all pretence that the bedraggled remains of allied forces were the armies of independent, sovereign states. On 8 September, the Council of Five Hundred passed three bills which recruited not only the *légion des francs du nord* from the annexed Rhineland, but, more controversially, another Polish legion and a *légion italique*. The Italian legion enlisted refugees from Piedmont and the Cisalpine, Roman, and Parthenopean Republics. The three units had identical organization, pay, and regulations. Their purpose was outlined in the decrees, which were reminiscent of those establishing the very first 'patriot' legions in 1792. The ranks of the *légion italique* were to be filled with Italian patriots in France who 'burn with desire to fight for the cause of liberty'. The new Polish legion, the *légion du Danube*, was established because 'if the coalesced kings deploy vast armies against free peoples, the latter must admit into their ranks all men whom a sublime fervour calls to fight for the sacred cause of liberty'. On the other hand, the preamble to the Italian decree was more blunt in recognizing the pressing French need for manpower: 'circumstances demand an augmentation of our armies, in order to repel the enemy'.[55]

There was more than a hint of irony to the verbiage of liberty. The idea for a *légion italique* had first been mooted by the Neapolitan exile Cesare Paribelli, who had met General Championnet, founder of the now dead Parthenopean Republic, at Grenoble on 5 July 1799. Both Paribelli and Championnet were supporters of Italian unity and their proposal for a legion was presented to the Council of Five Hundred by Talot, a former *conventionnel* and a member of the Jacobin Manège club. If at first the idea for an Italian legion was the brainchild of Italian unitarists and their French Jacobin sympathizers, the government itself soon recognized that such a legion might have other uses. The Directory regarded the Italian refugees with suspicion

[54] Fieffé, *Histoire des troupes étrangères*, ii. 31–3; Meller, '"Pour notre liberté et pour la vôtre"', 318.

[55] Fieffé, *Histoire des troupes étrangères*, ii. 32, 45.

because the aim of a united Italy did not coincide with French strategic concerns and because, since the Babeuf conspiracy, Italian patriots were considered extremists. When Italian refugees began to flow into France in their hundreds, therefore, a legion seemed to be a useful means to gather them in one place and to control them. On 29 October, the foreign minister, Reinhard, ordered the government's *commission des secours* to make sure that all Italians were gathered near the frontier. He urged, 'you cannot try too hard to press into the *légion italique* all those who can offer military service'. It was a dangerous strategy, as the government was arming and sustaining men whose political loyalties to the regime were suspect.[56]

The further flung the French campaigns, the less control the central government had over the recruitment of foreign troops by freelancing French generals, who needed cannon-fodder and, perhaps, who sought to enhance their personal prestige and power. In Malta on 13 June 1798, General Bonaparte reformed the military forces of the Order of Saint John and drafted some of the rest of the island's population into units of volunteer *chasseurs*. These troops were shipped to Egypt and organized into the *légion maltaise*, which fought at the Battle of the Pyramids on 21 July. Once the French army was cut off from reinforcement by the crushing defeat of Aboukir Bay on 1 August and then ravaged by plague, Bonaparte began to draw recruits from among the local people, first in Egypt and then in Syria. Yet, when combined with deserters from the Mameluke cavalry, these troops formed one single squadron.[57]

The fall of the revolutionary government on 9 Thermidor did not immediately herald brighter days for prisoners of war. The law of 7 Prairial was extended to include Spanish troops on 11 August 1794 (24 Thermidor), in retaliation for Spanish failure to honour the terms of a prisoner exchange. 'This example is needed to enlighten the soldiers who form the coalition armies,' explained Barère disingenuously, 'and to show them how little their generals care for their blood and for their

---

[56] A.-M. Rao, 'La Révolution française et l'émigration politique: Les Réfugiés italiens en 1799', *AhRf* 52 (1980), 254–7.

[57] Howard, *Letters and Documents*, i. 238–9; Fieffé, *Histoire des troupes étrangères*, ii. 47, 51.

existence.' With perverse reasoning, he concluded that executing Spanish prisoners would stir the Spanish people against their king.[58] The war continued to exert its ugly weight on attitudes towards prisoners, whose behaviour was also the subject of numerous complaints. On 6 August, the Convention received a demand by the Jacobins of Chaumont in the Haute-Marne for severe measures against foreign prisoners and deserters. Several deputies were prodded into making their own complaints, Beauchamp describing how they 'prowl in the departments to pillage, make threats and to murder'. It was also reported that Spanish deserters had slaughtered two French soldiers returning from leave in the Lot.[59]

The decrees of 7 Prairial and 24 Thermidor were finally repealed on 30 December 1794 'in the middle of applause'. Brival rose to condemn the orders as 'contrary to every law; they contradict the *droit des gens* and the laws of war . . . these laws are even opposed to the sentiments which drive our brave soldiers, who know how to conquer our enemies, but never to murder the vanquished'. An embarrassed sense of honour and humanitarianism was behind Brival's motion, but so too was shame. Brival excused his colleagues by explaining weakly that the laws 'were snatched from the Convention by surprise'.[60] What was left unsaid was that French soldiers might be subject to brutal reprisals if the law were ever rigorously enforced.

The repeal of these grisly decrees did not mean that the regime for prisoners of war was to be relaxed. Further news that prisoners had abused their liberty by leaving the communes in which they had been quartered, coupled with the ever-lurking fear of espionage and sabotage, provoked a further draconian law on 28 May 1795. Merlin de Douai reported to the Convention that some prisoners of war had filtered into Paris and that, only days after the Prairial uprising, 'what has attracted them here cannot be in doubt'. The Convention ordered that any prisoner who left his municipality without permission would be tried before a military commission and punished with six years in irons. Those found in the capital would be put to death unless they left within twenty-four

---

[58] *AP* xciv. 492; *Moniteur* (26 Thermidor II).
[59] *AP* xciv. 238, 241.
[60] *Moniteur* (12 Nivôse III).

hours. Those in Paris, argued Merlin, were not simple soldiers but 'lords, they are officers who understand French very well, and who spy on all government activities, on all the operations of the Convention'. Harsh as it was, the decree did not materially affect the everyday living conditions of those prisoners of war who remained in their assigned communes. Those who worked in the local community were considered to have government dispensation to move freely from their living quarters to their place of work.[61]

Exchanges continued as before and the Committee of Public Safety accepted petitions from individuals requesting repatriation. Enemy soldiers sent home surplus to those in the exchange cartels were simply counted against future exchanges. Officers could be freed on parole, by which they swore that they would not bear arms against France until a French counterpart was repatriated. Those who could not fulfil these conditions were honour-bound to return to France within three months. In some cases, the government permitted such exchanges on humanitarian grounds, to officers who were dangerously ill or wounded. Soldiers in the ranks, meanwhile, had to rely on cartels negotiated by their generals. The honour system for officers seems to have worked. On 29 June 1795, four French officers who returned from captivity in Britain petitioned the Committee of Public Safety and secured the release of two British prisoners in partial fulfilment of their parole.[62] Despite the rhetoric, both sides still observed some of the customs of eighteenth-century warfare. The revolutionaries were privately conscious that these were survivals of Ancien Régime practices. On 6 January 1797, shortly after the rebuttal of British peace overtures made since October 1796, the foreign minister, Delacroix, sent Truguet, the navy minister, copies of previous agreements for prisoner exchanges. They included those from the Seven Years War and the American War of Independence and were to give Truguet an idea as to how to proceed with talks with the British negotiator, Henry Swinburne.[63]

Those prisoners who remained in France were not always closely guarded or confined. In May 1795, after peace had been

[61] *Moniteur* (13 Prairial III).
[62] SHAT, Y^{i}1.
[63] MAE, CP, Angleterre, 590.

signed with their government, Prussian prisoners of war working as miners asked the inspector of glassworks, Daguilbel, if they might be permitted to remain in France 'by uniting with Frenchwomen'. On 10 July, the Committee of Public Safety agreed that the law permitted them to do so. Marriage between prisoners of war and local women hints at the freedom which they had to form relationships. The Prussians were not an isolated case. The law-abiding citizen Andoyer asked the Committee if he might give his daughter in marriage to Joseph Jabonesqui, a prisoner of war. On 28 July the Committee replied 'that every foreign prisoner of war is free to settle in France and to contract marriage there'.[64] These conditions were dictated by the persistence of eighteenth-century practices, which in turn survived out of necessity. Certain communities did not have the resources to impose a restrictive regime on prisoners of war, while in others the authorities sought to put them to productive use, working in manufactures, workshops, and agriculture. Prisoners who were locked up wasted resources.

The liberality of the regime was fragile. Vacillations in circumstances ensured that prisoners' freedom could be curtailed at any time. On 6 March 1798, during the organization of the *armée de l'Angleterre*, the Directory ordered the rearrest of any British prisoners of war freed on parole in the maritime departments. All prisoners were to be restricted to a band of territory 5 miles in width and 10 miles from the coast.[65]

To many revolutionaries, deserters were no better than prisoners of war. On 6 September 1794, the Convention received a complaint from the Jacobins of Perpignan, who spoke vibrantly of their 'fears relating to that class of men which royalism has vomited among us, called deserters'.[66] That frontier town had received a fresh influx of frightened, hungry men fleeing the war zone as the French marched into northern Spain. In August 1795, the administration of the Eure heard that foreign deserters were guilty of almost every cardinal sin. They were described as 'idlers, drunkards, recalcitrants, thieves, destroyers of property in the barracks; they sell their bread at twenty francs a pound, and roam the countryside where they forcibly take bread and

---

[64] SHAT, Y^{j}1.   [65] AN, F/7/7446.   [66] *AP* xcvi. 303.

cider'.[67] Deserters were no longer men who had come to share in the fruits of liberty, but were a nuisance, a menace, and probably spies.

On 24 August, therefore, the department of the Eure ordered all foreign deserters to Évreux, the *chef-lieu*. There, they were placed under the surveillance of the *procureurs-syndics*, who were empowered to reallocate them to other municipalities. Deserters would only work in rural communes if the authorities received written requests for such labour from the farmers, who would then be held responsible for any misdemeanours committed by the deserters. Anyone employing a deserter was to register him with the municipal authorities. Those who sold their bread, or who stole food or drink, were to be imprisoned.[68] By discouraging their employment in rural areas, the department sought to restrict as many as possible to the towns, where they might be more easily controlled.

In other departments, however, deserters were encouraged to earn their keep as before. The order of the Committee of Public Safety, issued on 17 July 1794, to arrest any deserter who refused to work still applied. This also meant, however, that those who could not work either through injury or lack of opportunity were still subsidized by the local authorities, who reclaimed their expenses from the *commission des secours publics*. Deserters unable to make ends meet were still given a daily handout of 10 *sous* and, more importantly, the inflation-proof bread ration of 24 ounces.[69]

Between 9 Thermidor and the coup of Brumaire, the opposition which had emerged in 1793 to recruiting foreign troops persisted and was encapsulated in the ban written into the constitution. The Thermidorians therefore finished what the Convention had nearly completed in 1793 and disbanded the last surviving legion. With Article 287, Dubois-Crancé's vision, expressed in 1789, for a truly 'national' army was at last fulfilled—at least on paper. Requests by Polish officers for their own legion, which might have been greeted enthusiastically in 1792, were met with cold indifference in 1795. Foreigners still served in the French army, although not in separate units, and the revolutionaries

---

[67] AN, F/9/137.   [68] Ibid.   [69] Ibid.

were soon obliged to circumvent the ban on foreign troops. When French military resources were strained across Europe, sister republics were urged, as nominally independent states, to raise armies. It was in this way that the Poles finally formed their legion early in 1797. This recruitment was indicative less of a revival in the cosmopolitan exuberance of 1792 than of a practical response to the strategic needs of the French Republic. The French required men to wage their campaigns, fought ever-further from home and across a wider extent of territory. As the war spread, generals were able to recruit foreigners into their armies when it suited their purposes, regardless of what the government thought. Meanwhile, as early as March 1796, the Directory was willing to turn a blind eye to the use of some foreigners, if they promised strategic advantage. Foreign prisoners and Irish soldiers were deployed in the ill-fated Bantry Bay expedition. The military defeats of 1799 persuaded the Directory to abandon all legal pretence and to accept the bedraggled troops from the overrun sister republics. By then, the Directory had broken the constitution enough times to make this departure from law seem positively innocuous.

If the use of foreign troops had little to do with cosmopolitan ideals, the revolutionaries now showed a similar disregard for their earlier universal pretensions in their treatment of prisoners of war and deserters. When the laws of 7 Prairial and 24 Thermidor were repealed at the end of 1794, humanitarian impulses were certainly among the reasons, but so too was shame, embarrassment and fear of reprisals. Otherwise very little changed in the day-to-day conditions of prisoners and deserters, because they were supervised by local authorities whose resources and attitudes varied across the country. The treatment of prisoners owed much to the persistence of eighteenth-century practices, even if they were couched in different terms. Perhaps most surprising of all, the government still accepted parole for enemy officers, a fine illustration of the weight of tradition among men who claimed to be waging a national war based on new principles.

III

The foreign clergy regained their freedom piecemeal between Thermidor and the spring of 1795, but they suffered penury because they had no access to their property. In December 1794, Thomas Walsh, superior of the Irish College, asked the Convention for help for his twenty-two students and priests who remained in Paris. On 2 March, the *commission des secours* told the Committee of Public Safety that it would provide the Irish with 'provisional aid and indemnities', until a decision was made on their property. The commission pointed out that the Irish clergy deserved such support because, in the first place, for three years the students had not studied theology, but literature, medicine, and surgery, while some 'are employed in the hospitals and armies of the Republic'. Others were ready to volunteer for the army. Such patriotism, despite their imprisonment, demonstrated the students' dedication to the new order.[70] Between 21 April 1795 and 16 September 1796, the residents of the Irish College in Paris were given monthly subsidies, totalling over 23,235 *livres*, drawn from the funds voted by the Convention on 4 March 1794 for refugees and foreign patriots and represented 27 per cent of the sums paid out in this seventeen-month period. The Irish students and clerics claiming financial support clearly impressed the *commission des secours* with their republican credentials.[71] The Thermidorians also sought to distance themselves from the Terror by compensating some of its victims. On 14 April 1795, the Convention voted to provide all English nuns in France with a provisional daily allowance of 40 *sous* each, payable by the *commission des secours*.[72]

If the Terror was over, the anticlericalism now enmeshed with the Revolution was not. James Burke was rearrested in Bordeaux and gaoled shortly after 9 Thermidor, as 'a priest, as an aristocrat and agent of *monseigneur* de Cicé', formerly archbishop of Bordeaux and *monarchien* in the Constituent Assembly.[73] As the Directory veered between the Scylla of Jacobinism and the Charybdis of royalism, Walsh felt threatened enough in March

[70] MAE, ADP, France, 10.
[71] AN, F/15*/17.
[72] *Moniteur* (28 Germinal III).
[73] AN, H/3/2561/A; Loupès, 'Irish Clergy', 37.

1796 to write to the foreign minister, Delacroix, asking for his protection. He had heard that he 'has just been included on the arrest warrants issued against ecclesiastics'. Having regained the college's confiscated property for the administrators, Walsh complained of 'the fears which are paralysing their activities'.[74] The resurgence of official persecution after Fructidor engulfed the foreigners. On 1 August 1798, the Directory authorized the passage of staff and students of the Scots, English, and Irish Colleges to Gibraltar. The minister of police called this a 'deportation', but not all the foreign clergy in France were included: it was as much a flight as a penal measure.[75]

Some foreign clergy did not need to be expelled, as they were revolted by life in revolutionary France. Meanwhile, developments in the British Isles promised better days for Catholics, who were being regarded with less suspicion than before 1789, thanks partly to the fact that French *émigré* clergy had made an impression as opponents of French republicanism. This combination of stick and carrot was central to the demise of the foreign ecclesiastical institutions in France. On their release, the English Benedictine nuns in Paris sold what remained of their linen and furniture to get enough money to travel to Britain in June 1795. Those at Cambrai decided not to struggle to regain their 'much-beloved but now lost' convent. They applied for passports and received money, via Hamburg, from a British sympathizer, sailing from Calais on 23 May. The staff and students of the English Colleges of Saint-Omer and Douai asked permission to return home and were possibly among those who left for Gibraltar in August 1798.[76]

For the British and Irish clergy who remained, the most serious threat to the survival of their institutions was the sale of their property. This did not go ahead without resistance from certain clergymen, who were confronted by ambiguities in the legislation. The release of foreigners' property from confiscation on 29 December 1794 gave them some leverage. There was, however, confusion over whether the property of the foreign houses was ecclesiastical wealth, and could be sold as such, or

[74] MAE, ADP, France, 10.
[75] AN, F/7/3081.
[76] MAE, ADP, France, 10.

whether it ought to be defined as private property because it belonged to foreigners. Local authorities, potential beneficiaries of the sales, and the superiors took their different interpretations to the authorities. On 21 February 1795, the Irish clerics of the Paris college petitioned the commission of *domaines nationaux*, claiming that the law of 29 December applied to their property. They stressed that it belonged by right to those fugitives who 'put the debris of their fortune under the safeguard of French loyalty, to provide for the education of their relations'. This tried and trusted argument did not immediately work. A year later, the Irish were given the right to administer the property, which fell short of full restitution. For as long as the nature of ownership remained in doubt, the superiors could not dispose or use the wealth as they saw fit.[77]

This was not the end of their troubles, because the law of 13 July 1797 (25 Messidor V), allocated the bursaries of all the old Paris colleges to a new military academy, the *Prytanée français*. It was, however, by no means clear that the foreign seminaries were to be included. The decree referred only to the ten colleges of the arts faculty at the University of Paris, of which the foreign institutions were affiliates, but not constituent parts.[78] The academy, of course, laid claim to the foreign property and the superiors were no closer to securing it for the benefit of their own students. This was a particularly cruel blow for Alexander Innes, procurator of the Scots College, who had succeeded in his struggle to regain its main building near the Panthéon in April 1796. He joined Walsh in besieging the French government with letters of protest up to and beyond the collapse of the Directorial regime. By December 1797, the Irish College in Paris was offered compensation to the value of two-thirds of its property, but Walsh understood the implications of accepting such an offer. It meant abandoning all claims to the buildings themselves.[79]

The efforts of the superiors were in vain. The Fructidorian Directory took a harsher line against both the British and the clergy and decided that the property of all the foreign institutions

---

[77] Ibid.; MAE, CP, Angleterre, 592.

[78] R. R. Palmer, 'Le Prytanée français et les écoles de Paris (1798–1802)', *AhRf* 53 (1981), 124–5.

[79] AN, H/3/2561/A; MAE, CP, Angleterre, 592; ADP, France, 10.

remained *domaines nationaux*. On 25 May and 23 July 1798, it ordered its sale in execution of the law of 1 February 1794. The foreign clergy protested, but the ruling was confirmed by decree on 17 November. The department of the Seine began to evaluate foreign ecclesiastical property and announced an auction for 30 August 1799. The superiors of the English Benedictine monastery, the Scots College, the English Augustinian, and the English Conceptionist nuns in Paris counterattacked in a joint petition to Reinhard, then foreign minister. Walsh persevered on his own for the Irish College.[80] They made little impact. Property belonging to the English Conceptionists, the buildings of the English Augustinian nuns, and those of the English Benedictine monastery were duly auctioned between 30 August and 5 September 1799.[81]

The wealth of the foreign seminaries in Paris was, however, ironically saved by their new adversary, the military academy. The administrators of the *Prytanée français* argued that an *arrêté* issued by the Directory on 1 July 1798, which ordered execution of the law of 25 Messidor, applied to foreign colleges. The property by which the bursaries were funded could not, therefore, be sold. The department of the Seine agreed and, by the end of the year, ordered the transfer of property from the seminaries to the military academy. The Scots College farm at Grisy had already been sold off and the department of the Seine-et-Marne was obliged to void the sale. The purchaser, Théodore La Roche, was prevented from taking possession of the land.[82] While the academy saved the colleges' property from sale, it left the superiors with a renewed battle for ownership, now with the administrators of the *Prytanée*. The dispute was not resolved until the Consulate.

The Irish College of Bordeaux was also offered a respite thanks to its use by the authorities. The college church of Saint-Eutrope was sold to a manufacturer of saltpetre on 22 February 1795. James Burke took upon himself the task of salvaging something from the wreckage. In prison, he drew up a petition and used his contacts outside to help him in his campaign. He enlisted the support of several Protestants in the

---

[80] MAE, CP, Angleterre, 592; AN, H/3/2561/A.
[81] AN, H/3/2561/A.
[82] Ibid.

departmental administration, which suspended the transfer of the deeds of the church. Burke was released shortly after this first victory, but he had a long struggle ahead. Further sales were prevented by an understanding with the mayor of Bordeaux, who proposed to use the seminary to house refugees from the devastated French colonies. It took Burke another eight years before he succeeded in definitively preventing the sale of the buildings, but he never managed to reopen the college. The other Irish colleges in the provinces were similarly never resurrected.[83]

Meanwhile, the remains of seminaries' movable property also remained open to dispute. Robert Watson, a Scot and leading member of the London Corresponding Society, fled to France after the arrest of five of his associates in January 1798. On 19 October 1799, he proposed that, until a permanent home be found for its fragile remnants, he be caretaker of the shattered library of the Scots College in Paris. It was, he proclaimed, 'the last monument to Scotland's political independence'. In the dying light of the Directory, Lindet, minister of finance, advised Reinhard that he was inclined to accept Watson's request, but the Brumaire coup intervened.[84]

With their efforts to restore their institutions frustrated by red tape and official hostility or indifference, the British and Irish Catholic clergy sought alternatives. Even the toughest campaigners began to think in terms of seeking compensation, instead of the restoration of their establishments. As early as June 1795, John Farquharson of the Scots College in Douai wrote that at the first whiff of peace, he hoped that 'some compensation on either side will be granted us'. The war, however, ground tortuously on almost continuously until 1815, and it was only then that such redress from the French government could be discussed seriously. In the long run, however, the most important reason for the failure of most foreign colleges to rise from the ashes was that conditions for Catholics were slowly improving in the British Isles. In 1795, the English Catholic clergy received a substantial private donation for a college. The smaller and poorer Scots Catholic

[83] Ibid.; Preston, 'Collège irlandais', 26; Loupès, 'Ecclésiastiques Irlandais', 96; Loupès, 'Irish Clergy', 37; Simms, 'The Irish', 652.

[84] MAE, CP, Angleterre, 593.

population received government aid to defray the building costs of two Catholic colleges, one of which opened in 1799, the other in 1803.[85] In Ireland, Maynooth College was founded in 1795. Some of the Irish clergy remaining in France opposed this development, because, as Walsh explained to Delacroix in March 1796, the Dublin government aimed to destroy the independence of the Irish clergy on the continent and control Catholic education.[86] Together, the Revolution and the slowly improving status of British and Irish Catholics signalled the end of an era for their institutions in France.

The prospects for the personal survival of the foreign clergy undoubtedly brightened after Thermidor, with their release from the squalor of imprisonment, but the struggle for their institutions was only just beginning. The Terror disgusted and intimidated some of the foreign clergy to the extent that certain orders made little attempt to recover their property and returned to Britain at the earliest opportunity. Others clung on until forced to emigrate in the hostile atmosphere after Fructidor. Unpleasant as incarceration and anticlericalism were, what made the prognosis for their institutions so bleak were the ambiguities over the fate of their property. Its dual status as clerical and as foreign left its liability for sale open to dispute. Before October 1793, foreign status had protected this wealth from ecclesiastical reforms. Once the revolutionaries had confiscated it as enemy property, however, they had broken the glass wall which sheltered foreign wealth from the revolutionary whirlwind. The authorities then regarded it increasingly as ecclesiastical land, liable to nationalization and sale. This equivocal position embroiled the foreign clergy in complex political battles to save their property. The decision to categorize it as *domaines nationaux* in the summer of 1798 stemmed from the anticlericalism which reawoke after Fructidor and ensured the destruction of more foreign institutions in France. Thereafter, dogged as foreign clerics such as Walsh, Innes, and Burke were in the struggle for their seminaries, the fate of the property was largely out of their hands. By the time they had made progress,

---

[85] Johnson, *Developments*, 119–25, 231.
[86] MAE, ADP, France, 10.

developments in the British Isles favourable to Catholics ensured that interest in the institutions in France would never reach pre-revolutionary levels.

IV

When the Terror collapsed, those foreign patriots who had been imprisoned were eventually released, while some of those who had fled reappeared to taste the new freedom. Mary Wollstonecraft returned to Paris from Le Havre in the late summer of 1794. On 23 September, she wrote approvingly to her wayward husband of the 'liberty of the press with the overthrow of the Jacobins'.[87] Not all foreign patriots felt such euphoria: the experience of imprisonment, expulsion, or harassment left them disillusioned with France and the Revolution. Paine was released on 4 November because his American citizenship was recognized by James Monroe, Morris's more sympathetic replacement as United States ambassador.[88] Ill from almost a year in the disease-ridden Luxembourg, he refused a pension from the Thermidorians. Monroe petitioned the Committee of Public Safety on his behalf on 4 January 1795, asking for him to be entrusted with a mission to the United States. The committee replied curtly that 'the position he holds will not permit him to accept it'.[89] Having been denied his seat in the Convention at the end of 1793, Paine was now being prevented from returning to his other adopted country on the grounds that he was, after all, a deputy. After her initial pleasure at Thermidor, Wollstonecraft travelled back to Britain in April 1795, possibly because, as Archibald Hamilton Rowan implied, laws against foreigners were being more rigorously enforced than during the Terror. She was also penniless, frustrated by the prolonged absence of Imlay and disappointed with Thermidorian Paris. On 10 February 1795 she wrote to her husband that 'this has been such a period of barbarity and misery' and that she wished that 'I had never heard of the cruelties that have practised here'.[90]

---

[87] Wardle, *Collected Letters of Mary Wollstonecraft*, 264.
[88] Conway, *Life of Thomas Paine*, ii. 142–9; Keane, *Tom Paine*, 416, 419.
[89] Conway, *Life of Thomas Paine*, ii. 154–5.
[90] Tomalin, *Mary Wollstonecraft*, 176–8; Rowan, *Autobiography*, 248; Wardle, *Collected Letters of Mary Wollstonecraft*, 279, 281, 282.

Some foreign patriots, burnt by the Terror, now avoided the unpredictable flame of politics altogether. In any case, many of the Germans saw the importance of the Revolution not so much in political as in moral terms. Bitaubé, freed from captivity, remained in France and successfully engaged in literary and philosophical pursuits. He was elected to the Institut national des sciences et des arts created by the Directory on 25 October 1795, to which foreign associates could be admitted. When Meyer arrived in March 1796, he found that Bitaubé had become an established member of the intellectual cream of French society.[91] Schlabrendorf now lived among his books, devoting as much attention to his interests in literature and philosophy as he did to politics.[92]

The post-Thermidor period still saw new arrivals with avow-edly political missions. As the French invaders swept across the frozen Dutch landscape in December 1794, the Patriots Jacob Blauw and Willem van Irhoven van Dam (replaced in March by Caspar Meijer) were sent to Paris. Their mission, which proved in vain, was to convince the Thermidorians to treat the Nether-lands as an ally rather than as a conquest.[93] Theobald Wolfe Tone, a leader of the republican United Irish movement, arrived at Le Havre from the United States in February 1796, to coax a French invasion of Ireland. The Scottish republican, Thomas Muir, who had escaped from the penal colony at Botany Bay, ended his global odyssey when he arrived at Bordeaux to a triumphal reception in November 1797. The last fourteen months of his life were employed writing memoranda to the French government, requesting military support for a revolution in Scotland.[94] John Ashley of the London Corresponding Soci-ety slipped across to France in the spring of 1798 and by Muir's good offices tried to convince Talleyrand of the desirability of a French invasion of Britain.[95]

Besides such individuals, whole new groups found refuge, namely the United Irishmen after the catastrophic uprising in 1798 and, from April 1799, 5,200 Italian 'Jacobins', when the

[91] Meyer, *Fragments*, ii. 53–4; Mathiez, *La Révolution et les étrangers*, 188.
[92] Gooch, *Germany*, 336.
[93] Schama, *Patriots and Liberators*, 185, 203.
[94] *Moniteur* (12 Frimaire VI); Bewley, *Muir*, 160–3; Francisque-Michel, *Les Écossais en France: Les Français en Écosse*, 2 vols. (London, 1862), ii. 465–71; MAE, CP Angleterre, 592.
[95] MAE, CP Angleterre, 592.

Austrians and Russians poured into Italy. The Italians arrived in waves: the Cisalpines in April, Piedmontese in June, Neapolitans in August, and Romans in October.[96] In the last months of the Directory, the refugees came from more exotic places, reflecting the far-flung campaigns waged by the French. In August and October 1799, the minister of the interior received petitions for financial aid from refugees hailing from Malta, Gozo, Corfu, and Cephallonia, protesting their 'devotion to the cause of the French'.[97]

Demands for political conformity were no longer as stringent as they had been during the Terror, but it was still possible for foreign patriots to fall foul of the authorities if they were too forthright. The outspoken José Marchena, a surviving friend of Brissot, was sharply critical of the Thermidorians for not being harsh enough on the Terrorists. While many Thermidorians might have applauded his demand for the expulsion of all Jacobins from every organ of the state, most baulked at his proposal to compromise with the constitutional monarchists. As Marchena also condemned the law of two-thirds, he was falsely accused of joining the royalist Vendémiaire uprising when it exploded on the streets of Paris. Arrested on 8 October, he was held captive for a month.[98]

More radical foreigners found themselves facing a moderate regime hostile to overly egalitarian propositions. On 7 July 1795, Paine made his only appearance in the Convention after his release. Still a proponent of direct representative democracy, he roundly condemned the proposed Thermidorian constitution. Murmurs arose from around the chamber as his speech was read out and some deputies violently opposed its publication. His opinions reaped an onslaught from Merlin de Douai two days later.[99] After the dissolution of the Convention, Paine would have nothing to do with the organization of the Directory which he had so eloquently attacked, until it was threatened by something even worse: royalism.[100]

---

[96] A.-M. Rao, 'Paris et les exilés italiens en 1799', in Vovelle, *Paris et la Révolution*, 226; Rao, 'Réfugiés italiens', 244.

[97] AN, F/15/3511.

[98] J. F. Fuentes, 'Les Écrits politiques de Marchena pendant le Directoire: Clés biographiques et intellectuelles', *AhRf* 69 (1997), 62–4.

[99] *Moniteur* (22, 25 Messidor III).

[100] Conway, *Life of Thomas Paine*, ii. 165.

As a rightward shift in revolutionary politics, Thermidor also exposed those foreign radicals who had succeeded in attaching themselves too closely to the Terrorist regime. Archibald Hamilton Rowan, who had been freed from captivity by orders of the revolutionary government at the height of its power, left France for the United States. He felt uneasy after Jacobins were blamed for the accidental explosion at the Grenelle gunpowder works on 31 August 1794.[101] The German doctor Saiffert, an associate of the Hébertists and a founder of the German legion, had enjoyed an acquittal by the Revolutionary Tribunal during the Terror. He now returned to Germany and tried to shed his extremist past.[102] Even Valckenaer, who had only escaped arrest during the Year II by keeping a low profile, was watched along with others of his kind as 'shrewd intriguers', who shared 'all the disruptive ideas which have desolated France'.[103] Some foreigners resident in Paris, who had been active in the popular movement, re-emerged to provide some local leadership in the Prairial insurrection against the Thermidorian Convention, succumbing to the repression which followed. The Germans Jean Schwerdfeger, Joseph Klaine, and Mathias Halm, the Bohemian Jean Krubert, the Belgian Joseph Biot, and the Swiss Pierre Cardinaux were all arrested. The nervous authorities freed them gradually over the summer, with Biot having to wait until August before being allowed back on the streets.[104]

The Robespierrist Filippo Buonarroti was recalled from his mission in Oneglia on 14 March 1795 and was arrested after a neutral complained of the confiscation of his property and its distribution among 'sans-culottes'. He was eventually released in October 1795, as the Convention sought Jacobin allies against the royalist surge which accompanied the Vendémiaire uprising. Buonarroti was no repentant Terrorist, however, and was later caught in the Babeuf conspiracy.[105] He was not the only foreigner to be implicated. The Liégeois general, Fyon, was a member of the Babouvist military committee. While he escaped

[101] Rowan, *Autobiography*, 240.

[102] Mathiez, *La Révolution et les étrangers*, 187–8.

[103] Schama, *Patriots and Liberators*, 256; Godechot, *Grande Nation*, 216.

[104] Monnier and Soboul, *Répertoire*, 278, 352, 354, 410, 431, 499; Cobb, *People's Armies*, 79, 627.

[105] *Moniteur* (3 Prairial IV); Rao, 'Réfugiés italiens', 236; Godechot, *Grande Nation*, 226.

arrest in May 1796, he was captured in the Jacobin attempt to foment revolt at the military camp at Grenelle on 9 September, only to be acquitted. The incorrigible Biot was a Babouvist agent in the 7th *arrondissement*. Sandoz, the Genevan, already identified by the police minister, Cochon, as 'a very dangerous scoundrel', was arrested as an Equal, but released. Like Fyon, he was then arrested at the Grenelle uprising, but, unlike the Liégeois, did not escape the death penalty. He was shot on 25 September.[106] Such people were not simply exposed, accidentally, on the 'wrong' side as the revolutionary tide moved away. They, at least, actively conspired against the Directorial regime.

Others, however, seem to have been accused of extremism merely because of their suspected political ties with Jacobins. A few days after the arrest of the Equals, the Director Reubell was warned that other Italian patriots, Selvaggi, Celentani, Serra, and Sauli, were in Paris 'under the auspices of the conspirator Buonarroti'.[107] When the authorities harassed him for the fact that Jacobins met at his café on the place de l'Estrapade, Cardinaux defended himself by limply explaining that 'I had the misfortune to have a large venue . . . where citizens met as a political society.' Foreigners also appeared on the lists of Parisian militants considered by Babeuf's agents to be dependable, including some of those implicated in Prairial. Yet these lists were often the product of the optimistic imaginations of the conspirators, who took past militancy as a sign of persistent commitment.[108]

Still, over the summer of 1796, the authorities insisted on seeing Jacobins under every Directorial bed. In June, the government demanded that its Dutch allies actually recall Valckenaer, now Batavian ambassador to Madrid, who was passing through Paris and who was suspected of Jacobinism. That same month, the Fribourg radical, François Roullier, was reported to hold sinister, nocturnal meetings in his home, propagating the 'ferocious and sanguinary maxims' of 'that monster', Marat. The police suggested his deportation back to Switzerland. In December, the Directory refused to recognize the credentials of the

---

[106] Monnier and Soboul, *Répertoire*, 24–5, 152, 445; Cobb, *People's Armies*, 621.
[107] Godechot, 'Jacobins italiens', 73–4.
[108] Monnier and Soboul, *Répertoire*, 352, 432, 499, 508; Cobb, *People's Armies*, 620–3, 627.

Genevan ambassador to France, Delaplanche, whom it suspected of *babouvisme*.[109]

Embroiled in a war and buffeted by real or imagined conspiracies, the jumpy government did not give foreign patriots the
same benefit of the doubt as the revolutionaries might have done
prior to the Terror. On 27 March 1796, Friedrich Cotta, a
Württemberg patriot and editor of the *Gazette allemande du
Rhin*, came to the attention of the authorities in the Bas-Rhin
for his repeated journeys between Strasbourg and Basle. Cochon
ordered his expulsion if he proved liable to the law of 23
Messidor III. An Italian refugee named Cetto was only allowed
to stay in France when he appealed to the Directory on 23
April.[110]

With the search for domestic stability proving elusive, the
French authorities continued to take no chances with foreign
refugees. Early in the morning of 15 June 1797, after the collapse
of the well-publicized mutinies in the British fleet, a fishing boat
carrying eleven mutineers from the *Inflexible* sailed into Calais.
'They were received as deserters, placed in an inn with two
sentries' and, the report added carefully, were treated gently.
The sailors brought with them a mutineer's hat ribbon and a
cockade, but the French had still approached the fugitives
warily.[111]

Suspicion of certain foreign patriots flowed with political shifts
within the republican regime. Marchena's achievement was to
fall foul of the Directory during its swings both to the left and to
the right. Arrested after the Vendémiaire uprising, he was
released only to have the Directory cite the law of 23 Messidor
against him and he was expelled from the country. The backlash
against the left, after Babeuf and the Grenelle uprising, enabled
him to return to France towards the end of 1796. Yet he
persisted in his attacks on the Directory in his journal, the
Spectateur français, which first appeared in February 1797. He
drew conclusions which tasted, of all things, like Jacobinism and
he was rearrested in April. For once, the political winds were in

---

[109] Schama, *Patriots and Liberators*, 255–6; Monnier and Soboul, *Répertoire*, 473;
Palmer, *Age of the Democratic Revolution*, ii. 187, 195–6; Godechot, *Grande Nation*,
231–2.
[110] AN, F/7/3081.
[111] MAE, CP Angleterre, 590.

his favour. The monarchists and royalists had done well in the recent elections and, despite his social commentary which had enraged the increasingly shrill right-wing press, the Council of Five Hundred, hostile to the government which had initially ordered his arrest, released him. Naturally, his relationship with the authorities remained rocky. No royalist, he attacked the right who were responsible for his freedom and he applauded the coup of 18 Fructidor. Even so, he spent a further seven months in prison between December 1798 and July 1799. Marchena was too much of a loose cannon to be tolerated by the Fructidorian Directory.[112]

The demands for orthodoxy certainly became more pressing after the coup. Thomas Paine was safe, as he had rallied to the Directory beforehand. He had joined the Swiss moderate, Benjamin Constant, in the republican Constitutional Club in reaction to the alarming royalist resurgence in elections of the spring of 1797. For Paine, the imperfect Directory was preferable to a restoration of the monarchy: 'the friends of the Republic should rally around the standard of the Constitution'. Yet even Paine was vulnerable to the anglophobia which seeped out following the breakdown of the Lille peace negotiations. In the autumn of 1798, he was questioned on his connections with the British secret service.[113] John Hurford Stone was an early supporter of the coup, describing it in a letter to Joseph Priestley, now in the United States, as 'a happy event for the country'.[114] The Liégeois Fyon, long suspected of Jacobin sympathies, redeemed himself by commanding troops loyal to the Directory at the *poste de Gravilliers* during the coup.[115]

Not all foreigners passed the litmus test so easily. In October 1797, Talleyrand asked Wolfe Tone to name all Irish refugees known personally to him and to assess their sincerity. Tone obliged on 15 October, producing a list of six Irishmen with a brief description of their virtues. He also took the opportunity to mention four others who had been imprisoned in Liège, victims of Fructidorian vigilance: 'I believe them all to be true patriots.' The screening procedure was formalized when, at the end of the

[112] Fuentes, 'Marchena', 64–70; *Moniteur* (30 Prairial, 19 Messidor V).
[113] Keane, *Tom Paine*, 433–6, 443.
[114] Stern, 'English Press', 330–3.
[115] Monnier and Soboul, *Répertoire*, 35.

year, Talleyrand suggested to Sotin, minister of police, that, as British agents might try to slip into France posing as Irish refugees, none should be allowed to remain unless vouched for by Tone.[116] Some of this vigilance was justified. On 9 November 1797, the United Irish contact in Hamburg, William Duckett, warned Talleyrand of 'an Irish priest named Ferris', describing him as an *émigré* 'closely tied to all the conspirators'. He also noted that Ferris had recently been in London. Richard Ferris was arrested on a charge of espionage in April 1799.[117]

After the catastrophic failure of the Irish insurrection in 1798 and Tone's suicide, Edward Lewins filled his shoes as the main judge of patriotism among the Irish in France. Fearful to the point of paranoia, he sought to restrict the number of Irish refugees entering France, in case there were British spies among them. On 28 October 1799, Lewins warned Reinhard that he did not wish to communicate with the 'central committee of the Society of United Irishmen' in Paris. He agreed with the foreign minister's view 'that such an association can do harm and even be used by the English Ministry as an instrument of espionage'.[118]

Italian exiles were also viewed nervously by the authorities. The discovery of Buonarroti among the Babouvists in 1796 ensured that Italian patriots became almost synonymous with Jacobin conspiracy. Carlo Salvador, who had lived in Paris during the Terror, was wrongly accused in 1798 by the French minister to the Cisalpine Republic as a one-time 'agent of Robespierre, assassin of September, judge at the Revolutionary Tribunal of Paris'.[119] The brief Jacobin resurgence which followed the Prairial parliamentary coup on 18 June 1799 therefore ensured that, when Italian refugees streamed into France, they would be welcomed as genuine patriots by a vocal body of French political opinion. Italian sufferings gave the French Jacobins a rod with which to chastize the Directory in its conduct of foreign policy and the war. Meanwhile, opponents of the Jacobins and of Italian unity played on the reputed extremism of

---

[116] MAE, CP Angleterre, 592; Tone, *Life*, ii. 457.

[117] MAE, CP Angleterre, 592; M. Purcell, 'The Strange Story of Richard Ferris', in L. Swords (ed.), *The Irish–French Connection 1578–1978*, (Paris, 1978), 103.

[118] MAE, CP Angleterre, 593; Elliott, *Partners in Revolution*, 265–71.

[119] Godechot, 'Jacobins italiens', 76.

the Italian exiles. On 8 September, Reubell accused them of being in league both with French *exagérés* and with the ambitious 'Jacobin' generals who had fought in Italy, Brune and Championnet.[120]

While bowing to Jacobin pressure to give the Italians refuge and financial support, therefore, the Directory also sought to contain their militancy through the very means by which the subsidies were allocated. On 4 August, the Directory urged the foreign minister to assemble them in the departments closest to the Italian frontier and encouraged the minister of war to enlist them as a unit in the French army. While making the distribution of handouts easier, this would also force the refugees to a safe distance from Paris and prevent them from settling too comfortably on French soil. On 23 October, the government appointed a commission of reliable Italian representatives, who were to screen applicants for financial assistance. Six days later, Reinhard ordered that only a select few of the Italians would be permitted to remain in Paris. Refusal to comply with all these regulations would mean withdrawal of the subsidies.[121]

The reception of foreign patriots in France did not only depend upon shifts in Directorial politics, but also upon the government's reading of French strategic interests. Renewed French advances into neighbouring countries created an atmosphere in which the 'crusade for universal liberty' seemed to have been rejuvenated after the apparent stagnation under the revolutionary government. Yet this hid the continuities between 'Robespierrist' attitudes, as they were emerging in the summer of 1794, and the post-Thermidor approach towards foreign patriots. Like every regime, the Thermidorians and the Directory put French security and strategic concerns above international fraternity. Foreign patriots in France were therefore negotiating with a government whose motives were at least partially concealed by a veil of secrecy. Most patriots sooner or later understood that the French had their own plans for their conquests and so they tried to adapt their negotiations accordingly. Their fortunes were therefore tied both to the fickle barometer of Directorial politics and to French strategic objectives, which were also inconsistent.

[120] Godechot, *Grande Nation*, 229; Rao, 'Réfugiés italiens', 243, 246–8, 254.
[121] Rao, 'Réfugiés italiens', 253–5.

As the French armies marched into Germany, the Mainz patriots in Paris clamoured for the annexation of the Rhineland in the summer of 1795. Initially, the Directory also supported this policy, as it coincided with the drive for natural frontiers. The government subsidized the exiles' paper, *Der Pariser Zuschauer*, edited by Anton Dorsch and Georg Böhmer. Monarchist successes in the elections of 1797, however, seemed to knock these aspirations on the head. The new, moderate Director Barthélemy, like his colleague Carnot, supported a peace on the basis of more modest territorial accessions. For those who hoped to see France batter the empire into relinquishing the Rhineland, the omens were not good. The Rhenish exiles switched, therefore, to the goal of a Cisrhenan sister republic under French protection, which, they hoped, would fit the Directory's new objectives. It also suited General Hoche who, like Bonaparte in Italy, sought to create a personal power-base for himself in Germany. Fructidor, however, brought in a government which once more demanded the annexation of the Rhineland. Having seen their plans sunk, yet again, by the treacherous tides of Directorial politics, the hapless Rhenish exiles were dealt the additional blow of Hoche's death a few weeks later.[122] Wolfe Tone, whose hopes for French military support were equally subject to fickle Parisian politics, sighed 'wretched . . . is the nation whose independence hangs on the will of another'.[123]

The post-Thermidor regimes did, at least, recognize that foreign patriots had their strategic and propaganda uses, which explains why the authorities persisted in supporting them financially while they were in France. The decree of 14 Ventôse II (4 March 1794), which allocated 20 million *livres* for the subsistence of refugees, remained in force until the money ran out on 16 September 1796. The Belgians and Liégeois were the main beneficiaries until 23 February 1795, taking 97 per cent of the 182,710 *livres*, 7 *sous*, distributed to foreign patriots, with the rest going to those from the Rhineland. From 24 February, however, Belgians and Liégeois accounted for progressively less of the handouts. The remaining funds were then shared between

---

[122] Ruiz, 'Jacobinisme allemand', 266; Godechot, *Grande Nation*, 217–19; Meyer, *Fragments*, i. 129–30.

[123] Tone, *Life*, ii. 93.

German and Irish exiles in Paris and a small group of Italian refugees in the Isère. The money which the Belgians and Liégeois did receive was to defray travel costs, decreed on 25 September 1794, for their homeward journey. These payments implied that, in return, foreign patriots were expected to serve the French occupiers, who had supported them in anticipation of such collaboration.[124]

Fresh demands were made on the French government's purse by the new waves of fugitives who came from Ireland in 1798 and Italy in 1799. In the spring of 1799, the minister of the interior, François de Neufchâteau, reminded the Directory that these people also deserved aid. The Cisalpine refugees were offered 200,000 francs by the Directory on 12 June 1799. After the Prairial coup six days later, which bolstered the influence of the sympathetic Jacobins, a further 100,000 francs were offered to exiles from other parts of Italy.[125] The Irish had to wait longer before they were promised assistance. The delay was due to the lack of trust which Lewins placed in these fresh and unfamiliar faces. As he screened the refugees on behalf of the French government, few were given passports to enter the country and fewer still, although wasting in dire personal hardship, received French subsidies. The Directory had been willing to ask the legislature for 60,000 francs, but the secrecy demanded by Lewins, ever-anxious over spies, made such a move impossible. It was not until 16 July 1799 that the Directory finally authorized François de Neufchâteau's successor, Quinette, to release 10,000 francs from his secret funds, giving each Irish exile 80 francs a month. Even so, between July 1799 and March 1800, only seven received money from the government.[126]

In the twilight of the Directory, cash may have been made available on paper, but it could take a while for it to reach the outstretched hands of the fugitives. In 1799, the Republic was struggling to survive heavy defeats inflicted by the Second Coalition and faced a shortage of funds. Consequently, at the very moment that foreign refugees flooded into France, the government lacked the means to support them. On 2 October

[124] AN, F/15*/17.
[125] AN, F/15/3511; Rao, 'Réfugiés italiens', 252.
[126] MAE, CP Angleterre, 592; AN, F/15/3511; Elliott, *Partners in Revolution*, 270–1.

1799, Bourdon de Vatry, the Directory's last naval minister, warned Reinhard that some of the Irish in Paris were 'reduced to desperation by the extreme misery which they have suffered for several months'.[127] The foreign minister replied four days later, explaining that the breakdown in the distribution of the money promised 'can only be blamed on the penury of funds in every branch of the administration of the republic'.[128] On 4 November, five days before Bonaparte's *coup d'état*, the Paris *bureau de surveillance* grumbled about the cost of providing Italian exiles with food and lodging.[129]

The rejection of the Terror brought about a new flourish in political activity. The release of political prisoners, the restoration of press freedom and the repeal of the law of suspects encouraged foreign patriots to re-emerge and participate more enthusiastically in the Revolution. Yet the problem of political orthodoxy did not disappear as a consideration altogether. Foreign radicals seemingly sympathetic to the Terror or to Jacobinism could still provoke surveillance or expulsion. Italian refugees were accused of extremism by the government which, with some justice, suspected them of links with the Jacobin opposition. Marchena, on the other hand, was imprisoned and harassed because he was suspected of monarchist sympathies in 1795 and then of Jacobinism in 1797. Friedrich Cotta was threatened with punitive action simply because his activities looked suspicious.

Concerns for French domestic security informed the authorities' approach to foreign patriots, as it had done during the Terror. Nervousness over British agents led the French government to be wary about being overly warm in their reception of British and Irish exiles. In the case of the Irish, the government told Tone to screen Irish patriots in France and then supported Lewins in his efforts to do the same. When foreign refugees were admitted in great numbers, as the Italians were, the government used subsidies and the formation of legions to control their behaviour. At the same time, foreign patriots like the Rhenish exiles and Wolfe Tone anxiously watched shifts in

---

[127] MAE, CP Angleterre, 593.
[128] AN, F/15/3511; MAE, CP Angleterre, 593.
[129] AN, F/15/3511.

French politics, as the nature of the regime determined French strategic aims.

The period after the fall of Robespierre did not see the emergence of any cosmopolitan era of fraternity. The post-Thermidor regimes did not need political equals, but administrators in the territories they occupied, to help them exploit local wealth, to protect French interests, and to place those interests above local aspirations. They hoped, as the revolutionary government had done in the last months of its existence, that foreign patriots would fulfil this role. Their personal freedom to express their views gained greater latitude after the Terror, but foreign radicals discovered that their aspirations would only be respected for as long as they supported French aims.

V

The uncertain direction of the Revolution immediately after 9 Thermidor was reflected in the Convention's treatment of those foreigners who contributed to French economic life. The Thermidorians did not immediately dismantle the controlled economy and, until property belonging to enemy merchants was released, neutrals would remain important to efforts to carry food and war materials into France. The trading partners of the German mercantile community in Bordeaux continued to be exploited. The Bordeaux-based Danish merchant, Meyer, worked as the Republic's intermediary with Hamburg and Copenhagen in its search for vital imports. Freedom of commerce was restored gradually. On 17 October 1794, the government lost its right to first purchase of all imports of prime necessity. Initially, only French merchants benefited from the withdrawal of this monopoly, as neutrals had to wait until 15 November before they were allowed to trade at will.[130]

On 24 December 1794, the same day that the Maximum was lifted, the government proposed to release confiscated foreign property and to reimburse the funds raised from its sale. Johannot, who pressed this measure, claimed that it would mean the resumption of free trade and restore confidence in

---

[130] Lefebvre, 'Commerce extérieur', 266, 274.

France as a commercial partner.[131] He provoked a lively debate. Those in favour argued that freedom of commerce was the best means of meeting French needs for raw materials and food. Ramel even reverted to the language heard before the Terror, that it was up to France to lead by example. The war was being waged against governments and not peoples, who were protected by the *droit des gens*. In opposition, Cambon and Thirion argued that the *droit des gens* commanded strict reciprocity: enemy property should be withheld until their governments released what belonged to French citizens. The more paranoid deputies warned that enemy merchants kept agents in Paris, who were engaged in dealings less wholesome than trade.[132]

The Thermidorians, therefore, were not entirely convinced of the wisdom of a return to free trade between French and foreigners. They were not against commercial freedom in principle, but some believed that, for now, its return might hand certain advantages to the Republic's enemies. Both sides pointed to malign foreign influence behind the arguments of their opponents. Girod, Richard, Ramel, and Réal, all supporters of the repeal of sequestration, suggested that the measure had been prompted by foreign speculators. The movement in favour of liberalizing trade was therefore due, not to cosmopolitanism, but to assumptions about the benefits of free trade for France herself. The xenophobic outbursts also reflected a deep anxiety about the consequences of so significant a change in economic policy. The Convention eventually accepted the proposals on 29 December, although in principle the Thermidorians retained the ban on British imports.

Some revolutionaries still felt strongly that strenuous efforts should be made to block British merchandise from France. On 31 October 1796, after sustained pressure on the government from French cotton manufacturers, who sought to protect their markets from cheaper British imports, a decree ordered that a long list of British articles be seized. Domiciliary visits, seizures, and the arrest of British merchants were authorized. Other imported goods were to be accompanied by a certificate of origin validated by a French consul.[133] On 23 November, the Directory ordered

---

[131] *Moniteur* (5 Nivôse III).
[132] *Moniteur* (11, 12 Nivôse III).
[133] Lefebvre, *French Revolution*, 216–17.

that the captains of all ships which had docked in Britain and then put into French ports be interrogated by the local authorities before being allowed to set sail again. American sailors who could provide proof of United States citizenship were supposed to be freed immediately, but the French authorities were nervous about the possibility of false papers, particularly after Fructidor. There was some justification for these suspicions. In August 1797, two Glasgow entrepreneurs, John and Benjamin Sword, tried to pass themselves off as Americans. They failed in this ploy in Hamburg, where the French representative refused them passports, but they succeeded at the Hague, from where they made their way to Dunkirk.[134] The brothers had French sympathies and their intentions appear to have been no more than commercial, but such duplicity justified the stringent measures which followed the Fructidor coup.

On 18 January 1798, the government, having broken off peace negotiations with Britain, ordered the seizure of any neutral ship carrying British commodities. Enforcement of this new order entailed a *guerre de course* against neutral shipping on the high seas. Americans, in particular, suffered. Between 1797 and 1800, 834 American vessels were seized by French corsairs, of which 419 were declared *bonne prise*. This probably amounted to thousands of American sailors being held captive in French seaports over the course of the crisis.[135]

The Directory's order of 26 February then permitted the arrest and questioning of American citizens in French ports. Neutrals had access to British harbours, so were regarded as potential conduits for British propaganda and possibly as enemy agents. American sailors were easily mistaken for British subjects, especially as the British still press-ganged American seamen. In the summer, the president of the administration of Clahar-Carnoët in the Finistère was suspended from his duties by the government. His crime was to have allowed an American merchantman, the *Iris*, to dock and then leave without interrogating the captain. The ship had just come from London and British newspapers were discovered on board.[136] Complaints

---

[134] H. W. Meikle, 'Two Glasgow Merchants in the French Revolution', *Scottish Historical Review*, 8 (1911), 153–4.
[135] Bonnel, *La France et les États-Unis*, 115.
[136] AN, F/7/7446; Bonnel, *La France et les États-Unis*, 91.

from American consuls led the naval minister, Admiral Eustace Bruix, to write two circular letters on 11 and 16 August 1798, reminding the port authorities that France and the United States were not at war. The embargo on British goods did not mean that neutral crews could be imprisoned. Yet he conceded that some Americans had abused their status so often that their countrymen were inevitably viewed with suspicion. So genuine Americans without the necessary proof of citizenship were still incarcerated. Even those with papers were detained. Cox Barnet, the American consul in Bordeaux, and Dobrée, his counterpart in Nantes, fired off their protests. In August 1799, they were particularly worried by the plight of forty-five American sailors held prisoner in Saumur, as half of them had proven their citizenship.[137]

Such measures against neutrals naturally threatened to disrupt commerce with foreign merchants, who were often the only carriers of raw materials, such as cotton, which came originally from British sources. After Fructidor, however, the French government gave priority to the prosecution of the war, even at the cost of friction with neutral powers. The risk of open conflict between France and the United States—and skirmishes between their ships—only subsided when President Adams sent a peace commission to Paris early in 1799 to negotiate. After Brumaire, when Bonaparte was keen to secure the quiescence of the United States, the Americans managed to make serious progress in securing the release of their captive sailors.

For the Thermidorians, foreign financiers posed a more sinister threat. When the Convention debated the return of property to enemy subjects, the Belgian banker Edouard Walckiers was accused of originally provoking the measure, to profit from the resultant shifts in exchange rates. The eighteenth-century fear of foreign banking networks emerged in these discussions, with London and Amsterdam as the centre of international speculation.[138] These suspicions only intensified with spiralling movements of prices which followed the abolition of the Maximum, then the demise of the *assignats* in February 1796 and, finally, the

---

[137] Bonnel, *La France et les États-Unis*, 92–4; AN, F/7/7446.
[138] *Moniteur* (11, 12 Nivôse III).

return to metal currency a year later. On 9 March 1797, Karl Reinhard reported from Altona that French credit was being steadily corroded by the manœuvres of an 'association of some London bankers with three or four Hamburg houses, united in their interests with the most considerable capitalists in Paris'.[139]

Some hostility towards foreign financiers was justified, if not on the scale that some revolutionaries believed. From 1795, Oberkampf used the Paris-based Genevan financier, Théodore Rivier, to channel French money to Britain via Basle. This allowed the entrepreneur to trade illegally with Britain, without having to draw the tell-tale British currency in Paris.[140] Vast fortunes were made by speculators who were willing to run the high financial risks. In 1798, Heinzmann remarked that some of his fellow Germans had come to France and got rich by 'an advantageous speculation'.[141] As the Genevan economist Francis d'Ivernois, now a confirmed counter-revolutionary, noted, such people made their fortune not from private enterprise, but off the state, through the purchase and resale of *biens natio-naux*.[142] On his return to Paris, Meister concurred with many revolutionaries in seeing foreigners as the worst of the speculators, believing that they had profited far more than French citizens from the sale of *émigré* property.[143]

While such evidence is highly subjective, it illustrates the extent to which the economic climate aggravated fears of foreign *agioteurs* who pillaged the Republic. Despite the persistent anxieties, however, foreign financiers still had their uses. The Swiss banker Perregaux, who had played a leading role in raising funds for the purchase of foreign currency during the Year II, was allowed to use some of this money to buy merchandise in Copenhagen.[144] When the government ceased printing *assignats* in February 1796, Perregaux was among the bankers appointed to a consortium which would issue new notes, the *mandats territoriaux*.[145]

[139] AN, AF/III/59.
[140] Chassagne, *Oberkampf*, 178.
[141] Heinzmann, *Voyage*, 16–17.
[142] Lyons, *France under the Directory*, 183.
[143] Meister, *Souvenirs*, 71–2, 79.
[144] Lefebvre, 'Commerce extérieur', 266.
[145] Woronoff, *République bourgeoise*, 111.

The only foreigners whom the Thermidorians and the Directory regarded in an unequivocally favourable light were foreign manufacturers and artisans. On 24 March 1795, the *bureau de commerce* warned the Committee of Public Safety that 'we cannot allow Britain to retain her superiority in innovation'.[146] Yet the war and the Terror had dissuaded newcomers from establishing new manufactures. Heinzmann met German artisans who had set up shop in northern France, but remarked that few seemed to have arrived since the Terror. German and Swiss artisans who had once come to France to ply their trade could, he suggested, make just as much money in their home countries.[147]

The revolutionaries, therefore, sought to encourage and protect those who remained because they bolstered the war-ravaged economy. On 25 December 1794, Boissy d'Anglas reported on 'one of the marvels of liberty'. He was speaking of the manufacture of clocks set up in Besançon in 1793. The attractions of the Republic had brought 'twelve thousand foreigners, skilled in the art of clockmaking' from Geneva, Neuchâtel, and London. Boissy sought a decree to encourage them to stay in France and to lure others. He suggested the payment of bounties to the entrepreneur who employed the most workers and produced the best quality. The enterprise, Boissy argued, would stimulate the growth of auxiliary industries such as tool-making and watch-chains.[148] To attract foreign craftsmen, the Thermidorians were using methods identical to those of the Ancien Régime *bureau de commerce*. They also shared the same long-term goal: to naturalize foreign skills and knowledge in France.

The revolutionaries faced an uphill struggle in trying to achieve these aims. Their financial and economic policies brought dramatic oscillations in the value of French currency, which made enterprise in France a risky business. Some artisans did flourish in the more relaxed social climate of the Directory, where an enriched few had money to burn. Meyer remarked that in Paris the Scottish glassmaker O'Reilly was doing very well by producing one vase in eight days of work, but to such a degree of

---

[146] Harris, *Industrial Espionage*, 381; Ballot, *L'Introduction du Machinisme*, 25.
[147] Heinzmann, *Voyage*, 16–17, 106–7.
[148] *Moniteur* (8 Nivôse III).

perfection and skill that he could charge a very high price. Meanwhile, a German porcelain manufacturer named Dihl showed Meyer the stores of his vast workshop, which were 'richly stocked', and the shop-floor where painters and gilders worked on his plates and vases.[149]

Others suffered, however, from the economic dislocation in the winter freeze of *nonante-cinq*, and the financial crisis of 1797. That year, Philemon Pickford blamed the effects of French paper money when production of his spinning-mules nearly collapsed. Goldschmidt's file manufacture at Annecy closed in 1798 when the government could no longer afford to pay the bounties which had been promised in 1794.[150] The war made the transfer of the most desirable technology and expertise from abroad very difficult. The semi-legitimate methods used to obtain new skills and processes were no different from the industrial espionage encouraged by the Ancien Régime. The teams of expert British workers needed to implement these processes were no longer so available, but there were exceptions. French determination to narrow the technological gap between France and Britain was such that, despite the seething brew of war and anglophobia, the authorities still encouraged British manufacturers and craftsmen to settle in France, even after Fructidor. In 1797, William Robinson brought a flax-spinning machine to France, while the dogged Charles Albert, the Alsatian arrested and imprisoned in Lancaster in 1791, was released in 1796, returned to France, and set up an agency to import British technology. He also installed a spinning mill at Coye-la-Forêt, north of Paris, with the help of some of the British artisans with whom he had once worked with Boyer-Fonfrède in Toulouse.[151] During his visit to France from the autumn of 1797 to the spring of 1798, the Glaswegian John Sword asked the interior minister, Letourneur, for permission to sink his personal wealth into a new muslin factory at Nantes, in which some of his own tradesmen would teach their skills to the locals. The plan came to nothing because, on a return visit to Scotland to collect his family in May 1798, Sword was arrested

---

[149] Meyer, *Fragments*, ii. 241–3.
[150] Ballot, *L'Introduction du machinisme*, 26.
[151] Henderson, *Britain and Industrial Europe*, 25, 32, 47.

with his brother. The charge was correspondence with the enemy.[152]

The French government, therefore, still thirsted for foreign skills and labour, but it was the war which dried up the supply. The Belgian manufacturer, Bauwens, opened a cotton mill in Paris in 1797 and narrowly escaped arrest on a recruiting trip to Britain between August and November. He enticed workers from Manchester with the promise of bounties and high wages, but he hid their ultimate destination from them. They had got as far as Gravesend when the abandoned wife of one of the artisans caught up with them and alerted the local magistrates. Escaping their clutches, the workers managed to reach Hamburg, but there they realized that their destination was France and, fearing charges of treason, denounced Bauwens to the British plenipotentiary minister. The hapless entrepreneur fled across north-eastern Europe, arriving in France with only two loyal artisans.[153]

When Britain proved inaccessible, prisoners of war were recruited. In another echo of Ancien Régime practice, a decree of 20 August 1794 released over a hundred prisoners with weaving skills to an entrepreneur in Bourges. The manufacturer Bourguet-Travanet had struggled since 1791 to establish a mechanized cotton mill at the old abbey of Royaumont at Gonesse, north of Paris. He finally succeeded in 1795, with the help of British prisoners of war. In 1798, La Rochefoucauld-Liancourt employed an Englishman named Gibson and four Irish prisoners at his cotton mill at Cire des Mello. Otherwise, the French looked elsewhere. Oberkampf succeeded in using his contacts in London to glean information about recent developments in fabric-printing processes, but he also contacted his sisters at Aarau in Switzerland to obtain sketches and notes about the methods of his competitors. In 1798, two Americans, Reynaud and Ford, were given a grant of 6,000 *livres* by the Directory to establish a textile factory with the most up-to-date technology, but the enterprise failed.[154]

The war and the economic crises of the post-Thermidor

---

[152] Meikle, 'Two Glasgow Merchants', 150, 157.

[153] Ballot, *L'Introduction du machinisme*, 100–1.

[154] Ibid. 26, 93; Henderson, *Britain and Industrial Europe*, 26; Chapman and Chassagne, *European Textile Printers*, 140–4; Chassagne, *Oberkampf*, 179.

period made life especially hard for the poorest foreign migrants. In April 1796, Meyer crossed the Pont-Neuf and noted, rather condescendingly, that 'even the poor little Savoyards, setting up their stands along the pavements to clean the shoes of passersby, find it very difficult to make a living; their great protectors have disappeared and the pedestrians are so different from their predecessors that it is rare for any of them to have their boots or shoes cleaned'.[155] Heinzmann stuffily cited a French pamphlet which claimed of Parisian prostitutes that 'they mostly come from abroad'. He haughtily concurred, saying that 'one finds among the *filles publiques* many Swiss, Italians, Spanish, Germans, Dutch and English . . . the most impure waste of all those countries'. The libertine decline in morals, explained Heinzmann, was caused by such foreigners who 'believe that here they have found the soil which suits them best'. In fact, of ninety-six prostitutes arrested in three Parisian sections between 1793 and 1795, only three were 'foreign', coming from Belgium.[156]

The return to free commerce certainly benefited foreign merchants, who were still able to trade despite the war. Foreign artisans who had remained in France could still prosper, as Meyer discovered, particularly if their skills were devoted to the luxury industries patronized by the *nouveaux riches*. Yet the French economy lurched from one crisis to another and the war was disruptive. Even neutral merchants were harassed and imprisoned because, after Fructidor, the government made the prosecution of the war against Britain a priority. In manufacturing, besides the financial hardship from which most people suffered, the continuing conflict meant that foreign skills and technology were not forthcoming, despite efforts made by both government and manufacturers to acquire them. Those rare British entrepreneurs and artisans willing to defect risked severe penalties. If the political repression of the Terror had disappeared, the vagaries of French finances made investment in anything other than land a risky venture, and this in turn aggravated the old suspicions of foreign financiers. The government was at least practical enough to use the connections of

---

[155] Meyer, *Fragments*, i. 18–19.
[156] Heinzmann, *Voyage*, 100; Cobb, *Police and the People*, 236–7.

some foreign bankers, such as Perregaux. Yet, despite the efforts of both the revolutionary government and its successors to retain the skills and services of foreigners, persistent economic difficulties and the conflict were discouraging. As both Meister and Heinzmann observed, the Terror had driven skilled foreigners out, but the regimes which followed failed to create the conditions which would attract many of them back.

VI

Conditions for foreigners in France improved with the end of the Terror. Most of the repressive measures against them were eventually lifted. The death sentence passed on British and Hanoverian prisoners was commuted, but not before it had been extended by the Thermidorians themselves to include Spanish troops. The decree of 26–7 Germinal, expelling enemy subjects from Paris, French ports, and frontier towns, was also rescinded. It took longer to repeal these measures, however, than it did to revoke those aimed more generally at French citizens. Moreover, both the Thermidorians and the Directory enacted their own legislation against foreigners, often reverting to measures similar to those taken in the Year II. This suggests that the punitive mentality of the Terror did not disappear with 9 Thermidor, but remained lurking beneath the surface of republican ideology and attitudes. Alternatively, it may mean that the urge to exclude, restrict, and watch foreigners was a response to real problems, such as the continuing conflict and the persistence of political instability. Both possibilities carry weight.

On the one hand, the revolutionaries still feared plots and subversion and they retained the exclusive, nationalizing implications of their ideology. The vast majority of revolutionaries usually accepted laws against foreigners, because they still feared their malign capabilities. They saw them at work behind the popular uprisings, royalist intrigues, and economic upheavals which battered the post-Thermidor regimes. On the other hand, xenophobia and a tendency to blame the crises on foreign agents and on conspiracies were not the only strings in the revolutionaries' rhetorical bows. The Terror had given most revolutionaries a jolt and, awake to the possibility of returning to those dark days, some objected to renewed measures against foreigners. They did not forget that action against foreigners had been the prelude to the repression of civil liberties for French citizens. If revolutionary ideology was so powerful a force in politics, it is necessary to explain why certain implications won out over others, why the exclusive and the xenophobic elements, rather than the libertarian and universalist, were carried over into legislation.

The answer lies in the war and the domestic crises. Even with military success, French regimes remained beset by domestic difficulties. For as long as the war continued, it was natural for revolutionaries to explain problems closer to home by reference to the conflict and to enemy influence. Conspiracy and counter-revolution genuinely existed in France and there was real evidence that some foreigners were involved in political intrigue. It was the failure to secure outright victory in the war that ensured that life for foreigners never returned to the freedom enjoyed before the Terror. Not only did war and instability bring out the punitive side of revolutionary mentality, but they persuaded the more reluctant revolutionaries that repressive measures against foreigners were necessary, if temporary. In these circumstances, the Thermidorian Convention and the Directory recast 'Terrorist' laws against foreigners. The rhythm of such legislation kept time with the problems of war and internal instability: until Fructidor, each crisis brought a new law or government directive.

After Fructidor, however, the revolutionaries did not require the stimulus of an emergency to take measures against foreigners. The order of 26 February 1798 was not so much a reaction to a crisis as an initiative reflecting the determination of the new government to prosecute the war to the utmost. Yet even the policies of the Fructidorian Directory were not so dominated by xenophobia and war fever as to be blind to the needs of the Republic. As before, useful foreigners were sheltered from the more repressive implications of revolutionary legislation.

Both the Thermidorians and the Directory attempted to attract foreign entrepreneurs and artisans, like every eighteenth-century regime in France, because they brought much-needed technology and skills. If foreigners were now officially excluded from the army by Article 287 of the new constitution, in reality the revolutionaries were still reluctant to demobilize seasoned troops and they were simply subsumed into regular French units. As resources were stretched in the widening conflict, the Directory circumvented the law by recruiting foreign legions under the theoretical command of the 'sister republics'. An expansive foreign policy also ensured that foreign patriots would be supported, but they were expected to serve French strategic interests. Ideology still mattered, as foreigners continued to fall foul of the authorities for their views. Some, like many hapless Irish, were prevented from seeking refuge in France because they were not trusted, while those Italians who surged onto French territory in 1799 were strictly controlled. Yet the demands on foreigners within France for political conformity were not as exacting as they had been during the Terror. They were given more space to express their ideas and to negotiate with the French government for assistance.

Foreigners who had little to offer still suffered from the possibility of exclusion and persecution. The foreign clergy, in particular, remained the targets of both popular and official hostility. Once the regime of the Terror had eliminated the distinction between foreign ecclesiastical property and that of the French church, subsequent authorities were reluctant to reassert it. For the foreign clergy, therefore, the end of the Terror simply signalled new struggles for survival. Financiers were treated with suspicion because their transactions were thought to have a damaging impact on the economy and to have corrupting influences on politics. Foreign manufacturers and artisans, however, even those from Britain, were still encouraged for the skills which they brought. Merchants were tolerated because they brought in important supplies.

The driving force behind this practical approach, in which inclusion and encouragement was interspersed with surveillance and persecution, was the ebb and flow of political instability and war. This brought out varying and sometimes conflicting attitudes towards foreigners. While in some cases the need for troops, material, money, and foreign allies ensured that certain foreigners would be welcomed, in other cases military and political crises stirred the darker, exclusive forces of revolutionary anxieties. The rhythms of these crises ensured the enactment of measures modelled on those of the Terror. They represented the continued intrusion of the state into foreigners' everyday lives. While they had retreated from the intense surveillance imposed in the Year II, the nervous authorities remained poised, ever watchful. The measures were not applied in so sweeping a manner as the letter of the law suggested, but the efforts of the regime to ensure its own security meant that, on paper, nationality remained an important criterion for legal distinctions between individuals. For as long as France was at war and was dogged by domestic instability, the Revolution would not—and could not—return to its earlier, universal promise.

Epilogue

Foreigners under Napoleon Bonaparte

On 18 October 1801, a group of ragged foreigners emerged from quarantine in Marseille. They were Egyptians who had fled their homeland in August, when the French capitulated there. The commandant at Marseille was nervous: more troops and refugees were due to arrive in the port, and the supplies in the magazine were being run down. For now, these homeless people could be housed in municipal buildings and even in the homes of the great mercantile families, but the new arrivals would put more pressure on his resources. On 26 October, he asked Carnot, minister of war, what he should do. Carnot in turn forwarded the question to Chaptal, minister of the interior. Meanwhile, one of the Egyptians had bypassed these official channels and petitioned the First Consul directly, the day after he was released from quarantine. The request for help bore his own, beautifully intricate signature, but the text itself was drafted by a sympathetic French hand. It was a story of the personal tragedy which befell those caught on the losing side after foreign occupation. George Ayde, one of the Coptic Egyptian minority, had acted for the French as customs officer at Damietta. He also joined Bonaparte on his campaign to Syria, where his brother was killed at Acre. He had felt understandably endangered by the advance of the Ottoman troops who poured into Egypt from Sinaï. Not only did he embark with his own eight children, but he had dutifully adopted his brother's six progeny. Now, famished and a long way from home, he begged Bonaparte for the means with which to support his huge brood. The First Consul received this letter on 3 November and in the margin scribbled, 'As this individual has rendered great services to me, the Minister of the Interior will let me know what I might do for him, when he presents his report on the assistance to be given to the Copts and other individuals who have arrived from Egypt.'[1]

---

[1] AN, F/15/3438–9.

Bonaparte's response suggests that, under the Consulate, usefulness to the state remained one of the crucial determinants of how different foreigners were treated by the authorities. This was no different to either the absolute monarchy or the Revolution, but Ayde's direct petition to the First Consul—and Bonaparte's note—implies that an important shift in focus was taking place. Ayde may have been unaware that it was usually the foreign minister or, in his case, the minister of war, who dealt with foreign refugees. In bypassing these channels, however, the petition suggests that the Egyptian saw where the real authority in the French state lay.

The First Consul's reply merely reinforces the impression that Ayde had the right idea and that such a view was being encouraged. Bonaparte did not commend him for his services to the Republic, but for those rendered to himself. For foreigners, this shift away from the abstract Republic to the person of Bonaparte was a process which was to continue gradually until 1809, when letters of naturalization were reintroduced and henceforth issued only as an act of the *chef de l'état*, Napoleon himself.[2] French nationality was being defined, once more, as a relationship between ruler and 'subject', a term which was legally revived in 1806, knocking the revolutionary 'citizen' from its pedestal.[3] This retreat back to the forms of the Ancien Régime was not absolute. The Consulate and the Empire claimed legitimacy from the consent of the French nation: Napoleon Bonaparte and the state apparatus which he commanded were deemed to embody the general will. Loyalty, obedience, and service to the head of state became the criteria for advancement both for his French subjects and for the inhabitants of his European conquests and client-states.[4] The treatment of foreigners, therefore, was no longer based on conformity to a set of revolutionary or republican values, but rather on usefulness to the state, which meant, above all, to Napoleon Bonaparte himself.

It was for this reason that naturalization was removed from the

---

[2] Gaudemet, 'L'Étranger', 50.

[3] B. Jenkins, *Nationalism in France: Class and Nation since 1789* (London, 1990), 36.

[4] M. Lyons, *Napoleon Bonaparte and the Legacy of the French Revolution* (Basingstoke, 1994), 160; M. Broers, *Europe under Napoleon 1799–1815* (London, 1996), 135.

hands of the law and placed into those of the emperor. During the discussions on the Constitution of the Year VIII and the debates on jurisprudence, it was suggested that naturalization might not be automatic on fulfilment of specific legal conditions, but was subject to government approval. Initially, the new constitution simply imposed a ten-year residence requirement on any foreigner who sought naturalization, the longest of any such prerequisite since 1789, but it was the only condition demanded of foreigners.[5] On 1 December 1801, however, Antoine Boulay de la Meurthe, one of Bonaparte's *conseillers d'état*, suggested that the acquisition of French nationality not be automatic, but be subject to the final decision of the government. He explained that the state ought not to naturalize unsavoury characters simply because they satisfied the legal conditions. The aim of the constitution was not only to enrich France with 'new citizens, useful and respectable', but also to exclude certain people: 'the nation can no longer be forced to receive . . . a foreigner which displeases it'. Meanwhile, foreigners themselves should not be compelled to become French citizens if they did not want to, a situation which might have occurred if naturalization was automatic.[6] On 18 October 1802, a *senatus-consultum*, or a special decree by the Senate, empowered the First Consul to naturalize any foreigner whom he deemed fit, and who need only to have lived in France for a year.[7] Eventually, the adoption of a foreigner as a French subject or citizen was determined not by fixed legal criteria, but by an arbitrary decision of the head of state. The law of 7 March 1809 reverted to Ancien Régime practice by placing the final decision regarding all naturalizations entirely in the hands of the emperor.

Moreover, Article 13 of the Civil Code stressed that foreigners only enjoyed full civil rights when they were permitted to settle in France by the government, a form of immigration control.[8] On 9 June 1803, the *conseil d'état* decided that foreigners who failed to obtain this permission would be ineligible for French citizenship. Moreover, permission could be modified, restricted, or even revoked by the police minister. The acquisition of French

---

[5] *Archives parlementaires: Recueil complet des débats législatifs et politiques des chambres françaises de 1800 à 1860*, 2ème sér., 127 vols. (Paris, 1862–1913) (AP/2), i. 1.

[6] AP/2, iii. 11. [7] Portemer, 'L'Étranger', 550. [8] AP/2, iv. 105.

nationality was therefore the outcome of two discretionary acts by the government: the initial authorization to live in the country and then naturalization. This last act was the result of a laboured process, involving a report by the minister of justice, the advice of the *conseil d'état*, and finally a decree by the head of state.[9]

Under the Consulate, more than any previous revolutionary regime, citizenship became an 'instrument of social closure',[10] as the boundaries of what foreigners could and could not do were redefined. The deregulation of the professions during the revolutionary decade had opened them up to all-comers, particularly in the practice of law. As part of the painstaking drift back to their reordering, the law of 10 March 1803 restricted the professions to citizens, although a foreign doctor or surgeon could be given special dispensation to practise in France.[11]

This shrinkage in the civil rights of foreigners was given momentum in the Civil Code, promulgated on 21 March 1804. On 5 March 1805, the *cautio judicatum solvi* eventually took its place as Article 16 and it followed the Ancien Régime practice closely. Boulay justified this simply, if weakly, as 'a wise measure found in every legal code'.[12] Additionally, imprisonment for debt had already been reintroduced under the Directory for foreigners. Now the Civil Procedure Code of 1806 denied foreign debtors resort to the *cession de biens* to escape incarceration, as the Ancien Régime had done.[13]

The Civil Code insisted on strict reciprocity between the treatment of French citizens abroad and foreigners in France. The Consulate abandoned the idea, cherished among the revolutionaries, that 'the natural land of liberty' should treat all foreigners equally under the law. Article 11, on the contrary, asserted that 'A foreigner in France will enjoy the same civil rights as those granted to the French by the conventions of the nation to which that foreigner belongs.'[14] The authors of the Code had precisely the *droit d'aubaine* and the *droit de détraction* in mind when they composed this wordy clause. The

[9] AN, F/7/3001; Schnapper, 'La Naturalisation', 212–13.

[10] Brubaker, *Citizenship and Nationhood*, p. x.

[11] Portemer, 'L'Étranger', 551.

[12] AP/2, iii. 8, 12.

[13] G. Lepointe, 'Le Statut des Étrangers dans la France du XIXe siècle', *Recueils de la Société Jean Bodin*, x. 569.

[14] AP/2, iv. 105.

conseil d'état had read a report compiled by one of its members, Pierre Louis Roederer, who drafted the article in August 1801. Roederer repeated the by now received wisdom that the *droit d'aubaine* was the product of 'that jealous, anxious and fierce spirit' among peoples in darker, distant times and helpfully reminded the *conseil d'état* that the Scythians ate foreigners. Yet he then focused on the persistence of the *droits d'aubaine* and *détraction*, still imposed on French citizens abroad. From the French point of view, it was overall 'a confused picture of an unfavourable balance with other nations'. After criticizing the reasoning of those 'philanthropists' who had supported unilateral abolition, Roederer proposed that the two impositions be resurrected against foreigners, whose own governments persisted in exerting similar rights against French citizens.[15]

The Civil Code was submitted to the legislature in a series of bills, the second of which, presented in December 1801, included the clause on reciprocity (initially Article 13). Its significance was lost on no one. The Tribunate, the debating forum of the Consular regime, was vocal in its opposition. On 31 December, one horrified deputy, Mathieu, denounced the *droit d'aubaine* as 'a languishing branch of the old tree of feudalism'.[16] The following day, the legislature rejected the first articles of the Code by 61 to 31 votes. Reluctance to restore the *aubaine* played no small part in this rare defeat for the Consulate.[17] The set-back was brief, however, for the Tribunate was purged in March and so it was a muted chamber which meekly listened to the slightly revised bill a year later. When the offending article came up for discussion on 5 March 1803, no one spoke and the Legislative Body passed it, formally restoring the *droit d'aubaine* in France.[18] It was not formally abolished until 14 July 1819, during a brief, liberal flourish under the Restoration monarchy, which desperately needed foreign credit to shore up its rickety finances.

While the Napoleonic regime retreated from some of the original revolutionary deeds regarding foreigners, it retained

---

[15] MAE, ADP, France, 1.

[16] Mathieu, *Opinion de Mathieu, sur l'article 13 du deuxième projet du Code civil: Séance du 11 nivôse an 10* (Paris, An X), 2.

[17] AP/2, iii. 373.

[18] AP/2, iv. 99, 111.

and developed the apparatus of surveillance and control. For as long as Bonaparte felt unsure of his hold on power, his police remained vigilant. Even after his victory at Marengo in June 1800 strengthened his domestic position, awareness of Jacobinism and royalist conspiracies, the first of which were discovered in the autumn, convinced the authorities that foreigners must remain under a watchful eye. Nowhere was vigilance more intense than in the capital. Foreigners who planned even a short-term stay in Paris needed a *permission de séjour*, issued by the *préfecture de police*. The general secretary of the *préfecture* maintained almost daily registers of these permits, noting the name, age, profession, country or city of origin, place of residence in Paris, length of permission to stay, and date of departure. There were three kinds of entry: those issuing the initial *permission*, usually for one or two months; the *renouvellements de séjour*, extensions which ranged in time from as little as one *décade* to a maximum, usually, of three months; and the *visa de départ*, which noted the ultimate destination of the foreigner now leaving the city. To contemporaries, for whom passports were once a startling infringement of personal liberty, this system might have seemed imposingly bureaucratic. Permits, however, were rarely refused: even a handful of British subjects were allowed to stay for a period, a year before the peace preliminaries opened between the two governments.[19] On 2 April 1800, Talleyrand forwarded a request by Louis Guyton de Morveau of the Institut national to allow three British scientists, including Thomas Wedgwood, son of the ceramics manufacturer, and John Leslie, the Scottish physicist and mathematician, to visit France. As their voyage 'appears only to have been taken for the perfection of human knowledge', Talleyrand recommended that the First Consul grant Guyton's request.[20]

It was only with the treaty of Lunéville, signed with Austria on 9 February 1801, and the preliminaries agreed with Britain on 1 October 1801 that enemy subjects were encouraged to visit France in any great numbers. No sooner had the ink dried on the latter than gaggles of British subjects set off for France. On 14 October, Bonaparte instructed Fouché to give them free passage, provided that they held valid British passports and

---

[19] AN, F/7/3501.   [20] MAE, CP, Angleterre, 593.

were not *émigrés*.[21] Anthony Merry, British ambassador in Paris until December 1802, estimated that at the crest of this wave, there were 5,000 British subjects in the city.[22]

Meanwhile, a clause in the treaty of Amiens, signed on 27 March 1802, provided for the restitution or compensation of British property seized by the French since 1793. Merry complained of 'clamorous demands', 'incessant and sometimes intemperate applications' from anguished or angry British subjects who sought to offset their losses from the Revolution.[23] Few, if any, of these demands were met before war broke out again. Like other foreign claimants, the British had to wait until after 1815 before they were compensated.

The relative freedom of movement across French frontiers collapsed along with the uneasy European peace. On 23 May 1803, eleven days after the departure from Paris of Whitworth, Merry's successor, the French government issued an order to arrest all British males in France aged between 18 and 60: in other words, those deemed liable for militia service. The order was repeated, but with wider application, in the Berlin Decrees of 1806. All British subjects, of every age and of either gender, found on any territory occupied by French or allied forces, were to be arrested.[24]

When the initial order was given in 1803, there were still travellers fleeing northwards, which probably explains the trickle of British subjects still trying to pass through Paris in May and June.[25] Some of these were imprisoned. On 26 May, an unfortunate British traveller without a passport, Henry Bate, was arrested in the capital and conducted to the *préfecture de police*.[26] Ernest Winckelmans, a Hanoverian clerk on his way to take up a position at a Parisian tobacco manufacture, was arrested at Montdidier in the Somme. The subprefect reported to his superior at Amiens that, besides the fact that he was an enemy subject, he was travelling with his brother's passport. Worse, Winckelmans's income could not account for his standard of living. With these circumstances shrouding the German in a fog of suspicion and despite the entreaties of his French

---

[21] Howard, *Letters and Documents*, i. 504.

[22] J. G. Alger, *Napoleon's British Visitors and Captives 1801–1815* (London, 1904), 23–4.

[23] Ibid. 95–6.   [24] Ibid. 257.   [25] AN, F/7/6338.   [26] Ibid.

employer, he was placed under house arrest, with two gendarmes maintained at his own expense. It was only when he
became dependent on the municipality for his keep that, on 27
September, the prefect authorized him to seek work in Montdidier.[27]

Bonaparte referred sinisterly to such unfortunate foreigners as
ôtages. According to the order of 23 May, they were to answer for
the French merchant sailors from two small craft captured off
Brest by British warships on 19 May, before the British declaration of war had been received in France. Yet the order was a
remarkably swift and disproportionate act, even as a measure of
représailles. Its main precedent, the mass incarceration of British
subjects in October 1793, can be explained by the beleaguerment
of the Year II, fear of treachery, and the (false) report that the
British had committed the heinous crime of executing a French
deputy. The extent of Bonaparte's action against British subjects, by contrast, is not so easily explained. He had encouraged
them to visit France during the peaceful interlude, so the order
seems extraordinarily hasty. It appears, in fact, to have been a
deliberate policy embarked upon at the outbreak of war.[28] It was
a subtle, but important departure from previous measures: up to
1803, all legislation and acts against foreigners had been reactive,
set off by panic or by events which seemed to dictate extreme
vigilance. Now the government was ordering internment as a
matter of course.

Not all enemy subjects were detained. The government did
not apprehend manufacturers and skilled workers whose products might be used for the war effort.[29] As with much previous
legislation, the authorities could be very flexible in their application of the order. William Dickinson, an artist and engraver
imprisoned at Verdun, and Samuel French, a language teacher
held at Fontainebleau, were given special permission by the
minister of war to live in Paris and exercise their craft or
profession. This dispensation was granted to French so that he
could provide for his family.[30] Such people were interned only in
the sense that they were not permitted to leave their designated

[27] Ibid.
[28] M. Lewis, *Napoleon and his British Captives* (London, 1962), 21.
[29] AN, F/7/6338.
[30] Ibid.; AN, F/7/6463.

town. At Verdun, the main entrepôt for British detainees, the captives were not confined to a prison: those who could afford it were allowed to live in townhouses, while others prospered as tradesmen and artisans.[31] Individuals who had long been established in France also remained at liberty, as did people of known French sympathies, such as John Hurford Stone and Helen Maria Williams.[32]

These exceptions, however, were accompanied by government attempts to perfect the system of surveillance. On 7 November 1803, the seaport mayors were ordered to provide the ministry of justice with a weekly list of travellers, of whatever nationality, who were obliged to have their passports stamped at the *mairie*. It is not surprising that, by mid-January 1804, the lists for Calais bore almost exclusively French names.[33] Some determined enemy subjects, however, still slipped through the net. Thomas Dickinson, son of William, stole into France with the passport of a Danish subject. He was arrested in Paris on 11 June 1805 and held in the Temple. Under interrogation, he convinced Dubois-Crancé, now minister of *police générale*, that he had only come to France out of an infatuation with Madame Gourbillon, whom he had met in London during the peace. What prevented his release was the fact that, while in custody, he had boasted of his friendship with certain leading *émigrés*.[34]

It was not just war which led to restrictions on foreigners: in November 1804, the government received news that an epidemic of yellow fever, which had ravaged Malaga in Spain, had now reached Livorno in Italy. The *conseil d'état* tried to seal the French borders from Bayonne to Port-Vendres and from Genoa to Lake Geneva. Two extraordinary *commissions de santé* were to be established, one for the Spanish frontier and the Atlantic ports, the other for the Italian border and the Mediterranean coast. 'These commissions, the *conseil* was told, 'will have a sort of Dictatorship', drawing into service as many doctors and health officers as they saw fit. Troops would form a double

---

[31] Lewis, *Napoleon and his British Captives*, 32, 116–18.
[32] Alger, *Napoleon's British Visitors*, 191–2, 231; Lewis, *Napoleon and his British Captives*, 298, 306.
[33] AN, F/7/6338.
[34] AN, F/7/6463.

cordon along the frontiers to prevent anyone from trying to slip into France.[35]

The Napoleonic regime adapted the precedents of both the Revolution and the Ancien Régime in its treatment of foreigners. The revolutionary inheritance was evident in the declared emphasis on foreigners' civil rights, in the setting down of clear, legal provisions for naturalization, but also in the policing and bureaucratic paraphernalia used to keep watch over foreigners, such as registers, passports, visas, and the mass arrests of enemy subjects. None of these means of control were unknown to the Ancien Régime, but the Revolution, and then the Napoleonic state, developed them into far more efficient and systematic tools.

The Revolution's libertarian influence steadily receded, however, and Ancien Régime precedents increasingly appeared to be the model. The Civil Code's emphasis on reciprocity and the re-establishment of the *aubaine* were accompanied by the government's explicit rejection of the Constituent Assembly's thinking over this issue, a thinking which, however, was not so easily repudiated by many veteran revolutionaries in the legislature. The Napoleonic state also returned, by stages, to Ancien Régime practice in its naturalization procedures. In order to assimilate only the most useful and loyal foreigners, acquisition of French citizenship became dependent on a government decision. Automatic naturalization, on the fulfilment of certain legal conditions, was therefore supplanted by the process by which the head of state accepted a foreigner as a subject. The law of 7 March 1809 essentially restored the Ancien Régime's *lettres de naturalité*. The determinant of French nationality now looked increasingly less like the revolutionary idea of acceptance into a community of citizens and more like the Ancien Régime vision of reciprocal, individual bonds between ruler and ruled.

The Napoleonic state did not retreat entirely into pre-revolutionary practice, but also innovated. The settlement of any foreigner in France became, like naturalization, dependent on government permission. Such control of immigration went further than the passports and registers demanded by successive

[35] AN, F/7/3001.

revolutionary regimes which, in any case, regarded such bureaucracy as a temporary expedient until more peaceful times. Under Bonaparte, the right of the government to decide whether or not a foreigner could remain in France was permanently enshrined in the Civil Code. The Napoleonic regime also seems to have gone further than either the Revolution or the Ancien Régime in its arrests of British subjects. By the order of May 1803, internment was implemented as a matter of wartime policy. It was not a reaction to any particular crisis brought on by the conflict. In practice, however, even the Napoleonic regime was not so draconian, and followed both the Ancien Régime and the Revolution in making exemptions as it saw fit.

Yet, by making detention of enemy subjects a matter of course, by further developing surveillance, by reintroducing the *droit d'aubaine*, by making both residence and naturalization dependent on a political decision, the Napoleonic regime reinforced state power over the lives of foreigners. It built on the foundations haphazardly laid by the Revolution, while also using fabric from the absolute monarchy. These measures demanded both a consolidation of existing mechanisms of control and an expansion of bureaucracy and policing which would enable the authorities to apply the various orders and decrees against foreigners. French citizens were also subject to police surveillance, with the reintroduction in 1803 of the Ancien Régime *livret*, a domestic passport without which artisans and labourers could not be employed. These measures did not mark a return to the intrusive, localized surveillance of the revolutionary committees of the Terror. Yet the attempts of the Napoleonic regime to control systematically foreigners' movements, their residence, their access to the capital, and their assimilation as French subjects consolidated the state apparatus which aimed at distinguishing them from citizens.

Conclusion

The French Revolution, Citizenship, and Nationality

In February 1997, the small town of Vitrolles near Marseille prepared for its second ballot in the mayoral elections. The Socialist incumbent faced a strong challenge from the candidate of the extreme right-wing, xenophobic Front National. A couple of days before voting, a local coalminer told a British journalist that, come the final vote on Sunday 9 February, 'a Republican reflex' would bring out enough people to destroy the Front National's attempt to take political control of yet another town.[1] This hope was not realized, but its persistence shows that the memory of the French Revolution retains its emotive power in current debates on nationality, citizenship, and immigration in the Fifth Republic. The doctrine of the rights of man implies that all men and women can be citizens, either in their own countries or in France, on fulfilment of certain basic conditions. As these rights are universal, race, religion, or language are theoretically irrelevant: being human and having a proven desire and ability to contribute to the life of the nation is sufficient. In the early years of the Revolution, the revolutionaries sought to attract and retain talented and diligent foreigners who would enjoy the fruits of liberty while enriching the country. Ultimately, these people would adopt France as their home—but at the price of abandoning all other forms of corporate or national identity.

Yet in France today, this revolutionary ideal of citizenship, which still seeks to assimilate immigrants by securing their exclusive allegiance to the secular Republic, has been challenged by two alternatives. The rise of the Front National, since the economic crisis of the early 1980s, has thrust one version of nationality onto the agenda. After its victories in the municipal

[1] *Independent* (7 Feb. 1997).

elections of 1983, its slogan of 'La France aux français!' appeared on posters and stickers everywhere. Given the party's policies towards immigrants and its outbursts of anti-Semitism, it is clear that, in this case, the French people are being defined ethnically.

The other challenge, however, has come from liberal intellectuals and immigrant groups, who no longer regard the revolutionary, assimilationist model for the nation as the most viable. Instead, they have moved towards a more pluralist idea (sometimes described as British or American), whereby immigrant groups and ethnic minorities can retain their separate cultural and religious identities, while sharing in French citizenship, which would be only one dimension of their identity. In legal terms, this might even mean that foreigners, by the virtue of their contributions to civil society, would acquire certain political rights, such as the suffrage, without having to assume French nationality.

The *cause célèbre* of the *affaire du foulard* in 1989 helped to crystallize the division between the 'Republican', assimilationist position and the liberal, pluralist view. Three Muslim girls were expelled from a French state school for refusing to remove their traditional Islamic headscarves, which raised the thorny issue of cultural pluralism within the secular Republic. Michel Rocard's Socialist government decided to let the girls wear their dress, provided that they did not try to convert their fellow pupils. In the end, the *conseil d'état* accepted this view: all pupils were free to wear religious symbols at school, provided that they did not interfere with the religious freedom of others. Not everyone was so willing to compromise the revolutionary idea of the nation. The editor of *Libération* summed up the debate as 'the seamlessness of assimilation, pure and simple, on one side; the promotion of Anglo-American-style ghettos on the other, in the name of exalting the right to be different'.[2] There are, however, two practical problems with the 'Republican' tradition.

---

[2] Hollifield, 'Immigration and Modernization', 139–40, 149–50.

I

The first is that, humans being as they are, the unity of few, if any, states can be bound merely by a sense, among its citizens, of equal submission to and benefit from the same laws and political structures. Of course, the constitution, the law, and the founding deeds which established these institutions might be a source of pride among the population, as they have been in the United States and France. The political symbolism bequeathed by the American and French Revolutions to succeeding generations of citizens do provide a cement which binds people together, even if the meanings of those symbols are often disputed. In the backlash against the French Revolution in the 1790s, the British political élites played on popular loyalty to the monarchy, 'constitution', and 'liberties' to defeat the challenge of the British radicals. In these instances, however, the founding deeds, political institutions, and the attendant political and legal symbolism take on a historical value. They have become part of the national myth or tradition, which, any viability aside, partly explains why the assimilationist ideal in France is so tenacious.

Yet, in themselves, the political and legal framework are usually insufficient as a means by which states secure the loyalty of their citizens. They often make additional appeals to something more emotive. Under the old regime, it may have been the monarchy, or religion, or a sense of community among the social élites and their retainers. The American and French Revolutions, however, elevated the nation—meaning the whole people—to this position.[3] If the revolutionaries defined the nation as the result of a political contract between equal citizens, without any cultural reference, it is not clear that most French people saw themselves only in that light. Nicolas Chauvin, the soldier who has been both exalted and ridiculed for his zealous patriotism, did not (if he existed at all) feel French because he was a citizen in a wider political community. The Chauvin penned by Jacques Arago in 1845 was a terrifying sight: a horribly mutilated face, a shattered shoulder, and three amputated fingers complement the seventeen other wounds (all taken, naturally, in the front, never in the back), sustained during every

[3] J. D. Mabbott, *The State and the Citizen*, 2nd edn. (London, 1967), 154–5.

campaign in the revolutionary and Napoleonic wars. Now he is *le vieux grognard*, the cranky, aged veteran who proudly wears his decorations, draws his 200 franc pension and basks in the sun in his native village, perhaps retelling the stories of his campaigns, beguiling children, and probably frightening old ladies.[4] It was the experience of war, his part in the imperial dream of French dominance and his attachment to his *pays*—meaning, not France, but his rural home—which gives Chauvin his identity. While devoid of appeals to blood or ethnicity, it still draws on something more concrete than an abstract political community: a feeling of comradeship evoked by military glory and a sense of belonging to a particular locality.

This localism, 'the curse of rurality',[5] took a long time to overcome. Variations in idiom, in weights and measures, in custom and superstition, and in isolation from the rest of the country persisted deep into the nineteenth century.[6] During the Revolution, the most important agencies of change were the representatives of the state and its laws. That meant, above all, the bearers of such unwanted assaults on local well-being as taxation, conscription, and secularization. A natural reaction for many peasants was to take refuge in their traditional identities, linguistic, religious, provincial.[7] Such loyalties would only be slowly eroded over the course of the next two centuries. Much as the revolutionaries insisted on defining nationality on political or contractual lines, culture, language, and specific political and social circumstances were (for better or worse) inescapable contexts for the development both of national identity and of the various forms of nationalism across the globe.[8]

The evolution of French national identity was therefore as much the result of long-term political, social, and cultural conditioning as it was of the ideology and experience of the Revolution. Such longer term developments shaped national identities elsewhere in the world. For Linda Colley, British

---

[4] G. de Puymège, 'Le Soldat Chauvin', in P. Nora (ed.), *Les Lieux de Mémoire*, ii, part 3. *La Nation* (Paris, 1986), 46.

[5] T. Nairn, *Faces of Nationalism: Janus Revisited* (London, 1997), ch. 5.

[6] Weber, *Peasants into Frenchmen*, Part One.

[7] C. Emsley, 'Nationalist Rhetoric and Nationalist Sentiment in Revolutionary France', in Dann and Dinwiddy, *Nationalism*, 52.

[8] L. Greenfeld, *Nationalism: Five Roads to Modernity* (Cambridge, Mass., 1992), 1–26, 490–1.

identity was shaped by the interlinked responses to war with France, the defence of Protestantism against Catholicism, the growth of commerce, and the expansion of empire. It was, moreover, active engagement in these activities which led British subjects ultimately to lay claim to 'a much broader access to citizenship'. Germany also experienced the growth of a 'primitive nationalism' and a sense of a separate national identity in reaction to French conquest. It was claimed that the French version of liberty and equality was an abstraction and that under their enlightened rulers, Germans enjoyed true freedom, which meant freedom from arbitrary oppression and moral liberty. Germans, it was argued, were also different from—and superior to—the French in character. In the United States, the Alien and Sedition Act may have been a 'concerted legislative attempt to define what it meant to be an American, and the definition tended to exclude precisely those people who showed the greatest inclination to support "French" ideas'.[9] These political and cultural responses helped to develop a sense of collective identity in the countries concerned. Ideological forces such as nationalism are given potency and relevance by the specific political and cultural contexts in which they arise.

In France, the contractual idea of citizenship therefore developed alongside a national identity which was emerging both from the experience of the Revolution itself and from long-term political, social, and cultural conditions peculiar to France. Despite their claims for universality, in the long term the revolutionaries could not forestall the linguistic and the cultural from lending their weight in determining attitudes towards nationality and, above all, towards what it was to be French. While on a day-to-day basis, this means simply that individual French men and women have to balance the political conception of the nation with their cultural and linguistic attachments, at a legal level, it has serious implications. It suggests that assimilation means more than just political loyalty to the Republic, but that it also requires a deeper cultural immersion.

---

[9] Colley, *Britons*, 1–6; Blanning, *Reform and Revolution in Mainz*, 293–5; L. S. Kramer, 'The French Revolution and the Creation of American Political Culture', in J. Klaits and M. H. Haltzel (eds.), *The Global Ramifications of the French Revolution* (Cambridge, 1994), 45.

II

The second problem with the 'Republican' definition of the nation is that there are two important contradictions within the French Revolution, the event which gave the republican ideal its historic legitimacy. First of all, within revolutionary ideology, there was tension between, on the one hand, the claim that rights were universal and, on the other, the idea of the nation. The former implied that political rights could be obtained not only by all French people, men, women, rich, or poor, but perhaps also by all human beings. In practice, of course, this universalism had limits, both within French territory (with the exclusion of women, the poor, most Jews until 1791, and blacks until 1794) and outside France. For it was understood that to make universal claims for rights of citizenship meant that potentially the nation had no geographical boundaries. The revolutionaries recognized that there had to be some territorial limits if they were to avoid war without end. Only Anacharsis Cloots was willing to countenance all-engulfing conflict to achieve global citizenship in a one-world state. Geographical limits to the nation implied some exclusion. People who lived beyond French frontiers had the same rights as French people, but they were to be realized in a different national context. This also raised the problem as to how the French nation was to be defined internally: what, in other words, was to be the status of foreigners who, while resident on French territory, were reluctant to abandon their allegiances to societies or sovereigns beyond the frontier? This question goes to the heart of revolutionary notions of nationality and citizenship.

Citizenship is the legal membership of a state, which gives its members entitlement to certain social and political rights. Nationality is the belonging to a community which identifies itself as a single political, or ethnic, or cultural group and which claims control over its own domestic and external affairs. Where that people defines itself ethnically or culturally, membership of the state is dependent on birth within the ethnic, racial, or linguistic group. Where the nation is defined politically, as a result of a contract between equal citizens, membership of the state becomes a matter of individual choice. The acquisition by a foreigner of the rights of citizenship gives that person his or her nationality.

The French Revolution took the latter view, which was probably why the revolutionaries never used the term *nationalité*: they assumed that by exercising the rights and duties of citizenship, one was already a *national*, a term which they did use to mean a member of the nation. Yet both the state and the nation had geographic limits, which meant that, in practice, in order to be defined as a citizen in France, one had to be defined as French first. The French Revolution, therefore, made citizenship dependent on nationality. In every constitution of the 1790s, a precondition for the exercise of the rights of citizenship was either birth within French territory, or, for foreigners, the fulfilment of certain conditions which turned them into nationals. The nation, therefore, was deemed to exist before the state, which was the product of the nation's will. Yet the Revolution never defined the nation in an ethnic or cultural sense. The conditions for naturalization ensured that no one was barred for their ethnicity, religion, or language. To have done so would have meant denying that Bretons, German-speaking Alsatians, and others were French.

To be French meant, simply, to have been born on French territory or to have made an evident commitment to settle there and to contribute to the life of the nation. These very qualities gave an individual a claim to citizenship. When the Constituent Assembly excluded large numbers of people from political rights, it did not deny that women and the poor were French, but suggested that they were merely inactive citizens. In response, excluded groups such as women, the poor, Jews, and some *gens de couleur* from the colonies claimed that their very membership of the nation entitled them to the full rights of citizenship.

Foreigners had no such recourse. They could not exercise political rights unless they abandoned their original allegiances and chose to live as members of the French nation. Those foreigners who did not do so would be excluded from the attributes of citizenship. The Revolution sought to assimilate foreigners with this argument, but it appeared to set limits on the universality of the rights of man. A person was only a citizen within his or her own nation. Elsewhere, one was merely a human being. Yet political exclusion of foreigners was not the only implication in revolutionary ideology. The revolutionaries were reluctant to admit that their fight against most of Europe was for anything but a universal cause. This perversely allowed them to deny the very humanity of some of those who were struggling against them, including Louis XVI and, by the law of 7 Prairial, the British, but it also raised the question as to the status of individuals who were not French, but who contributed to the Republic's combat for survival.

Such people seemed to show that, regardless of nationality, all men were capable of patriotism, the virtue which placed self-interest last and the triumph of the new order first. The problem was that as the Revolution pursued its radical path, that patriotism became increasingly exclusive, not on lines of nationality, but along those of political allegiance. By the Year II, when patriotism focused on loyalty to the government, this circle of true patriots was very exclusive indeed. Within revolutionary politics, 'good' foreigners were so hard to find that the Republic of Virtue might just as well have been an exclusively French paradise. Beyond politics, however, the larger numbers of foreigners who contributed to the war effort were still serving the *patrie* in other ways, particularly in commerce and manufacturing. The message of the Terror appeared to be that foreigners could work for the Republic in society, but not within the political structures of the state, which could only be the reserve of French citizens. Yet, when it came to their dealings with foreigners in practice, the revolutionaries trod gingerly, rarely following the logic of their principles through.

The second contradiction within the Revolution is suggested by this protection of foreigners who contributed to French political, social, and economic life. This tension lies between ideology and practice. The exclusive implications of the idea of the nation were only understood by the Constituent Assembly when it began to reform France in accordance with its principles and was stalled by the stumbling block of foreigners in the army, the clergy, and in state administration. Some revolutionaries, such as Dubois-Crancé for the army and Grégoire for the clergy, argued for foreigners to be squeezed out of these institutions, which, they argued, should be run by nationals for the sake of the nation. From the very outset, however, diplomatic, economic, and political circumstances demanded special care in the treatment of foreigners. The sweeping terms of legislation which excluded them from the structures of the state were rarely applied in full, because the revolutionaries were unwilling to lose the expertise, skills, and the support which certain types of foreigners might offer, particularly with the outbreak of war. Even during the Terror, the revolutionaries retained foreign soldiers and gave administrative positions to reliable foreign patriots.

Many foreigners were undeniably excluded from the structures of the state and even from civil society. Those who were least protected from the heavy axe of xenophobia were the foreign clergy. The revolutionaries had allowed them their own corporate existence on French territory, provided that they did not try to minister to the spiritual needs of French citizens. The foreign clergy were therefore the most 'foreign' of any other type in France, because their immunity from French ecclesiastical laws lay in their separateness from the nation. When the revolutionaries finally confiscated their land and buildings from October 1793, they were not only committing reprisals on enemy subjects, but they were destroying what appeared to be a cosseted survival from the absolute monarchy. Likewise, the dismissal of the Swiss regiments in August 1792 fit comfortably with the 'nationalizing' impulse within revolutionary ideology, pushing foreigners out of the military arm of the state. Even so, there were practical considerations behind this act: the revolutionaries calculated that the diplomatic upset with Switzerland was worth the elimination of an apparently counter-revolutionary force at the heart of the military.

In fact, when most foreigners were expelled from positions occupied in the French state, it was less from any nationalizing logic, than due to the emergence of new considerations which outweighed the original and equally practical reasons against their exclusion. The idea of the nation, in other words, was not the prime factor in decisions over the fate of foreigners. At the very most, it took certain circumstances for the revolutionaries to follow up its exclusive implications with concrete action.

The gap between what revolutionary rhetoric implied and how the revolutionaries actually behaved in practice suggests that ideology alone was not the dynamic which drove the Revolution

along its radical course. Instead, the revolutionaries were pragmatic, restraining, even denying, the implications of their principles as circumstances dictated. This was true not just for those
foreigners who worked within the structures of the state, but also
in French society at large. In practice, the revolutionaries never
fully realized the implications of national exclusion, because they
feared diplomatic furores or a haemorrhaging of much-needed
skills and manpower. The expediency demanded by the pressures of war and economic crisis led the revolutionaries to
exempt from even the most sweeping legislation those whom
they believed would be of some use, putting them to work for the
Republic. Above all, the persistence of some foreign patriots on
local committees, within the government bureaucracy, and the
redistribution of foreign soldiers among French units suggests
that there was limited space for foreigners, even within the brutal
machinery of the Terrorist state. In principle, the Revolution
made citizenship explicitly dependent on nationality, but in
practice the revolutionaries occasionally—and perhaps accidentally—disentangled the two.

As the service of the state never became the exclusive preserve
of French citizens, the model provided for women in revolutionary France by Joan Landes's work is not, therefore, applicable to foreigners.[10] More apt, perhaps, is the suggestion by
Darline Gay Levy that the meanings of citizenship were often
contradictory, diverse, and unstable, which meant that they were
also open to challenge and to flux.[11] Unlike Landes's women,
there was no concerted effort to exclude foreigners from the
'public sphere', despite legislation to the contrary and despite the
implications of both xenophobia and the politically exclusive
patriotism which rapidly emerged.

The experience of the French nobility, described by Patrice
Higonnet, offers a striking parallel to that of foreigners. Both
groups were on the fringes of the new order, whose limits were
eventually defined so as to exclude them in theory. Both groups
were classified as potential suspects and were subjected to a
range of oppressive legislation which took their origins to be a
sign of subversive potential. Nobles were banned from primary

---

[10] Landes, *Women in the Public Sphere*.
[11] Levy, 'Women's Revolutionary Citizenship', 169, 182.

assemblies on 17 December 1792, from the *comités de surveillance* on 21 March 1793, and by the Law of Suspects all nobles who had not demonstrated active loyalty to the Revolution could be proscribed. For the very sin of their birth, former aristocrats were also purged from certain military units early in 1794. The law of 26–7 Germinal prohibited them, along with foreigners, from attending *sociétés populaires* and sectional assemblies. Many ex-nobles, even those who were pro-revolutionary, therefore found it hard to wash away 'their intrinsic immorality' as aristocrats. After Fructidor, the law of 29 November 1797 excluded all nobles from eligibility for public office and decreed their deportation.[12]

In fact, the former aristocracy probably suffered more than foreigners. Besides the greater intensity of the popular hatred towards them, legislation debarring nobles from citizenship and even from social rights often ran ahead of similar measures against foreigners, which reflects where the revolutionaries' deeper anxieties lay. Yet, when both nobles and foreigners were theoretically cast out of the ideal Republican city envisaged by Saint-Just on 26 Germinal, the government requisitioned individuals from both groups. The registers of the Committee of Public Safety carry substantially more exemptions for nobles than for foreigners, although this also reflects the greater numbers of the former in positions of social, economic, and political importance.[13] The idea that the original sin of their birth could be erased by patriotic virtue applied to both foreigners and nobles. In the Manichaean struggle between liberty and despotism, the battlelines were determined by moral qualities, not accidents of birth.[14] In the restrictive definition of political orthodoxy in the Year II, it was very hard for both nobles and foreigners to prove their republican worth, but individuals from both groups did survive in important positions in both state and society.

For all their ideological claims to a new order, therefore, the revolutionaries did not entirely 'nationalize' the state. Initially bound by the same conditions which dictated the Ancien

---

[12] P. Higonnet, *Class, Ideology, and the Rights of Nobles during the French Revolution* (Oxford, 1981), 127–31, 136–43, 235–7.

[13] AN, AF/II/61.

[14] Higonnet, *Class, Ideology*, 130, 139, 154, 166, 236–8.

Régime's approach to foreigners, their solutions to the problem represented a continuity from the absolute monarchy. Both regimes based their decisions on a careful weighing of the interests of the state, even if the language used and specific laws may have differed. The resulting persistence of foreigners in the army and administration suggests that, in practice, the legal differences between citizens and foreigners remained blurred during the Revolution. Foreigners continued to serve the regime in capacities which would be unusual in most modern nation-states.

Foreigners undoubtedly found more opportunities beyond or semi-independent of the state, in civil society. In some cases, foreigners engaged in normal social and economic activities even found themselves co-opted or drawn in by the state because they performed tasks which were useful to the war effort. Foreign patriots were protected by successive French governments both out of an ideological affinity and for their potential, strategic use. This meant that they were permitted to produce their own newspapers, organize themselves politically, and, for a while, to raise legions. The state gave foreigners room to engage in political activities, even to attempt to influence French policies for the furtherance of their particular interests. Such activities were not always welcomed by French politicians, which meant that the freedom of manœuvre allowed to these foreigners fluctuated throughout the 1790s. Yet if the legions were disbanded, a number of foreign political clubs persisted even during the Terror. What mattered to their survival was not their nationality, but their tact and their political orthodoxy. Foreign patriots were treated in much the same way as their French counterparts. In the Year II, they were expected to chant the same dreary psalm of loyalty to the revolutionary government. This does not say much for the regime's tolerance of political dissent, but it does suggest that foreigners could try to pursue their political interests at the very juncture of state and society, even as they conformed to demands for orthodoxy.

Similarly, despite all the hostility towards them, foreign financiers pursued their social and economic activities which, from the start, also led them into frequent contact with the state. Some were drawn into the arguments over the financial crises, including the debates over the creation of the *assignats* under the

Constituent Assembly. Eventually, those who remained at liberty in France were drawn into the government machinery for the acquisition of foreign exchange during the Year II. Foreign merchants were likewise employed, becoming agents of the state, exploiting their networks and overseas contacts in order to buy vital supplies for the hungry, threadbare Republic. Without becoming state employees, foreign artisans were requisitioned by the Committee of Public Safety, so that they could join the chorus of hammers and saws at work for the war effort. Every revolutionary regime sought to encourage the spread of skills which such artisans brought to France.

The persistence of foreigners in French society, and the protection of those who were useful and who posed no apparent threat, suggests that, even in the most xenophobic days of the Terror, the Revolution never created a closed society which excluded along lines of nationality. Moreover, the survival of foreigners within the structures of the French state, and the greater numbers who were co-opted by it when their expertise was needed, suggests that the revolutionaries never quite succeeded in making all the rights and duties of citizenship the exclusive reserve of French nationals. If foreigners could not vote or sit in the Convention, they remained on local committees and within the administration. There were, moreover, plenty of other ways in which they could prove their patriotism and, usually inadvertently, challenge the restriction of citizenship to nationals. That foreigners could still play a role within both state and society, without fully assimilating into the revolutionary model of the nation, suggests that the revolutionaries themselves were still fumbling towards the realization of the new political order. If only by accident, nationality was not always an essential prerequisite for the assumption of some of the rights and duties of citizenship.

III

The failure of the Revolution, in practice, to make the boundaries of citizenship and nationality coincide exactly is all the more remarkable because, inevitably, the anxiety which many revolutionaries felt at the presence of foreigners could be ranted in the most xenophobic terms. Such foreigners were given good cause to tremble and sweat. No matter how much the revolutionary authorities protected them from their own legislation, from the issue of passports in August 1792 to the expulsion of enemy subjects from ports in February 1798, the rules themselves were discriminatory. They marked foreigners out for the very fact of their nationality. The enforcement of the law required an expansion of the state apparatus down to the most localized level, to check registers, passports, certificates, to take declarations, and to investigate and watch foreigners.

This represented an intrusion of the state into the lives of ordinary people on an unprecedented scale. The Revolution had begun the process of rationalizing the administrative apparatus before the outbreak of the war, with the establishment of the departments, for example. From 1792, however, the conflict and the accompanying domestic crises increased the demands of the state on its citizens for loyalty and for resources, which accelerated bureaucratic and political intrusion. French people were subject to surveillance as much as foreigners, but the laws aimed specifically at the latter encouraged people to discriminate more between citizens and non-citizens. This surveillance and the attendant bureaucracy made nationality matter almost on a daily basis. The authorities demanded from individuals details such as place of birth and nationality as they issued documents like passports and *cartes de sûreté*. Surveillance and control of foreigners was nothing new, but the apparatus by which the laws were implemented entered the lives of individuals with an efficiency and intensity which was unfamiliar to most people. In 1793–4, decrees were applied by local committees who may have known many of the foreigners by sight and who had the ability either to protect them, or to make life very unpleasant. Such a legal capacity to discriminate against foreigners became less localized after the Terror, as the committees of surveillance, and then the sections themselves, were abolished, but similar powers remained with municipalities and the police bureaux. Controls over the movement of foreigners were further developed by Bonaparte. This bureaucratization of everyday life made nationality significant and demanded clarity in one's origins and allegiances.

Yet, demanding as the French revolutionary state was, the

passports and surveillance imposed on foreigners were only the beginning of the process. As Albert Mathiez suggests, action against enemy aliens still had a long way to develop before matching those which have characterized the 'total wars' of the twentieth century.[15] State surveillance during the Revolution made differences between foreigners and citizens more explicit, but not absolute. The indistinct line of demarcation between citizens and non-citizens in the revolutionary period stemmed from the peculiar circumstances of the 1790s. The domestic crises and the war dictated that certain foreigners had to be protected or tolerated, even in positions which the nationalizing tendencies of revolutionary ideology implied should be reserved for French citizens. Moreover, it is perhaps all too easy to overemphasize the pervasive power of the state. The chaotic way in which the Unité section of Paris sought to implement legislation against foreigners suggests that the revolutionaries were stumbling uncomfortably as they entered unfamiliar terrain.

Nor were the measures entirely original. In crises, the revolutionaries naturally reverted, sometimes very reluctantly, to repressive measures enacted under the Ancien Régime before innovating further. Furthermore, the intensity of police measures taken by many other countries in this period—often against French citizens—also represented an expansion of state surveillance over ordinary people. Such acts sometimes predated those imposed by the revolutionaries in France.

Spain was the first country to take these steps, even before she entered the European conflict. As early as November 1789, foreigners were expelled from Madrid. In July 1791, all foreigners in Spain had to register with the authorities, 'transients' required permission from the secretary of state to remain in the country, and they were not permitted to work. In March 1793, when Spain entered the war, and months before the French took comparable measures, the king ordered all non-domiciled French citizens to abandon their homes within forty-eight hours and to leave the kingdom. The original order was actually dated 26 February 1793, almost two weeks before the commencement of hostilities. It was an explicitly pre-emptive

---

[15] Mathiez, *La Révolution et les étrangers*, 177.

measure.[16] Catherine II of Russia went further still. On the news of the execution of Louis XVI, the *ukaz* of 8/19 February 1793 prohibited all trade between Russia and France and expelled all French citizens, unless they swore to renounce 'the godless and subversive principles professed in their native country'. All the tsarina's subjects were recalled from France and imports of French newspapers and journals into Russia were forbidden.[17] Britain also enacted police measures against French citizens, just before she joined the coalition powers. On 15 December 1792, the Alien Bill was presented to parliament, which aimed to control the movements of French citizens in Britain. The Alien Act of 7 January 1793, in force for a period of ten years until its expiry in 1803, was enforced by the police and led to a 'complete system of surveillance for suspects, whether British or foreign'.[18] Even the republic of the United States succumbed, passing the Alien and Sedition Act in 1798, empowering the authorities to expel foreigners who might have subversive intentions.[19]

Such measures had their precedents in Ancien Régime practices in times of war, and had been exercised under the concept of the *droit des gens*. What was novel was the intensity with which the legislation was enforced. It was not only the political culture of the French Revolution which was at the source of the state's harsh discrimination between citizens and foreigners. It was also produced by the reaction of other powers *against* the contagion of revolutionary ideology. Likewise, in the twentieth century, citizenship has given governments a means by which to control the movement of apparently dangerous ideas into the country, by denying visas or resident permits to foreigners believed to harbour troublesome thoughts. Now, however, such discrimination has also taken on greater importance, as the state has expanded from an almost purely political role, to a provider of social services. Citizenship is used to protect pros-

---

[16] MAE, CP Espagne, 635; Herr, *Eighteenth Century Revolution*, 256–7, 269–70, 311, 380–1.

[17] G. Vernadsky *et al.* (eds.), *A Sourcebook for Russian History from Early Times to 1917*, ii. *Peter the Great to Nicholas I* (New Haven, Conn., 1972), 422; I. de Madariaga, *Russia in the Age of Catherine the Great* (New Haven, Conn., 1981), 442.

[18] E. Sparrow, 'The Alien Office, 1792–1806', *Historical Journal*, 33 (1990), 362.

[19] J. Godechot, *France and the Atlantic Revolution of the Eighteenth Century, 1770–1799*, tr. H. H. Rowen (New York, 1965), 233; Kramer, 'American Political Culture', 45.

perous states from the migrant poor, barring them from entry and excluding foreigners from certain rights, benefits, and obligations.[20] It was not primarily the French Revolution, but the modern urge to protect standards of living and to ensure that work, health, and social security remain available to citizens which has given distinctions between citizens and foreigners the urgency with which they are invested today.

IV

It is possible to recognize twentieth-century practices and ideals of citizenship and nationality in the French Revolution. Yet, at the time, the revolutionaries were awkwardly feeling their way through a dark fog in which they encountered successive economic, financial, political, and military crises. In its contributions to the development of notions of nationality and citizenship, the French Revolution did not so much create modern political culture, as help to begin its construction, adopting and adapting old materials and then, out of necessity, adding its own fabric in an often ramshackle way. The resulting expediency explains the persistence of Ancien Régime practice, the blurring of distinctions between foreigners and nationals, the overlapping of the roles assigned to citizens and foreigners in the state.

The experience of war, xenophobia, and state interference makes the balance sheet look bleak for foreigners during the French Revolution. Yet the revolutionaries' practice of quietly retaining the services of foreigners, even within French political structures; the protection, for a while, of special rights such as those of the clergy and foreign regiments; the tolerance, if not the encouragement, of the political organization of foreign patriots; and the protection of foreign financiers, merchants, and artisans implies two conclusions. First of all, that while the revolutionary state drew legal, day-to-day distinctions between foreigners and citizens, it never entirely closed French society to foreigners, even to enemy aliens. It always permitted the participation of foreigners in civil society (even if it was severely restricted by security measures), thereby keeping open their ultimate access to

---

[20] Brubaker, *Citizenship and Nationhood*, pp. ix–x.

citizenship. Secondly, despite the assimilationist idea of the nation, some foreigners were permitted to work within the structures of the state without abandoning their original identities. The Revolution, therefore, left cracks in the edifice of the national order. In fact, if not in theory, these cracks permitted the limited existence of a cosmopolitan practice of citizenship.

Bibliography

MANUSCRIPT SOURCES

Of special use were the Archives du Ministère des Affaires Etrangères, Paris, where the *Affaires diverses politiques* (France), *Mémoires et documents* (Allemagne and Angleterre) and the *Correspondance Politique* (Allemagne, Angleterre and Espagne) were consulted. The archives of the Service Historique de l'Armée de Terre, Vincennes, were consulted, particularly series X^g (*Suisses*) and X^k (*Troupes spéciales*). The main source, however, were the Archives Nationales, Paris. Of most use, although not the only series consulted, were F/7 (*Police générale*), F/12 (*Commerce et industrie*), F/15 (*Hospices et secours*) and AF (*Pouvoir exécutif, 1789–1815*). Materials in the Scottish Catholic Archives, Edinburgh, were also read. For all that, there is still plenty of room for further research on foreigners in France.

PRINTED SOURCES

Primary Sources

Almanach Royal.

Archives parlementaires de 1787 à 1860: Recueil complet des débats législatifs et politiques des chambres françaises, 1ère sér., 96 vols. (Paris, 1877–1990).

Archives parlementaires: Recueil complet des débats législatifs et politiques des chambres françaises de 1800 à 1860, 2ème sér., 127 vols. (Paris, 1862–1913).

Aulard, F.-A., *La Société des Jacobins: Recueil de documents pour l'histoire de club des Jacobins de Paris*, 6 vols. (Paris, 1889–97).

—— *Recueil des Actes du Comité du Salut Public*, 28 vols. (Paris, 1889–1951).

Besenval, P.-V., *Mémoires de M. le baron de Besenval*, 3 vols. (Paris, 1805).

Campe, J. H., *Été 1789: Lettres d'un Allemand à Paris*, tr. J. Ruffet (Paris, 1989).

Chew, W. J., *A Bostonian Merchant Witnesses the Second French Revolution: James Price, a Voyage and a Visit to France in 1792* (Brussels, 1992).

Christie, T., *Letters on the Revolution of France* (London, 1791).

Cochin, A., *Les Actes du Gouvernement Révolutionnaire (23 août 1793–27 juillet 1794)*, 3 vols. (Paris, 1935).

Collow, T, *Le Citoyen Thomas Collow à la Convention Nationale* (Paris, An II).

Courrier de Provence.

Courtois, E. B., *Rapport fait au nom de la commission chargée de l'examen des papiers trouvés chez Robespierre et ses complices* (Paris, An III).

Desmoulins, C., *Révolutions de France et de Brabant* (1790).

——*Le Vieux Cordelier.*

Diderot, D., and J. d'Alembert, *Encyclopédie, ou dictionnaire raisonné des sciences, des arts et des métiers, par une société des gens de lettres*, 23 vols. and 4 suppls. (Neuchâtel, 1751–77).

Doppet, F.-A., *Mémoires politiques et militaires du général Doppet* (Carouge, 1797).

Dumont, E., *Souvenirs sur Mirabeau et sur les deux premières assemblées législatives*, ed. J. Bénétruy (Paris, 1951).

Elliott, G. D., *Journal of my Life during the French Revolution* (n.pl., 1955).

Ferrière, C.-J. de, *Dictionnaire de droit pratique contenant l'explication des termes de droit, d'ordonnances, de coutumes et de pratique: Avec les jurisdictions de France*, 2 vols. (Toulouse, 1779).

Gazette Nationale, ou le Moniteur Universel.

Genlis, Mme de, *Mémoires inédits de Madame la Comtesse de Genlis*, 8 vols. (Paris, 1825–6).

Goethe, W., *The Autobiography of Goethe. Truth and Poetry: From my Life*, tr. P. Godwin, 2 vols. (London, 1847).

Heinzmann, J. G., *Voyage d'un Allemand à Paris, et retour par la Suisse* (Lausanne, 1800).

Historical Manuscripts Commission, *The Manuscripts of J. B. Fortescue, Esq., preserved at Dropmore*, 10 vols. (1892–1927).

Howard, J. E., *Letters and Documents of Napoleon: The Rise to Power* (London, 1961).

Hunt, L., *The French Revolution and Human Rights: A Brief Documentary History* (New York, 1996).

Isambert, Jourdan, and Decrusy, *Recueil général des anciennes lois françaises depuis l'an 420 jusqu'à la Révolution de 1789*, 31 vols. (Paris, 1822–33).

Jefferson, T., *The Papers of Thomas Jefferson*, ed. J. P. Boyd and W. H. Gaines, 21 vols. (Princeton, 1950–83).

Karamzin, N. M., *Voyage en France 1789–1790*, tr. A. Legrelle (Paris, 1885).

Marat, J.-P., *L'Ami du peuple.*

—— *Les Pamphlets de Marat*, ed. C. Vellay (Paris, 1911).

Mathieu, *Opinion de Mathieu, sur l'article 13 du deuxième projet du Code civil: Séance du 11 nivôse an 10* (Paris, An X).

Meister, H., *Souvenirs de mon dernier voyage à Paris (1795)*, ed. P. Usteri and E. Ritter (Paris, 1910).

Mercier, L.-S., *Paris pendant la Révolution (1789–1798), ou Le Nouveau Paris*, 2 vols. (Paris, 1862).

—— *Le Tableau de Paris*, ed. J. Kaplow (Paris, 1989).

Meyer, F. J. L., *Fragments sur Paris*, 2 vols. (Hamburg, 1798).

Montesquieu, C.-L. de S., *De l'esprit des loix* (Amsterdam and Leipzig, 1758).

Moore, J., *A Journal during a Residence in France from the Beginning of August to the Middle of December, 1792*, 2 vols. (London, 1793).

Morris, G., *A Diary of the French Revolution 1789–1793*, ed. B. C. Davenport, 2 vols. (London, 1939).

O'Connell, D., *The Private Correspondence of Daniel O'Connell*, ed. W. J. Fitzpatrick, 2 vols. (London, 1888).

Pardiellan, P. de, *Mémoires d'un vieux déserteur: Aventures de J. Steininger* (Paris, 1898).

Procès-Verbal de la Convention Nationale, 72 vols. (Paris, 1792–An IV).

'Relation de la Prise de la Bastille, le 14 juillet 1789, par un de ses défenseurs', *Revue Rétrospective*, 1ère sér. 4 (1834).

Rigby, E., *Dr. Rigby's Letters from France, etc., in 1789* (London, 1880).

Robespierre, M., *Œuvres de Maximilien Robespierre*, ed. M. Bouloiseau, G. Lefebvre, and A. Soboul, 10 vols. (Paris, 1939–67).

Rousseau, J.-J., 'Considérations sur le gouvernement de Pologne et sur sa réformation projettée', in *Œuvres Complètes*, iii (Paris, 1964).

Rowan, A. H., *The Autobiography of Archibald Hamilton Rowan*, ed. W. H. Drummond (Shannon, 1972).

Sieyès, E., *Qu'est-ce que le tiers état?*, ed. J.-D. Bredin (Paris, 1988).

Smollett, T., *Travels through France and Italy* (London, 1907).

Tone, T. W., *Life of Theobald Wolfe Tone*, ed. W. W. Tone, 2 vols. (Washington DC, 1826).

Vernadsky, G., *et al.* (eds.), *A Sourcebook for Russian History from Early Times to 1917*, ii. *Peter the Great to Nicholas I* (New Haven, Conn., 1972).

Wardle, R. M., *Collected Letters of Mary Wollstonecraft* (Ithaca, NY, 1979).

Wille, J.-G., *Mémoires et journal de Jean-Georges Wille, graveur du roi* (Paris, 1857).

348 *Bibliography*

Williams, D., *Incidents in my Own Life which have been Thought of Some Importance*, ed. P. France (Brighton, 1980).

Williams, H. M., *Letters Written in France in the Summer of 1790* (London, 1790).

——*Letters Containing a Sketch of the Politics of France, from 31 May 1793 till 28 July 1794*, 2 vols. (London, 1795).

Young, A., *Travels in France during the Years 1787, 1788 and 1789*, ed. C. Maxwell (Cambridge, 1929).

Secondary Sources

Acomb, F., *Anglophobia in France 1763–1789: An Essay in the History of Constitutionalism and Nationalism* (Durham, NC, 1950).

——*Mallet du Pan (1749–1800): A Career in Political Journalism* (Durham, NC, 1973).

Alger, J. G., *Englishmen in the French Revolution* (London, 1889).

——'The British Colony in Paris, 1792–93', *English Historical Review*, 13 (1898).

——*Napoleon's British Visitors and Captives 1801–1815* (London, 1904).

Anderson, M. S., *War and Society in Europe of the Old Regime, 1618–1789* (London, 1988).

Arendt, H., *The Origins of Totalitarianism*, 3rd edn. (London, 1967).

Avenel, G., *Anacharsis Cloots: L'Orateur du genre humain* (Paris, 1976).

Ballot, C., *L'Introduction du machinisme dans l'industrie française* (Paris, 1923).

Beckles, H. M., 'Social and Political Control in the Slave Society', in F. W. Knight (ed.), *General History of the Caribbean*, iii. *The Slave Societies of the Caribbean* (Basingstoke, 1997).

Bénétruy, J., *L'Atelier de Mirabeau: Quatre proscrits genevois dans la tourmente révolutionnaire* (Paris, 1962).

Bewley, C., *Muir of Huntershill* (Oxford, 1981).

Black, J., 'The Archives of the Scots College Paris on the Eve of their Destruction', *Innes Review*, 43 (1992).

Blanning, T. C. W., *Reform and Revolution in Mainz, 1743–1803* (Cambridge, 1974).

——*The Origins of the French Revolutionary Wars* (London, 1986).

——*The French Revolutionary Wars 1787–1802* (London, 1996).

Bodin, J., *Les Suisses au service de la France de Louis XI à la Légion étrangère* (Paris, 1988).

Boizet, J., 'Les Lettres de naturalité sous l'Ancien régime', Thèse de droit (Paris, 1943).

Bonnel, U., *La France et les États-Unis et la guerre de course (1797–1815)* (Paris, 1961).

Boulle, P. H., 'Les Gens de couleur à Paris à la veille de la Révolution', in M. Vovelle (ed.), *L'Image de la Révolution française: Congrès Mondial pour le Bicentenaire de la Révolution, Sorbonne, Paris 6–12 juillet 1989*, 4 vols. (Paris, 1990), i.

Bouloiseau, M., *La République jacobine: 10 août 1792–9 thermidor an II* (Paris, 1972)

Broers, M., *Europe under Napoleon 1799–1815* (London, 1996).

Brubaker, R., *Citizenship and Nationhood in France and Germany* (Cambridge, Mass., 1992).

Burstin, H., *Le Faubourg Saint-Marcel à l'époque révolutionnaire: Structure économique et composition sociale* (Paris, 1983).

Césaire, A., *Toussaint Louverture: La Révolution française et le problème colonial* (Paris, 1961).

Chacon, V., 'Étudiants brésiliens à Montpellier et Révolution française', *Annales historiques de la Révolution française*, 62 (1990).

Chagniot, J., *Paris et l'armée au XVIIIe siècle: Étude politique et sociale* (Paris, 1985).

Chapman, S. D., and S. Chassagne, *European Textile Printers in the Eighteenth Century: A Study of Peel and Oberkampf* (London, 1981).

Chassagne, S., *Oberkampf: Un entrepreneur capitaliste au siècle des Lumières* (Paris, 1980).

Cherry, A., 'The Scots College Books in Paris', *Innes Review*, 44 (1993).

Cobb, R., *The People's Armies. The Armées révolutionnaires: Instrument of the Terror in the Departments, April 1793 to Floréal Year II*, tr. M. Elliott (New Haven, Conn. 1987).

—— *The Police and the People: French Popular Protest 1789–1820* (Oxford, 1970).

—— 'Quelques aspects de la mentalité révolutionnaire (avril 1793–thermidor an II)', *Revue d'histoire moderne et contemporaine*, 6 (1959).

Colley, L., *Britons: Forging the Nation 1707–1837* (London, 1994).

Conway, M. D., *The Life of Thomas Paine with a History of his Literary, Political and Religious Career in America, France, and England*, 2 vols. (New York, 1892).

Coquard, O., 'Le Paris de Marat', in M. Vovelle (ed.), *Paris et la Révolution* (Paris, 1989).

Craton, M., 'Forms of Resistance to Slavery', in F. W. Knight (ed.), *General History of the Caribbean*, iii. *The Slave Societies of the Caribbean* (Basingstoke, 1997).

Crook, M., *Elections in the French Revolution: An Apprenticeship in Democracy, 1789–1799* (Cambridge, 1996).

Czouz-Tornare, A.-J., 'Les Troupes suisses à Paris et la Révolution 1789–1792', in M. Vovelle (ed.), *Paris et la Révolution* (Paris, 1989).

Danjou, C., *La Condition civile de l'étranger dans les trois derniers siècles de la monarchie* (Paris, 1939).

Delange-Janson, L., *Ambroise: Chronique d'un Liégeois de France* (Brussels, 1959).

Doyle, W., *Origins of the French Revolution* (Oxford, 1980).

—— *The Oxford History of the French Revolution* (Oxford, 1989).

Dubost, J.-F., and P. Sahlins, *Et si on faisait payer les étrangers? Louis XIV, Les immigrés et quelques autres* (Paris, 1999).

Dupuy, A., 'Voyageurs italiens à la découverte de la France (1789–1848)', *Revue d'histoire moderne et contemporaine*, 9 (1962).

Durden, R. F., 'Joel Barlow in the French Revolution', *William and Mary Quarterly*, 3rd ser. 8 (1951).

Echeverria, D., *Mirage in the West: A History of the French Image of American Society to 1815* (Princeton, 1957).

Elliott, M., *Partners in Revolution: The United Irishmen and France* (New Haven, Conn. 1982).

—— *Wolfe Tone: Prophet of Irish Independence* (New Haven, Conn., 1989).

Emsley, C., 'Nationalist Rhetoric and Nationalist Sentiment in Revolutionary France', in O. Dann and J. Dinwiddy (eds.), *Nationalism in the Age of the French Revolution* (London, 1988).

Erdman, D. V., *Commerce des Lumières: John Oswald and the British in Paris, 1790–1793* (Columbia, Mo., 1986).

Eude, M., 'Une interprétation "non-Mathiézienne" de l'affaire de la Compagnie des Indes', *Annales historiques de la Révolution française*, 53 (1981).

Fehér, F. (ed.), *The French Revolution and the Birth of Modernity* (Berkeley, Calif., 1990).

Fieffé, E., *Histoire des troupes étrangères au service de France*, 2 vols. (Paris, 1854).

Fitzsimmons, M. P., 'The National Assembly and the Invention of Citizenship', in R. Waldinger, P. Dawson, and I. Woloch (eds.), *The French Revolution and the Meaning of Citizenship* (Westport, Conn., 1993).

Folain-Le Bras, M., 'Un projet d'ordonnance du chancelier Daguesseau: Étude de quelques incapacités de donner et de recevoir sous l'Ancien Régime', Thèse pour le doctorat (Paris, 1941).

Francisque-Michel, *Les Écossais en France: les Français en Écosse*, 2 vols. (London, 1862).

Fuentes, J. F., 'Les Écrits politiques de Marchena pendant le Directoire: Clés biographiques et intellectuelles', *Annales historiques de la Révolution française*, 69 (1997).

Furet, F., *Interpreting the French Revolution*, tr. E. Forster (Cambridge, 1981).

Gaudemet, J., 'L'Étranger: De l'image au statut', in Y. Lequin (ed.), *Histoire des étrangers et de l'immigration en France* (Paris, 1992).

Gauthier, F., *Triomphe et mort du droit naturel en Révolution: 1789–1795–1802* (Paris, 1992).

Gerbod, P., 'Visiteurs et résidents britanniques dans le Paris révolutionnaire de 1789 à 1799', in M. Vovelle (ed.), *Paris et la Révolution* (Paris, 1989).

Giblin, C., 'The Irish Colleges on the Continent', in L. Swords (ed.), *The Irish–French Connection 1578–1978* (Paris, 1978).

Gillispie, C. C., *Science and Polity in France at the End of the Old Régime* (Princeton, 1980).

Godechot, J., 'Les Jacobins italiens et Robespierre', *Annales historiques de la Révolution française*, 30 (1958).

—— *France and the Atlantic Revolution of the Eighteenth Century, 1770–1799*, tr. H. H. Rowen (New York, 1965).

—— 'Nation, patrie, nationalisme et patriotisme en France au XVIIIᵉ siècle', *Annales historiques de la Révolution française*, 43 (1971).

—— 'La Révolution française et les juifs', *Annales historiques de la Révolution française*, 48 (1976).

—— *La Grande Nation: L'Expansion révolutionnaire de la France dans le monde de 1789 à 1799*, 2nd edn. (Paris, 1983).

—— 'The New Concept of the Nation and its Diffusion in Europe', in O. Dann and J. Dinwiddy (eds.), *Nationalism in the Age of the French Revolution* (London, 1988).

Gooch, G. P., *Germany and the French Revolution* (London, 1920).

Goodwin, A., *The Friends of Liberty: The English Democratic Movement in the Age of the French Revolution* (London, 1979).

Gough, H., 'Politics and Power: The Triumph of Jacobinism in Strasbourg, 1791–1793', *Historical Journal*, 23 (1980).

Greenfeld, L., *Nationalism: Five Roads to Modernity* (Cambridge, Mass., 1992).

Haas, R., *Un régiment suisse au service de France: Bettens 1672–1792* (Pont l'Abbé, 1967).

Halloran, B. M., *The Scots College Paris 1603–1792* (Edinburgh, 1997).

Hampson, N., *The Life and Opinions of Maximilien Robespierre* (London, 1974).

—— 'François Chabot and his Plot', *Transactions of the Royal Historical Society*, 5th ser. 26 (1976).

—— *Danton* (Oxford, 1978).

Hampson, N., 'La Patrie', in C. Lucas (ed.), *The French Revolution and the Creation of Modern Political Culture*, ii. *The Political Culture of the French Revolution* (Oxford, 1988).

—— *Saint-Just* (Oxford, 1991).

—— 'The Idea of the Nation in Revolutionary France', in A. Forrest and P. Jones (eds.), *Reshaping France: Town, Country and Region during the French Revolution* (Manchester, 1991).

—— *The Perfidy of Albion: French Perceptions of England during the French Revolution* (Basingstoke, 1998).

Harris, J. R., 'The Transfer of Technology between Britain and France and the French Revolution', in C. Crossley and I. Small (eds.), *The French Revolution and British Culture* (Oxford, 1989).

—— 'John Holker: A Lancashire Jacobite in French Industry', *Newcomen Society Transactions*, 64 (1992–3), 132–5.

—— *Industrial Espionage and Technology Transfer: Britain and France in the Eighteenth Century* (Aldershot, 1998).

Harris, R. D., *Necker: Reform Statesman of the Ancien Régime* (Berkeley, Calif., 1979).

Harsin, P., *La Révolution liégeoise de 1789* (Brussels, 1954).

Hartmann, E., *La Révolution française en Alsace et en Lorraine* (Paris, 1990).

Hayes, R., 'Liens irlandais avec Bordeaux', in R. Hayes, C. Preston, and J. Weygand, *Les Irlandais en Aquitaine* (Bordeaux, 1971).

Henderson, W. O., *Britain and Industrial Europe, 1750–1870: Studies in British Influence on the Industrial Revolution in Western Europe*, 3rd edn. (Leicester, 1972).

Herr, R., *The Eighteenth Century Revolution in Spain* (Princeton, 1958).

Higonnet, P., *Class, Ideology, and the Rights of Nobles during the French Revolution* (Oxford, 1981).

—— *Sister Republics: The Origins of French and American Republicanism* (Cambridge, Mass., 1988).

Hollifield, J. F., 'Immigration and Modernization', in J. F. Hollifield and G. Ross (eds.), *Searching for the New France* (London, 1991).

Hufton, O., *The Poor of Eighteenth-Century France 1750–1789* (Oxford, 1974).

Hulot, F., *Le Maréchal de Saxe* (Paris, 1989).

Hunt, L., *Politics, Culture, and Class in the French Revolution* (London, 1986).

Hyslop, B. F., *French Nationalism in 1789 According to the General Cahiers* (New York, 1968).

Jarrett, D., *The Begetters of Revolution: England's Involvement with France, 1759–1789* (London, 1973).

Jenkins, B., *Nationalism in France: Class and Nation since 1789* (London, 1990).

Johnson, C., *Developments in the Roman Catholic Church in Scotland 1789–1829* (Edinburgh, 1983).

Jones, E. H. S., *The Last Invasion of Britain* (Cardiff, 1950).

Jones, P. M., *Reform and Revolution in France: The Politics of Transition, 1774–1791* (Cambridge, 1995).

——(ed.), *The French Revolution in Social and Political Perspective* (London, 1996).

Kafker, F. A., 'Paris, centre principal de l'entreprise encyclopédique', in M. Vovelle (ed.), *Paris et la Révolution* (Paris, 1989).

Kaplow, J., 'Sur la population flottante de Paris à la fin de l'Ancien Régime', *Annales historiques de la Révolution française*, 39 (1967).

—— *The Names of Kings: The Parisian Laboring Poor in the Eighteenth Century* (New York, 1972).

Kates, G., *The Cercle Social, the Girondins, and the French Revolution* (Princeton, 1985).

—— 'Jews into Frenchmen: Nationality and Representation in Revolutionary France', in F. Fehér (ed.), *The French Revolution and the Birth of Modernity* (Berkeley, Calif., 1990).

Keane, J., *Tom Paine: A Political Life* (London, 1995).

Knight, F. W., *The Caribbean: The Genesis of a Fragmented Nationalism* (New York, 1978).

Kramer, L. S., 'The French Revolution and the Creation of American Political Culture', in J. Klaits and M. H. Haltzel (eds.), *The Global Ramifications of the French Revolution* (Cambridge, 1994).

Kristeva, J., *Strangers to Ourselves*, tr. L. S. Roudiez (New York, 1991).

—— *Nations without Nationalism*, tr. L. S. Roudiez (New York, 1993).

Landes, J., *Women in the Public Sphere in the Age of the French Revolution* (Ithaca, NY, 1988).

Le Cour Grandmaison, O., and C. Withol de Wenden, *Les Étrangers dans la cité: Expériences européennes* (Paris, 1993).

Lee, O., *Les Comités et les clubs des patriotes belges et liégeois (1791–An III)* (Paris, 1931).

Lefebvre, G., 'Le Commerce extérieur en l'an II', in *Études sur la Révolution française* (Paris, 1954).

—— *The French Revolution from 1793 to 1799*, tr. J. Friguglietti and J. H. Stewart (New York, 1964).

Lepointe, G., 'Le Statut des Étrangers dans la France du XIXe siècle', *Recueils de la Société Jean Bodin*, x. *L'Étranger* (Brussels, 1958).

Lešnodorski, B., *Les Jacobins polonais* (Paris, 1965).

Lewis, M., *Napoleon and his British Captives* (London, 1962).

Levy, D. G., 'Women's Revolutionary Citizenship in Action, 1791:

Setting the Boundaries', in R. Waldinger, P. Dawson, and I. Woloch (eds.), *The French Revolution and the Meaning of Citizenship* (Westport, Conn., 1993).

Loupès, P., 'Les Ecclésiastiques irlandais dans le Diocèse de Bordeaux sous l'Ancien Régime', in Fédération Historique du Sud-Ouest, *Bordeaux et les Îles britanniques du XIIIe au XXe siècle: Actes du colloque, York, 1973* (Bordeaux, 1975).

—— 'The Irish Clergy in the Diocese of Bordeaux during the Revolution', in D. Dickson and H. Gough (eds.), *Ireland and the French Revolution* (Dublin, 1990).

Lüthy, H., *La Banque Protestante en France, de la révocation de l'Édit de Nantes à la Révolution*, 2 vols. (Paris, 1959–61).

Lyons, M., *France under the Directory* (Cambridge, 1975).

—— 'Regionalism and Linguistic Conformity in the French Revolution', in A. Forrest and P. Jones (eds.), *Reshaping France: Town, Country and Region during the French Revolution* (Manchester, 1991).

—— *Napoleon Bonaparte and the Legacy of the French Revolution* (Basingstoke, 1994).

Mabbott, J. D., *The State and the Citizen*, 2nd edn. (London, 1967).

McMillan, J. F., 'Scottish Catholics and the Jansenist Controversy: The Case Reopened', *Innes Review*, 32 (1981).

—— 'Thomas Innes and the Bull "Unigenitus"', *Innes Review*, 33 (1982).

Madariaga, I. de, *Russia in the Age of Catherine the Great* (New Haven, Conn., 1981).

Maradan, E., 'L'Échec de la propagande du club helvétique auprès du Régiment des Gardes 1789–1791', in M. Vovelle (ed.), *Paris et la Révolution* (Paris, 1989).

Marion, M., *Dictionnaire des institutions de la France aux XVIIe et XVIIIe siècles* (Paris, 1984).

Mathias, P., 'Skills and the Diffusion of Innovations from Britain in the Eighteenth Century', *Transactions of the Royal Historical Society*, 5th ser. 25 (1975), 93–113.

Mathiez, A., *La Conspiration de l'étranger* (Paris, 1918).

—— *La Révolution et les étrangers: Cosmopolitisme et défense nationale* (Paris, 1918).

—— 'Les Citra et les Ultra', *Annales historiques de la Révolution française*, 3 (1926).

—— 'Le Comité de Salut Public et le Complot de l'Étranger (octobre–novembre 1793)', *Annales historiques de la Révolution française*, 3 (1926).

—— *La Vie chère et le mouvement social sous la terreur*, 2 vols. (Paris, 1973).

Mathorez, J., *Les Étrangers en France sous l'Ancien Régime: Histoire de la formation de la population française*, 2 vols. (Paris, 1919–21).

Méautis, A., *Le Club helvétique de Paris (1790–1791) et la diffusion des idées révolutionnaires en Suisse* (Neuchâtel, 1969).

Meikle, H. W., 'Two Glasgow Merchants in the French Revolution', *Scottish Historical Review*, 8 (1911).

Meller, S., ' "Pour notre liberté et pour la vôtre": 200ᵉ anniversaire des légions polonaises qui combattirent aux côtés de l'armée française sous le commandement du général Bonaparte', *Annales historiques de la Révolution française*, 70 (1998).

Monnier, R., *Le Faubourg Saint-Antoine (1789–1815)* (Paris, 1981).

—— and A. Soboul, *Répertoire du personnel sectionnaire parisien en l'an II* (Paris, 1985).

Moran, P. A., 'Grisy, the Scots College Farm near Paris', *Innes Review*, 43 (1992).

Mouffe, C. (ed.), *Dimensions of Radical Democracy: Pluralism, Citizenship, Community* (London, 1992).

Muret, P., 'L'Affaire des princes possessionnés d'Alsace et les origines du conflit entre la Révolution et l'Empire', *Revue d'histoire moderne et contemporaine*, 1(1899–1900).

Nairn, T., *Faces of Nationalism: Janus Revisited* (London, 1997).

Necheles, R., 'L'Emancipation des juifs 1787–1795', *Annales historiques de la Révolution française*, 48 (1976).

Nicolas, J., *La Savoie au 18ᵉ siècle: Noblesse et bourgeoisie*, 2 vols. (Paris, 1978).

Palmer, R. R., *The Age of the Democratic Revolution: A Political History of Europe and America, 1760–1800*, 2 vols. (Princeton, 1959–64).

—— 'Le Prytanée français et les écoles de Paris (1798–1802)', *Annales historiques de la Révolution française*, 53 (1981).

Parra-Pérez, C., *Miranda et la Révolution française* (Paris, 1925).

Peabody, S., *'There are no Slaves in France': The Political Culture of Race and Slavery in the Ancien Régime* (New York, 1996).

Pfister-Langanay, C., *Ports, navires et négociants à Dunkerque (1662–1792)* (Dunkirk, 1985).

Philp, M., *Paine* (Oxford, 1989).

Portemer, J., 'L'Étranger dans le droit de la Révolution française', *Recueils de la Société Jean Bodin*, x. *L'Étranger* (Brussels, 1958).

Poussou, J.-P., 'Recherches sur l'immigration anglo-irlandaise à Bordeaux au XVIIIe siècle', in Fédération Historique du Sud-Ouest, *Bordeaux et les Îles britanniques du XIIIe au XXe siècle: Actes du colloque, York, 1973* (Bordeaux, 1975).

—— 'Mobilité et migrations', in J. Dupâquier (ed.), *Histoire de la population française*, 4 vols. (Paris, 1988), ii.

Poussou, J.-P., 'A l'école des autres', in Y. Lequin (ed.), *Histoire des étrangers et de l'immigration en France* (Paris, 1992).

—— 'Les Internationales de l'"honnête homme"', in Y. Lequin (ed.), *Histoire des étrangers et de l'immigration en France* (Paris, 1992).

—— 'Un monde plein', in Y. Lequin (ed.), *Histoire des étrangers et de l'immigration en France* (Paris, 1992).

Preston, C., 'Le Collège irlandais de Bordeaux', in R. Hayes, C. Preston, and J. Weygand, *Les Irlandais en Aquitaine* (Bordeaux, 1971).

Purcell, M., 'The Strange Story of Richard Ferris', in L. Swords (ed.), *The Irish–French Connection 1578–1978* (Paris, 1978).

Puymège, G. de, 'Le Soldat Chauvin', in P. Nora (ed.), *Les Lieux de mémoire*, ii, part 3. *La Nation* (Paris, 1986).

Rao, A.-M., 'La Révolution française et l'émigration politique: Les Réfugiés italiens en 1799', *Annales historiques de la Révolution française*, 52 (1980).

—— 'Paris et les exilés italiens en 1799', in M. Vovelle, *Paris et la Révolution* (Paris, 1989).

Rapport, M., 'The Treatment of Foreigners in Revolutionary France, 1789–1797', Ph.D. thesis (Bristol, 1997).

—— '"A Languishing Branch of the Old Tree of Feudalism": The Death, Resurrection and Final Burial of the *Droit d'Aubaine* in France', *French History*, 14/1 (2000).

Raxhon, P., 'Les Réfugiés liégeois à Paris: Un état de la question', in M. Vovelle (ed.), *Paris et la Révolution* (Paris, 1989).

Réau, L., *L'Europe française au siècle des Lumières* (Paris, 1971).

Robertson, W. S., *The Life of Miranda*, 2 vols. (New York, 1969).

Rose, R. B., *The Enragés: Socialists of the French Revolution?* (London, 1965).

Rosendaal, J., 'Qui était l'être suprême pour les réfugiés bataves?', *Annales historiques de la Révolution française*, 61 (1989).

Ruiz, A., 'Un regard sur le jacobinisme allemand: Idéologie et activités de certains de ses représentants notoires en France pendant la Révolution', in F. Furet and M. Ozouf (eds.), *The French Revolution and the Creation of Modern Political Culture*, iii. *The Transformation of Political Culture 1789–1848* (Oxford, 1989).

Sacquin, M., 'Les Anglais à Montpellier et à Nice pendant la seconde moitié du siècle', *Dix-huitième siècle*, 13 (1981).

Sahlins, P., 'Natural Frontiers Revisited: France's Boundaries since the Seventeenth Century', *American Historical Review*, 95 (1990).

Schama, S., *Patriots and Liberators: Revolution in the Netherlands 1780–1813*, 2nd edn. (London, 1992).

Schnapper, B., 'La Naturalisation française au XIXe siècle: Les Variations d'une politique', *La Condition juridique de l'étranger hier et aujourd'hui: Actes du colloque, 1988* (Nijmegen, 1988).

Scott, S. F., *The Response of the Royal Army to the French Revolution: The Role and Development of the Line Army, 1787–93* (Oxford, 1978).

—— 'The French Revolution and the Irish Regiments in France', in D. Dickson and H. Gough (eds.), *Ireland and the French Revolution* (Dublin, 1990).

Scott, W., *Terror and Repression in Revolutionary Marseilles* (London, 1973).

Simms, J. G., 'The Irish on the Continent, 1691–1800', in T. W. Moody and W. E. Vaughan (eds.), *A New History of Ireland*, iv. *Eighteenth-Century Ireland 1691–1800* (Oxford, 1986).

Slavin, M., *The Hébertistes to the Guillotine: Anatomy of a 'Conspiracy' in Revolutionary France* (Baton Rouge, La., 1994).

Soboul, A., *Les Sans-Culottes parisiens en l'An II: Histoire politique et sociale des sections de Paris, 2 juin 1793–9 thermidor an II* (La Roche-sur-Yon, 1958).

—— 'Anacharsis Cloots: L'Orateur du genre humain', *Annales histor-iques de la Révolution française*, 52 (1980).

Sorel, A., *L'Europe et la Révolution française*, 8 vols. (Paris, 1885–1904).

Sparrow, E., 'The Alien Office, 1792–1806', *Historical Journal*, 33 (1990).

Stern, M. B., 'The English Press in Paris and its Successors', *Papers of the Bibliographical Society of America*, 74 (1980).

Thornton, J. K., ' "I Am the Subject of the King of Congo": African Political Ideology and the Haitian Revolution', *Journal of World History*, 4 (1993).

Tomalin, C., *The Life and Death of Mary Wollstonecraft* (London, 1974).

Vidalenc, J., 'Quelques cas particuliers du cosmopolitisme en France au XVIIIe siècle', *Annales historiques de la Révolution française*, 35 (1963).

Villers, R., 'La Condition des Étrangers en France dans les trois derniers siècles de la monarchie', *Recueils de la Société Jean Bodin*, x. *L'Étranger* (Brussels, 1958).

Wadsworth, A. P., and J. de L. Mann, *The Cotton Trade and Industrial Lancashire, 1600–1780* (Manchester, 1931).

Wahnich, S., *L'Impossible Citoyen: L'Étranger dans le discours de la Révolution française* (Paris, 1997).

Wallon, H., *Histoire du Tribunal révolutionnaire de Paris, avec le journal de ses actes*, 6 vols. (Paris, 1880–2).

Weber, E., *Peasants into Frenchmen. The Modernization of Rural France, 1870–1914* (Stanford, Calif., 1976).

Weygand, J., 'Le Régiment de Dillon', in R. Hayes, C. Preston, and J. Weygand, *Les Irlandais en Aquitaine* (Bordeaux, 1971).

Woodward, L. D., *Une Anglaise amie de la Révolution française: Hélène Maria Williams et ses amis* (Paris, 1930).

Woronoff, D., *La République bourgeoise de Thermidor à Brumaire 1794–1799* (Paris, 1972).

Zeldin, T., *France 1848–1945: Intellect and Pride* (Oxford, 1980).

Zurich, P. de, 'Les Derniers Serments des troupes suisses au service de France sous l'ancien régime', *Zeitschrift für Schweizerische Geschichte*, 22 (1942).

Index